Rhythm and Critique

Technicities

Series Editors: John Armitage, Ryan Bishop and Joanne Roberts, Winchester School of Art, University of Southampton

The philosophy of technicities: exploring how technology mediates art, frames design and augments the mediated collective perception of everyday life.

Technicities will publish the latest philosophical thinking about our increasingly immaterial technocultural conditions, with a unique focus on the context of art, design and media.

Editorial Advisory Board
Benjamin Bratton, Cheryl Buckley, Sean Cubitt, Clive Dilnot, Jin Huimin, Arthur Kroker, Geert Lovink, Scott McQuire, Gunalan Nadarajan, Elin O'Hara Slavick, Li Shqiao, Geoffrey Winthrop-Young

Published
Lyotard and the Inhuman Condition: Reflections on Nihilism, Information and Art
By Ashley Woodward

Critical Luxury Studies: Art, Design, Media
Edited by John Armitage and Joanne Roberts

Cold War Legacies: Systems, Theory, Aesthetics
Edited by John Beck and Ryan Bishop

Fashion and Materialism
By Ulrich Lehmann

Queering Digital India: Activisms, Identities, Subjectivities
Edited by Rohit K. Dasgupta and Debanuj DasGupta

Zero Degree Seeing: Barthes/Burgin and Political Aesthetics
Edited by Ryan Bishop and Sunil Manghani

Rhythm and Critique: Technics, Modalities, Practices
Edited by Paola Crespi and Sunil Manghani

Forthcoming
Photography Off the Scale: Technologies and Theories of the Mass Image
Edited by Tomáš Dvořák and Jussi Parikka

www.edinburghuniversitypress.com/series/TECH

Rhythm and Critique

Technics, Modalities, Practices

Edited by Paola Crespi and
Sunil Manghani

EDINBURGH
University Press

Edinburgh University Press is one of the leading university presses in the UK. We publish academic books and journals in our selected subject areas across the humanities and social sciences, combining cutting-edge scholarship with high editorial and production values to produce academic works of lasting importance. For more information visit our website: edinburghuniversitypress.com

© editorial matter and organisation Paola Crespi and Sunil Manghani, 2020, 2022
© the chapters their several authors, 2020, 2022

First published in hardback by Edinburgh University Press 2020

Edinburgh University Press Ltd
The Tun – Holyrood Road
12(2f) Jackson's Entry
Edinburgh EH8 8PJ

Typeset in 11/13 Adobe Sabon by
IDSUK (DataConnection) Ltd

A CIP record for this book is available from the British Library

ISBN 978 1 4744 4754 6 (hardback)
ISBN 978 1 4744 4755 3 (paperback)
ISBN 978 1 4744 4756 0 (webready PDF)
ISBN 978 1 4744 4757 7 (epub)

The right of Paola Crespi and Sunil Manghani to be identifiedastheeditorsofthiswork has been asserted in accordance with the Copyright, Designs and Patents Act 1988, and the Copyright and Related Rights Regulations 2003 (SI No. 2498).

Contents

List of Illustrations   vii
Notes on Contributors   xii

INTRODUCTIONS

Rhythm, *Rhuthmos* and Rhythmanalysis   3
Paola Crespi and Sunil Manghani

Could Rhythm Become a New Scientific Paradigm for the Humanities?   20
Pascal Michon

A Genealogy of Rhythm   30
Paola Crespi and Sunil Manghani

I   MODALITIES OF RHYTHM

1   Drawing Rhythm: On the Work of Rudolf Laban   55
Paola Crespi

2   What is at Stake in a Theory of Rhythm   79
Henri Meschonnic (trans. Chantal Wright; introduced by Marko Pajević)

3   Rhythm and Textural Temporality   101
Sha Xin Wei and Garrett Laroy Johnson

II   SITES AND PRACTICES

4   Attunement of Value and Capital in the Algorithms of Social Media   127
Simon Yuill and Beverley Skeggs

5   Idiorrhythmy: An (Unsustainable) Aesthetic of Ethics   150
Sunil Manghani

6   Adventures of a Line of Thought: Rhythmic Evolutions of Intelligent Machines in Post-Digital Culture   173
Stamatia Portanova

III RHYTHMANALYSIS

7 The Configuring of 'Context' in Rhythmanalysis   201
   Yi Chen

8 City Rhythms: An Approach to Urban Rhythm Analysis   218
   Caroline Nevejan and Pinar Sefkatli

9 Rhythm, Rhythmanalysis and Algorithm-Analysis   242
   Julian Henriques

Index   267

List of Illustrations

Figure I.1	'A Genealogy of Rhythm'. © Jane Birkin and Sunil Manghani, 2019.	31
Figure 1.1	R. Laban, n.d., L/C/3/47. Figure Drawings/Figures within Energy Lines. A crayon drawing by Rudolf Laban of two figures within spiralling lines. © Rudolf Laban Archive, National Resource Centre for Dance Archive, University of Surrey.	58
Figure 1.2	R. Laban, n.d., L/C/3/48. Figure Drawings/Figure within Energy Lines. A crayon drawing by Rudolf Laban of a figure within swirling lines. © Rudolf Laban Archive, National Resource Centre for Dance Archive, University of Surrey.	58
Figure 1.3	R. Laban, n.d., L/C/3/94. Figures/Figure in Icosahedron. A black-crayon drawing by Rudolf Laban showing a figure surrounded by short, overlapping lines making an icosahedral shape. © Rudolf Laban Archive, National Resource Centre for Dance Archive, University of Surrey.	59
Figure 1.4	R. Laban, n.d., L/C/5/123. Single and Double Figures in Spatial Forms/A Figure in a Dodecahedron. Pencil drawing of a figure within a line tracing a continuous path around some edges of a dodecahedron. © Rudolf Laban Archive, National Resource Centre for Dance Archive, University of Surrey.	60
Figure 1.5	R. Laban, n.d., L/C/5/129. Single and Double Figures in Spatial Forms/A Figure in a Dodecahedron. Pencil drawing of a figure within a line tracing a continuous path around some edges of a dodecahedron. © Rudolf Laban Archive, National Resource Centre for Dance Archive, University of Surrey.	60

Figure 1.6   R. Laban, n.d., L/C/5/126. Single and Double Figures in Spatial Forms/A Figure in a Dodecahedron. Drawing by Rudolf Laban of a figure within a line tracing a continuous path around some edges of a dodecahedron. In pencil, and green, black, and red crayon. © Rudolf Laban Archive, National Resource Centre for Dance Archive, University of Surrey.   60

Figure 1.7   R. Laban, n.d., L/C/5/130. Single and Double Figures in Spatial Forms/A Figure in a Dodecahedron. Pencil drawing by Rudolf Laban of a figure within a dodecahedron. © Rudolf Laban Archive, National Resource Centre for Dance Archive, University of Surrey.   60

Figure 1.8   R. Laban, n.d., L/C/6/69. Relationship between Groups of Figures/Six Figures. Drawing by Rudolf Laban of six figures encircled by a line. In pencil and green crayon. © Rudolf Laban Archive, National Resource Centre for Dance Archive, University of Surrey.   61

Figure 1.9   R. Laban, n.d., L/C/6/70. Relationship between Groups of Figures/Three Figures. Drawing of three figures with swirling lines superimposed on them. In pencil and blue and red crayon. © Rudolf Laban Archive, National Resource Centre for Dance Archive, University of Surrey.   61

Figure 1.10   R. Laban, n.d., L/C/10/95. Relationships between Groups of Figures. Pencil diagram of three figures with curving lines superimposed on them. © Rudolf Laban Archive, National Resource Centre for Dance Archive, University of Surrey.   62

Figure 1.11   R. Laban, n.d., L/C/6/81. Relationship between Groups of Figures/Three Figures. Drawing of three figures in green crayon. © Rudolf Laban Archive, National Resource Centre for Dance Archive, University of Surrey.   63

Figure 1.12   R. Laban, n.d., L/C/6/86. Relationship between Groups of Figures/Three Figures. Drawing of three figures. Done in his short-stroke style in green crayon. © Rudolf Laban Archive, National Resource Centre for Dance Archive, University of Surrey.   63

List of Illustrations   ix

Figure 1.13   R. Laban, n.d., L/C/6/79. Relationship between Groups of Figures/Three Figures. Drawing of three figures within a line tracing a continuous path around edges of an icosahedron. In black, brown, blue and green crayon. © Rudolf Laban Archive, National Resource Centre for Dance Archive, University of Surrey.   63

Figure 1.14   R. Laban, n.d., L/E/33/8. Lecture notes on various subjects/Notes and diagrams. Diagram of primary scale as basis for other patterns, diagrams of dial structures, physiology of work, the discovery that man continually lives in two different media, notes on types of movement, personal abilities. © Rudolf Laban Archive, National Resource Centre for Dance Archive, University of Surrey.   65

Figure 1.15   R. Laban, n.d., L/E/5/21. Choreology (Effort)/Indulging in élan is. Handwritten manuscript relating to combinations of two effort elements. © Rudolf Laban Archive, National Resource Centre for Dance Archive, University of Surrey.   69

Figure 1.16   R. Laban, n.d., L/E/40/11. Rhythm/The Language of Rhythm. Handwritten manuscripts. © Rudolf Laban Archive, National Resource Centre for Dance Archive, University of Surrey.   70

Figure 1.17   Effort Graph. Source: Wikimedia. Available at: <https://upload.wikimedia.org/wikipedia/commons/2/27/Laban-effort-graph.jpg> (last accessed 16 June 2019).   73

Figure 1.18   R. Laban, n.d., L/E/53/4. Books, Manuscripts, Outlines/The Method of Drawing an Effort Graph. Typed instructions and handwritten diagrams. © Rudolf Laban Archive, National Resource Centre for Dance Archive, University of Surrey.   74

Figure 1.19   R. Laban, n.d., L/E/10/16. Choreutics/Rhythmologie [Rhythmology]. Manuscript for an article about crystal forms; handwritten notes, symbols and drawings. © Rudolf Laban Archive, National Resource Centre for Dance Archive, University of Surrey.   76

Figure 3.1   Rhythm kit by Julian Stein. © Synthesis Center, Arizona State University.   106

Figure 3.2	Adrian Freed's semblance typology of entrainments. Courtesy of Adrian Freed.	111
Figure 3.3	Correlation of streams of quaternion-valued orientation normals to points on bodies. © Synthesis Center, Arizona State University.	112
Figure 3.4	Correlation of orientations, as sensed by body-borne sensors. © Synthesis Center, Arizona State University.	113
Figure 3.5	Balloon game: five people bat and volley balloons among themselves. © Synthesis Center, Arizona State University.	114
Figure 3.6	Lanterns suspended from ceiling. Sound and lamp intensity vary according to the lanterns' movement. © Synthesis Center, Arizona State University.	115
Figure 3.7	Semblance typology for interaction with lanterns. © Synthesis Center, Arizona State University.	117
Figure 4.1	Example diagrams from *Rhythms of Use*. © Beverley Skeggs and Simon Yuill.	131
Figure 4.2	The *Rhythms of Interaction* showing the different types of data composited into the diagram. © Beverley Skeggs and Simon Yuill.	132
Figure 4.3	A comparison of two of the participants from the project showing *Interaction* and *Tracking*. © Beverley Skeggs and Simon Yuill.	133
Figure 4.4	The *Rhythms of Attention* showing the ordering of posts in a News Feed and how these change over time for a given participant. © Beverley Skeggs and Simon Yuill.	134
Figure 4.5	Two diagrams from the *Rhythms of Tracking*. © Beverley Skeggs and Simon Yuill.	136–137
Figure 4.6	One of Marx's diagrams of the circuit of capital as it transforms through cycles of investment, production and sale. Courtesy of Simon Yuill, based on Karl Marx (1978: 142).	138
Figure 5.1	Tokihiro Sato, *Photo-respiration # 87 Shibuya* (1990). Gelatin-silver print, 41.9 × 58.4 cm; or black and white transparency over light box, 96.5 × 121.9 cm. © Tokihiro Sato, Courtesy Leslie Tonkonow Artworks + Projects, New York.	163
Figure 5.2	Jitish Kallat, *Allegory of the Endless Morning*, 2011–12. Five panels. Courtesy of the artist.	164–165

List of Illustrations   xi

Figure 5.3	Li Wei, *040-02*, *040-01*, *29 Levels of Freedom* series, Beijing, 120 cm × 175 cm, 24 July 2003. Courtesy of the artist LiWei (www.liweiart.com).	167
Figure 8.1	Linear and circular documentation of the daily activities in the central square of Assendelft, Zaanstad. (Source: Pinar Sefkatli, inspired by the student work Minor Responsible Innovation).	222
Figure 8.2	Map of informal networks in Amsterdam Zuidoost that the single mothers are part of. (Source: Pinar Sefkatli, inspired by the student work Minor Responsible Innovation).	225
Figure 8.3	Diagram showing the comparison of rhythms of the elderly and rhythms of the younger residents in Keizerswaard, Rotterdam. (Source: Pinar Sefkatli, inspired by the student work Minor Responsible Innovation).	228
Figure 8.4	Visualisation of the methodology for Urban Rhythm Analysis. (Source: Caroline Nevejan and Pinar Sefkatli).	233
Figure 8.5	Visualisation of steps 1, 2, 3 of the methodology for Urban Rhythm Analysis. (Source: Caroline Nevejan and Pinar Sefkatli).	234
Figure 8.6	Linear representation of morning and evening rhythms in Tulpstraat, Helmond. (Source: Pinar Sefkatli, inspired by student work Minor Responsible Innovation 2016).	235
Figure 8.7	Functional analysis of Meerzicht Shopping Centre Square shown in a linear fashion and on a map with the routes of the visitors. Zoetermeer, The Netherlands. (Source: Pinar Sefkatli, inspired by the student work Minor Responsible Innovation 2016).	236
Figure 8.8	Linear representation of the daily rhythms of the residents in Zwaardvegersgaarde, Den Haag. (Source: Pinar Sefkatli, inspired by the student work Minor Responsible Innovation 2016).	236
Figure 8.9	Visualisation of steps 4, 5 and 6 of the methodology for Urban Rhythm Analysis. (Source: Caroline Nevejan and Pinar Sefkatli).	237

Notes on Contributors

Yi Chen is Lecturer in Contextual and Theoretical Studies at the University of the Arts London. Yi's research interests include cultural theory, art and design history and research methodology. She recently published her monograph *Practising Rhythmanalysis: Theories and Methodologies* (2016) with Rowman and Littlefield International.

Paola Crespi is a Visiting Research Fellow at the Topology Research Unit (Goldsmiths). She completed a PhD in Media and Communications (Goldsmiths) with a focus on rhythm in the work of Rudolf Laban. Paola has taught in various universities as an Associate Lecturer and her work has been published in international peer-reviewed journals such as *Body & Society* (2014, print) and *Theory, Culture & Society* (2015, online). She is Section Editor for Cultural Studies and Critical Theory for the *Open Journal of the Humanities* and a member of the editorial board of *Evental Aesthetics: An Independent Journal of Philosophy*.

Julian Henriques is Professor of Media, Communication and Cultural Studies at Goldsmiths, University of London, convenor of the MA Scriptwriting and Cultural Studies programmes and director of the Topology Research Unit. In 2015 Julian co-founded Sound System Outernational, an agency organising events to develop the relationship between academic researchers and sound system practitioners. Julian is also a co-founding director of Sonic Womb Productions Ltd, which, with partners in UCL, conducts biomedical research to better understand what the foetus hears from inside the womb. Among other books and several articles, Julian's *Sonic Bodies: Reggae Sound Systems, Performance Techniques and Ways of Knowing* was published by Continuum in 2011, the special issue of the journal *Body & Society* entitled 'Rhythm Movement, Embodiment' that he co-edited with Pasi Valiaho and Milla Tiainen was published in 2014 and his edited collection *Stuart Hall: Conversations, Projects and Legacies* (co-edited with David G Morley) was published by Goldsmiths Press in 2017. His *Sonic Media: The Street Technology of the Jamaican Sound System* is forthcoming (2020).

Garrett Laroy Johnson is media art researcher at the Synthesis Center and Center for Philosophical Technologies, Arizona State University, where he pursues interests including responsive environments, new materialisms, alternative economies and process theory through a research-creation practice in computational media. He is also co-founding director of PHuN (Posthuman Network) and a co-founding member of ITITITinc, a speculative engineering firm.

Sunil Manghani is Professor of Theory, Practice and Critique at Winchester School of Art, University of Southampton (UK). He is Managing Editor for *Theory, Culture & Society*. His primary research has been concerned with the concepts of the image and visual culture across a range of historical, philosophical and cultural contexts, and his work includes writings on visual arts practices. He co-curated *Barthes/Burgin* at the John Hansard Gallery (2016) and is the co-editor of *India's Biennale Effect: A Politics of Contemporary Art* (2017), which examines the development of the Kochi-Muziris Biennale. He is also author of *Image Studies: Theory and Practice* (2013) and *Image Critique and the Fall of the Berlin Wall* (2008); editor of the four-volume set *Images: Critical and Primary Sources* (2013); and co-editor of *Seeing Degree Zero* (2019), *Barthes/Burgin: Notes Towards an Exhibition* (2016), *Farewell to Visual Studies* (2015), *Images: A Reader* (2006) and *Painting: Critical and Primary Sources* (2015).

Henri Meschonnic (1932–2009) was a French poet, linguist, essayist and translator. He is best known as a theoretician of language and as a translator of the Old Testament. *Critique du rythme. Anthropologie historique du langage* (1982) is his most famous theoretical work, an element of which is translated into English for this book. As a translator of the Old Testament he published many volumes, including *Les cinq rouleaux* (1970); *Jona et le signifiant errant* (1998); *Gloires* (2000); *Au commencement* (2002); *Les Noms* (2003); *Et il a appelé* (2005); and *Dans le désert* (2008).

Pascal Michon is a Professor in Classes Préparatoires aux Grandes Écoles in Paris, a historian as well as a philosopher. He was a member of the Collège International de Philosophie. He is the director of the publishing company Rhuthmos and the editor of a website dedicated to rhythm, www.rhuthmos.eu. Pascal recently authored two volumes of the Rhuthmos series *Elements of Rhythmology* (2017), and he has previously published several books on rhythm: *Rhythme, povoir, mondialisation* (2005); *Les rhythmes du politique. Démocratie et capitalisme mondialisé* (2007); *Marcel Mauss retrouvé. Origines de l'anthropologie du rhythme* (2010); *Rhythmologie baroque. Spinoza, Leibniz, Diderot* (2015).

Caroline Nevejan is Professor of Designing Urban Experience at the Amsterdam School for Social Science Research, University of Amsterdam, and Chief Science Officer for the City of Amsterdam. She is a researcher and designer who has been involved with the emerging network society and digital culture since the 1980s. For over a decade she has been working on how people make trade-offs for trust in the new merging of online and offline realities to which 'integrating rhythm' seems to be vital. In this context she is now directing a large research project into Designing Rhythms for Social Resilience.

Marko Pajević studied Comparative Literature, Philosophy and Slavic Studies in Munich, Berlin and Paris. Henri Meschonnic was his research director. After teaching positions in Paris, Belfast, London and a Senior Research Fellowship at the Centre Marc Bloch (Humboldt University Berlin), he took up the Chair of German Studies at the University of Tartu in January 2018. Following books on Paul Celan and Franz Kafka, Pajević developed a poetic anthropology in a monograph around the notion of poetic thinking. He pursued this further in a project on 'Thinking Language(s)' funded by the British Academy. Outputs of this project were special issues on Wilhelm von Humboldt (*Forum for Modern Language Studies* 2017/1) and on Henri Meschonnic (*Comparative Critical Studies* 2018/3), as well as a Meschonnic Reader in English translation for Edinburgh University Press (2019). This is part of his overarching research project on poetic thinking; see the website apt.ut.ee.

Stamatia Portanova is a Research Fellow at the Università degli Studi di Napoli 'L'Orientale' (Naples), where she is also part of the Technocultures Research Unit. Her research focuses on digital culture and philosophy. She is the author of *Moving without a Body: Digital Philosophy and Choreographic Thoughts* (MIT Press, Technologies of Lived Abstraction series), and of several articles published in books and journals such as *Body and Society*,

Computational Culture, Space and Culture, Fibreculture, Angelaki, Anglistica AION and *Inflexions*.

Pinar Sefkatli is an architect and a PhD candidate at the Amsterdam Institute for Social Science Research. Part of the consortium Designing Rhythms for Social Resilience (2018–23), she explores the rhythmic qualities in the social dynamics of cities as a framework for urban analysis. The research is the continuation of City Rhythm (2016–17), where Pinar contributed as a research assistant. Supervised by Professor Caroline Nevejan, the issue of social safety was studied in six cities in the Netherlands from the rhythm perspective in urban and data domains.

Sha Xin Wei is Director of the Synthesis Center for experimental art, philosophy and technology at ASU. He obtained a PhD in 2001 on differential geometric performance and the technologies of writing in Mathematics, Computer Science, and History and Philosophy of Science at Stanford University. Sha's early work was in scientific simulations and human-computer systems architecture. His art and scholarly work include gestural media, movement arts, realtime media environments, critical studies and philosophy of technology. Currently, Sha is Professor and Director of the School of Arts, Media and Engineering in the Herberger Institute for Design and the Arts at Arizona State University, Fellow of the ASU-Santa Fe Center for Biosocial Complex Systems and Professor at the European Graduate School. He published his monograph *Poiesis, Enchantment and Topological Media* with MIT Press in 2013.

Beverley Skeggs is Professor of Sociology, University of Lancaster, and Consultant to the Atlantic Fellows Programme and the International Inequalities Institute at the London School of Economics. She is an ethnographer who researches the relationship between values and different aspects of social life, including class, space, violence, sexuality, reality TV and subject formation.

Chantal Wright is a Reader at Warwick University, where she convenes the MA in Literary Translation Studies. She is also a literary translator working from German and French into English: in 2012 she was awarded the inaugural Cliff Becker Book Prize in Translation, and she has twice been shortlisted for the Marsh Award for Children's Literature in Translation (2011 and 2015). She is the coordinator of the Warwick Prize for Women in Translation.

Simon Yuill is an artist, programmer and researcher who develops custom research software and works in the fields of Software Studies and Digital Sociology. He was the inaugural winner of the Vilém Flusser Theory Award (Berlin, 2008) and has been a Research Resident at the Piet Zwart Institute (Rotterdam, 2005), Visiting Fellow at the University of Warwick (2013). He is a Visiting Research Fellow with the Digital Culture Unit at Goldsmiths, University of London, where he has also worked within the Department of Sociology.

Introductions

Rhythm, *Rhuthmos* and Rhythmanalysis

Paola Crespi and Sunil Manghani

Rhythm remains one of the most productive terms for critical enquiry into our social, political and cultural lives. References to temporality, flow, measure, pattern, variation and metre occur across a wide range of critical literatures concerned with the arts, philosophy, technology, critical theory and studies of the everyday. Yet, conceptually, rhythm is rarely made explicit, instead being perhaps more readily only in the service of critique. As Derrida put it: 'Rhythm has always haunted our tradition, without ever reaching the centre of its concerns' (Derrida 1989: 33). On the one hand the claim is made specifically for the discipline of philosophy, in which rhythm is said to be present yet peripheral. Yet, as Lexi Eikelboom (2018) notes, a more general and arguably more important point is being made:

> Like a ghost, rhythm is barely visible and therefore rarely noticed, but it is also ever-present. Rhythm does not easily adhere to the channels through which communication operates. [We might] define it as a periodic oscillation between strong and weak beats, or point to repetitions of visual patterns, but as we will see and as many of us may already suspect, these indications do not sufficiently capture all that is involved with rhythm. They do not, for example, explain why we talk about 'getting into a rhythm'. (Eikelboom 2018: 1–2)

In the context of a *haunting* of rhythm, and with an attempt to work variously through the difficulties of communicating critically about/with rhythm, this book brings together a set of new essays that explore and challenge our understanding of the term. This introduction, which sets out the main parameters and themes, and which provides an overview of the book, is the first of three opening entries. The second is Pascal Michon's essay 'Could Rhythm Become a New Scientific Paradigm for the Humanities?', which is offered as a parallel introductory text.

Michon sets out succinctly how we can understand rhythm as presenting a new kind of paradigm, one that differs from the earlier unifying paradigmatic concepts of 'structure' and 'system'. Crucially, he argues that these earlier, dominant paradigms, which span the first half of the twentieth century, no longer correspond well to the analysis required of our 'neo-capitalist world'. In a key line, he writes: 'What looked critical when the world was dominated by hierarchical, stable and stifling classification systems, seems less and less relevant since the world has become open, mobile and fluid.' It is now rhythm, he suggests, that becomes the more operative term. It is worth noting that his account has been an important factor in helping to shape the overall editorial process of this book and in establishing key issues and concerns. Michon is notable for his prolific scholarship in the area of rhythm, including his extensive, multi-volume *Elements of Rhythmology* (2017–19), which traces the term through its long philosophical (and etymological) history, from antiquity to the present. He has also been a champion of a community of research, having founded *Rhuthmos* (http://rhuthmos.eu/), an international and transdisciplinary platform for research on rhythm in science, philosophy and the arts. Publishing primarily in French, and including open access to all of Michon's work, this online network and publisher has galvanised a broad community of researchers.

Drawing directly upon Michon's historical account, Crespi and Manghani's 'A Genealogy of Rhythm' completes the three-part introductory texts. It presents a genealogy of rhythm as it occurs through critical theory literatures of the twentieth century (and with reference back to early Greek thought). The approach taken has been to curate key passages from a variety of thinkers, with the aim of helping to map out links and lineages of thought, and crucially to prompt further investigation and development of the field. The selection of texts cannot in any way be taken to be exhaustive (indeed it is something that could fill a book all of its own), and inevitably there are varying terminologies and aspects of rhythm that get woven into the different styles and hues of critical accounts. Nonetheless, the selected materials help to show how pre-Socratic thinking on rhythm and form is echoed in the post-structuralist writings of the 1970s. In fact, it is evident that rhythm emerges as an underlying interest among a number of the prominent thinkers of the French intellectual scene. In this case, the concept of rhythm provides an alternative to the rigidities of structuralism, and also stands against an emphasis on individualism (for which phenomenological and postmodernist critiques can often be criticised). However, while ideas about rhythm and its application can be located in a wide range of writings, it has generally remained implicit. It has not led, for example, to a set of common concepts or critical terms. The different contributions to this book go some way towards examining just what those concepts might look like (and the various tensions at stake), and together they demonstrate how rhythm might now emerge more forcefully and pertinently as a critical framing for contemporary culture.

Rhythm can be seen to regulate much of the discourse on time, speed and efficiency from the turn of the twentieth century onwards, as in the work, for example, of Henri Bergson, Georg Simmel, Carl Buecher, Frederick Taylor and William Wundt. Moreover, rhythm was instrumental in the political propaganda of the National Socialists in Germany and in the Soviet Union. There is also an earlier philosophical debt towards the Romantics such as Friedrich Schelling and, later, Friedrich Nietzsche. We can consider connections here to authors and practitioners such as Rudolf Bode, Ludwig Klages and Rudolf Laban, all associated with *Koerperkultur* during the early part of the twentieth century, which marked a sustained consideration of physical education and bodily practices in the wider context of culture and society. As forms of materialist phenomenology, studies pertained to dance, playing sport, outdoor activities and other forms of movement. There are connections here to the ideology of National Socialism during this period, but more broadly speaking, links are established between the body and the 'rhythms' of politics, economics and ethics; ideas which are later picked up in new critical work on the body in the 1980s (not least drawing on the work of Michel Foucault). In another direction, there is the implied importance of rhythm in regard to the dialectic of Marx's historical materialism. While Marx represents a critique of capitalism, his observation of factory work etc. relates to Taylorism, the scientific analysis and management of labour and production that had such a profound impact on the shaping of modernity. Rhythm as a critical concept resurfaces in the post-war period, discernible in the work of a wide variety of authors such as Hannah Arendt, Rudolf Laban, Gaston Bachelard, Henri Lefebvre, and later with the writings of Gilles Deleuze and Félix Guattari, Henri Meschonnic, Michel Foucault, Jacques Derrida, Michel Serres, Paul Virilio and Jean Baudrillard, among others. Rhythm is also pertinent to feminist writings, relating to critical ideas of enunciation, style, performance and the body, as found in the work of Luce Irigaray, Hélène Cixous, Donna Haraway and Judith Butler. Julia Kristeva's account of language as a 'signifying process' (*signifiance*), and her account of the 'chora' as rhythms and forces, is frequently acknowledged, while not necessarily afforded sufficient critical attention. Notably, however, in English-speaking academia, a noticeable shift occurs in the first decade of the new millennium with the translation of Henri Lefebvre's *Rhythmanalysis* (2004).

Nonetheless, despite or maybe because of its complex heritage, rhythm remains ambiguous. It is synonymous with 'order', 'harmony' and 'measure'; and yet equally with 'chaos', 'disharmony', 'idiosyncrasies' and, more particularly, for the purposes of this book, as a composite term for form and patterning. The complexity of the term makes rhythm a *productive* concept for contemporary critical enquiry. A recent symposium under the title of 'Chasing Rhythm', for example, brought together a diversity of thinkers concerned with education, sociology, cultural studies, critical theory and topology. The subtitle to the event referred to 'encounters at the edge of academic and epistemological traditions', and there was an evident attempt to 'interrogate the historical, cultural and societal conditions and moods that seem to invite and propel the return of rhythm'.[1] An underlying question was whether or not rhythm could be viewed as an emerging 'field' and if so, how it might be marked out in terms of distinct theoretical and methodological explorations. As with the development of the field of visual culture studies and the associated Visual Turn of the 1990s, there are inevitable dilemmas in announcing a new academic trend. It was certainly the case that those attending the 'Chasing Rhythm' event were not able to come to a consensus; suffice to say that rhythm was roundly welcomed as a new force for thinking that could ably work across different disciplinary boundaries. W. J. T. Mitchell's (1995) view on interdisciplinarity and visual culture is perhaps instructive. He notes how his interest has always been less in terms of interdisciplinarity *per se*, and more 'in forms of "indiscipline", of turbulence or incoherence at the inner and outer boundaries of disciplines' (541). In this vein, the difficulties in defining rhythm, devising methods and/or *getting into a rhythm*, can all be viewed as a productive force. In our present context, in which the gains of post-structuralism and deconstruction have largely been acknowledged and subsumed into mainstream political thinking, at least in terms of how we relate to questions of power, identity and representation, but which have arguably coalesced less strongly in offering a critical response to globalisation and digital, network culture, there is a pressing need for a new, or at least a renewed agenda.

Rhythm Thinking

As we enter more deeply into the ensuing debates, it becomes apparent that rhythm can be used both as a conceptual tool and as a subject of investigation. This gives rise to what we might call 'rhythm thinking' – albeit with the reminder that 'thinking' here refers to a wide range of modalities and to allow for *practice* as a form of critical thought. Nonetheless, we adopt this phrase in a manner similar to Caroline Knowles' phrase of 'mobilities thinking'. In her case, it is a phrase she uses to critique a body of work, but one that she nonetheless maintains sympathy with. Her book *Flip Flop* (2014) is an extended study of the seemingly simple and innocuous footwear, the flip-flop, which she works through methodically from the extraction of raw materials to manufacture, distribution and consumption. It is a very thorough form of *material* sociology. She positions herself against a wider body of work in both anthropology and sociology concerned with material culture, which she would argue moves too quickly, avoiding certain 'frictions' that come of materials and their itineraries. It is worth quoting Knowles in her explanation of the problem, which she calls 'mobilities thinking':

> In attending to the social textures of mobility it becomes apparent that the 'mobilities thinking' of many contemporary social theorists . . . is deficient. It is over-theorised and under empirically demonstrated. Specifically, mobility thinking supports two serious deficiencies. The first is evident in the use of terms like 'scape' and 'flow' to establish force fields in which movement is part of the architecture of space. Flow conveys an unreal ease with which people and things move from place to place. [. . .] The second deficiency extends from the first. Mobility thinking erases the social textures of travel in calling movement flow. Where people and objects travel, how they travel and the knowledge with which they travel matters: making lives through the journeys in which they are cast. (Knowles 2014: 7)

Given her evident interest in 'movement' (and query over the term 'flow'), there are many ways in which rhythm poses interesting connections and intersections (see Lyons 2019). However, for the purposes of this introduction, it is the parallels of the problem of mobilities thinking that are of note. In bringing together a dozen different authors for this edited volume, it is not necessarily desirable to set a single, overarching set of definitions and parameters – as such, we present a variety of forms of thinking around rhythm. Philosophically, we might argue certain 'deficiencies' (or frictions) emerge between one chapter and another, though we take this to be productive in working through the difficult concept of rhythm. The temptation to over-theorise and under-empiricise is evident in much that is written about rhythm – going all the way back to the early Greek writings on rhythm. Nonetheless, as detailed in the outline below, this volume comprises a mix of the theoretical and the empirical. Hopefully, then, in *looking across* all of the contents, the book avoids inventing any kind of 'force field' or metaphysics of rhythm, but instead maintains a dialogue with a complex set of social, cultural and material textures that we can understand *through* investigations of rhythm.

Unlike Knowles' evocation of 'mobilities thinking' (which is to define a field in need of critique), the point here of positing 'rhythm thinking' is to help stake out a field that is arguably much less defined, though it is pervasive and 'haunting' once one starts to look. As shown in the supplementary introduction, 'A Genealogy of Rhythm', it is possible to map philosophical thinking regarding rhythm across a long history of varying trends and developments. We can begin with Greek antiquity, with reference, for example, to Heraclitus' 'Theory of Flux', or Leucippus' and Democritus' ideas of the 'atom'. This leads us to the term *rhuthmos*, as explicated by Émile Benveniste's widely read essay 'The Notion of "Rhythm" in its Linguistic Expression' (1971: 281–8). But we can also look to more recent history, to the different phases of the industrial revolution, for example, to consider how mechanisation, electrification, mass production, computing and data have all impacted on ourselves as rhythmic beings and on the rhythms of society. Here, as suggested above, we might consider thinkers such as Nietzsche and Bergson, as well as the practitioner Rudolf Laban (discussed in Crespi's chapter), but then also traced through to the modern period, with the French theorists who emerged at the cusp of change as structuralism declined. Michon (2011) notes how with the decline of structuralism there was evidently an underlying interest in rhythm among a number of the prominent thinkers of the French intellectual scene. Foucault, Barthes and Derrida, in particular, Michon suggests, were 'reflecting on this concept, explicitly or implicitly using it as an alternative after the collapse of structuralism and against the coming methodological individualism; maybe also . . . as a tool to curb the tendency of certain kind[s] of Nietzscheism and Heideggerism to overplay dispersion, difference and chaos'. Foucault's *Discipline and Punish* (1975), Barthes' late lecture course at the Collège de France in 1977, *Comment vivre ensemble?* (as explored in Manghani's chapter on idiorrhythmy), Michel Serres' writings on physics, and Deleuze and Guattari's *A Thousand Plateaus* (1980), as well as Deleuze's *Difference and Repetition*, are all examples where rhythm represents if not a central, certainly an important, recurrent underlying concern.

Nonetheless, for various reasons, specific readings of rhythm – a specific 'rhythm thinking' – has not been adequately drawn out from these works. As Michon puts it: 'Rhythm, which could have been a new common concept for critical thought, disappeared until the second half of the 1990s, when it was rediscovered in many different disciplines but with very few references to this short period of obscure glory.' The apparent disappearance might lead us to consider this merely a broken branch of knowledge, disconnected from more current interests in rhythm. Nonetheless, it would seem pertinent to look for ways in which a critical history (and key source materials of rhythm and rhythmanalysis) can provide a proper framing for current debates, so encouraging a contemporary dialogue between our present interest in rhythm and past literatures. The nature of rhythmanalysis itself – whether we root this back purely to Lefebvre's volume *Rhythmanalysis*, or as a more generally adopted term – undoubtedly draws upon *interdisciplinary* thinking, working across areas of philosophy, aesthetics, critical theory, anthropology, sociology and cultural studies. It takes time for interdisciplinary work, through its varying attempts and outcomes, to show itself as a distinctive undertaking. Some of the contributions to this book – particularly those that are more empirically driven – are quite explicit about adopting or at least seeking an interdisciplinary approach. Other contributions, while less concerned with staking out an 'approach', are still nonetheless wide-ranging in their terms and referencing. A certain dividing line that emerges from the various contributions might be described as between rhythm-based 'approaches' and 'critiques'.

Of the former, rhythm as an approach or a 'method' (even if not always fully defined) has purchase across a wide range of areas, notably within the social sciences. Dawn Lyon's (2019) *What Is Rhythmanalysis?* is a testament to this widening interest. Her book is part of a series on research methods 'at the forefront of developments in the social sciences'. Alongside traditional interests in qualitative and quantitative methods, the book sits alongside those which consider a variety of approaches: diary method, discourse analysis, inclusive research, narrative research and online methods, etc. Placed in this way, rhythmanalysis becomes part of a broader discourse that legitimates methods and approaches. Indeed, cutting across a wide range of areas and disciplines, including, for example, geography, sociology, anthropology, economics, architecture and urban studies, there is both an interest in developing methods and their application. Such work is under way in dedicated units and centres at numerous universities. The Synthesis Center at Arizona State University, for example, has a dedicated rhythamanalysis research group looking at cities, movement of people and computational media as 'biosocial complex systems'; the Sunkhronos Institute in Switzerland includes the Temporalities, Rhythms and Complexity lab, and has published on these themes in relation to education; City Rhythm is a long-standing research programme at Delft University and Amsterdam Institute for Advanced Metropolitan Solutions (working across six cities in the Netherlands, as recounted in Nevejan and Sefkatli's chapter in this book); and the Topology Research Unit at Goldsmiths draws upon the concept of rhythm as part of its development of conceptual language for understanding relationships, intensities and transformations. These various research clusters are just a snapshot of a range of interdisciplinary activities taking place at an international level, leading to a network of likeminded scholars and practitioners. Overall, there is an emergent and committed audience for writings on rhythm as a critical term within the sciences, arts and humanities, with a number of notable publications having been published over the last decade. Tim Edensor's (2010) edited volume *Geographies of Rhythm: Nature, Place, Mobilities and Bodies* brings together fifteen contributors who, primarily based on the work of Lefebvre, consider current ideas in human geography and social sciences. Alhadeff-Jones (2017) offers enquiry into the temporal dimensions of education, providing insights into how diverse experiences of time structure our educational and learning experiences; and Morris (2017), in looking at rhythm in acting and performance, offers the analysis of rhythm as embodied and understood by performers, directors, educators, playwrights, designers and scholars.

On the other side, however, there is equally an interest in rhythm as critique, which, if not always explicit, remains within a critical, historical and theoretical tradition. There are different directions in which such critique can be applied, as is seen across this book. Some notable, book-length studies include Ikoniadou's (2014) *The Rhythmic Event*, which is published in the MIT book series edited by Massumi and Manning, 'Technologies of Lived Abstraction'. This monograph presents a philosophical introduction to rhythm specifically in relation to affective technology and sonic art. Yi Chen (2016), in *Practising Rhythmanalysis: Theories and Methodologies*, provides a focused account and application of Lefebvre's rhythmanalysis as a philosophy and research method; here combined with an interest in cultural studies. Jonathan Culler and Ben Glaser's (2019) edited volume *Critical Rhythm* looks at new approaches to poetic rhythm, looking beyond merely the literary mode to consider what it means to 'think rhythm' and what it is to experience rhythm. Lexi Eikelboom's *Rhythm* (2019), which draws explicitly from Michon's opening up of the field, develops the term beyond the human to consider it as a theological category, as a means to underpin ideas about faith and one's relationship to a deity. Taken together, whether we are concerned with rhythm as an approach or as a type of critique, there has been a steady, growing interest and significance. As an overall trend it represents some kind of 'rhythm thinking', but it remains hard to pin down. In many cases the root interest stems from the work of Lefebvre, which can be attributed to the relatively late, posthumous publication of his slim book *Rhythmanalysis*. While the tone of this book is confident and optimistic about the establishment of a new field of critical thinking, it reads in many ways as merely suggestive and even ambiguous. The hope, here, in bringing together the essays for this book, has been to build upon the clear appetite for thinking about contemporary social and culture phenomena in terms of rhythms, but equally to seek to hone more rigour and definition in how we relate to this critical term.

Overview of the Book

Following the three introductory elements, this book consists of nine chapters, which are placed within a three-part structure. These chapters each examine specific issues and ideas on rhythm. In Part I, 'Modalities of Rhythm', three essays set out theoretical and cross-cultural considerations of rhythm as a critical concept. Part II, 'Sites and Practices', explores rhythm as *situated* within questions of value, politics and ethics. It opens up different scenarios of the everyday and the contemporary economy, with reference to immaterial labour, affective capitalism and financial algorithmic technologies. Finally, the third part of the book, 'Rhythmanalysis', provides distinct case studies and critical discussions of the *application* of rhythmanalysis, turning attention to the research and analysis of political conjunctures, urban analysis and the algorithmic, with reference to pattern of life analysis and Artificial Intelligence.

The collection of essays offers a bridging of language and cultural divide thanks to the translation and discussion of French and German scholarship. The insights of Émile Benveniste, noted above, become a recurrent point of reference. As outlined in Crespi and Manghani's 'A Genealogy of Rhythm', Benveniste provides an etymological account of *rhuthmos*, which elucidates how the term 'rhythm' operates as a key oscillating term from the pre-Socratics through to the present day when attending to issues of matter, form, movement and repetition. Rhythm is revealed here as a fundamental problematic, pertinent to social, political and aesthetic analysis. In addition, there are chapters which examine the specific work of Rudolf Laban, Henri Lefebvre and Roland Barthes, among others. Part I includes archive materials of Rudolf Laban and a newly translated text by Henri Meschonnic. In the case of Laban, Crespi's chapter locates the practice-based approach to rhythm of this feted choreographer and movement-thinker. In doing so, she adds a significant and overlooked voice to the ongoing debate on rhythm as it has unfolded in Western thought, and argues for the value of a practitioner's insight into an otherwise prominently if not exclusively theoretical discourse. The chapter draws upon Laban's artistic output and philosophy through an exploration and analysis of unpublished manuscripts and diagrams held at the National Resource Centre for Dance at the University of Surrey. Anticipating what Henri Lefebvre famously argued in *Rhythmanalysis*, rhythm is for Laban at the same time a quantifiable phenomenon unfolding in space and a qualitative variable 'in contact', suggestive of what Lefebvre would later describe as 'what is least rational in human being: the lived, the carnal, the body' (2013: 18). Laban studied rhythm's *intensities* in his 'Effort theory' in English factories in the post-war period. This work resonates with, but at the same time differs from, Taylor's project of time-motion studies, in that rhythm plays the central role of resisting the impact of machine work on individual workers. In order to understand and reconcile the inner (Effort) and outer (Choreutics) study of rhythm, Laban later in life relied on topological structures such as knots and Mobius strips to devise his theories, which resonate with the work of Gilles Deleuze and Félix Guattari, Jacques Lacan and Michel Serres among others. These topological models sought to overcome the binary division of inside–outside and, also, to conceive of a continuous space of transformation without interruption, something that comes to define Laban's understanding of rhythm.

In the case of Henri Meschonnic, whom we might equally consider a 'visionary' thinker, a translation is presented from his magnum opus *Critique du rythme. Anthropologie historique du langage* (1982). Meschonnic was a French linguist, poet and translator of the Bible who developed a theory of language based on the notion of rhythm. The translation provided here gives some of the tenets of Meschonnic's theory, which, based on Benveniste's account, leads him to argue for rhythm as '*form in movement*'. As such, Meschonnic's 'poetics of rhythm' is concerned with 'signifiance' for the *way* its meaning is constituted. It is explicitly an attempt to go beyond semiotics, which was the dominant field at the time of his writing. Part I concludes with a contemporary essay, 'Rhythm and Textural Temporality', by Sha Xin Wei and Garrett Laroy Johnson, which takes us towards a posthumanist and radical empiricist approach to rhythm. Suspending all commitment to the anthropic subject, whether phenomenological, psychological or cognitive, their approach shares with pragmatism and process philosophy the proposition of experience without a subject. Drawing directly upon the work of the aforementioned Topological Media Lab and the Synthesis Centre at Arizona State University, the chapter offers key insights from experimental, gestural media and performative techniques. In thinking back to Knowles' concerns for theory overstepping the empirical, this chapter gives an example of a clear attempt to work from both ends, to use both theory and practice to interrogate and challenge one another in an unfolding process.

Part II of the book, 'Sites and Practices', opens with Yuill and Skeggs' chapter, 'Attunement of Value and Capital in the Algorithms of Social Media', which, while drawing directly upon Lefebvre's *Rhythmanalysis* (2004), provides an account of the authors' own application and adaptation of rhythm for their Values & Value project. This project is an empirical investigation into how social media transforms personal value into financial value, so recalibrating the relations between value, capital and technics. Picking up on concerns around 'immaterial labour' and 'emotional capitalism' and the related impact of social media platforms, this chapter provides a way of thinking about time and value. In the context of platforms such as Facebook, the *rhythms* of its users' daily lives, not just their data, become a part of the accumulation of capital and underpin the algorithms that then perpetuate such accumulations.

Taking a more philosophical approach, Manghani's 'Idiorrhythmy: An (Unsustainable) Aesthetics of Ethics' raises questions about how we *choose* to navigate the rhythms of the everyday. In particular, it draws on Barthes' account of idiorrhythmy, which is concerned with how individual rhythms are established among the rhythms of others. Akin to debates of the political aesthetic – in which we consider politics as form, as mediation and sensibility – this chapter looks to the aesthetics that must underline the 'rhythm' of ethics, our choosing how to live together. A key motif is our 'framing' of rhythm. This picks up from Lefebvre's chapter 'Seen from the Window', in which he performs a rhythmanalysis by looking down upon the streets of Paris through a window frame; a passage that lends itself to a reading of Lefebvre as poet or artist. In writing on rhythm as a philosophy of the present, Lefebvre himself raises the question as to whether the rhythmanalyst is in some way akin to the poet. This point is extrapolated through Barthes' account of 'idiorrhythmy', which in turn prompts a critical reading of Benveniste's essay on the notion of rhythm; and which is further illuminated with reference to three artists' work in the context of city spaces, who each offer distinctive 'windows' or viewpoints of rhythm. Echoing the account of Laban as a *practitioner* of rhythm, this chapter, drawing on Barthes' ethical interest in idiorrhythmy (based upon his posthumously published lecture courses *How to Live Together* and *The Neutral*), examines the *writing* of rhythm in important ways, not least in allowing for a more *writerly* account of rhythmanalysis, which in turn opens out to an ethics of rhythm: to question less what rhythm is and what it does, and instead to consider what kinds of rhythms we want and desire; i.e. to shift from ontological questions of rhythm to ethical ones. Manghani's essay closes with a reminder of the fragility of our chosen rhythms. While there is a need to divert instrumentalist uses of rhythm, we also need to attend to the fact that rhythm is always a form of *idio*rrhythmy, which is far from sustainable.

Unlike the preceding chapters (though chiming with Manghani's post-structuralist interest in rhythm), Part II closes with a more 'writerly' essay. 'Adventures of a Line of Thought' by Stamatia Portanova can be read as a *performance* of rhythmanalysis. Specifically, in working with the idea of the 'line' (as something that must proceed, must be between points), Portanova offers a speculative reading of the concept of rhythm in relation to capital in the context of financial technologies such as trading algorithms, bitcoin and the blockchain. Based on a reading of the posthumanist philosophy of Gilles Deleuze and Félix Guattari, rhythm might be defined as that which continuously changes direction along critical, although infinitesimal, differentiations. Departing from this definition, Portanova describes different financial milieus as rhythmic, which in her case is to be more than mere metric repetition.

The final part of the book, 'Rhythmanalysis', presents three different accounts of how rhythm can be understood and *put to use* as a form of analysis or method. In the opening chapter of this section, Yi Chen's 'The Configuring of "Context" in Rhythmanalysis', we gain two main conceptual configurations: rhythm as a meta-sense and rhythm as temporal-spatial relations in which social entities are (dis)ordered. In the main, Chen's account is drawn directly from Lefebvre, but is presented as a methodology for cultural historical research. Taking her cue from Lawrence Grossberg's observation that cultural studies is about making 'radical contexts', Chen questions what it means to contextualise something, i.e. what parameters and mechanisms are brought to bear in forming a context to a text. There is a need, she argues, to identify and assemble social entities at the level of rhythms, which enables a more radical conception of the identity of 'subjects' and 'objects'. In turn, this is to develop alternative ways of conceiving and conducting social research. One key implication is the transgression of linear progress in research, and the need for modes of contextualisation that are characteristically experimental, 'obtuse' and nuanced in configuration and their articulation of cultural historical experience. Using the same term, albeit written as 'rhythm analysis', an almost opposite approach is taken by Caroline Nevejan and Pinar Sefkatli in their chapter 'City Rhythms: An Approach to Urban Rhythm Analysis'. While introducing terminology such as rhythmic tuning, matching and balancing, which could all find their corollary in Chen's work, this account is interventionalist. Indeed, working with city planners, councils and residents, the City Rhythms project at the heart of this chapter, which involved fieldwork in six cities, invokes rhythm analysis as a normative and pragmatic methodology. They define rhythm as a 'boundary object', enabling conversations across varying divides, helping a range of stakeholders to identify new solutions for key social issues within urban contexts. Rhythm here, unlike Chen, is not about disjunctures or alternative readings; it is about consensus-building through empirical validation. In presenting data about rhythms of different actors within a shared city space, the aim is to bring disparate groups together with a new understanding of one another (something that chimes, for example, with Lyon's (2016) account of the everyday rhythms of a London fish market). In this case, Nevejan and Sefkatli offer a sharable, repeatable approach, i.e. rhythm as method, which has clear impact on the lives of the city residents involved in the project. However, unlike Chen, Nevejan and Sefkatli present a universalist and arguably 'power neutral' account. Against such a view, Henriques, in concluding this section and the book, examines the underlying appeal of rhythm and algorithm, and indeed the concerns we can hold for the commercial application of both terms. Again, reference is made back to the origins of rhythm in ancient Greek thought (via Benveniste and, more recently, Pascal Michon), which in turn opens up questions about the origins of algorithm. Henriques posits the notion of 'algorithmanalysis', being distinct from the analysis of algorithms, to define the process of recoding data as pattern, in contrast to quantisation that encodes the patterning of continuous analogue variation as digital data. The chapter brings to the fore our current situation in which algorithmanalysis has already been put to use in the commercial world, whether in predicting consumer behaviours, in the political world by identifying particular groups of UK voters via social media or, indeed, in warfare, through the targeting of drone missiles. Henriques' account makes for a foreboding message on which to end this book. However, when viewed through the lens of all the contributions to the book, it can be read as one of a series of viewpoints that rhythm and rhythmanalysis open up. As a field of enquiry, we are still at a threshold moment. The task is not only to define how rhythm relates to our understanding of contemporary culture, but also to refine the skills and methods of enquiry that we can bring to the rich phenomenon of rhythm.

Rhythmic Futures

Today, the term 'rhythm' seems ever more prescient – not least where our everyday existence is underpinned by the rhythms of high-speed networks, Big Data and the choreography of satellites and computing, which at any single instant are hard to comprehend, yet undoubtedly regulate so much of what we do. Rhythm lies at the heart of our experience of shifting dynamics ruling neoliberal society in terms of life patterns, economic growth and decay, and our systems of mediation and communication. Our lives are shaped and partake of rhythmical fluctuations: the regular happening of events and its sudden variations, the negotiations between different degrees of speed, as in the way we produce and consume food or think and practise art, and the balance and alternation between our moods, affects and desires. Nevertheless, as soon becomes apparent, rhythm is difficult to grasp, pin down, describe. It is more something we feel, sense and intuit. Its study inevitably encompasses a wide diversity of disciplines and fields.

In the opening of *Rhythmanalysis*, Lefebvre boldly asserts the idea of a new science. His book, he writes, 'does not conceal its ambition. It proposes nothing less than to found a science, a new field of knowledge [*savoir*]: the analysis of rhythms; with practical consequences' (2013: 13). Yet, equally, he notes how this field of study shares characteristics with psychoanalysis and poetry. It is perhaps no surprise that today we are still in a similar position, partly asserting the prospect of a new science and yet remaining open to what its modality might be. To return to the opening suggestion of a *haunting* of rhythm, we might usefully adopt the related term of *spectre*. Perhaps as much as rhythm already pervades our thinking and actions, it is also something, as a form of study, that is still to come. As Derrida writes of 'the "scholar" of the future, the "intellectual" of tomorrow . . . [we] should learn to live by learning not how to make conversation with the ghost but how to talk with him, with her, how to let them speak or how to give them back speech, even if it is in oneself, in the other, in the other in oneself' (1994: 176). In this case, the ghost, the spectre to which we wish to give voice, is rhythm itself.

Finally, then, building on the contributions to this book, we might suitably establish the following four key interests and trajectories for a growing community of researchers. Firstly, akin to how we refer to the 'political aesthetic' – as a means to consider forms and conditions of the political – we can look to an underlying form or precept: to the notion of *rhythm politics*, which, as traced through by most of the chapters of this book, is to consider rhythm as a pervading critical 'currency' or analytic. Secondly, in conjunction with this sense of a rhythm politics, we need to pay attention to what we mean by *rhythm objects*, which, as noted for example in Manghani, Chen and Henriques' chapters, is to recalibrate the 'units of analysis' pertinent to new forms of social and cultural investigation. Thirdly, we can be open to what we might call *worldly rhythms*. It is important to acknowledge that this book has been worked through almost exclusively in relation to a Western canon. This can be taken as a deficiency, but it was arguably necessary to excavate key critical ideas across this canon that have not been explored sufficiently before. However, an important next step is undoubtedly to look at rhythm from a more *worldly* perspective: to examine rhythm in terms of its cross-cultural meanings and applications, as well as to draw upon a much wider set of literatures, philosophies and histories (reaching further too among feminist and queer literatures). Such an expanded field of research will undoubtedly open up significant ideas for rhythm research, benefiting from a rich canvas of historical, philosophical and cultural ideas. In drawing these three interests together we can lead to a general critical enquiry into *rhythms of life*. The philosophical interest in forms of life, as that which makes meaning itself possible, root back to a tradition of anthropological and sociological texts such as Émile Durkheim's *The Elementary Forms of the Religious Life* ([1912] 2008). It is certainly possible to return to such studies through the lens of rhythm, as well as equally attending to our own contemporary forms of life. Today's *rhythms of life* will span a wide range of issues and interests, relating to the environment, energy, well-being and logistics to name just a few areas. Each in itself presents vast complexities, but it is the drawing together of all elements – to turn to rhythms of life very much in the plural – that surely marks the most significant forward trajectory of critical rhythm studies.

Acknowledgements

This book has been devised and developed through a series of sustained scholarly dialogues. It began with an interview between the editors for *Theory, Culture & Society* (Crespi and Manghani 2015), in which they discuss Paola Crespi's contributions to a special issue of *Body & Society* (2014; vol. 20, nos 3–4) on 'Rhythm, Movement, Embodiment'. This exchange can also be set in the context of a conference Crespi convened, *Rhythm as Pattern and Variation: Political, Social & Artistic Inflections*, held at Goldsmiths College, 23 April 2016. The critical and primary sources presented in the chapter 'A Genealogy of Rhythm' were originally brought together in preparation for a seminar series on 'rhythmanalysis', supported by the AHRC-funded Consortium of Humanities and the Arts South-East England. The series took place at Goldsmiths College between February and May 2017 (in collaboration with Winchester School of Art, University of Southampton). The seminars sought to foreground the nature and import of rhythm and rhythmanalysis by highlighting their relevance and richness as methodological perspectives and practices within the humanities. Six sessions explored various approaches to time and rhythm as found in the work of key critical theorists such as Gilles Deleuze, Henri Lefebvre, Rudolf Laban, Roland Barthes, Henri Meschonnic, Émile Benveniste, Gaston Bachelard and others. The editors would like to thank Yi Chen, Stamatia Portanova, Eleni Ikoniadou and Pascal Michon for each offering very insightful and engaging seminar sessions as part of the series; and subsequently, a special thanks for their respective contributions to this book as a result. Thanks also to Mike Featherstone, who very kindly supported the project funding application. In addition, thanks to Fadia Dakka, who convened 'Chasing Rhythm: Encounters at the Edge of Academic and Epistemological Traditions', an international symposium on rhythm held at Birmingham City University, UK, 29 May 2019. The discussions held at this event helped to prompt some of the suggestions made above regarding 'rhythmic futures'.

Note

1. 'Chasing Rhythm: Encounters at the Edge of Academic and Epistemological Traditions', an international symposium on rhythm held at Birmingham City University, UK, 29 May 2019. Convened by Dr Fadia Dakka, Deputy Director of the Centre for the Study of Practice and Culture in Education, Birmingham City University.

References

Alhadeff-Jones, M. (2017), *Time and the Rhythms of Emancipatory Education: Re-thinking the Temporal Complexity of Self and Society*. London: Routledge.
Benveniste, É. (1971), *Problems in General Linguistics*, trans. M. E. Meek. Coral Gables: University of Miami Press.
Chen, Y. (2016), *Practising Rhythmanalysis: Theories and Methodologies*. London and New York: Rowman & Littlefield International.
Crespi, P., and S. Manghani (2015), 'Rhythmanalysis: An Interview with Paola Crespi', *Theory, Culture & Society*, <https://www.theoryculturesociety.org/rhythmanalysis-an-interview-with-paola-crespi/> (last accessed 28 December 2019).

Culler, J., and B. Glaser (eds) (2019), *Critical Rhythm: The Poetics of a Literary Life Form*. New York: Fordham University Press.
Derrida, J. (1989), 'Introduction', in Philippe Lacoue-Labarthe, *Typography: Mimesis, Philosophy, Politics*, trans. C. Fynsk. Cambridge, MA: Harvard University Press, pp. 1–42.
Derrida, J. (1994), *Specters of Marx: The State of the Debt, the Work of Mourning, and the New International*. New York: Routledge.
Durkheim, É. (2008), *The Elementary Forms of the Religious Life*, trans. C. Cosman. Oxford: Oxford University Press.
Edenso, T. (ed.) (2010), *Geographies of Rhythm: Nature, Place, Mobilities and Bodies*. Farnham: Ashgate.
Eikelboom, L. (2018), *Rhythm: A Theological Category*. Oxford: Oxford University Press.
Ikoniadou, E. (2014), *The Rhythmic Event*. Cambridge, MA: MIT Press.
Lefebvre, H. (2013), *Rhythmanalysis: Space, Time and Everyday Life*, trans. S. Elden and G. Moore. London: Continuum.
Lyon, D. (2016), 'Doing Audio-Visual Montage to Explore Time and Space: The Everyday Rhythms of Billingsgate Fish Market', *Sociological Research Online*, 21(3), 12, <http://www.socresonline.org.uk/21/3/12.html> (last accessed 28 December 2019).
Lyon, D. (2019), *What Is Rhythmanalysis?* London: Bloomsbury Academic.
Meschonnic, H. (1982), *Critique du rythme. Anthropologie historique du langage*. Lagrasse: Verdier.
Michon, P. (2011), 'A Short History of Rhythm Theory Since the 1970s', *Rhuthmos*, 6 December 2011, <http://rhuthmos.eu/spip.php?article462> (last accessed 28 December 2019).
Michon, P. (2017–19), *Elements of Rhythmology*, vols 1–3. Paris: Rhuthmos.
Mitchell, W. J. T. (1995), 'Interdisciplinarity and Visual Culture', *Art Bulletin*, LXXVII (4), pp. 540–3.
Morris, E. (2017), *Rhythm in Acting and Performance Embodied Approaches and Understandings*. London: Bloomsbury.

Could Rhythm Become a New Scientific Paradigm for the Humanities?

Pascal Michon

The first thing that becomes obvious when one is documenting the studies in human and social science dedicated to rhythmic phenomena or using rhythm as operating concept – whatever its definition – is the rapid increase in their number. Whereas thirty years ago rhythmic studies were very few and confined to sociology, economics, philosophy, musicology and poetics, they now both multiply and spread into new disciplines. For the last twenty years, rhythmic research has been developing in psychiatry, psychoanalysis and cognitive science. It emerged in anthropology, history, geography, urbanism. We saw it rising in linguistics and communication science – even in fields of knowledge that are more art than science, such as management and learning sciences. To make it short, we are witnessing a quite remarkable blooming of studies on rhythm or using rhythm as a tool.

This initial finding raises a question: should we see this re-emergence of rhythm as more than a fad? Should we see it, more specifically, as a transformation of knowledge or what one might call a 'paradigm shift'? Assuming that we define the concept of 'paradigm' as Thomas Kuhn did in the early 1960s, this would require that some problems, methods, concepts or certain findings would effectively be shared by a sufficiently large number of science and would provide a framework or a common epistemological support. Nowadays, obviously, this is not the case. Although increasingly frequent and spread in various fields, attention to rhythmic thematics remains dispersed and borrowings between disciplines are still rather rare.

This can be interpreted in three ways. The first, the most radical, would be that there is no and there will never be such thing as a 'rhythm paradigm.' This interpretation cannot be excluded from the outset but it has the flaw to close the debate even though we have not yet verified whether other interpretations are possible. The second, which is already a little more favorable, would be that the various examples, that have just been quickly listed, suggest that we would be at the mere beginning of a paradigmatic shift. This shift would be advanced enough to be detectable but not enough to be effective. The substitution of the new epistemological framework to the previous one would not be completed yet but it could happen in a foreseeable future. The last one would be that we may need to question Kuhn's view of scientific paradigms, which is itself a byproduct of a particular conception of science inspired by systemism/structuralism. Is it not possible indeed, that a paradigm supports, enlivens, irrigates some science without constituting an *a priori*, unconscious, uniform framework without exception? Could we not see the rhythmic paradigm rhythmically, i.e. as a simultaneously unitary and multiple ensemble of specific yet shareable ways to make the thought flow?

To put it in a nutshell, it is the third hypothesis which seems to me the most likely in view of the research that has been conducted on the web platform *Rhuthmos*. Rhythm is indeed a new paradigm but in quite a new way which implies diversity of approaches and flexible articulations. It is in this sense that we will use the term paradigm here.

Towards a New Kind of Paradigm?

In order not to remain too abstract, I would like to present three examples: one taken in sociology, another one in anthropology and finally one in theory of language and poetics.

Sociology can rightly pride itself on numerous and ancient studies on rhythms of daily life, rhythms of work, rhythms of leisure. Time, labor, urban and entertainment sociologies are today flourishing. In most of these studies, the concept of rhythm is taken either in its traditional periodic sense or as mere speed of action. The change of rhythm is identified in the first case to a change of accentuation, that can sometimes lead to dissolution and complete fluidity (Bauman 2000), and in the second to a change of pace that supports the very fashionable theme of 'acceleration' (Rosa 2010). But one sees in the work of young urban planners, sociologists and geographers new concerns that give to the concept of rhythm a different and quite remarkable meaning.

Given the space available, I will mention only one of these young researchers. In 2010, Benjamin Pradel defended a PhD thesis entitled *Temporary Urbanism and Event Urbanity: The New Collective*

Rhythms (2011). In this research he sought to challenge the common idea that life in large cities is becoming increasingly arrhythmic and dominated by movement and fluidity. He showed instead that the number of rhythms continue to organise the generation, support and destruction of singular and collective identities. But by so doing, he was not content with reintroducing discontinuity into continuity, or accentuation into fluidity. His aim was to dismiss both holistic and individualistic conceptions of social time and to show that the temporality of action is built in a constant back and forth between individual and collective level, local and global scale. In great cities, rhythms of interaction certainly have no longer the regularity they had in urban societies of the past, but they are not completely dissolved either in what is often presented as a Brownian motion without term or form. To understand what is happening, we must, as Gilbert Simondon (1958) said, 'start from the middle'. These interaction rhythms are new ways to produce social ties, which combine hypermodern features (e.g. the ceaseless weaving of weak ties) and updated legacy features (e.g. regular festive gatherings).

In anthropology, the notion of rhythm – which, in an already broader sense, was crucial to Franz Boas, Marcel Mauss and E. E. Evans-Pritchard – was dismissed after World War II and rejected from the circle of scientific concern (Michon 2016, Michon 2015a). But in recent years, a mutation occurred through the emergence of what François Laplantine (2005) suggested calling a 'modal anthropology'. This, he said, is:

> an approach to apprehend lifestyle, action and knowledge, ways of being, and more precisely modulations of behavior, including the most seemingly trivial, in the dimension of time, or rather the duration. While structural logic is a combinational logic presupposing the discontinuity of invariant signs likely to dispose and rearrange in a finite ensemble, a modal approach is much more attentive to transition processes and rhythmic transformations. Its main concern is less the nature of the relationship of the elements to the whole than the question of tone and intensity, that is to say the graduations oscillating between acceleration and deceleration, moving body and body at rest, contraction and relaxation. (Laplantine 2011)

This new anthropology rejects any eleatic perspective but also any structuralist elementarism. It wants to focus on continuity, modality, mutation, derailment and ultimately event – all kinds of phenomena that are not covered by traditional categories and deterministic logic. The rhythm, explicitly taken in the sense of mode of flowing, is thus becoming a leading operational concept. Without clearly saying it, this anthropology revives reflections by Georg Simmel, Mauss, Evans-Pritchard and many authors of the first half of the twentieth century, who considered rhythm a key anthropological issue. In the 1930s, Mauss said in one of his lectures: 'Socially and individually, man is a rhythmic animal' (1947: 85).

Last example: theory of language and poetics. For Henri Meschonnic, first of all, linguistics must be included in a more general discipline he called 'theory of language' – in French, *théorie du langage*. Unlike traditional linguistics, which poses the primacy of *la langue*, i.e. of a separate linguistic body linked to a social group – even when it includes the concept of enunciation – the theory of language is characterised by the primacy it gives to speech and language as an activity. It is part of a Humboldtian legacy that Meschonnic sees passing through Saussure and Benveniste. Moreover, this theory of language takes into account not only the ordinary discourse, as linguists and philosophers of language do, but also the literary discourse. So instead of considering poetics as external to linguistics, it places it instead at its centre (Michon 2010).

This double theoretical reversal is the frame that gives its meaning to Meschonnic's quite innovative use of the rhythm concept. The language activity is characterised, Meschonnic says, by:

> a relational morphological performativity, [which] neutralizes the opposition between signifier and signified. [. . .] This neutralization involves a representative function of language as discourse at all linguistic levels, in intonation, phonology, syntax (word order), organization of speech [. . .], etc. The signifier is no longer opposed to the signified; there is only one multiple, structural signifier, that brings about meaning from any part, a signifiance [. . .] constantly in the making and de-making. (Meschonnic 1975: 512)

Thus, far from being conceived, as in the dominant metric tradition, as a succession of strong and weak beats more or less strictly arithmetically organised, rhythm for Meschonnic means the continuing organisation of this unique and at once multiple signifier, which produces *signifiance*:

> I define rhythm in language as the organization of the marks by which the signifiers, be they linguistic or non-linguistic (especially in the case of oral communication), produce a specific semantics, separate from lexical meaning, that I call signifiance: that is to say the values specific to a discourse and to only one. These marks can be at all 'levels' of language: accentuation, prosody, lexis, syntax. (Meschonnic 1982: 216–17)

As we see, these three uses of the rhythm concept do not completely overlap. While the sociology of urban life still gives an important space to its metric definition and the anthropology of traditional groups adopts the opposite view by making rhythm the pure modality of a flow, theory of language and poetics seeks to elaborate a concept taking on the tension between form and flow.

These three various investigations share what one might call a 'family resemblance', which makes them reject any structural and even systemic model, without falling either into the differentialistic or individualistic views. They develop new perspectives from concepts neglected by previous paradigms: rhythms, modes and ways or manners of flowing. These differences as well as these common theoretical rejections and choices make these studies form a constellation whose elements are relatively independent from each other but share some important features.

Historical Differences with Previous Paradigms

In the 1950s and more than ever in the 1960s, the concept of 'structure', defined as a stable organisation based on a set of internal differences, provided a formal model for many human and social sciences. At the same time, it allowed these sciences to be organised around a discipline queen: linguistics. Language – at least as it was defined by phonology, i.e. as *la langue* – was a type of organisation that seemed to be generalisable to many other realities. Simultaneously, but over a significantly longer period of time, the concept of 'system' represented a second 'universal' formal model, used both in social and natural science. This time it was not linguistics that provided the central model, but cybernetics. Like structure, system was defined as a stable organisation, but its stability resulted from the divergent yet in the long run balanced interaction of differentiated elements.

Since the 1970s and especially the 1980s, both models have been regularly challenged and two other concepts began to occupy the space left by their progressive withdrawal: on the one hand, the concept of 'difference', which was presented as a legacy of Nietzsche's and Heidegger's critiques of metaphysics but which also presupposed a number of principles drawn from structuralism; on the other hand, the concept of 'individual' that first, in the 1980s, openly challenged the concept of system, but eventually, in the 1990s, combined with it in new syntheses based on hermeneutical, interactionist or neo-dialectic methodologies. While in the first case – the difference model – the philosophy of temporality replaced linguistics as paradigm core, in the second – the individualist model – economy took the place of cybernetics.

Opinions on what remains today of these four paradigms diverge sharply. While everyone agrees that the structural paradigm collapsed a long time ago, the fate of the other three is still the subject of lively debate. It seems to me that none of these paradigms correspond any longer to the way our neo-capitalist world – both fluid and full of shocks and divides – operates, and that this fact alone already opens a space for rhythm. The radical break we have experienced in the last twenty-five years has made these theoretical models obsolete, while it gave again to rhythm an operative character. If our societies are penetrated by forces that fragment them and increasingly individualise us, this does not entail a greater capacity for action and experience. It is rather the opposite: we are more and more individualised, but we become less easily subjects. Therefore, except for the economists of the classical school and some sociologists, very few scientists still support the view that individuals can be considered as the primary elements of reality from which any human or social science should be built.

Overall, systemic approaches have not lost all legitimacy. But here too there are questions about their appropriateness to a universe that has been largely de-systematised for at least two decades. While the world as it emerged from World War II was composed of relatively stable systems fitting inside one another – United Nations Organization, blocks, free trade areas, states, businesses, families, even individuals – the events that have occurred in the last decades have questioned all these modes of organisation one after the other. The blocks have disappeared; the UN has been ruled out at least for a time; production, consumption and information have been globalised through transport, telecommunication and information networks that grid now the entire globe. The states have been liberalised; businesses reorganised into networks; the traditional family has had to accept periodic reconfigurations and individuals to demonstrate capabilities of faster engagement and disengagement. None of these new forms still pertains to the traditional system theories.

Finally, approaches based on the various philosophies of difference, whether ontological, semiotic or pragmatist, continue, meanwhile, to be a great success – at least quantitatively. But one may question the relevance of the critiques they have been developing, for a good twenty years now, with regard to the contemporary world, whose operation consists for a great part in the deconstruction of oppositions and frontiers, the questioning of hierarchical systems and the commoditisation of alternative lifestyles. One wonders even if, in some cases, these approaches have not become more or less willingly mere auxiliaries of the current capitalist revolution. What looked critical when the world was dominated by hierarchical, stable and stifling classification systems seems less and less relevant since the world has become open, mobile and fluid.

As in the late nineteenth and early twentieth centuries, we are now faced with an intensification of economic globalisation, a fluidisation of societies, an increase in social inequality and a reorganisation of the balance of power in the world. And that is why, as a hundred and thirty years ago, when rhythm began to be taken into account by human and social science, we need new thinking models that are adequate to the new world, at once fluid and fractured, in which we have entered. Indeed, it is precisely a model of this kind that the rebirth of the concept of rhythm suggests.

Conceptual Characteristics of the Rhythmic Paradigm

We may turn now to the main features that give the new emerging concept of rhythm its particular potential in the historical and theoretical context just described. The first is the *rejection of the metric model* that has dominated Western thought since Plato, Aristotle and Aristoxenus of Tarentum. By explicitly abandoning for poetics the Platonic model of rhythm as simple 'order of movement' (*hê tês kinêseôs táxis – ἡ τῆς κινήσεως τάξις*, Pl. *Lg.* 665a), or 'regular recurring motion' (*pâs rhuthmòs hôrisménêi metreîtai kinêsei – πᾶς ῥυθμὸς ὡρισμένῃ μετρεῖται κινήσει*, Arist. *Pr.* 882b2) (see Michon 2018a), Meschonnic anticipated what happened later, more or less explicitly, in other disciplines: he returned to the pre-Socratic view reported by Benveniste (1971: 281–8) in his famous article 'The Notion of "Rhythm" in its Linguistic Expression' (see Michon 2018a). The rhythm recovered its ancient meaning of *rhuthmos*, that is to say not only, as we read too often in hasty comments, 'a configuration at a given moment of a reality that is soon going to change', but a real 'way of flowing'. Now this is one of the most significant elements of the current scientific changes: the best of them are made in the name of what we call a *rhuthmological* conception of rhythm (Michon 2018b).

The second important feature of the new concept of rhythm concerns its *ontogenetic dimension*. Far from being a mere sensitive phenomenon, consequently pertaining only to *aesthesis*, rhythm is considered as the support of *individuation* phenomena, i.e. the generation of entities separate from each other but which are nevertheless in permanent if not constant mutation. Finally, the third significant feature of the new concept of rhythm is its *ethical and political dimension*. If rhythm supports individuation, it may sometimes support subjectivation as well, in the sense of a becoming-agent of the individuals that or who are concerned. Then rhythm has a critical dimension that makes it a fundamental tool for understanding our past, but also the new world we are now living in. These three features explain – although the analysis should certainly be further refined – the epistemological, ethical and political effectiveness of the new concept of rhythm. Once redefined as *rhuthmos* and with its dimensions of *individuation* and possible *subjectivation*, the concept of rhythm becomes a very powerful tool.

Conclusion

Owing to historical studies that have multiplied in recent years, we begin to understand that the current emergence of rhythm actually re-actualises a number of previous artistic, philosophical and scientific endeavours: before the twentieth century, the Platonic metric model had already been challenged. I think of Diderot in France in the eighteenth century or of the group of artists and art theorists that in Germany in the late eighteenth century included Moritz, Goethe, Schiller, Schlegel, Hölderlin. I also think of the constellation that marked the second half of the nineteenth century with Baudelaire, Wagner, Nietzsche, Hopkins, Mallarmé, Debussy, Mahler (Michon 2015b and 2018b). Finally, I think of the scholars who, in the late nineteenth century and the first half of the twentieth, set rhythm at the centre of their concerns, while implicitly or explicitly challenging its Platonic definition: Tarde, Simmel, Mauss, Evans-Pritchard, Granet, Bergson, Whitehead (Michon 2016). To this list, we should add all thinkers who reflected on rhythm in the late 1970s and the early 1980s: Foucault, Barthes, Serres, Deleuze, Lefebvre and Meschonnic, who is one of the most articulate on the matter (Michon 2015a).

Taking rhythm as *rhuthmos* – let us repeat it because it is the source of persistent misunderstandings – is not intended to oppose the fact that there are phenomena ordered by a succession of strong and weak beats distributed arithmetically, or by recurring periods or cyclical oscillations. But simply put, as already pointed out by Aristotle in his *Poetics*, it is not rhythm that is in the metre, but metre in rhythm. All metric organisations are organisations of dynamic phenomena and are therefore rhythms. But many rhythms are not reducible to the concept of measured order of movement that the Greeks called *metron*. The contrast between rhythmics and metrics is therefore not only conceptual, it is primarily strategic: it is about how to fit these concepts into one another. The concept of *rhuthmos* is broader and more powerful than the traditional concept of rhythm. It includes more cases in extension while it describes better their specificities.

Now we see what may be the main reason that explains the emergence of rhythm as we have witnessed for the last twenty years. Rhythm, when redefined as *rhuthmos* – i.e. as a way of flowing resulting in individuation and possibly subjectivation – is much better suited to the needs of any science that deals with objects that manifest themselves as organised flows. Whether those are the flows of speech, writing or information, the flows that ceaselessly intertwine in major global cities and tourist places or the personal and social flows that the new modal anthropology tries to understand, every time modern science must solve the same type of problem: the observer faces a dynamic reality that runs continuously, and whose particularity is that it can never be stopped and fixed in a stable form. But it is not either a totally liquid, amorphous, unorganised reality, as some claim a bit hastily. It is a moving organisation, or an organised mutation.

Studying beings from the rhythms that make them emerge fulfils the vow of Simondon to 'start from the middle' (Simondon 2007); that is to say, from the activities in which they are constantly generated and destroyed, while they seem falsely to exist by themselves and retain a substantial identity. Instead of starting from *individuals* or *systems*, as if they already existed *per se*, and look how they eventually interact, but also instead of looking only to the countless ways linguistic *différance* or temporal difference subvert identity, the new sciences study the singular and collective individuation-deindividuation processes, i.e. the processes of simultaneous generation-destruction of individuals and systems, concurrently at body, language and social levels. That kind of approach certainly removes any ethical and political guarantee based on individual or collective consciousness, but it does not indulge in relativism either, because these processes can always be classified and criticised accordingly: firstly, to the degree of *life power*, that is to say of *subjectivation*, each of them guarantees to singular and collective individuals; and secondly, the degree of *shareability* of this power. A process generating individuals by discriminating or even destroying other individuals is clearly the lowest it can exist. On the contrary, a process generating individuals by including and empowering others is the best one can hope for.

I conclude with a few words of praise and encouragement to all researchers engaged in recent years in rhythmanalytical or rhythmological research. Apart from a few seniors, such as François Laplantine, Jean-Claude Schmitt and myself, most of those researchers are young. They form a group of people who, without always being fully aware of it, share common formal and methodological concerns. These young researchers stumble against many obstacles: lack of jobs, rejection of innovation, fierce resistance against anything that might question the scientific legitimacy of existing authority relying on outdated paradigms. We have no less confidence in their future. We believe a new 'rhythm-generation' is slowly emerging: a generation that will, I am confident, introduce a radical change of rhythm in human and social science.

References

Bauman, Z. (2000), *Liquid Modernity*. Cambridge: Polity.
Benveniste, É. (1971), *Problems in General Linguistics*, trans. M. E. Meek. Coral Gables: University of Miami Press.
Laplantine, F. (2005), *Le social et le sensible. Introduction à une anthropologie modale*. Paris: Téraèdre.
Laplantine, F. (2011), 'Le vivant et le vécu, l'expérimentation et l'expérience, la catégorie et l'énergie', *Rhuthmos*, <http://rhuthmos.eu/spip.php?article276> (last accessed 28 December 2019).
Mauss, M. (1947), *Manuel d'ethnographie*. Paris: Payot.
Meschonnic, H. (1975), *Le signe et le poème*. Paris: Gallimard.
Meschonnic, H. (1982), *Critique du rythme. Anthropologie historique du langage*. Lagrasse: Verdier.
Michon, P. (2010), *Fragments d'inconnu: Pour une histoire du sujet*. Paris: Le Cerf.
Michon, P. [2007] (2015a), *Les rythmes du politique: Démocratie et capitalisme mondialisé*. Paris: Rhuthmos.
Michon, P. (2015b), *Rythmologie baroque: Spinoza, Leibniz, Diderot*. Paris: Rhuthmos.
Michon, P. [2005] (2016), *Rythme, pouvoir, mondialisation*, Paris: Rhuthmos.
Michon, P. (2018a), *Elements of Rhythmology I: Antiquity*. Paris: Rhuthmos.
Michon, P. (2018b), *Elements of Rhythmology II: From the Renaissance to the 19th Century*. Paris: Rhuthmos.
Pradel, B. (2011), 'Le rythme : une question de recherche urbaine' – introduction to PhD thesis, *Rhuthmos*, <http://rhuthmos.eu/spip.php?article460> (last accessed 28 December 2019).
Rosa, H. [2005] (2010), *Accélération: Une critique sociale du temps*. Paris: La Découverte.
Simondon, G. [1958] (2007), *L'individuation psychique et collective*. Paris: Aubier.

A Genealogy of Rhythm

Paola Crespi and Sunil Manghani

As outlined in the introduction to this book, and traced in detail in Pascal Michon's *Elements of Rhythmology* (2017–19), rhythm as a critical, philosophical concept has a long history. Yet equally, it is still not easy to define and is only rarely worked through explicitly. In response to this problem, a series of source materials are presented here with the aim of helping to unpack and map various connections and differences across the critical literatures. Offered as a supplement to the main introduction and Michon's essay on rhythm as a new paradigm within the humanities, the idea here is to aid familiarity with key texts and to consider various 'genealogies' of critical thought on rhythm. At a general level, we might identify three main perspectives or routes through which to consider the concept of rhythm, which we can label as materialism, phenomenology and language (or semiotics broadly defined). However, crucially, there are no simple lineages, and there is certainly plenty of crossover. The diagram shown here, 'A Genealogy of Rhythm' (Figure I.1), along with the selected texts, should in no way be taken as definitive or exhaustive. Rather the materials are presented in the form of a heuristic, as a means to prompt further thought, discussion and research.

There are various points at which we might wish to start a critical, historical account of rhythm. Prior to the industrial revolution, René Descartes formulated his thoughts on the animal as machine, as a non-thinking entity. La Mettrice later picks this up as a critique of the human. Such thinking – as well as, for example, Bentham's notion of the panopticon – works upon the discourse of the industrial revolution. The Cartesian split allies with the new ways of thinking about efficiencies in production. The ability to rationalise our bodily movements, and to command these movements, is epitomised by Taylorism, as developed through the mass production and assembly lines of the second phase of the industrial revolution. All of this goes on to define a particular 'rhythm of life', which we still negotiate to

A Genealogy of Rhythm 31

Pre-Socratics: Theory of Flux (Heraclitus) / Atoms (Leucippus, Democritus)
Rhuthmos (form in the instant)
PLATO (measure; movement organized in time)
Aristotle

| cc. 1760-1840 | René Descartes, Bête-machine (c.1649)   La Mettrice, L'Homme Machine (1747) | cc. 1760-1840 |

INDUSTRIAL REVOLUTION I
(mechanization, steam power)

'Immanent rhythm' of the dialectical movement of Spirit   Panopticon (1843) Jeremy Bentham
G.W.F. Hegel - *The Phenomenology of Spirit* (1807)

Late 1800s   INDUSTRIAL REVOLUTION II   Late 1800s
(mass production, assembly line, electrification)
The Factory
Karl Marx, *Das Kapital* (1867)
Studies of Motion 1870s (Eadweard Muybridge)   Dionysian/Apollonian – Rhythm/Restraint
Nietzsche, *The Birth of Tragedy* (1872/1886)

TAYLORISM 1880s – 1890s

Reality as duration (motion and flux)   cinematography – 1895-
Henri Bergson – *Matter and Memory* (1896)   (Lumière brothers)
Koerperkultur
Karl Buecher, *Arbeit und Rhythmus* (1899)
Georg Simmel, *The Philosophy of Money* (1900)
     FORDISM - early 1900s
WORLD WAR I
Rudolf Bode, *Rhythm and its Importance for Education* (1920)
     NAZISM (1920 – 1940s)   Metropolis – 1927
Rudolf Laban, *Kinetography*, c.1928
La Rythmanalyse Lucio Alberto Pinheiro dos Santos, , 1931
Ludwig Klages – *Vom Wesen des Rhythmus* (1934)   Triumph of the Will (1935)
     Olympia (1938)
WORLD WAR II
Industrial Rhythm   Laban and Lawrence, *Effort* (1947)

1950s   INDUSTRIAL REVOLUTION III   1950s
(computing, semiconductors, digital)
'Rhythmanalysis'
Gaston Bachelard,
La dialectique de la durée (1950)   **RUTHMOS** (particular manner of flowing)
     Emile Benveniste – *Problèmes de linguistique* (1966)
Heraclitus Seminar (1966-67) Martin Heidegger and Eugen Fink
     Gilles Deleuze - *Difference and Repetition* (1968)
significance Chora / Pulsional: Julia Kristeva - *La revolution du langage poétique* (1974)
Henri Meschonnic – *Le signe et le poème* (1975)
     1970s: écriture feminine - Hélène Cixous, 'The Laugh of the Medusa' (1975)

Idiorrhythmy   Michel Foucault - *Surveiller et punir* (1975)
Roland Barthes, *Comment vivre ensemble* (1977)   Paul Virilio - *Vitesse et Politique* (1977)
Desistance
Jacques Derrida, Philippe Lacoue-Labarthe *Typographies* (1979)
Henri Meschonnic – *Critique du rythme* (1982)   *Refrain*
     Deleuze and Guattari, *A Thousand Plateaus* (1987)
RHYTHMANALYSIS
Henri Lefebvre – *Éléments de rythmanalyse* (1992)

2011-   INDUSTRIAL REVOLUTION 4.0   2011-
(AI, Big Data, Cloud Computing, cyber physical systems)
RUTHMOS – Online Platform
(Pascal Michon)

Figure I.1 A Genealogy of Rhythm.

this day. The analysis of movement and rhythms that led to ideas about efficiency and productivity in factories and commerce more generally is situated within the perspective of materialism (which in turn relates to writings on new materialism, even where the emphasis is placed upon a discontinuity with the rhythms of modernity).

A second key strand of thinking on/through rhythm can be situated within the various developments of phenomenology. We can go as far back as G. W. F. Hegel. In *The Phenomenology of Spirit* ([1807] 1977), he refers to the notion of 'immanent rhythm' when outlining the dialectic of Spirit. And in his *Lectures on the History of Philosophy* (1861), he references Heraclitus, known for the pre-Socratic 'theory of flux'. Nietzsche (2008) also draws upon Greek thought, in his case the mythologies of Apollo and Dionysius, to present two different senses of rhythm: measured 'form' and a fuller, gestural movement respectively. While these rhythms stand opposed to one another, they work together to constitute reality (Miller 1999). This combined, non-dualistic account of rhythm recurs in much later literatures, as represented here, for example, with excerpts from Laban, Lefebvre, and Deleuze and Guattari. Reference can also be made to Heidegger as a phenomenological thinker influenced by Nietzsche. There is a connection too with Heraclitus, with a description of rhythm appearing in his *Heraclitus Seminar* (Heidegger 1979). Here, Heidegger refers to rhythm as a binding force, or imprint, in a way that is not dissimilar to the Dionysian force of Nietzsche's writings. The thread of phenomenological thought on rhythm is also picked up through the work of Bergson, Bachelard and later Lefebvre, each of whom is represented below.

Finally, we can consider the strand of thought that operates around issues of language and literary analysis. As already noted in the introduction to this book, Pascal Michon (2011) notes how with the decline of structuralism there was evidently an underlying interest in rhythm among a number of the prominent thinkers of the French intellectual scene that straddles structuralism and post-structuralism. Foucault, Barthes and Derrida, in particular, Michon notes, were 'reflecting on this concept, explicitly or implicitly using it as an alternative after the collapse of structuralism and against the coming methodological individualism; maybe also ... as a tool to curb the tendency of certain kind[s] of Nietzscheism and Heideggerism to overplay dispersion, difference and chaos'. In the introductory essay to Philippe Lacoue-Labarthe's *Typographies* (1989), Derrida develops a reading of rhythm along the lines of *différance*, suggesting that rhythms come before the subject as both repetition and spacing. Lacoue-Labarthe similarly considers rhythm as that which makes the subject possible, yet, equally, is inherently unstable and so as much disrupts the subject (again, we might hear echoes of Nietszche's Apollonian and Dionysian rhythms). The significance of space and spacing (as much as time) is evident with semiotic readings of rhythm. It emerges clearly with Émile Benveniste's much-cited essay on rhythm in *Problems in General Linguistics* (1971). His etymological account of rhythm through the Greek term *rhuthmos* – outlined below – reveals a technical term for an improvised, fluid 'form', which is directly referenced in the work of Roland Barthes and Henri Meschonnic (both represented in this book) and also importantly in the work of Julia Kristeva, whose term 'chora' in her *Revolution in Poetic Language* (1984) reframes the semiotic as a pre-verbal force, energy or drive. In turn, this gives rise to the term 'signifiance', which adds a sense of 'movement', rhythm and play to significations, and becomes key to post-structuralist thought. Deleuze and Guattari's *A Thousand Plateaus* (2013), as well as Deleuze's (1986; 1989) volumes on cinema, are also significant examples – albeit not sitting so neatly within a single strand of either materialism, phenomenology or language – where rhythm represents a central, or at least significant underlying concern.

Nonetheless, despite these various genealogies and connections, it remains the case that a specific reading of rhythm is rarely drawn out. With respect to the French milieu specifically, Michon explains how, unfortunately, 'Barthes and Foucault died rapidly in 1980 and 1984, and Meschonnic and Deleuze had no relation whatsoever, although they were teaching at the same university.' So, while rhythm *might* have become a 'new common concept for critical thought', he notes, in fact it 'disappeared until the second half of the 1990s, when it was rediscovered in many different disciplines but with very few references to this short period of obscure glory' (2011).

Émile Benveniste

'The Notion of "Rhythm" in its Linguistic Expression' is a short, unassuming essay tucked away towards the end of Émile Benveniste's *Problems in General Linguistics* (1971: 281–8), originally published in French in 1966. There are two main reasons for placing these extracts at the very start of the selected entries. Firstly, its etymological account provides a historical perspective, taking us back to the Ancient Greek root of the word ρυθμός [*rhuthmós*], which while an abstract noun of ῥεῖν, to flow, has to be understood to bear a specific meaning of rhythm as 'form'. Secondly, due to its careful historical and linguistic account, the essay is widely read and cited – with direct references, as noted, appearing in the work of Roland Barthes, Henri Meschonnic, Julia Kristeva, Deleuze and Guattari and others. It is also referenced in numerous places in the contributions to this book.

Benveniste's account of rhythm as *rhuthmos* is laid out as follows:

> In Greek itself, in which ῥυθμός [*rhuthmos*] does indeed designate rhythm, where does the notion come from and what does it properly mean? An identical answer is given by all the dictionaries: ῥυθμός is an abstract noun from ῥεῖν 'to flow,' the sense of the word . . . having been borrowed from the regular movements of the waves of the sea. This is what was taught more than a century ago, at the beginnings of comparative grammar, and it is what is still being repeated.
>
> [. . .] But the semantic connection that has been established between 'rhythm' and 'to flow' by the intermediary of the 'regular movement of the waves' turns out to be impossible as soon as it is examined. [. . .] what flows, ῥεῖ, is the river or the stream, and a current of water does not have 'rhythm'. If ῥυθμός means 'flux, flowing,' it is hard to see how it could have taken on the value proper to the word 'rhythm.' There is a contradiction of meaning between ῥεῖν and ῥυθμός, and we cannot extricate ourselves from the difficulty by imagining – and this is a pure invention – that ῥυθμός could have described the movement of the waves. What is more, ῥυθμός in its most ancient uses never refers to flowing water, and it does not even mean 'rhythm.' (Benveniste 1971: 281–2)

The term takes on a technical meaning, not least through the account widely disseminated by Aristotle. The fundamental relationship between bodies is established by mutual difference, which Aristotle differentiates in three ways: by form (*rhuthmos*), order and position. He gives an illustration with the letters of the alphabet. Consider letters such as 'A' and 'N', for example, from a graphic point of view: if we look at the strokes in drawing the letters, they can be said to share various elements, yet still result in different overall configurations of form, order and position. Benveniste's explication of this more technical meaning leads us to the overall understanding that *rhuthmos* never meant rhythm in the obvious sense; it was never applied to the movement of waves; and, despite quite varied conditions, its meaning is constant as 'distinctive form, proportioned figure, arrangement, disposition', etc. He goes on to explain as follows:

> the relation of ῥυθμός to ῥέω does not in itself give rise to any objection. It is not this derivation itself that we have criticized, but the wrong sense of [ῥυθμός] that was deduced from it. Now we can take up the analysis again, basing it on the corrected meaning. The formation

in $-(\theta)\mu\delta\varsigma$ deserves attention for the special sense it confers upon 'abstract' words. It indicates, not the accomplishment of the notion, but the particular modality of its accomplishment as it is presented to the eyes. For example ὄρχησις is the act of dancing, ὀρχηθμός, the particular dance seen as it takes place; [. . .] But it is especially the meaning of the radical which must be considered. When Greek authors render ῥυθμός by σχῆμα, and when we ourselves translate it by 'form,' in both cases it is only an approximation. [. . .] On the other hand, ῥυθμός, according to the contexts in which it is given, designates the form in the instant that it is assumed by what is moving, mobile and fluid, the form of that which does not have organic consistency; it fits the pattern of a fluid element, of a letter arbitrarily shaped, of a robe which one arranges at one's will, of a particular state of character or mood. It is the form as improvised, momentary, changeable. Now, ῥεῖν is the essential predication of nature and things in the Ionian philosophy since Heraclitus, and Democritus thought that, since everything was produced from atoms, only a different arrangement of them produced the difference of forms and objects. We can now understand how ῥυθμός, meaning literally 'the particular manner of flowing,' could have been the most proper term for describing 'dispositions' or 'configurations' without fixity or natural necessity and arising from an arrangement which is always subject to change. (Benveniste 1971: 285–6)

Crucially, there is an important secondary step in defining the modern meaning of 'rhythm', which comes about around the middle of the fifth century. Benveniste (1971: 286) does not assign a date as such, but rather a 'circumstance': 'It is Plato', he writes, 'who determined precisely the notion of "rhythm", by delimiting the traditional value of ῥυθμός in a new acceptation':

Plato still uses ῥυθμός in the sense of 'distinctive form, disposition, proportion'. His innovation was in applying it to the form of movement which the human body makes in dancing, and the arrangement of figures into which this movement is resolved. The decisive circumstance is there, in the notion of a corporal ῥυθμός associated with μέτρον and bound by the law of numbers: that 'form' is from then on determined by a 'measure' and numerically regulated. Here is the new sense of ῥυθμός: in Plato, 'arrangement' (the original sense of the word) is constituted by an ordered sequence of slow and rapid movements, just as 'harmony' results from the alternation of high and low. And it is the order in movement, the entire process of the harmonious arrangement of bodily attitudes combined with metre, which has since been called ῥυθμός. We may then speak of the 'rhythm' of a dance, of a step, of a song, of a speech, of work, of everything which presupposes a continuous activity broken by metre into alternating intervals. (Benveniste 1971: 287)

Rudolf Laban and *Koerperkultur*

As part of a special issue of *Body & Society* on 'Rhythm, Movement, Embodiment' (2014; vol. 20, nos 3–4), Crespi (2014) outlines how key texts, previously untranslated, by Rudolf Bode – *Rhythm and its Importance for Education* (1920) – and Rudolf Laban – 'Eurhythmy and Kakorhythmy in Art and Education' (1921) – give us insights into the rhythm-related discourse of Germany in the 1920s. Both Bode and Laban, as renowned exponents of German body-culture (*Koerperkultur*) and German expressionist dance (*Ausdrucktanz*) respectively, had far-reaching influence. An excerpt here from Laban's text on eurhythmy and kakorhythmy reminds us of the centrality of rhythm to his philosophy and practice as a choreographer and movement theoretician, which in turn connected with the then emerging conceptions of education, aesthetics, psychology and economics in Germany prior to the dominance of National Socialism. Citing Wedemeyer-Kolwe's study *Der Neue Mensch* (2004), Crespi (2014: 33) remarks how '*Koerperkultur* was also seen as a way to reform life and society in general and give birth to a "higher *Mensch*" whose "duty" was "to consider the body as a sacred temple".' The text below, by Laban, is an early elaboration of his polyrhythmic ontology, whereby rhythm takes shape through three key terms: Ur-rhythm, Eu-rhythm, and Kako-rhythm. Laban suggests the co-dependency of rhythm, movement and space, but also considers rhythm to access a socio-ethical dimension culminating in the Festival, or art of celebration:

> 'Eurhythmy' is a term that has been used for thousands of years, and it originally meant 'a beautiful or harmonious flow of movement [*Wohlfluss*] perceivable through our senses'. The totality of all imaginable sequences of movement is rhythm in nature. But does anything exist that is not an outcome of movement? The easily definable, clearly visible good order [*Wohlordnung*] of sequences of movement is beautifully rhythmic, eurhythmic. However, in the end does anything exist that is not well ordered, that is, perceivable as being composed of the basic elements?
>
> [...]
>
> Every phenomenon [*Erscheinung*], including those which are perceived by us as immobile, is in constant motion, and it is therefore intrinsically rhythmic: for it receives its unique quality – the hallmark of its unity – due to the resonance of specific nodal points [*Knotenpunkte*] of an infinite range of phenomena. But this resonance is nevertheless always movement. Every regularity, symmetry and proportionality and harmony is caused by forces [*Teilspannungen*] which, turbulently flowing into and around each other, generate structures

[*Gebilde*] of clearly perceptible harmonious rhythm [*Wohlrhythmus*]. Good order in all forms, whether moving or apparently still, is also eurhythmy. (Laban 2014: 75–6)

Laban goes on to ask a rhetorical question as to where the dividing line might be between eurhythmy and kakorhythmy. His answer seeks in fact to avoid this dualism. As Crespi explains, '[t]he divide between eurhythmy and kakorhythmy, between rationality and irrationality, between cosmos and chaos, between movement and form is difficult to discern' (2014: 46). Instead, we need to consider their 'delicate balance; this seems to be, for Laban, the nature of the rhythm phenomenon. In this sense, Laban and his project can be said to overcome the dichotomy *Takt*/rhythm in a way that anticipates later treatments of rhythm such as Lefebvre' (46). Something similar is at stake for Deleuze and Guattari, when – in reference to both Virilio on 'smooth space' and Democritus on atomism – they refer to 'rhythm without measure, which relates to the upswell of a flow, in other words, to the manner in which a fluid occupies a smooth space' (2013: 424). It is worth noting, here, Deleuze and Guattari directly query Benveniste's essay on rhythm, and specifically the notion that rhythm 'has nothing to do with the movement of waves' (424). Their point is seemingly to critique Plato's layering of 'measure' and 'cadence' rather than the idea of rhythm as 'form'. They accept 'that the forms made by atoms are primarily large, nonmetric aggregates, smooth spaces such as the air, the sea, or even the earth' (424). Crucially, they wish to assert the idea of 'rhythm without measure' as something fluid and less defined. This would seem to chime with Laban's polyrhythmic account, in which he suggests 'we identify as kakorhythmic those phenomena whose constituent subrhythms we cannot perceive as being regular or symmetric, or flowing into each other in good proportions' (Laban 2014: 76). Laban goes onto to write:

> The boundary between eurhythmy and kakorhythmy is, however, fluid. [. . .] all that exists and happens emerges from a more or less complex metamorphosis of simpler base rhythms [*Grundrhythmen*]. The origin of these base rhythms was always sensed as being Ur-rhythm. The rhythmic metamorphoses follow regularly from a simple to a more complex and progressive chain of events. When our organs of perception perceive these chains of events with a spatial arrangement, speed, amplitude and intensity appropriate to their perceptivity, we gain the impression of something ordered, comprehensible and clear, and then we speak of understanding, beauty, positive flow – eurhythmy. But if we are suddenly catapulted from extreme to

extreme and are even carried away outside the extremes, we then, in distress, call what we don't understand kakorhythmy.

The individual has two options in order to harmonize or connect their personal rhythm [*Eigenrhythmus*] with the rhythm of all other happenings. They can either close their mind to what is alien to them or beyond their level of development, that is, to whatever is kakorhythmic relative to their skills; they will hedge themselves around with rules and practices, impose technical schematas on what is natural, and install security measures in order to exclude what they perceive as kakorhythmic. Or they can aspire to increase their skills to the ultimate in order to comprehend, and thus experience as eurhythmic, as large a part as possible of the all-encompassing rhythm [*Allrhythmus*].

At this point Laban turns to the idea of 'Festival', as a site of *practice*, a meeting of art and education as eurhythmic:

> The art of the celebration [*Festkunst*] is freer than pedagogy, philosophy, the applied arts [*Werkkunst*] and all other forms of development grounded in everyday life. The art of celebration is meant to connect to the all-encompassing rhythm in its complete and infinite variability through dance. Essentially, the Festival knows no kakorhythmy. However, this type of art should not misuse its freedom, and should serve people's hearts, blending the inspiring with the astounding. Only when the Festival unveils the deeper eurhythmic meaning of what seems kakorhythmic by way of affectionate human guidance – only then has it accomplished its task as mediator of the experience of the all-encompassing dance [*Alltanzes*]. (Laban 2014: 77)

Henri Bergson/Gaston Bachelard

Gaston Bachelard can be credited – in part – for gaining more currency for the term 'rhythmanalysis', at least by dint of the fact that it is from here that Henri Lefebvre appropriates the term:

> Philosophers (including Nietzsche, the philosopher-poet) only presaged the importance of *rhythm*. It is from a Portugeuse, dos Santos, that Bachelard, in *The Psychoanalysis of Fire*, borrows the word 'rhythmanalysis', though without developing the meaning any more than did dos Santos. However, the concept of rhythm, hence the rhythmanalytical project, emerges bit by bit from the shadows. (Lefebvre 2013: 19)

The reference to dos Santos is in regard to his book of 1931, *La Rythmanalyse: Société de Psychologie et de Philosophie.* Nonetheless, as Lefebvre remarks, rhythm as a critical term is not developed in an explicit fashion. Instead we have to weave through various writings and look to the incremental changes. A notable consideration in looking at Bachelard is his direct critique of Henri Bergson, who was writing at the turn of the twentieth century (with Bachelard's key texts coming half a century later). Bergson cannot be said to write explicitly about rhythm, but it pervades his account of reality as 'duration', understood in terms of constant motion and flux. It is on the notion of duration that Bachelard responds, countering what he sees as Bergson's metaphysics of rhythm. Excerpts from two of Bergson's texts offer a flavour of his reading of rhythm. In his essay, *Time and Free Will* ([1927] 2001), he writes:

> The sounds of the bell certainly reach me one after the other; but one of two alternatives must be true. Either I retain each of these successive sensations in order to combine it with the others and form a group which reminds me of an air or rhythm which I know: in that case I do not count the sounds, I limit myself to gathering, so to speak, the qualitative impression produced by the whole series. Or else I intend explicitly to count them, and then I shall have to separate them, and this separation must take place within some homogeneous medium in which the sounds, stripped of their qualities, and in a manner emptied, leave traces of their presence, which are absolutely alike. (Bergson 2001: 86–7)

The idea of an entity not being held by a single rhythm, but that other rhythms can open out, is suggestive. In the book *Matter and Memory* ([1939] 1991), the concept of duration is developed, whereby rhythm mediates duration into different levels of being and consciousness:

> [Duration] is not ours, assuredly; but neither is it that homogeneous and impersonal duration, the same for everything and for every one, which flows onward, indifferent and void, external to all that endures. This imaginary homogeneous time is, as we have endeavoured to show elsewhere, an idol of language, a fiction whose origin is easy to discover. In reality there is no one rhythm of duration; it is possible to imagine many different rhythms which, slower or faster, measure the degree of tension or relaxation of different kinds of consciousness and thereby fix their respective places in the scale of being. (Bergson 1991: 207)

Bachelard argues against Bergson's view of duration as continuous flow. Instead he considers the discontinuities of being, as interrupted by 'nothingness'. His account is of a dialectic of being and nothingness (which can be placed within the debates at the time of existentialism and phenomenology). In *The Dialectic of Duration* ([1950] 2016), he writes as follows:

> We shall now go on to criticise this school of thought on one specific point. Since any critique is clarified by its end-point, let us say straight-away that of Bergsonism we accept everything but continuity. Indeed to be even more precise, let us say that from our point of view also continuity – or continuities – can be presented as characteristics of the psyche, characteristics that cannot however be regarded as complete, solid, or constant. They have to be constructed. They have to be maintained. Consequently, we do not in the end see the continuity of duration as an immediate datum but as a problem. We wish therefore to develop a discontinuous Bergsonism, showing the need to arithmetise Bergsonian duration so as to give it more fluidity, more numbers, and also more accuracy in the correspondence the phenomena of thought exhibit between themselves and the quantum characteristics of reality [. . .] We shall see that there is a fundamental heterogeneity at the very heart of lived, active, creative duration, and that in order to know or use time well, we must activate the rhythm of creation and destruction, of work and repose. Only idleness is homogeneous. (Bachelard 2016: 20–1)
>
> [. . .]
>
> In order to really *continue* an act initially adapted to space, you must therefore make another effort and add a second act. This is one of our main arguments and must, we consider, be emphasised. [. . .] Effort is dependent on the brain, which is as much as to say that it is dependent on the intellect. Continuation is not natural at the level of reflexes. [. . .] In this way, the clear far-sighted will opens duration like a perspective; it places a sequence of supplementary acts behind the first impulse; it shows itself to be a synthesizing power determining an organic convergence. We obtain duration by progressively bringing more and more muscles into play. The analysis of continuity of effort would lead us to repeat almost term for term Bergson's detailed work developed with regard to the *intensity* of effort. There is plurality in the development of continuity just as there is plurality in an increasing intensity of effort. It can be seen that this intensity and this continuity are in a way homologous, and that the arithmetic sum of particular efforts which accumulate to give an intensity is dispersed the length of a succession to give a duration. Of course, if we look fairly closely at it, we shall see that continuation of this kind is made up of separate impulses. Any psychology of effort must accede not just to the geometrisation of effort Bergson indicates when he reads intensity in the volume of muscles progressively brought into play but also to the arithmetisation of effort that counts the muscles which are progressively alerted. (Bachelard 2016: 46)

Michel Foucault

In *Discipline and Punish* (1977), Michel Foucault presents his influential account of the 'docile body', which is the product of various operations of the body, or disciplines, with time and rhythm being key. His account looks at a shift in the late eighteenth century, whereby not only has the body become analysable, but also manipulable: 'A body is docile that may be subjected, used, transformed and improved' (1977: 136). Foucault is of course well aware that there is nothing new to power being exercised upon the body. However, he argues for certain important changes:

> To begin with, there was the scale of the control: it was a question not of treating the body, *en masse*, 'wholesale', as if it were an indissociable unity, but of working it 'retail', individually; of exercising upon it a subtle coercion, of obtaining holds upon it at the level of the mechanism itself – movements, gestures, attitudes, rapidity: an infinitesimal power over the active body. Then there was the object of control: it was no longer the signifying elements of behavior or the language of the body, but the economy, the efficiency of movements, their internal organization; constraints bears upon the forces rather than upon the signs [. . .] Lastly, there is the modality: it implies an uninterrupted, constant coercion, supervising the processes of the activity rather than its result and it is exercised according to a codification that partitions as closely as possible time, space, movement. These methods, which made possible the meticulous control of the operations of the body, which assured the constant subjection of its forces and imposed upon them a relation of docility-utility, might be called 'disciplines'. (Foucault 1977: 136–7)

Foucault's analysis ranges across various settings, including monasteries, armies, workshops, hospitals, schools and factories. A common and evolving feature of these settings is a management of time and the rhythms of the body:

> The *time-table* is an old inheritance. The strict model was no doubt suggested by the monastic communities. It soon spread. Its three great methods – establish rhythms, impose particular occupations, regulate the cycles of repetition – were soon to be found in schools, workshops and hospitals. [. . .] For centuries, the religious orders had been masters of discipline: they were the specialists of time, the great technicians of rhythm and regular activities. But the disciplines altered these methods of temporal regulation from which they derived. They altered them first by refining them. One began to count in quarter hours, in minutes, in seconds. [. . .] In the elementary schools, the

division of time became increasingly minute; activities were governed in detail by orders that had to be obeyed immediately: 'At the last stroke of the hour, a pupil will ring the bell, and at the first sound of the bell all pupils will kneel, with their arms crossed and their eyes lowered . . .' [. . .] The gradual extension of the wage-earning class brought with it a more detailed partitioning of time [. . .] But an attempt is also made to assure the quality of the time used: constant supervision, the pressure of supervisors, the elimination of anything that might disturb or distract [. . .] Precision and application are, with regularity, the fundamental virtues of disciplinary time. (Foucault 1977: 149–51)

With a specific example of the marching of troops, Foucault describes a 'temporal elaboration', or shift in quality and precision. Whereas in the early seventeenth century reference can be found to troops marching to the beat of a drum (starting on the right foot to ensure the troop marches in unison), by the mid eighteenth century there is much greater attention to detail. Citing an ordinance of 1766 as a source, Foucault details four different kinds of steps:

The length of the short step will be a foot, that of the ordinary step, the double step and the marching step will be two feet, the whole measured from one heel to the next; as for the duration, that of the small step and the ordinary step will last one second, during which two double steps would be performed; the duration of the marching step will take one second; it will be at most eighteen inches from one heel to the next . . .' [. . .] What the ordinance of 1766 defines is not a time-table – the general framework for an activity; it is rather a collective and obligatory rhythm, imposed from the outside; it is a 'programme'; it assures the elaboration of the act itself; [. . .] We have passed from a form of injunction that measured or punctuated gestures to a web that constrains them or sustains them throughout their entire succession. A sort of anatomo-chronological schema of behavior is defined.

[. . .] Discipline defines each of the relations that the body must have with the object that it manipulates. [. . .] It consists of a breakdown of the total gesture into two parallel series: that of parts of the body to be used (right hand, left hand, different fingers of the hand, knee, eye, elbow, etc.) and that of the parts of the object manipulated (barrel, notch, hammer, screw, etc.); then the two sets of parts are correlated together according to a number of simple gestures (rest, bend); lastly, it fixes the canonical succession in which each of these correlations occupies a particular place. This obligatory syntax is what the military theoreticians of the eighteenth century called '*manoeuvre*'. The traditional recipe gives place to explicit and obligatory prescriptions.

Over the whole surface of contract between the body and the object it handles, power is introduced, fastening them to one another. It constitutes a body-weapon, body-tool, body-machine complex. One is as far as possible from those forms of subjection that demanded of the body only signs or products, forms of expression or the result of labour. The regulation imposed by power is at the same time the law of construction of the operation. Thus disciplinary powers appear to have the function not so much of deduction as of synthesis, not so much of exploitation of the product as of coercive link with the apparatus of production. (Foucault 1977: 151–3)

Foucault's account ranges across numerous settings, as mentioned, and indeed draws upon a variety of historical sources. Some have argued that he is too liberal with his arrangement of sources, so undermining a 'proper' handling of history. Yet what he helps demonstrate through a network of historical facts is a broader 'discourse' that shapes all social techniques and technologies. Crucially, rhythms are not simply imposed upon the subject, but are constitutive and *productive* of the subject; our bodies move in the ways that 'become' us: 'The body, required to be docile in its minutest operations, opposes and shows the conditions of functioning proper to an organism. Disciplinary power has as its correlative an individuality that is not only analytical and "cellular", but also natural and "organic"' (Foucault 1977: 156).

Roland Barthes

In his late lecture course *How to Live Together* (2013), Barthes offers a particular, underlying interest in rhythm. He draws directly upon Benveniste's account of rhythm as form and flowing, and in doing so presents an account of rhythm that is rather more spatial than temporal. He presents what he calls a fantasy of 'idiorrhythmy'. As he alludes, this has a connection with Nietzsche's account of a 'pathos of distance', but also more evidently with Foucault's account of regimes and 'technologies of the self'. Barthes explains as follows:

> [It's] a fantasy of a life, a regime, a lifestyle, *diaita*, diet. Neither dual nor plural (collective). Something like solitude with regular interruptions: the paradox, the contradiction, the aphoria of bringing distances together – the utopia of a socialism of distance (apropos of strong, ungregarious ages such as the Renaissance, Nietzsche speaks of 'a pathos of distance'). [. . .]

> Now, it was in the course of a chance reading (Lacarrière, *L'Été grec*) that the fantasy encountered the word that would set it to work. On Mount Athos: coenobitic convents + monks both isolated from and in contact with one another within a particular type of structure . . . idiorrhythmic clusters. Where each subject lives according to his own rhythm. (Barthes 2013: 6)

As it turns out, his research into the monastic forms does not open up as much as he would hope. However, it sets off a reading of rhythm as both a co-ordinating temporality and as a form that is related to issues of space and proximity. He turns, then, to Benveniste's account of *rhuthmos*, which he describes as:

> a distinctive form, a proportioned figure, an arrangement; very close to and yet very different from *schema*. *Schema*: a fixed, fully developed form that's set down like an object (statue, orator, choreographical figure). *Schema* ≠ form, the instant it's assumed by something moving, mobile, fluid, the form of something that lacks organic consistency. *Rhuthmos* = the pattern of a fluid element (a letter, a *peplos*, a mood), an improvised, changeable form. In atomism, one manner in which atoms flow; configuration without fixity or natural necessity: a 'flowing' (the musical, that is to say, modern meaning: Plato, *Philebus*). (Barthes 2013: 7)

In taking rhythm as a fluid and changeable element, Barthes is aware of the potential tautology in placing the prefix 'idio':

> Since *rhuthmos* is by definition individual, idiorrhythm is almost a pleonasm: the interstices, the *fugitivity* of the code, of the manner in which the individual inserts himself into the social (or natural) code.
> [. . .] It's because rhythm acquired a repressive meaning (I refer you to the life-rhythm of a coenobite, or a phalansterian, whose activities are scheduled to the nearest quarter of an hour) that it was necessary to add the prefix *idios*:
>
> *idios* ≠ rhythm
> *idios* = *rhuthmos*
>
> [. . .] Perhaps there are such things as idiorrhythmic couples? [. . .] likewise in shadow: macro-groupings, large communes, phalansteries, convents, coenobitism. Why? By which I mean: Why doesn't the fantasy encounter these larger forms? It's obvious: because their structure is based on an architecture of power . . . and because they're openly hostile to idiorrhythmy [. . .] I refer you to the fundamental inhumanity of Fourier's Phalanstery: with its *timing* of each and every quarter hour, it's the exact opposite of idiorrhythmy: barracks, boarding schools.

[. . . W]hat we're looking for is a zone that falls between two excessive forms:

- an excessively negative form: solitude, eremitism.
- an excessively assimilative form: the (secular or nonsecular) *coenobium*.
- a median, utopian, Edenic, idyllic form: idiorrhythmy. Note that as a form it's very eccentric: it never really caught on in the Church (on Mount Athos, through *disaffiliation*); in fact, the Church always resisted it [. . .] What's more, psychoanalysis has never really engaged with the question of 'small groups'. It's either the subject in his familial straitjacket or the crowd [. . .] In sum: neither the monastery, nor the family, the idea being to eschew those grand repressive forms.

To bring this introduction to idiorrhythmy to a close, I shall present a trait that seems to me to characterize the problem in a specific, localized manner. From my window (December 1, 1976), I see a mother pushing an empty stroller, holding her child by the hand. She walks at her own pace, imperturbably; the child, meanwhile, is being pulled, dragged along, is forced to keep running, like an animal, or one of Sade's victims being whipped. She walks at her own pace, unaware of the fact that her son's rhythm is different. And she's his mother! → Power – the subtlety of power – is effected through disrhythmy, heterorhythmy. (Barthes 2013: 8–9)

Gilles Deleuze and Félix Guattari

In *Difference and Repetition* ([1968] 1994), Gilles Deleuze's first monograph, he sets out to analyse the essential difference between these two modes of being, something that will constitute the core of his thought also in his subsequent works. At the onset, he opens up his discussion of repetition by stressing that the latter is to be thought of as an alternative to the principle of representation. That is, as he puts it, that: 'Our problem concerns the essence of repetition. It is a question of knowing why repetition cannot be explained by the form of identity in concepts or representations; in what sense it demands a superior "positive" principle' (1994: 19). Deleuze answers this question by introducing a double nature of repetition, one static and one 'dynamic', and taking rhythm as an example:

Similarly, the study of rhythm allows us immediately to distinguish two kinds of repetition. Cadence-repetition is a regular division of time, an isochronic recurrence of identical elements. However, a period exists only in so far as it is determined by a tonic accent, commanded by intensities. Yet we would be mistaken about the function of accents if we said that they were reproduced at equal intervals. On the contrary, tonic and intensive values act by creating inequalities or incommensurabilities between metrically equivalent periods or spaces. They create distinctive points, privileged instants which always indicate a poly-rhythm. Here again, the unequal is the most positive element. Cadence is only the envelope of a rhythm, and of a relation between rhythms. The reprise of points of inequality, of inflections or of rhythmic events, is more profound than the reproduction of ordinary homogeneous elements. As a result, we should distinguish cadence-repetition and rhythm-repetition in every case, the first being only the outward appearance or the abstract effect of the second. A bare, material repetition (repetition of the Same) appears only in the sense that another repetition is disguised within it, constituting it and constituting itself in disguising itself. Even in nature, isochronic rotations are only the outward appearance of a more profound movement, the revolving cycles are only abstractions: placed together, they reveal evolutionary cycles or spirals whose principle is a variable curve, and the trajectory of which has two dissymmetrical aspects, as though it had a right and a left. It is always in this gap, which should not be confused with the negative, that creatures weave their repetition and receive at the same time the gift of living and dying. (Deleuze 1994: 21)

Deleuze delineates already here, then, a difference between cadence and rhythm, that is, between mere repetition and rhythm intended as a dynamic, vitalist force giving birth to the emergence of the new, of the event. Much later, in 1980, Deleuze speaks about rhythm again in his much celebrated work with Félix Guattari, *A Thousand Plateaus* ([1980] 2013), and famously in relation to the refrain and the milieu. And here again the concern lies in working between the relation between metre and rhythm:

From chaos, *Milieus* and *Rhythms* are born [...] Every milieu is vibratory, in other words, a block of spacetime constituted by the periodic repetition of the component [...] Every milieu is coded, a code being defined by periodic repetition; but each code is in a perpetual state of transcoding or transduction. Transcoding and transduction is the manner in which one milieu serves as the basis for another, or conversely is established atop another milieu, dissipates in it or is constituted in it. The notion of the milieu is not unitary: not only does the living thing continually pass from one milieu to another, but the milieus pass into one another; they are essentially communicating. The milieus are open to chaos, which threatens them with exhaustion or intrusion. Rhythm is the milieus' answer to chaos. What chaos and rhythm have in common is the in-between – between two milieus, rhythm-chaos or the chaosmos [...] There is rhythm whenever there is a transcoded passage from one milieu to another, a communication of milieus, coordination between heterogeneous space-times. Drying up, death, intrusion have rhythm. It is well known that rhythm is not meter or cadence, even irregular meter or cadence: there is nothing less rhythmic than a military march [. . .]. Meter, whenever regular or not, assumes a coded form, whose unit of measure may vary, but in a noncommunicating milieu, whereas rhythm is the Unequal or the Incommensurable that is always undergoing transcoding. Meter is dogmatic, rhythm is critical: it ties together critical moments, or ties together passing from one milieu to another [. . .] This easily avoids an aporia that threatened to introduce meter into rhythm, despite all the declarations of intent to the contrary. How can one proclaim the constituent inequality of rhythm while at the same time admitting implied vibrations, periodic repetitions of components? A milieu does in fact exist by virtue of a periodic repetition, but one whose only effect is to produce a difference by which the milieu passes into another milieu. It is the difference that is rhythmic, not the repetition, which nevertheless produces it: productive repetition has nothing to do with reproductive meter. That is the 'critical solution of the antinomy'. (Deleuze and Guattari 2013: 364–5)

Henri Lefebvre and Catherine Régulier

The following extract is from an essay by Henri Lefebvre and Catherine Régulier, 'The Rhythmanalytical Project', originally published in French in *Communications* in 1985, with its English translation appearing at the end of Lefebvre's short volume *Rhythmanalysis* (2013), which became available in 2004, following the French publication in 1992 (a year after Lefebvre's death). While chronologically this entry comes at the end of the selections offered here, it is fair to say Lefebvre held a long-term interest in ideas about rhythm, space and movement. His theory of 'moments' (2014: 634–52; 800–7), for example, appears in the second volume of *Critique of Everyday Life*, which was originally published in French in 1961. Nonetheless, it is interesting to note how despite the posthumous publication of *Rhythmanalysis*, as late as the 1990s, it is this text more than any other that is now cited in reference to critical debates about rhythm and rhythmanalysis. When Michon remarks that rhythm as a critical term fades from view until the mid-1990s, it is certainly Lefebvre's text that plays a key role in the revival of interest.

Lefebvre takes specific interest in our everyday experiences, of which rhythm forms an important part. As Lefebvre and Régulier (2013: 86) remark, we tend to think we know what this word 'rhythm' means, but, as they point out, 'everybody senses it in a manner that falls a long way short of knowledge'. Furthermore, they suggest, we tend only to become conscious of rhythms 'when we begin to suffer from some irregularity'. Despite the affirmative account of rhythmanalysis that Lefebvre offers across the entirety of his book ('This little book does not conceal its ambition. It proposes nothing less than to found a science' [Lefebvre 2013: 13]), it is fair to say that it is difficult to draw out extracts that offer concise explanations. The choice here to present Lefebvre and Régulier's earlier essay is that it perhaps better encapsulates the project of rhythmanalysis.

> For there to be rhythm, there must be repetition in a movement, but not just any repetition. The monotonous return of the same, self-identical, noise no more forms a rhythm than does some moving object on its trajectory, for example a falling stone; though our ears and without doubt our brains tend to introduce a rhythm into every repetition, even completely linear ones. For there to be rhythm, strong times and weak times, which return in accordance with a rule or law [. . .] must appear in a movement. Rhythm therefore brings with it a differentiated time, a qualified duration. The same can be said of repetitions, ruptures and resumptions. Therefore a measure, but an *internal measure*, which distinguishes itself strongly though without separating itself from an *external* measure, with time t (the time of a clock or a metronome) consisting in only a quantitative and homogeneous parameter. In a reciprocal action, the external measure can and must superimpose itself on the internal measure, but they cannot be conflated. They have neither the same beginning, nor the same end or final cause. This double measure enters into the definition and quality of rhythm, irreducible to a simple determination, implying on the contrary complex (dialectical) relations. As such only a non-mechanical movement can have rhythm: this classes everything that emerges [*relève*] from the purely mechanical in the domain of the quantitative, abstractly detached from quality. [. . .]
>
> [. . .] Through this double aspect, rhythm enters into a general construction of time, of movement and becoming. And consequently into its philosophical problematic: repetition and becoming, the relation of the Same to the Other. It is to be noted at this point that by including a measure, rhythm implies a certain memory. While mechanical repetition works by reproducing the instant that precedes it, rhythm preserves both the measure that initiates the process and the re-commencement of this process with modifications, therefore with its multiplicity and plurality. Without repeating identically 'the same', but by subordinating the same to alterity and even alteration, which is to say, to difference. (Lefebvre and Régulier 2013: 86–8)

We can hear an echo with Deleuze and Guattari's *A Thousand Plateaus*, considered above. Seemingly at odds with Benveniste's etymological study, yet equally offering a further nuancing of the idea of rhythm as form in movement, Lefebvre and Régulier make a direct link between rhythm and waves: 'To grasp rhythm and polyrhythmias in a sensible, preconceptual, but vivid way,' they write, 'it is enough to look carefully at the surface of the sea. Waves come in succession: they take shape in the vicinity of the beach, the cliff, the banks. These waves have a rhythm . . .' (88). They go on to offer the following 'open' definition:

> there is not yet a general theory of rhythms. Entrenched ways of thinking, it has already been stressed, separate time from space, despite the contemporary theories in physics that posit a relationship between them. Up until the present, these theories have failed to give a unitary concept that would also enable us to understand diversities (differences).
>
> And now there is the hypothesis of rhythmanalysis. The body? Your body? It consists in a bundle of rhythms. Why not say: a bouquet? Or a garland? Because these terms connote an aesthetic arrangement, as if nature – an artist – had intentionally arranged and designed the beauty and harmony of bodies. That is perhaps not wrong, but it comes prematurely. The living – polyrhythmic – body is composed of diverse rhythms, each 'part', each organ or function having its own, in a perpetual interaction, in a doubtlessly 'metastable' equilibrium, always compromised, though usually recovered, except in cases of disruption. How? By a simple mechanism? By homeostasis, as in cybernetics? Or more subtly, through a hierarchical arrangement of centres, with one higher centre giving order to relational activity? This is one of our questions. But the surroundings of the body, the social just as much as the cosmic body, are equally bundles of rhythms ('bundles' in the sense that we say, not pejoratively, that a complex chord reuniting diverse notes and tones is a 'bundle of sounds'). Now look around you at this meadow, this garden, these trees and these houses. They give themselves, they offer themselves to your eyes as in a simultaneity. Now, up to a certain point, this simultaneity is mere appearance, surface, a spectacle. Go deeper. Do not be afraid to disturb this surface, to set its limpidity in motion. Be like the wind that shakes these trees. Let your gaze be penetrating, let it not limit itself to reflecting and mirroring. Let it transgress its limits a little. You at once notice that every plant, every tree has its rhythm. And even several rhythms. Leaves, flowers, fruits and seeds. On this cherry tree, flowers are born in springtime along with leaves that will survive the fruits, and which will fall in the autumn, though not all at once. Henceforth you will grasp every being [*chaque être*], every entity [*étant*] and every body, both living and non-living, 'symphonically' or 'polyrhythmically'. You will grasp it in its space-time, in its place and its approximate becoming: including houses and buildings, towns and landscapes. (Lefebvre and Régulier 2013: 88–9)

Overall, the excerpts given here offer some key examples of the three main strands of materialism, phenomenology and language. Inevitably, however, as presented in 'A Genealogy of Rhythm' (Figure I.1), there are numerous other routes, emphases and connections that could be traversed. The *haunting* of rhythm through intellectual history, as suggested in the introduction to this book, spans a long period of time, and is often more implicit than explicit. In her *Sequel to History*, which offers a blend of literary analysis and social theory, Elizabeth Deeds Ermarth (1992: 45) proposes that 'it is musical rhythm that best suggests the nature of postmodern temporality'. She sets a challenge to explore our contemporary condition through ideas of rhythm and timing; she cites Nabokov from *Ada, or Ardor*: 'Maybe the only thing that hints at a sense of Time is rhythm; not the recurrent beats of the rhythm but the gap between two such beats, the grey gap between black beats: the Tender Interval' (cited in Ermarth 1992: 45). The genealogies presented here (and other potential patterning they inspire) hopefully help begin a process of getting in amongst the gaps of rhythms, both to understand a longer history and to help inform a forward-going agenda. Much more can be explored with regard to the intellectual history of rhythm, but equally this work helps bring to the fore new, contemporary considerations. The Industrial Revolution 4.0 within which we are currently situated gives rise to a whole host of interests and concerns that rhythm is well placed to play a key role in understanding our present conjuncture, and in providing a means of critical response.

References

Bachelard, G. (2016), *The Dialectic of Duration*, trans. M. McAllester Jones. London and New York: Rowman & Littlefield International.

Barthes, R. (2013), *How to Live Together: Novelistic Simulations of Some Everyday Spaces*, trans. K. Briggs. New York: Columbia University Press.

Benveniste, É. (1971), *Problems in General Linguistics*, trans. M. E. Meek. Coral Gables: University of Miami Press.

Bergson, H. (1991), *Matter and Memory*, trans. N. M. Paul and W. S. Palmer. New York: Zone Books.

Bergson, H. (2001), *Time and Free Will: An Essay on the Immediate Data of Consciousness*, trans. F. L. Pogson. Mineola, NY: Dover Publications.

Crespi, P. (2014), 'Rhythmanalysis in Gymnastics and Dance: Rudolf Bode and Rudolf Laban', in *Body & Society*, Special Issue: *Rhythm, Movement, Embodiment*, 20: 3–4 (September and December), pp. 30–50.

Deleuze, G. (1986), *Cinema 1: The Movement-Image*, trans. H. Tomlinson and B. Habberjam. London: Athlone Press.

Deleuze, G. (1989), *Cinema 2: The Time-Image*, trans. H. Tomlinson and R. Galeta. London: Athlone Press.
Deleuze, G. (1994), *Difference and Repetition*, trans. P. Patton. New York: Columbia University Press.
Deleuze, G., and F. Guattari (2013), *A Thousand Plateaus: Capitalism and Schizophrenia*. London: Bloomsbury.
dos Santos, L. A. P. (1931), *La Rythmanalyse*. Rio de Janeiro: Société de Psychologie et de Philosophie.
Ermarth, E. D. (1992), *Sequel to History: Postmodernism and the Crisis of Representational Time*. Princeton: Princeton University Press.
Foucault, M. (1977), *Discipline and Punish: The Birth of the Prison*, trans. A. Sheridan. London: Penguin.
Hegel, G. W. F. (1861), *Lectures on the Philosophy of History*, trans. J. Sibree. London: H. Bohn.
Hegel, G. W. F. (1977), *Phenomenology of Spirit*, trans. A.V. Miller. Oxford: Clarendon.
Heidegger, M. (1979), *Heraclitus Seminar, 1966/67*, trans. C. H. Seibert. Tuscaloosa: University of Alabama Press.
Laban, R. (2014), 'Eurhythmy and Kakorhythmy in Art and Education', trans. P. Crespi, in *Body & Society*, Special Issue: *Rhythm, Movement, Embodiment*, 20: 3–4 (September and December), pp. 75–8.
Lacoue-Labarthe, P. (1989), *Typography: Mimesis, Philosophy, Politics*, trans. C. Fynsk. Cambridge, MA: Harvard University Press.
Lefebvre, H. (2013), *Rhythmanalysis: Space, Time and Everyday Life*, trans. S. Elden and G. Moore. London: Bloomsbury.
Lefebvre, H. (2014), *Critique of Everyday Life*, vols 1–3, trans. J. Moore. London: Verso.
Lefebvre, H., and C. Régulier (2013), 'The Rhythmanalytical Project', in H. Lefebvre, *Rhythmanalysis: Space, Time and Everyday Life*, trans. S. Elden and G. Moore. London: Bloomsbury, pp. 81–92.
Michon, P. (2011), 'A Short History of Rhythm Theory since the 1970s', *Rhuthmos*, 6 December 2011, <http://rhuthmos.eu/spip.php?article462> (last accessed 28 December 2019).
Michon, P. (2017–19), *Elements of Rhythmology*, vols. 1–3. Paris: Rhuthmos.
Miller, E. P. (1999), 'Harnessing Dionysos: Nietzsche on Rhythm, Time, and Restraint', *Journal of Nietzsche Studies*, 17, pp. 1–32.
Nietzsche, F. W. (2008), *The Birth of Tragedy*, trans. D. Smith. Oxford: Oxford University Press.
Wedemeyer-Kolwe, B. (2004), *Der Neue Mensch: Koerperkultur im Keiserriech und in der Weimarer Republik*. Wuerzburg: Koenigshausen und Neumann.

1 Modalities of Rhythm

Chapter 1

Drawing Rhythm: On the Work of Rudolf Laban

Paola Crespi

This chapter locates the practice-inspired approach to rhythm of choreographer and movement-thinker Rudolf Laban (1879–1958) in the wider context of critical theory focusing on rhythm and rhythmanalysis. In doing so, its aim is both to add a significant and overlooked voice to the ongoing debate on rhythm which has unfolded in Western thought, and to argue for the value of a practitioner's insight into this prominently if not exclusively theoretical arena. Laban's attempts to define, analyse and understand rhythm are here discussed in relation to his artistic output and his philosophy through an exploration and analysis of unpublished manuscripts and drawings held at the National Resource Centre for Dance at the University of Surrey in the United Kingdom.

Anticipating what Henri Lefebvre famously argued in *Rhythmanalysis* (2004), rhythm is for Laban at the same time a quantifiable phenomenon (*Takt*) unfolding in space and a qualitative variable (rhythm itself), suggestive of what Lefebvre would later describe as 'what is least rational in human being: the lived, the carnal, the body' (9). Laban studied rhythm's intensities in his 'Effort theory' in English factories in the post-war period. This work resonates with but at the same time differs from Taylor's project of time-motion studies, in that rhythm plays the central role of resisting the impact of machine work on individual workers. Rhythm's effects on space and its impact on the dynamics of the moving body are also explored by Laban in his Choreutic theory, of which several models in the form of sketches and drawings are discussed in this chapter. In order to understand and reconcile the inner (Effort) and outer (Choreutics) study of rhythm, Laban, later in life, relied on topological structures such as knots and Mobius strips to devise his theories, something that resonates with the work of Gilles Deleuze and Félix Guattari, Jacques Lacan and Michel

Serres among others. These topological models sought to overcome the binary division of inside–outside and also to conceive of a continuous space of transformation without interruption, something that, it will be argued, comes to define Laban's understanding of rhythm.

Laban is a controversial artistic figure: he is regarded by some as a mystical charlatan with dubious political ties, and by others as the master of modern and community dance, argued to have elevated dance to the same level as the other arts. This controversy, however, has been kept on the fringes of aesthetic and dance theory and of philosophy, seemingly because this has been the place of dance as such. Laban's main achievement is to have devised a well-known system of notation of bodily movement (Kinetography), as well as a lesser-known system of notation of the internal emotional tensions underlying bodily movement, known as Effort theory, and a series of studies on movement known mainly to modern dancers as Choreutics, which take inspiration from geometrical structures and aim to analyse the patterns and syntonies of movement.

In general, Laban was exploring the relation between time, space and movement (often also intended in a more abstract manner than bodily movement) set against the background of philosophical and scientific approaches that were emerging during his lifetime, i.e. in the last decades of the nineteenth century and the first half of the twentieth century. The fact that most of his intuitions did not reach the state of more developed arguments, and that they were for the most part in the form of unpublished, handwritten notes, does not detract from their importance. In the context of this book Laban's work is here argued to add to that of his and our contemporaries in regard to the concept of rhythm. As some have argued, rhythmanalysis has to date remained somewhat abstract; nonetheless, Laban's account, while developed partially on an abstract level, derives from his being a practitioner, and aims in part to fill this void. Laban had a particular way of utilising drawing to theorise rhythm, to explore it and to *express* it. In order to get at Laban's 'philosophy' we can as much look at his drawings as read his account of rhythm. Indeed, the material explored in this chapter suggests that the drawings *are* his philosophy of rhythm, or at least a means of attending critically to the very modality of rhythm itself. Furthermore, what emerges from juxtaposing Laban's exploration of rhythm with his interest in the scientific investigations of his time is that the interplay of intensive and extensive space seen in his drawings goes hand in hand with an understanding of rhythm and time. Rhythm is at the same time, so to say, intensive and topological and, intended as *Takt* and cadence, a metric, geometrical, extensive property of lived experience.

Drawing as Method

Laban's philosophy is based on a fundamental understanding of the primacy of movement. He sees movement as the fundamental aspect of reality and in this sense, it is possible to speak of Laban's philosophy of process. Laban also sees movement as primary to cognition, as when he states that the primary task of a philosophy of movement is to understand that 'movement and mind [are] not an antithesis in which two opposite faculties of man have to be reconciled, but a unity of which man can become aware more clearly to-day than was hitherto possible for him' (L/E/26/70). Moreover, Laban speaks of a creative force or *élan* from which movement originates, and he explains how the 'strength or power that moves us is not in us but around us, it is a combination of fluid tensions' (ibid.). In this sense, it blurs the boundaries of our body and, what is more, shapes our bodies as such similarly to the way in which a streaming of water plastically shapes a stone. Our bodies are moved and move, movement moves through our bodies and shapes reality in a rhythmical exchange between creative flux and structured form.

In Figures 1.1 and 1.2, movement is as much generated by the bodies as it is a force that shapes them from the outside. Movement becomes a frame in itself in these drawings, a moving structure. Bodies, which are more prominent in Laban's early work and tend to give space to a more abstract movement in his late studies, are for the artist always studied tangentially – it is always about what they do, how they can be represented, what they express. In a sense, then, Toepfer was right in asserting that Laban was ambivalent towards dance and the body, i.e. 'he saw that creating a higher value for dance depended on treating it as a huge, abstract system that functioned independently of dances and even bodies' (Toepfer 1997: 107).

Laban's response to the study of rhythm moves from a more 'representational' to a more 'vectorial' approach over the course of his life. In Figure 1.3, Laban's attempts to express the rhythmicity emanated by the moving body focuses on its propagation in, or rather, its impact on the creation of space. In a piece that reminds us of modernist artistic renditions of movement, Laban works here on the relationship between body, geometry and rhythm by encapsulating geometry in the body and rendering the body itself geometrical. This drawing is powerful in its emanations of rhythm and in its clash of body and pattern: the dancer's body propagates and evolves into crystalline lines without ever losing its momentum.

58   Paola Crespi

Figure 1.1 R. Laban, n.d., L/C/3/47. Figure Drawings/Figures within Energy Lines. A crayon drawing by Rudolf Laban of two figures within spiralling lines. Reproduced with the kind permission of the © Rudolf Laban Archive, National Resource Centre for Dance Archive, University of Surrey.

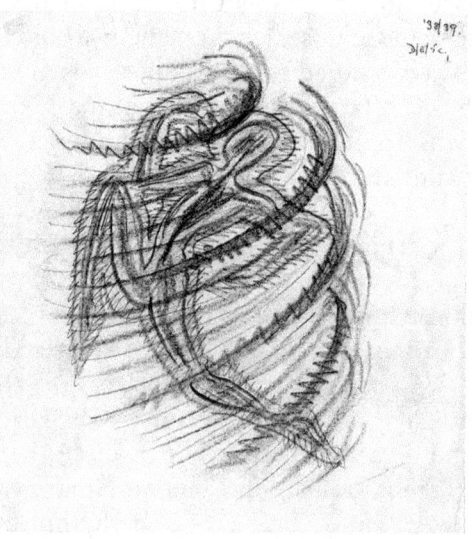

Figure 1.2 R. Laban, n.d., L/C/3/48. Figure Drawings/Figure within Energy Lines. A crayon drawing by Rudolf Laban of a figure within swirling lines. Reproduced with the kind permission of the © Rudolf Laban Archive, National Resource Centre for Dance Archive, University of Surrey.

Drawing Rhythm: On the Work of Rudolf Laban   59

Figure 1.3 R. Laban, n.d., L/C/3/94. Figures/Figure in Icosahedron. A black-crayon drawing by Rudolf Laban showing a figure surrounded by short, overlapping lines making an icosahedral shape. Reproduced with the kind permission of the © Rudolf Laban Archive, National Resource Centre for Dance Archive, University of Surrey.

In the dynamic sequence visible in Figures 1.4 to 1.7, the subsequent sedimentation of the vibrational, polyrhythmic matter is visible. Figure 1.4 is caught in the hysterical rhythms of matter and body, something that is here propagating also to the trace-form surrounding the figure. The frame is shaken in the propulsion of the swing. Slowly the movement is slowing down, but still visible in Figure 1.5 and Figure 1.6. Figure 1.7 represents the complete geometricalisation of rhythm. This sequence shows the movement from rhythm to measure, from polyrhythmia to cadence, from difference to repetition. The rest of the constant flux would then redevelop following the sequence inversely, so that from cadence one is led back into vital unrestricted rhythm.

As these two series of drawings suggest (Figures 1.8–1.9), Laban's compositions arise from a chaotic state and take form progressively. This first chaotic state is traceable in these drawings.

In this chaotic stage (Figures 1.8–1.9), which is yet unformed, what is more notable are the lines of movement which connect bodies and provide a vectorial understanding of dynamic space. This is the

Figure 1.4 (top left) R. Laban, n.d., L/C/5/123. Single and Double Figures in Spatial Forms/A Figure in a Dodecahedron. Pencil drawing of a figure within a line tracing a continuous path around some edges of a dodecahedron.

Figure 1.5 (top right) R. Laban, n.d., L/C/5/129. Single and Double Figures in Spatial Forms/A Figure in a Dodecahedron. Pencil drawing of a figure within a line tracing a continuous path around some edges of a dodecahedron.

Figure 1.6 (bottom left) R. Laban, n.d., L/C/5/126. Single and Double Figures in Spatial Forms/A Figure in a Dodecahedron. Drawing by Rudolf Laban of a figure within a line tracing a continuous path around some edges of a dodecahedron. In pencil, and green, black, and red crayon.

Figure 1.7 (bottom right) R. Laban, n.d., L/C/5/130. Single and Double Figures in Spatial Forms/A Figure in a Dodecahedron. Pencil drawing by Rudolf Laban of a figure within a dodecahedron. Reproduced with the kind permission of the © Rudolf Laban Archive, National Resource Centre for Dance Archive, University of Surrey.

Drawing Rhythm: On the Work of Rudolf Laban 61

Figure 1.8 R. Laban, n.d., L/C/6/69. Relationship between Groups of Figures/Six Figures. Drawing by Rudolf Laban of six figures encircled by a line. In pencil and green crayon. Reproduced with the kind permission of the © Rudolf Laban Archive, National Resource Centre for Dance Archive, University of Surrey.

Figure 1.9 (Top) R. Laban, n.d., L/C/6/70. Relationship between Groups of Figures/Three Figures. Drawing of three figures with swirling lines superimposed on them. In pencil and blue and red crayon.

Figure 1.10 (Bottom) R. Laban, n.d., L/C/10/95. Relationships between Groups of Figures. Pencil diagram of three figures with curving lines superimposed on them. Reproduced with the kind permission of the © Rudolf Laban Archive, National Resource Centre for Dance Archive, University of Surrey.

intensive ground from which geometrical figures arise in quantifiable space. Figure 1.10 presents us already with a metric representation of the same group of dancers: the lines that flow freely and continuously, interconnecting flesh and space, are now segmented and divided in measurable sections.

In the next sequence (Figures 1.11–1.13), the progressive materialisation of bodies and movement in relation to geometry and structure is seen from the point of view of a group. Again, it is as if from the indistinct enmeshment of body/rhythm/movement, form is encapsulated first inside the structures of the bodies, freezing the ensemble and then exteriorised. This movement from intension to extension is the rhythmical genesis of form. This is particularly useful in helping to define the action of rhythm in between intensive and extensive space and time. In its actualisation into metric space, rhythm is in a process of becoming-measure or cadence from the non-metric and topological realm of intensities that originates it. Never only virtual, not actual, the play of oscillation between form and movement is the 'essence' of rhythm.

Drawing Rhythm: On the Work of Rudolf Laban   63

Figure 1.11 (top left) R. Laban, n.d., L/C/6/81. Relationship between Groups of Figures/Three Figures. Drawing of three figures in green crayon.

Figure 1.12 (top right) R. Laban, n.d., L/C/6/86. Relationship between Groups of Figures/Three Figures. Drawing of three figures. Done in his short-stroke style in green crayon.

Figure 1.13 (bottom left) R. Laban, n.d., L/C/6/79. Relationship between Groups of Figures/Three Figures. Drawing of three figures within a line tracing a continuous path around edges of an icosahedron. In black, brown, blue and green crayon. Reproduced with the kind permission of the © Rudolf Laban Archive, National Resource Centre for Dance Archive, University of Surrey.

Intensive/Extensive: The Rhythmical Genesis of Form

In Figure 1.14, found in the midst of Laban's notes, the author maps the exchange between inner and outer, intensive and extensive movement. He focuses particularly on the intensive process of the filtering of impressions and the ways in which this might end up determining action. This is the map of the inner territory of effort. The course of action starts as a follow-up of previous action, with impressions reaching first the five senses and what Laban here calls the 'receptacle of the five shapes'. From here the movement continues turbulently, chaotically, indistinctly towards the bottom left of the page, where it separates in different strands. Some movement instigates 'simple responses as mood signs, awakened by pure or pseudo-significant impressions'. This gives rise to 'reflexes'. This sensomotoric aspect manages to trespass the porous boundary of inside/outside, passing through another indistinct zone where Laban locates 'rebounce movements' and to be expressed in 'shadow moves'. Laban describes these as 'tiny muscular movements [. . .] usually done unconsciously [that] often accompany movements of purposeful action like a shadow' (Laban 1950, p. 12). In his last unpublished manuscript, *Effort and Recovery*, Laban states: 'The struggle between shadow-moves and functional action is one of the most interesting subjects for the movement observer' (Laban, n.d., quoted in North 2011: 258). This tension is what is expressed in this map.

Laban writes at the top of the page: 'Re-bounce meets a thin layer between the actively outgoing and reflexively inwards-going movements'. It is this thin elastic and resilient layer which loosely contains moves that are the result of moods, that don't have the strength and decision to break through towards action. They extend but are recaptured towards the inside. Instead of heading towards the extensive plane, some impressions are projected inwards and are 'worked out as thought and emotions' and give birth to conscious 'volitions, attentions, intellect, decision and precision'. As highlighted by a direct thick arrow decisively cutting across the layer, these aspects of consciousness materialise into 'physical movements and communication' and are the ones that result in action. This map provides an incredibly vivid clue to how Laban thought of movement in its intensive state and in its process of extension. Process is here expressed by dynamic vectors and arrows travelling through the space of the page, creating it anew: this is for Laban a presentation of a process embodied through vortices, changes of direction, dead ends and blurred, chaotic areas.

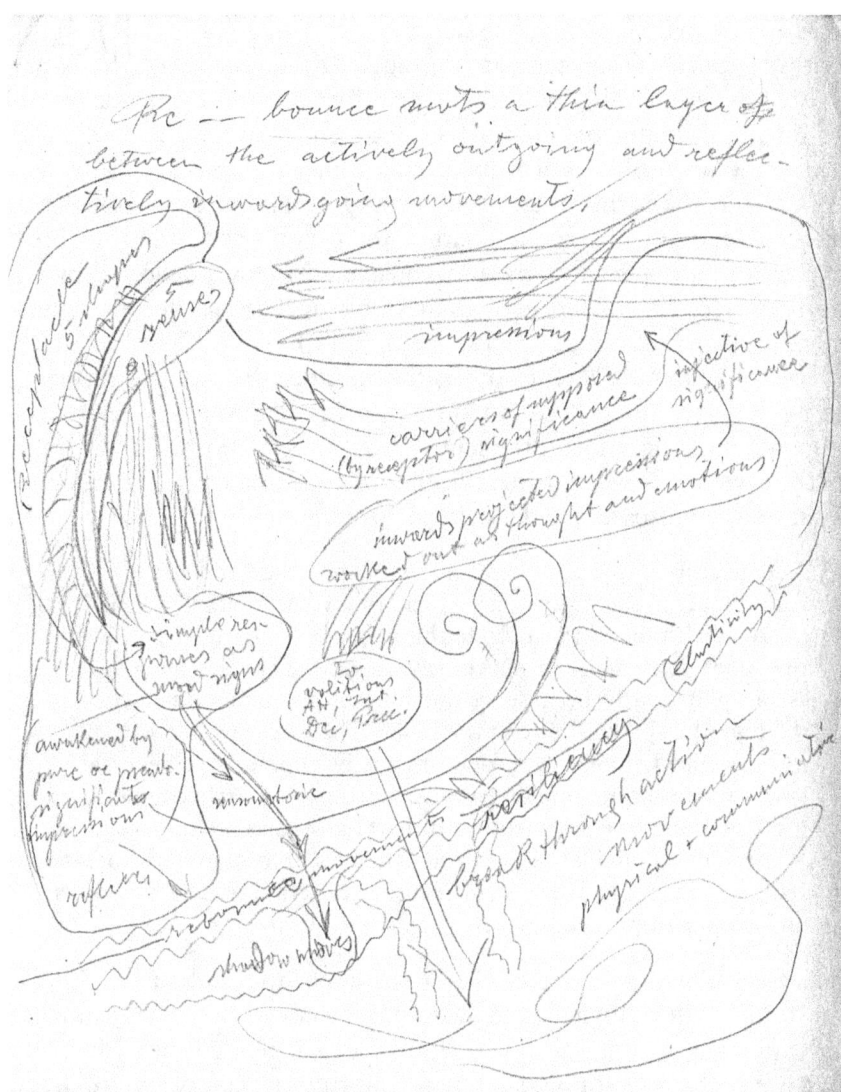

Figure 1.14 R. Laban, n.d., L/E/33/8. Lecture notes on various subjects/Notes and diagrams. Diagram of primary scale as basis for other patterns, diagrams of dial structures, physiology of work, the discovery that man continually lives in two different media, notes on types of movement, personal abilities. Reproduced with the kind permission of the © Rudolf Laban Archive, National Resource Centre for Dance Archive, University of Surrey.

The 'Science' of Rhythm

Having explored ways to describe or transcribe rhythm, Laban went on to call for a 'new kind of mathematics' (n.d., L/E/26/47), opposed to a mere metrical one. This 'new' mathematics should treat 'not the concept of magnitude, but the concept of living form (motor-form, effort-shape) as its subject matter' (ibid.). Around the year 1950 Laban started experimenting with topological forms, and in general, thanks to his pupil, mathematician Sylvia Bodmer, he explored topology as that 'new science' in which magnitudes 'merged into qualitativeness as, e.g. directions into the tectonic reality of lemniscates, knots, etc.', and in which in absence of matter 'there is no space and no time' (ibid.). In particular, it is the movement and rhythm deflected by the body that for Laban here evolves in topological fields, such as 'lemniscates and knotted bands of space-plan' (ibid.).

In the text of a lecture-presentation aided by the projection of drawings and models, Laban speaks of the relation between a particular topological form, the lemniscate, and the body. Laban states that movement does not form in the manner of a circle, but is more akin to a lemniscate. He defines the latter as follows:

> A lemniscate is a tape of movement, or the inside and outside alternate; that is to say: if we trace a line of movement along this tape we obtain a path that, in relation to this line, affords to move partially in the concave, partially in the convex direction. This lemniscate interests us particularly, because we find it in the anatomic construction of the body [. . .] specifically in the limbs. The forearms, the legs allow for movement similar to those of the helix of an aeroplane, creating in this way a certain force, a torque. Because not every movement will need this kind of energy expenditure, these studies are important for research into muscular tension and dynamics of force and because the spatial influence of these forms causes accelerations and slowdown and is therefore the cause of rhythm. (L/E/5/1; my translation)

What should be noted here is not so much how Laban thought of the body as topological, but how movement and rhythm, moving topologically in the guise of a lemniscate, depended on it. It is the body here that is a topological field, and rhythm that originates from it. In particular, it is through tension (of the limbs) and changes in speed that rhythm is born. The lemniscate is also interesting for Laban because 'it doesn't offer a stand point in his [sic] middle, in his [sic] surrounding or in his [sic] surface [. . .] which allows us to show exactly an "inside" or "outside" and to have the appropriated feeling of finished end' (Laban, n.d., L/E/25/24). In this sense, it is adequate to express movement in its constant flux and the capacity of movement to blur the boundaries of inside/outside, intensive, extensive.

In order to better understand this scientific basis of Laban's philosophy and practice, it is the dynamic of alternation between intensive and extensive space that will be the focus of the next section. As a start, one must lay down the postulates of a system that is concerned with intension and extension. This will be a system, as Manuel Delanda explains (2002), that owes some of its fundaments to a vision of science that focuses on quantum physics on the one side and topology on the other side. Moreover, it will partake of an ontology that is processual. A process ontology discards essences in favour of dynamic flow, something that strongly resonates with Laban's approach. Moreover, as we have seen, Laban was using both quantum physics and topology in his work in the last period of his life.

Laban's definition of topology is standard. He maintains that it is a fundamental branch of mathematical science that investigates non-metric spatial relationships and therefore 'deals with properties of position, which are not altered by the size or shape of the object in which such properties are present. Such properties remain the same in spite of any stretching or bending of an object' (n.d., L/E/56/10). Similarly, the structure and function of the body does not follow primarily metrical rules. For Laban, 'the properties of its functions are positional and are independent of the size and shape of the body' (ibid.). Laban is here referring to intensive properties, which cannot be metrically understood. He refers to effort motion factors, saying that they are 'in the first instance qualitatively and not quantitatively selected and united. It is this selective synthesis which typifies the effort made by living beings' (ibid.), and, with it, its rhythms.

Topological forms, in a genesis of physical forms and of actualisation of intensities as found in the theory of dynamic systems, give rise to geometrical forms. Contrary to the relation of ideal form to the particular, as found in Platonism and the Enlightenment, the dynamic between intensive and extensive space is one of emergence and expression based on difference. This is because, as Delanda explains,

> intensive differences are productive [. . .] wherever one finds an extensive frontier (for example, the skin which defines the extensive boundary of our bodies) there is always a process driven by intensive differences which produced such a boundary (for example, the embryological process which creates our bodies). (Delanda 2005: 81)

Similarly, Laban's geometrical constructs, as found earlier in this chapter, should be seen in direct dialogue with the intensive forces from which they originate. For Laban, the intensive space of the movements of effort gives rise to extensive movements as seen in action. This kind of 'science' goes hand in hand with a philosophical approach that favours process over stability. In the next section, the foundation of Laban's philosophy of process will be uncovered.

Takt, *Élan* and Rhythm

The modernist interest in movement and its 'flow' has been traced back to the work of Henri Bergson. Commentators have suggested that Laban's work seems to have been influenced directly by the philosophy of Bergson. This becomes evident in Laban's mentioning of an '*élan*' in relation to effort rhythm in Figure 1.15.

This reference concerns Bergson's concept of vital impulse in relation to rhythmic inflections, with particular focus here on the motion factor of 'weight', part of Laban's Effort theory (more below). This points towards a clarification of Laban's concept of effort and its relation to *élan vital* as a practical exploration of Bergson's philosophy. As I have explored elsewhere (Crespi 2014), Laban was not the only commentator aiming to define rhythm in relation to Bergson's philosophy. Of particular interest is Rudolf Bode's approach in this sense. The main thesis put forward by Bode was that rhythm is a continuum and as such not graspable rationally:

> it can only be looked at and experienced: moreover, rhythm has to take part in the Irrational. Rhythm is irrational, i.e. it is not subject to the judgmental, comparative, measuring functions of the intellect. And now we understand why everything spatial and temporal happens at the same time in rhythm, because our experience is a continuum in space and time at once. If I divide space and time, then I am immediately outside what is lived, outside rhythm. Because each division is a coming into force of the rational functions [of the intellect]. The continuum, or, as we may want to say: that which is not divided, is the fundamental characteristic of rhythm ([1920] 2014: 55)

Bode's philosophical approach, as he goes to great lengths to explain, derives from that of Ludwig Klages. The latter was an influential thinker at the turn of the century in Germany and his arguments for the separation of *Geist* (intellect) and *Seele* (soul), *Takt* (measure) and rhythm, rational and irrational were highly popular in the *Koerperkultur* milieu (Lubkoll 2002: 90–3). It has been argued that by counterpoising the continuity of rhythm to the staccato of *Takt*, Klages, and with him Bode, followed the Bergsonian differentiation between *temps* and *durée* (Lubkoll 2002: 87–90), giving birth to a philosophy of rhythm exemplified by Klages' affirmation: 'Takt repeats, rhythm renews' (1934: 33; my translation). In his *Machinic Unconscious*, Félix Guattari discusses his theory of the refrain in relation to Klages' theory of rhythm that can be summarised, as Guattari puts it, as 'th[e] distinction between vital elementary rhythms and socialised cadences' (147). Guattari explores Klages' claim that vital rhythm has been transformed by human culture in cadence. It is not too far-fetched

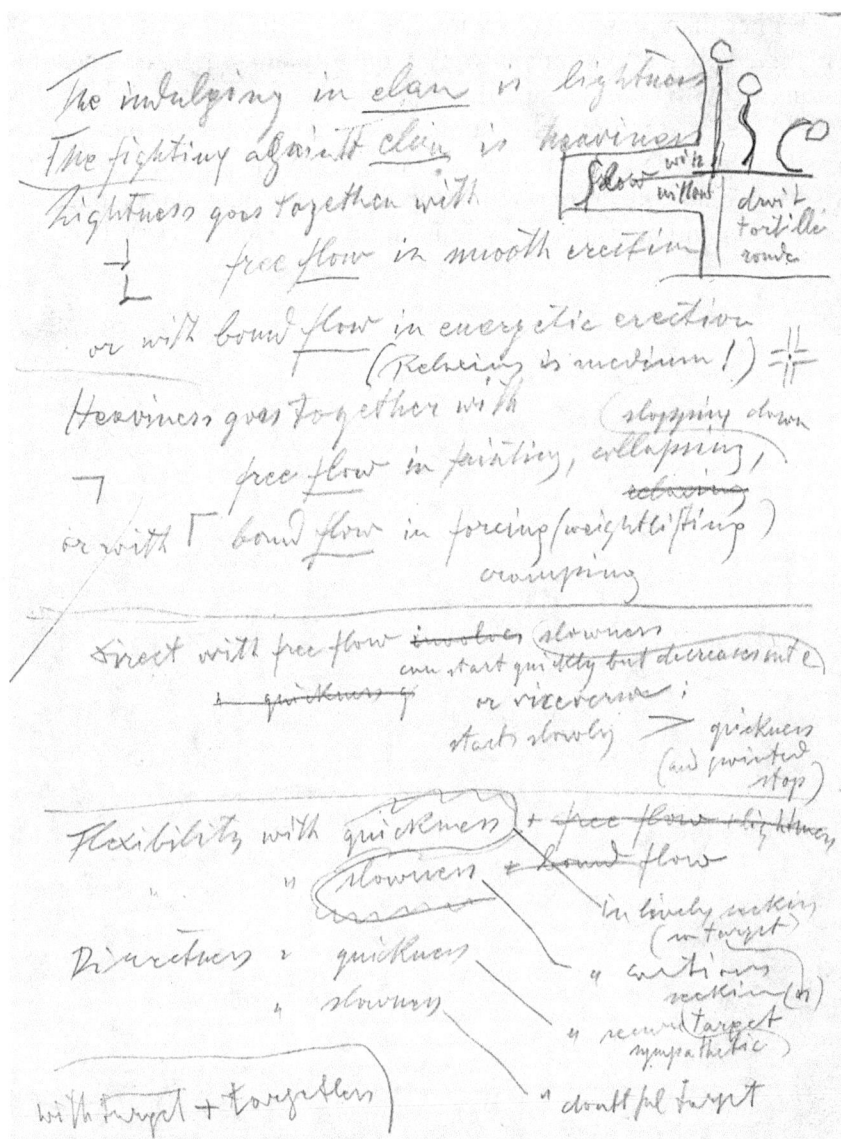

Figure 1.15 R. Laban, n.d., L/E/5/21. Choreology (Effort)/Indulging in élan is. Handwritten manuscript relating to combinations of two effort elements. Reproduced with the kind permission of the © Rudolf Laban Archive, National Resource Centre for Dance Archive, University of Surrey.

to suggest that Deleuze and Guattari's discussion of the refrain in *A Thousand Plateaus* [1980] (1988) owes also to this earlier German heritage represented by Bode's, Klages' and, as will be shown, Laban's distinction between *Takt* and rhythm.

Rather than presenting us with a eulogy of the unrestricted flow of rhythm, Laban's 'rhythmanalysis' is polyrhythmic and the phenomenon of rhythm takes shape through the manifold way in which it is verbalised: Ur-rhythm, Eu-rhythm, Kako-rhythm, sub-rhythm, Wohl-rhythm, Everyday-rhythm (see also Laban [1921] 2014). This is also visible in a document found in the archive, something that highlights a continuum in Laban's polyrhythmic approach (Figure 1.16). This also

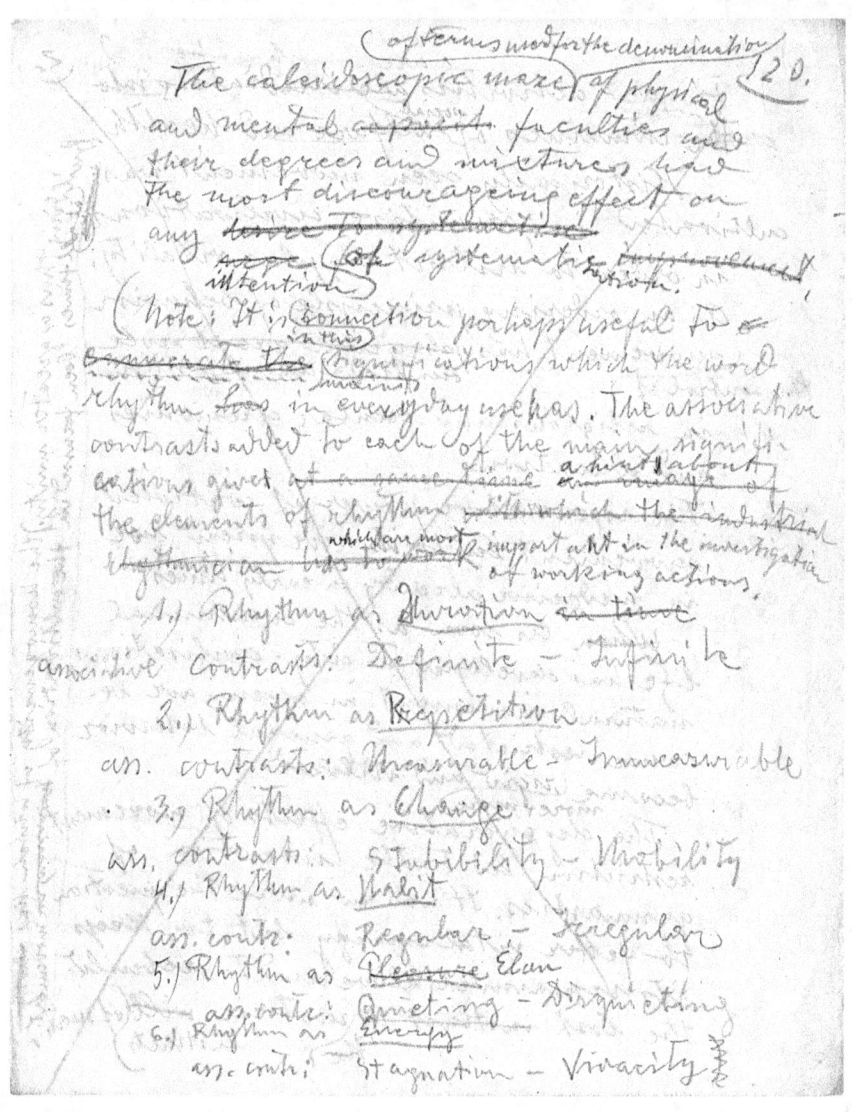

Figure 1.16 R. Laban, n.d., L/E/40/11. Rhythm/The Language of Rhythm. Handwritten manuscripts. Reproduced with the kind permission of the © Rudolf Laban Archive, National Resource Centre for Dance Archive, University of Surrey.

resonates with the concept of qualitative multiplicity found in Bergson. These different rhythms all pertain, in fact, to a unity: they can be said to express different qualities of an all-subsuming Ur-rhythm.

Economy of Effort: Rhythm and Labour

Karl Buecher's monograph *Arbeit und Rhythmus* (1899) was without any doubt the most influential study published on rhythm at the turn of the twentieth century (see Rabinbach 1992). Indeed, Georg Simmel draws on Buecher's study, published a few years earlier, in the rhythm-related chapter of his masterpiece *The Philosophy of Money* ([1900] 2004). Simmel's definition of rhythm as a 'rationalistic-systematic principle' which annihilates human spontaneity and his intuition that work in a factory 'brings about a deadening of the sense of rhythm as such' brings to mind Bucher's earlier work. Through a meticulous exploration of songs accompanying the work of tribal communities, Buecher shows how rhythm comes from the bodily movement of labour and how with modernisation and the loss of bodily activity in factories, rhythm changes. For Buecher, 'the ordered organisation of movement in its temporal progress', which is rhythm, 'originates from the individual's organic being. [Rhythm] seems to regulate the economical use of energy of all natural operations of the animal body' (Buecher 1899: 358; my translation).

The artificially standardised rhythm of the machines, then, upsets the natural unrestrained rhythms of the body: capitalism's quantisation wins over rhythm's qualitative nuances. Rather than longing to reinstate the original condition, however, Buecher hopes for a fruitful synchronisation between human and machine rhythm. It is in this context that Laban's application of his Effort theories in the English factories during the post-World War II period should be placed. Laban's acquaintance with Buecher's theories has been underscored by Evelyn Doerr (2008). She describes how Laban's pupils in Ascona (the Swiss retreat where Laban spent most of World War I, and that he visited during the summer on a number of occasions) were working and chanting under the master's supervision. 'This work', she explains, 'was carried out rhythmically with the help of self-composed work songs in accordance with the approach Karl Buecher described in his 1896 *Arbeit und Rhythmus*' (Doerr 2008: 32). The reason for amplifying the natural rhythm of labour with chants is to be found in Buecher's discovery that an increase of efficiency and 'happiness' derives from the application of this method.

Although certainly influenced by the 'Time and Motion' studies introduced by Taylor, Rudolf Laban's and businessman Frederick

Lawrence's method, which they baptised 'Laban-Lawrence Industrial Rhythm', allegedly 'proved to be more than a timesaving device. Throwing new light on the nature of effort, it revealed itself as a method of instruction and training leading to increased enjoyment of work through the awareness and practice of its rhythmic character' (Laban and Lawrence 1947: xi). Laban and Lawrence devised a 'complete technique' in order to analyse the endless variations of rhythm. What they studied, indeed, was not postures, but the movements in between them. Central to the method is effort, or 'effort-rhythm' (Laban and Lawrence 1947: xv). In order to 'compile a systematic survey of the forms effort can take in human action' (Laban and Lawrence 1947: 2), it is explained, it becomes necessary to study bodily rhythms.

Although commentators such as Moore equate effort with volition or voluntary movements (Moore 2009: 151), it is not clear, from what we can read of Laban's Effort theory, what he means by this notion. It is likely, as can be evinced from examples brought above, that effort should be equated with an 'impulse' (as the German translation 'Antreib' suggests), which might be the very Bergsonian *élan vital* that Laban mentions elsewhere. Laban speaks indeed of effort in relation to civilisations as well as moving bodies. Effort is not entirely defined by Laban, but it is comparable with force, both pertaining to the individual and more generally to an all-encompassing vital urge. The study of effort is therefore the study of how energy is inflected by gestures, something that gives rise to the qualitative rhythms of actions. Effort graphs express the intensity of force and rhythm of movements instead of postures; they are black vectors indicating qualities of movement and not position in space.

Laban saw four motion factors or elements of effort: weight, space, time and flow. Although Laban's concepts shift over the years, it can be said that motion factors of effort were set by the 1930s, then developed in the 1940s and later in England. Laban constructs a binary system around the embodiment of effort: each motion factor can be either seconded or resisted. Flow can be either bound or free, weight strong or light, time fast or slow and space direct or indirect. In this way Laban creates the fundamentals of effort's taxonomy, something that allows him to cover in a 'system' the nuances or qualities of effort in movement.

Effort states are a combination of two motion factors; effort drives of three; and complete efforts are a combination of four qualities. Effort states total 24 configurations, effort drives 32 and complete efforts 16, for a total of 72 mood states describable and expressible by way of the graph system. Effort motion factors and drives vary following a rhythmic dynamic of exertion and recuperation, so that effort moods change continuously. Rhythm, stresses Laban, 'speaks' to us in a language beyond words: it 'conveys something by which we are influenced: we may be excited, depressed, or tranquilised' (Laban and Lawrence 1947: xiv). Rather than meaning *per se*, then, rhythm speaks an affective language. This language is that of effort in its relation to the four Movement Factors. The attitude of the moving body towards these can be of either 'indulging' or 'resisting', giving birth to the eight basic qualitative aspects of movement.

Laban defines the effort/rhythm-graph (Figure 1.17) at first as a symbol and as a 'representation of the effort content of a movement by combination of strokes or bars' (Laban and Lawrence 1947: 8). The action 'punching' is expressed in Figure 1.18 in its dynamic of appearing and disappearing. In its emerging from the flux of continuous movement, a first effort/rhythm appears: it is strong in relation to weight, direct in relation to space (Figure 1.18, first top line left) and sudden in its attitude to time (Figure 1.18, first top line middle). In its diverse composition, the resulting action takes place through its polyrhythmicity and it is embedded in the diagram, from which it then moves on towards dissipation and anticipation of further action.

Laban traces here the rhythm and effort of the action by cutting it off from the continuous flow of movement, but at the same time by allowing for a detailed yet anexact exploration of a phraseology of rhythmical movement. The different accents result in the rhythmical nuances of punching, in this case a direct, strong and sudden quality

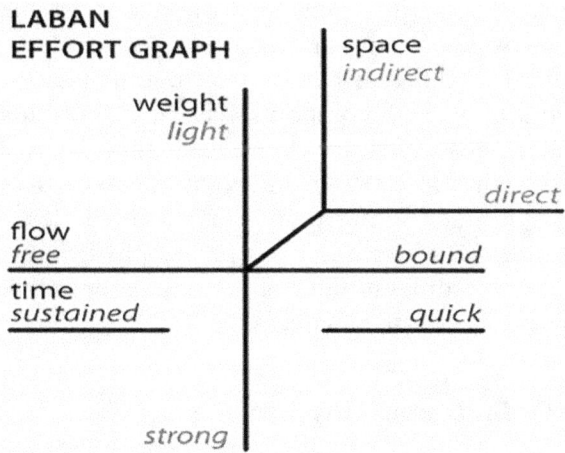

Figure 1.17 Effort Graph. Source: Wikimedia. Available at: <https://upload.wikimedia.org/wikipedia/commons/2/27/Laban-effort-graph.jpg> (last accessed 16 June 2019).

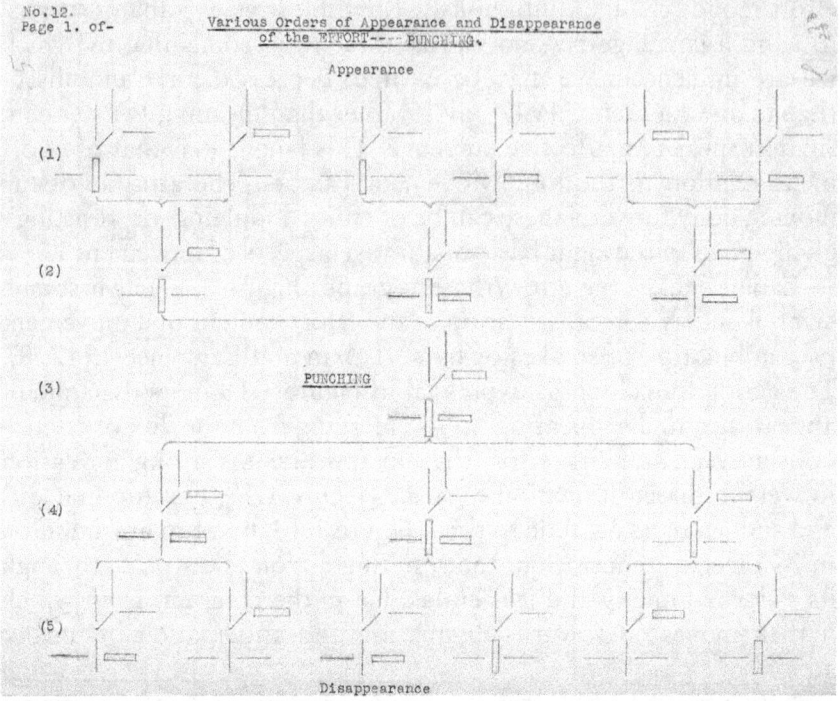

Figure 1.18 R. Laban, n.d., L/E/53/4. Books, Manuscripts, Outlines/The Method of Drawing an Effort Graph. Typed instructions and handwritten diagrams. Reproduced with the kind permission of the © Rudolf Laban Archive, National Resource Centre for Dance Archive, University of Surrey.

of movement with either 'fluent flow' (striking punch) or 'bound flow' (hitting punch). The action 'punching', moreover, is chosen for the sake of clarity by Laban among numerous actions that express the same rhythmical qualities in relation to the four factors of weight, space, time and flow. Each compound/assemblage of movement factors of an action gives birth to a specific rhythm. Each effort graph expresses the rhythm of a movement, what Laban calls a movement-drive or *rhythm-drive*. Rather than a personalised effort-rhythm, it is useful to think, in line with Laban's philosophy of movement, of a movement that overcomes notions of personality or individuality and expresses these in qualitative nuances.

Towards a Definition of Rhythm

Laban also refers to rhythm in terms of both difference and repetition, stating that 'the notion of recurrence in time is so prevailing that we overlook all the other rhythmical implications' (L/E/24/23). He adds that 'rhythmical recurrence of resembling chance-happenings might delude our practical mind with hopes and beliefs of security. We think and feel' he continues, 'to swim in an uninterrupted and continuous flow of causally connected situations without perceiving the frightening leaps of nature' (L/E/25/49). Laban is here referring to rhythm as repetition of happenings. On the other hand, he also sees discontinuity in the flow of existence as a source of novelty: 'We never know which curious rhythm might break out like lightening from the chaos. There is hope!' (ibid.). Elsewhere Laban would refer to repetition and difference in relation to hope by stating: 'The only thing that seems to be invariable is change [. . .] This is a most consoling idea. It is the base of hope, the base of striving, the base of the possibility of directing our intentions and our will towards aims' (L/E/24/27).

As a consequence of quantum physics and the 'new mathematics', i.e. topology, rhythm is therefore both repetition and difference for Laban, who can be said to subscribe to an eventful rhythmic ontology (Goodman 2010). 'There is no obstacle', states Laban, 'to our regarding time in the non-Euclidean sense (like space, for example as finite and returning upon itself (leminscatic field?)) . . . rhythm is a – so to speak – plastical whole (see lemniscate). It is only our incapacity to embrace the whole, which induces us to explore the phenomenon bit by bit (sound by sound or arabesque by arabesque)' (ibid.).

In Figure 1.19, rhythm is palpable in its shape. The Cartesian plane is stretched and bent into a sinuous transparent net, the ends of which are not to be discerned. In commenting on the 'new physics', Laban states that when magnitudes will be merged into the qualitativeness of a new mathematics (that is, topology), 'a much more general world-view will then result'. This will be one where 'metrical rule will be merged into the rhythmical one' (L/E/25/49).

Laban struggles in his writings to define rhythm. In his graphic philosophy, however, this notion acquires further depth. The clearest definition of rhythm comes in *Effort and Recovery*. Laban is here concerned with the topological aspects of bodies and space, and states that:

> In its essence rhythm is a non-metric entity. [. . .] Rhythm is one of the non-metric positional relationships which appear in variable sizes and shapes in functional movements. Rhythm cannot be abstracted from happenings in space and is always the result of successive changes of non-metric spatial relationships. (L/E/56/10)

Going back to Laban's concern with intensities and non-metric qualities, from this definition of rhythm it can be evinced that Laban thought of rhythm in the last stages of his career as both a topological, non-metric phenomenon, and as metre.

Figure 1.19 R. Laban, n.d., L/E/10/16. Choreutics/Rhythmologie [Rhythmology]. Manuscript for an article about crystal forms; handwritten notes, symbols and drawings. Reproduced with the kind permission of the © Rudolf Laban Archive, National Resource Centre for Dance Archive, University of Surrey.

References

Bode, R. [1920] (2014), 'Rhythm and Its Importance for Education', in *Body & Society*, Special Issue: *Rhythm, Movement, Embodiment*, 20: 3–4 (September and December), pp. 51–74.
Buecher, K. (1899), *Arbeit und Rhythmus*. Leipzig: Teubner.
Crespi, P. (2014), 'Rhythmanalysis in Gymnastics and Dance: Rudolf Bode and Rudolf Laban', in *Body & Society*, Special Issue: *Rhythm, Movement, Embodiment*, 20: 3–4 (September and December), pp. 30–50.
Delanda, M. (2002), *Intensive Science and Virtual Philosophy*. London: Bloomsbury Academic.
Delanda, M. (2005), 'Space: Extensive and Intensive, Actual and Virtual', in I. Buchanan and G. Lambert (eds), *Deleuze and Space*. Edinburgh: Edinburgh University Press.
Deleuze, G. and Guattari, F. [1980] (1988), *A Thousand Plateaus: Capitalism and Schizophrenia*. London: Continuum Books.

Doerr, E. (2008), *The Dancer of the Crystal*. Lanham, MD: Scarecrow Press.

Goodman, S. (2010), *Sonic Warfare: Sound, Affect and the Ecology of Fear*. Cambridge, MA, and London: MIT Press.

Guattari, F. [1979] (2011), *The Machinic Unconscious: Essays in Schizoanalysis*. Los Angeles: Semiotext(e).

Klages, L. (1934), *Vom Wesen des Rhythmus*. Kampen auf Sylt: Niels Kampmann Verlag.

L/E/5/1. 'Choreology (Effort)/La cristallographie dynamique' [Dynamic crystallography]. Typed manuscript, with handwritten corrections and additions, by R. Laban. Reproduced with the kind permission of the © Rudolf Laban Archive, National Resource Centre for Dance Archive, University of Surrey.

L/E/24/23. 'Philosophical comments/The rhythm of living energy'. Handwritten manuscript by R. Laban, with typed copy, of an article that appeared in the Laban Art of Movement Guild Magazine in 1959, with a synopsis of a lecture under the same title. Reproduced with the kind permission of the © Rudolf Laban Archive, National Resource Centre for Dance Archive, University of Surrey.

L/E/24/27. 'Philosophical comments/Stability and mobility in the rhythm of life'. Handwritten manuscript by R. Laban concerning the dynamic symbolisation of the events of existence. Reproduced with the kind permission of the © Rudolf Laban Archive, National Resource Centre for Dance Archive, University of Surrey.

L/E/25/24. 'Philosophical comments/The nothing is not big not little'. Handwritten manuscript by R. Laban. Reproduced with the kind permission of the © Rudolf Laban Archive, National Resource Centre for Dance Archive, University of Surrey.

L/E/25/49. 'Philosophical comments/Further thoughts on readings about the new physics'. Handwritten manuscript by R. Laban, with a typed copy. Reproduced with the kind permission of the © Rudolf Laban Archive, National Resource Centre for Dance Archive, University of Surrey.

L/E/26/47. 'Philosophical comments/Umwege zu 1' [Detour to 1]. Handwritten notes and drawings by R. Laban. Reproduced with the kind permission of the © Rudolf Laban Archive, National Resource Centre for Dance Archive, University of Surrey.

L/E/26/70. 'Philosophical comments/Movement and mind'. Two typed manuscripts by R. Laban of the same article, one with handwritten corrections. Reproduced with the kind permission of the © Rudolf Laban Archive, National Resource Centre for Dance Archive, University of Surrey.

L/E/56/10. 'Books, Manuscripts, Outlines/Effort and Recovery/Topological Explanations, Qualitative Aspects'. Original typed manuscript, with handwritten amendments, of a section of Laban's *Effort and Recovery*; photocopies of the original. Reproduced with the kind permission of the © R. Laban Archive, National Resource Centre for Dance Archive, University of Surrey.

Laban, R. (1950), *The Mastery of Movement*. Alton: Dance Books.

Laban, R. [1921] (2014), 'Eurhythmy and Kakorhythmy in Art and Education', in *Body & Society*, Special Issue: *Rhythm, Movement, Embodiment*, 20: 3–4 (September and December), pp. 75–8.

Laban, R., and F. C. Lawrence (1947), *Effort*. London: Macdonald & Evans.

Lefebvre, H. [1992] (2004), *Rhythmanalysis: Space, Time and Everyday Life*. London and New York: Continuum.

Lubkoll, C. (2002), 'Rhythmus: Zum Konnex von Lebensphilosophie und Aesthetischer Moderne um 1900', in C. Lubkoll (ed.), *Das Imaginaere des Fin de Siècle: Ein Symposion für Gerhard Neumann*. Freiburg und Breisgau: Rombach Verlag, pp. 83–110.

Moore, C., and K. Yamamoto (1988), *Beyond Words: Movement Observation and Analysis*. London: Routledge.

North, M. (2011), 'Shadow Moves', in D. McCaw (ed), *The Laban Sourcebook*. London and New York: Routledge.

Rabinbach, A. (1992), *The Human Motor: Energy, Fatigue, and the Origins of Modernity*. Berkeley: University of California Press.

Simmel, G. [1900] (2004), *The Philosophy of Money*. London and New York: Routledge.

Toepfer, K. (1997), *The Empire of Ecstasy*. Berkeley: University of California Press.

Chapter 2

What is at Stake in a Theory of Rhythm

Henri Meschonnic

Translated from French by Chantal Wright[1] with an introduction by Marko Pajević

Henri Meschonnic (1932–2009) was a French linguist, literary scholar, poet and translator of the Bible who developed a theory of language based on the notion of rhythm. He was a major French intellectual of his generation and had a particularly strong influence in translation studies.[2] His theory of language, however, concerns many fields and aims at transforming notions such as rhythm, the subject, sense, the poem and, indeed, the episteme altogether, thus developing a poetics of society (cf. Pajević and Smith 2018).

Meschonnic is difficult to read since he developed his own terminology and an often elliptic style, working against convention. All his concepts – such as rhythm, the continuous, the subject, modernity, the poem, orality – are interrelated, and only by reading him widely and having one concept illuminate the others, can one fully grasp them as an ensemble (Pajević 2011). Meschonnic published a good sixty books.

Proceeding from Émile Benveniste's (1966) linguistic archaeology of the notion of rhythm, and discovering that this term, before Plato, designated a particular configuration of movement or a characteristic arrangement of parts in an ensemble (Benveniste 1966), Meschonnic developed his poetics of rhythm and made of the traditional formal notion of rhythm a semantic one. Rhythm thus becomes central to signifiance, that is, the way meaning is constituted. In Meschonnic's definition, rhythm is the organisation of sense in discourse. And since sense is an activity of the subject, rhythm – as a configuration of the subject in its discourse – produces and transforms the subject. His theory of rhythm thus is also a theory of the subject and develops a historical anthropology of language. Throughout his life, Meschonnic attacked 'the sign' and 'semiotics', particularly their claim to an exclusive representation of language, demonstrating that they cannot explain important activities of language. He presented rhythm as an alternative approach to language and hence to the subject and society, based on the continuous of language in discourse.

The following text is an extract from his magnum opus Critique du rythme. Anthropologie historique du langage.[3] It exposes in a nutshell some of the main notions of his theory, the relation of his theory of rhythm to the concepts of sense, discourse, subject and semiotics. The text presents itself from the outset as a critique of sense. As opposed to the traditional distinction between rhythm and sense, Meschonnic positions rhythm within semantics instead of within a theory of the sign which separates form from sense. If we accept with Benveniste the original meaning of rhythm as form in movement and, consequently, Meschonnic's definition of rhythm as organisation of sense in discourse, rhythm is inseparable from sense. This idea strengthens the signifier and all other elements of discourse, including the speech situation, against the traditional fixation on the signified. The term Meschonnic uses here is signifiance, by which he means the ensemble of signifiers, the way of signifying. Rhythm then has more sense than the sense of words. This formulation shows another problem with translating Meschonnic, since the French word sens can be 'sense' or 'meaning' in English. The French word sens is employed by Meschonnic in its semantic fullness, to encompass 'direction', an individual 'meaning' and a more generalised 'meaningfulness', and also the 'senses' themselves. Particularly noteworthy here is that 'sense of language' (sens du langage) can mean a sense for language, a sense of language, but also 'sense' such as it takes place in language and languages. Since both 'sense' and 'meaning' are ambiguous terms, with 'sense' being more often contextualised than 'meaning', it is impossible to be fully consistent in translating sens; I decided on 'sense' here to underline the physical dimension of the term.

Since sense is the activity of a subject, Meschonnic claims a close connection between his theory of rhythm and the theory of the subject. They mutually determine each other. Rhythm therefore not only configures the utterance, but also the uttered, and, by extension, transforms the utterer. The theory of language taking rhythm into account goes beyond a theory of communication. It takes into consideration the creative, cognitive aspect of language. The theory of rhythm thinks language as an activity, not as a product, to refer to Wilhelm von Humboldt, who is one of Meschonnic's major references. Language is not only about passing on preconceived ideas *but more about conceiving ideas. That is what makes the poetic element of this approach, poetics coming from* poein, *which means to make / create. When Meschonnic talks about the poem, he is actually not referring to the literary form but to this transforming activity of language which cannot be grasped by the category of the sign because it does not reside in the sense of the signified but in the entirety of* signifiance.

Meschonnic thus wants to oppose the dominance of semiotics in the theory of language and beyond, understood as a totalising claim of everything being reducible to signs. Building on Benveniste, his critique of semiotics presents a counterforce to the sign, bringing to light aspects of language covered up by the sign. Another aspect of Meschonnic's ideas about rhythm as inseparable from the subject is that language and life are interconnected. He will later in his oeuvre define poetics as the interaction of the form of language and the form of life.

Referring to Freud, Marx, Adorno, Tynianov, Gerard Manley Hopkins and others, Meschonnic positions his theory, inscribing it in the discourses of the time, in line with his conviction that thinking always takes place in interaction with others, which means also against others – as he states: 'In language, there is always war.' But this is life, 'the undefined empirical'. For this, Meschonnic critiques criteria: they work for metrics but not for rhythm. That is why Meschonnic also defines rhythm as the sense of the unpredictable, which only in retrospect seems to be 'an interior necessity'. It represents the inscription of a subject in its history. And that is why rhythm, as anti-unity, is also anti-totality – which actually makes the political necessity of thinking rhythm.

Marko Pajević

The internal relationship between rhythm and sense ruins sense as unity, as totality. It shifts *langage* away from *langue* towards discourse, away from the language of pretend didactic-scientific neutrality towards the discovery of strategies, of stakes. Rhythm is the critique of sense. This has to be stipulated prior to any definition of rhythm. Beginning with a definition turns out not only to be an uncritical step, but an anti-critical one.

* * *

and it would, perhaps, be rather difficult to exclude the dimension of life from those who speak. – Jacques Lacan, trans. Bruce Fink (1999: 30)[4]

Rhythm, Sense, Subject

There is something at stake in the theory of rhythm, within language, and it is not the notion of rhythm, but that of sense, the status of sense, and thus the entire theory of language. From the beginning one can posit that a theory of rhythm, whatever it may be, is a critical situation for a theory of language. What is at stake with sense is either the question of its belonging to the theory of the sign, or the establishment of a theory of discourse. From one to the other, the definition of rhythm has changed. The relationship between sign, language, discourse has changed. I will outline a critique of the current notion of rhythm following an analysis of what is at stake, because that is the framework and the orientation of the conflict, and determines its terms. Their sense.

It suffices, in order to pose the question, to invoke the fact that the current notion of rhythm is compatible with the theory of the sign. Because it is included within it. It makes of rhythm a formal element. Relations with sense, where it sees them, are imitative relations. Juxtaposed, secondary. Rhythm is not a semantic notion. It is a structure. A level. The distinction between form and sense, rhythm and sense, is homologous with distinctions between the categories of grammar, lexis, syntax, morphology. Traditional and unproblematic. Allowing for philological study, the essence of structuralism.

Benveniste, in his critique[5] of the etymology that furnishes, and more or less constitutes, the current definition, has destabilised, turned upside down not only the notion of rhythm, but its insertion into the theory of the sign, and at the same time, destabilised the theory of the sign itself. In rewriting the history of the word, it is in fact not only the sense of the notion that has changed. It is that it no longer fits solely within a form, it is no longer an auxiliary of dualism. Characterised as an arrangement, 'the particular configurations of moving' (Benveniste 1971: 286) or as 'the characteristic arrangement of the parts in a whole' (ibid. p. 283), *'form of movement'* (ibid. p. 287), rhythm has abandoned a static definition which kept it within the sign and within the primacy of language. It can enter into discourse.

The paradox is that Benveniste did not develop this work, even though he was the first and the only one to have made it possible. That is because he created a linguistics of discourse and, perhaps, a poetics of discourse was necessary – which analyses the poem as revelatory of the functioning of rhythm in discourse. And Benveniste makes this poetics possible, but doesn't himself establish it.

Following Benveniste, rhythm can no longer be a sub-category of form. It is the organisation (disposition, configuration) of an ensemble. If rhythm is in language, in discourse, it is the organisation (disposition, configuration) of that discourse. And since discourse is inseparable from its sense, rhythm is inseparable from the sense of this discourse. Rhythm is the organisation of sense in discourse. If it is an organisation of sense, it is no longer a distinct, juxtaposed tier. Sense is created in and via all the elements of discourse. The hierarchy of the signified is now only one variable within it, depending on the discourse and situation. Rhythm in a discourse can have more sense than the sense of words, or a different sense. The 'suprasegmental' of intonation, always excluded from sense by linguists, can have all the sense, more than the words. It is not only the hierarchy of the signified that is disturbed, it is the 'traditional divisions', as Saussure put it: syntax, lexis ... Sense is no longer the signified. There is no longer a signified. There are only signifiers, present participles of the verb *signifier* [to signify].

In the theory of the sign, the language unit [*la langue*] is first and discourse second. It cannot be any other way. Within this theory, discourse is a use of signs, a choice, a series of choices within the pre-existing system of signs. In relation to language, the speaker can only have a grammatical definition: the one that is furnished by this choice. Which is where style and stylistics come from. Corresponding to this grammatical definition is Marxism's social definition, which makes the individual the creature of social relations.[6] Choice or the absence of choice, the subject-individual is therefore the creature of the systems of signs, whose social relationships are only a category. In this, Marxism is not only compatible with the theory of the sign but constitutes a culmination, a perfection of the politics of the sign.

In the theory of rhythm that Benveniste made possible, discourse is not the use of signs, but the activity of subjects in and against a history, a culture, a language – which is only ever discourse, where the definition of language appears essentially grammatical, a particular relation of the syntagmatic to the paradigmatic which takes up, *redistributes* old categories. Rhythm as the organisation of discourse, and therefore of sense, brings back to the fore what is empirically obvious, that there is only sense by and through subjects. That sense is in discourse, not in language. The notion (and the privilege) of the signified was not only the product of a description, its result and its stakes were also to exclude the subject. The extreme form of this linguistics was without a doubt Bloomfield's, the most coherent from this point of view, and which therefore also excluded sense.

If sense is an activity of the subject, if rhythm is an organisation of sense in discourse, rhythm is necessarily an organisation or configuration of the subject in their discourse. A theory of rhythm in discourse is therefore a theory of the subject in language [*langage*]. There cannot be a theory of rhythm without a theory of the subject, nor theory of the subject without theory of rhythm. Language is an element of the subject, the most subjective element, of which the most subjective in turn is rhythm.

The theory of language is therefore privileged terrain for the theory of the subject. Perhaps more so than psychoanalysis, which has been made to play the role of furnishing such a theory, for Marxism, or for anthropology in general. Like Sartre in *Questions de méthode* [*Search for a Method*] or *L'Idiot de la famille* [*The Family Idiot*]. The anthropological interest of literature, its effect as a social laboratory, is, from this point of view, to reveal – at the price of vulnerability – the functioning of the subject, through which society itself is revealed. A theory of discourse, of the subject, is therefore above all a theory of literature. And the theory of literature is perhaps the last thing the discovery of which Freud makes possible.

The subject is comparable to the origins of language. Searched for as though it were indefinitely hidden. Nothing is hidden in language. But what is shown there slips through seeing. Like the origin, it is produced in all mouths and all ears constantly. It is the very functioning of language, the *I* of interchangeable utterance. Moving from the linguistic sphere to literature, it extends from the use of the agents of utterance to organisation into a system of an entire discourse. The subject of utterance is a relation. A dialectic of the unique and the social. A linguistic, literary, anthropological notion, not to be confused with that of the individual, which is cultural, historical, emerging from histories of individuation. The subject is an ahistorical linguistic universal: subject has always existed, everywhere language has existed. The individual is historical: it didn't always exist. Whence the history of relations between subject and individual. In discourse, the subject of discourse is historical, socially and individually.

Writing, exposing the political state of the subject in a society, shows and creates of the subject of writing a trans-subject. But there is only a subject of writing when there is a transformation of the subject of writing into a subject of re-utterance.

Just as there is only sense by and for subjects, there is only rhythm by and for subjects. The relation of rhythm to sense and to subject, in discourse, frees rhythm from the sphere of metrics. Studying rhythm no longer begins with verse (identified with poetry), as is normally the case, but with ordinary discourse, in all discourses. The theory of rhythm demonstrates that a poetics is worth what its theory of ordinary language is worth. And that it is certainly more difficult to develop a theory of prose than a theory of poetry. Caught in the paradigmatic and syntagmatic of discourse, sense- and subject-rhythm create a generalised semantics, a function of the ensemble of signifiers, which is *signifiance*.[7]

Rhythm in sense, in the subject, and the subject, sense, in rhythm, make rhythm a configuration of uttering just as much as of the utterance. This is why rhythm is the major signifier. It encompasses, with the uttered, the infra-notional, the infra-linguistic. *Rhythm is not a sign*. It shows that discourse is not only made up of signs. That the theory of language further exceeds the theory of communication. Because language includes communication, signs, but also actions, creations, relations between bodies, the shown-hidden of the unconscious, everything that the sign cannot manage and that means we move from one attempt to another. There can be no semiotics of rhythm. Rhythm entails an anti-semiotics. It shows that the poem is not made of signs, even if linguistically it is composed only of signs. The poem slips through signs. This is why the critique of rhythm is an anti-semiotics.

Rhythm, particularly in the poem, places the theory of the sign in difficulty. Not that it prevents it from functioning. The theory has functioned perfectly, from the Stoics to the present day. But it functions because it isn't merely a linguistic theory of the sign. It is also a pragmatics and a politics of the sign. Those of instrumentalism. Of the State. Of reason and of State reason. Which the centralising policies of language reinforce. The State can have no theory of language other than instrumentalism. In this, structuralism has been the good conscience of the theory of the sign. This theory can only exclude the poem, as a deviation, or as anti-arbitrary. This exclusion – which is also adoration, luxury, *celebration* – shows that in rhythm, the subject, the poem, the same thing is at stake, that of the historical anthropology of language, which also has a political sense, through the primacy of discourse, which is to say of the multiple in the empirical, of the indefinite dialectic of subjects and of the State. Historicity, plurality are indissociable.

Rhythm is therefore the primary anthropological element in language, more so than the sign: because it pressures the theory of the sign, and pushes towards a theory of discourse. Exceeding signs, rhythm comprehends language with all the might of the corporeal. It necessitates a shift from sense as totality-unity-truth to a sense that is no longer totality, nor unity, nor truth. *There is no unity of rhythm*. The only unity would be a discourse as the inscription of a subject. Or the subject itself. This unity can only be fragmented, open, undefined.

The question of rhythm maintains what is inseparable between a theory of language and a theory of literature. Because if a subject can be a unity of rhythm, if a discourse can be a unity of rhythm, this is only possible when a subject inscribes itself to the maximum degree possible into its discourse, inscribes its situation to the maximum degree possible into its discourse, and this becomes the system of it – maximal constraint. Whereas the majority of discourses are inscribed into a situation, and only make sense with it. Unity therefore is made up of them and their situation. When the situation shifts, they shift with it. But the unity of the text, which can fragment (the poem, the collection of poems, the novel, the entire work), is a unity of writing, subjective (in the sense of a transformation of the social), distinct from the rhetorical, narrative, metric unities that it contains and that it informs.

Rhythm brings to life the conflict between an epistemology that is specific to the problems of language and the ascendancy of science, or philosophy, with its idealising effects. Its paradox is the fact of being the most empirical activity, the most common to all discourse, like *I*. And theorised as belatedly, if not even later so.

Against Semiotics

Semiotics currently takes up the greater part of the theory of language. After structuralist triumphalism, semiotic triumphalism. It presents itself both as a science, and therefore universal, and omnipresent, therefore international.[8] Science, 'new scientific *savoir-faire*' (Coquet in Helbo 1979: I1). It is not merely an epistemology, but also an ethics, and a politics, that are at stake in a theory of sense, because a theory of sense also influences theories of history and society. An epistemology is not merely a technical evaluation, it is also a strategy. Whence the importance of semiotics, and the urgency of a critique of semiotics.

If everything is sign and systems of signs, everything is semiotisable, and semiotics is the science of sciences – 'the method of methods' – to cite Sebeok (Sebeok in Helbo 1979: B28).[9] This totalitarianism is part of the history of American semiotics,[10] from Peirce to Charles Morris. It is indissociable from the temptations of unity, of totality. Its ambition leads it to integrate everything, to the detriment of rigour, and at the price of taxonomic difficulties. The sign therefore includes, for Sebeok, the medical symptom, which makes Hippocrates the first semiotician. Along with Saussure and Pierce, therefore, following a metaphor that is just as rickety as the table that it suggests, a 'semiotic tripod'; the third leg 'unequal' but 'the most deeply rooted' – medicine. This would be unobjectionable were it not for the state in which semiotics places language, in offering itself as a common denominator for incommensurable units.

Poetics, rhetoric, stylistics, semiotics not only have a different history, so that they cannot be 'synchronically harmonised' (Arrivé in Helbo 1979: J7). Their strategies are different, their units, their relations with the theory of the sign. Like Hjelmslev's linguistics, semiotics has an ambiguous relationship to epistemology: as if it both constituted it and assumed it to be anterior, exterior: 'linguistics depends on an *episteme* which is not constitutive of it and over which it has no control. The epistemology that, in a given era, governs the majority of the humanities influences both the choice of method and the choice of object. This is why all epistemological slippage in the humanities inevitably has consequences for the linguistic field' (Thomas in Helbo 1979: B5). Epistemology is not an outside, does not entrust itself to others. Each piece of work develops and critiques its very being. Hjelmslev's work is invalidated by its epistemological weakness, by the theorisation that masks its empiricism, its approximations, even its grammatical work on cases. Semiotics is positioned through its linguistics: Hjelmslev's – a few specifics notwithstanding – not Saussure's. Linguistics orients semiotics towards an ahistorical formalisation.

What is at stake for the humanities can only be the historicity of anthropology, or the variants of its status outside history. This is the situation and the sense of the conflict between the sign and the poem. Now, *the more semiotics acts like a science, the more it reinforces the metaphysics of the sign.* This is its constitutive contradiction. It both masks it and augments it by ever increasing totalisation, increasing scientificity. Its effects are: the reciprocal maintenance of post-structuralism and phenomenology; compartmentalisation into specialisms (a semiotics of painting, cinema etc.), which augments the blurriness of the notion of the sign, and the blurriness of borrowings from an ideology of pleasure that is derived from an 'articulation' with psychoanalysis. The strategy of a polemic of details, for internal use, like generative grammar, masks what is at stake through technical discussion, striving only to reinforce its academic standing. The manoeuvres of conventional theory, to cite Horkheimer. Semiotics therefore contributes to the current confusionism. It lends its dehistoricisation to millenarian irrationalism. It leaves the field open to it, offering the prospect of an absence of critique that is the political effect of its epistemology.

Because there is a radical ahistoricity to semiotics. The sign is a universal which, as such, knows neither historicity nor historicisation. This is what Jean-Claude Coquet emphasises, perhaps without wanting to, when he speaks of the 'achronic structure' of Greimas' 'constitutional model' (Coquet in Helbo 1979: I7). The 'Locke-Peirce-Morris pattern', as Sebeok says (1975: 4), is Leibniz's lineage. The sign has lost what was linguistic about it in its trajectory from Saussure to contemporary semiotics, just as narrative function, in its trajectory from Propp to Greimas, has lost what was historical about it.

Going in a different direction from Peirce, whom Sebeok cites, for whom 'all this universe is perfused with signs, if it is not composed exclusively of signs' (Sebeok 1975: 25),[11] an attentiveness to empirical discourse reduces the sign component in the strict sense (doubly articulated), and multiplies the pseudo-signs component. The semiotisable is lessened. It is unclear whether there is interest, either among the natural sciences or the linguistic sciences, in understanding the universe as a system of signs. The immediate effect of this is a generalised metaphor. Its effect on biology, genetics, is scarcely more than an effect of pan-semiotic discourse, via the usage of terms such as *code, message*... Its effect on language is an insertion into the cosmic to the detriment of empirical significance. The classic privilege of the signified is thus reinforced, as is the blurriness between sign, signal, symptom, indication.... But this blurriness is of a fashionable sort.

The myth of the totality-unity that drives semiotics can also be found in theories of rhythm. To combat this myth, I will try to show that a *general* theory of rhythm – encompassing all rhythms, everything that is rhythm – inevitably finds itself to be a metaphysics of rhythm, as semiotics finds itself to be a metaphysics of the sign. Since only discourse is historical, not the sign, a theory of language must constitute itself in accordance with the specificity of its object. It can only lose its historicity by merging with semiotics. This is why a theory of rhythm in discourse would not necessarily have a relationship with a theory of rhythm anywhere other than in discourse. As if the sense of the notion of rhythm in language could only be the particular realisation of a universal, which presupposes a universal rhythm, or rather a universal notion of rhythm. Which, curiously, is the very one that Benveniste recognised and condemned. Even though he deprived the notion of rhythm of the historical foundations of its sense, in fact, nothing has changed.

Against semiotics and its effect on language, on literature, Benveniste did more than simply sketch a strategy, in 'The Semiology of Language' ([1974] 1985: 228–46). Against the attempt at 'one system alone' (ibid. p. 229), Benveniste noted the insurmountable difference between Saussure and Peirce, where Sebeok's already rickety 'tripod' – which placed these two 'feet' into a continuous series, made them *equal*, since the only 'unequal' was Hippocrates – starts to break down. There is a 'non-convertibility of systems with different bases' (ibid. p. 235); 'There is no sign [. . .] that is transystemic' (ibid.). Benveniste showed that there is no *unity*, in the plastic arts for example, therefore no semiotics. Only 'the work of a particular artist' (ibid. pp. 237–8) would be an 'approximation' (ibid. p. 237) of such unity – in other words, 'individual characteristic' (ibid. p. 238): unity ruins the notion of unity. It becomes one unicity: 'Art is nothing more than a specific work of art' (ibid. p. 239). The double 'relationship of *interpretance*' (ibid. p. 240) instituted by Benveniste allows us to distinguish systems that are purely semiotic from those that are purely semantic. If there is occasion to 'go beyond Saussure's concern for the sign as a unique principle' (ibid. p. 243). Benveniste's analysis is the only one to uphold the historicity and specificity of each practice. He outlined the programme, announcing on the one hand a linguistics of discourse, and on the other, 'the translinguistic analysis of texts and other manifestations through the elaboration of a metasemantics founded on the semantics of enunciation' (ibid.). This is where a poetics of rhythm takes off. It is inscribed in an investigation of semantics, the theory of the particular. But semiotics, with its dream of a universal science, has got its epistemology wrong.

In semiotics, binarism – with its phonological origins – indefinitely repeats the dualism of the sign. Just as the Saussure-Peirce-Hippocrates triad is unstable, so too the concept of *seme*, constantly employed by vulgate semiotics, is confused. An introductory textbook defines it as follows: 'an element of signification rigorously determined by these two relations of disjunction on the basis of conjunction' (Hénault 1979: 49, my translation). Disjunction, conjunction refer to phonology, and binarise difference, which is plural in Saussure. Retaining, despite an allusion to the critiques directed at it, the isomorphism of expression and content, in Hjelmslev, the notion of a minimal element of signification bases its combinatory principle on the logic of identity and the primacy of the signified, conjoined in the notion of *isotopy*. Greimas defined isotopy as a 'bundle of redundant semantic categories underlying considered discourse' (Greimas 1970: 10). Isotopy is the repetition of the same, the 'thing resulting from the repetition of elements of signification of the same category'

(Hénault 1979: 81). One proceeds to its 'extraction'. In other words, to a series of conceptual reductions. A variant on the paraphrase concealed by scientism. Classification into categories rests on binarism (euphoria/dysphoria); mimics the generative: the 'manifest text' of the surface, 'abstract elements' in their depth (ibid. p. 103); divides polysemy into monosemies; has an almost non-existent power of discovery: the 'semiotic square' of oppositions into contraries and contradictories is only 'universally applicable' (ibid. p. 133) by finding abstract categories everywhere, by being vague, where *death* contrasts with *life*.

Confusionism and regression combine to give the semiotic definition of discourse. The same introductory textbook includes in its glossary: '*Discourse* (or parole) is the result of choices made by a given speaker, from the stock of language, in order to realise a particular message, inscribed in a concrete and specific situation' (ibid. p. 181). Giving *parole* as equivalent to *discourse* muddies the entire history of linguistic concepts, from Saussure to Benveniste, rendering Saussure unintelligible and the term unusable for a linguistics of discourse. The notion of *choice* reveals the primacy of *langue*, towards a stylistics that cannot work either because it is an individualism without a theory of the subject, since *langue* reduces the subject to a structure. Finally, *stock*, which reshapes language as a nomenclature of words instead of a system, discovers both, like a slip of the tongue, the anti-Saussure and the pre-Saussure at work in semiotics.

This degeneracy of the sign is not a timely failing, which would scarcely merit a mention. It is the combined product of a linguistics borrowed from Hjelmslev, of a pseudo-scientific formalisation, of the very history of American semiotics, particularly after Charles Morris. Confusion and regression are precisely most visible where discourse is at stake. Cinema, painting tolerate this scienticism better. But there too, semiotics is less and less in touch with the reality of those practices.

Rhythm rejects semiotics. It rejects it on its own account, first of all. It can also signal a critique that semiotics itself does not appear ready to grasp, labouring under the illusion that it is partaking in a 'gold rush' (ibid. p. 175).

Semiotics and poetics are only one aspect of a conflict revealed by poetics. This conflict is insurmountable. It reveals that it is impossible to think language without thinking in terms of conflict. In language, it is always war. Whether it is a matter of discourse that is an endless *agon*, or the status of the subject, or the relationship between words and things. Semiotic science is caught up in its positivity. And in the poise of the semiotician.

Negativity of Rhythm

If rhythm, sense, subject are in a relationship of reciprocal inclusion where the critique of rhythm and discourse are concerned, linguistics, by contrast, says nothing about rhythm, for reasons which meant that Bloomfield left sense out of linguistics.

Neither a theory of rhythm, nor a theory of sense, nor a theory of the subject are constituted. But no theory is ever constituted. The initial mistake would be to wait for one before an other can be further determined. None of the three is a prerequisite for the rest. That would mean waiting indefinitely. If sense, subject, rhythm are linked, working on one means working on all of them.

A theory of rhythm is necessary for a theory of the subject and of the individual, since it finds fault with the metaphysics of the sign. This metaphysics operates through the effacement of the subject-observer, conflated with the truth of what is observed, the *object*, as if the conditions of observation were not inseparably subjective-objective. This is the solidarity of the sign and of the dualist anthropology of the logical and the pre-logical. And the solidarity of discourse with a decentred anthropology. Which also underlines the fact that a theory is only a 'mode of representation' (Bergson 1972: 213, my translation), not an objective truth-universal of the object.

If theory recognises itself as relative, as a 'mode of representation', it is in a better state than the metaphysics of the sign to recognise that its object of knowledge is an empirical variable – sense, not truth. The literary work, grasped as a discourse among discourses, no longer allows for an aesthetics of mimicry, of the lie, nor an aesthetics of the truth. No more than is the case on the logical level of true or false. Adorno contrasted truth with *mimesis*: 'The spirit of works of art is neither their meaning nor the intention behind them but their truth content' (Adorno 1984: 398, A-56). He added: 'Jettisoning the idea of imitation from aesthetics would be just as wrong as accepting it uncritically' (ibid. p. 399, A-58). The subjectivity of sense, of reception, changes, prevents – at least in part – the moralisation that is truth. Adorno wrote: 'Great works of art are unable to lie', hence 'it is only the botched and misconceived ones that are untrue' (ibid. p. 188). Which reduces art to psychology. But subjectivity stands in the way of mimetics by withdrawing its transcendence to make of it an adventure of subjects.

The historicity of discourse no longer makes of the work a beautiful lie or a truth. Because it doesn't trace it back to an intention, as Adorno continues to do, nor to a content (cf. ibid. 187, 209). The link between sense and subject neutralises these oppositions.

The organisation of sense as signifiance, value, means in turn that rhythm can no longer be envisaged as a form, which would be the 'logicality' (ibid. p. 197), the coherence of works of art. That are 'determined objectively' (ibid. p. 198).

Adorno wanted to eliminate the concept of 'aesthetic enjoyment': 'The concept of aesthetic enjoyment was a bad compromise between the social essence of art and the critical tendencies inherent within it' (ibid. p. 20) and further on: 'the very idea that enjoyment is of the essence of art deserves to be thrown overboard' (ibid. p. 22). The critique of rhythm is a critique of pleasure. But Adorno cannot eliminate this concept, which carries an entire aesthetics along with it, by remaining, as he does, with art-as-imitation. *Mimesis* remains, for Adorno, the 'ideal of art' (ibid. p. 164). Adorno adapts Kant's 'purposefulness without a purpose' (ibid. p. 201) to an instrumentalist idea of language. But rhythm as the sense of the subject is both subjective and social, sense and history. The theoretical division therefore eliminates this 'aesthetic enjoyment as a constitutive concept'. It eliminates it as a product of dualism. Pleasure is the organisation of signifiance via the integration of the body and history in discourse. It is no more an aesthetic concept than one can differentiate between rhythm and metaphors in the 'thrill of the new' that Hugo perceived in Baudelaire.

At the same time, a maximalist rejection of the very notion of investigation into the subject suggests itself in a particular Marxist position. It has to be refuted but also analysed for its strategic importance, for the weakness of its arguments, and for what it indirectly anticipates: 'There can be no more a "theory of sense" or a "theory of the subject" than there can be "theories of God"; these objects are ideological categories, not objects of knowledge' (Henry 1977: 20). Althusserian Marxism presupposes in this the identification between science and theory that is necessary for it to radically contrast itself with the ideological. The object of knowledge actually belongs to science. Or at least to this particular concept of science. But the rejection of sense in ideology does not recognise the effect of its own action on the theory of language.

It is the logical continuity from Marx to Marr that, taking up or rejecting together both sense and ideology, places ideology in *langue*, rejects the philosophy of *langage* along with the language of philosophers (in *The German Ideology*) and prepares the unthinkable of *langage* via superstructure. Hence the unthinkable of the subject. The *articulation* of Marxism and structuralism is by itself the negation of the subject: 'social formation is not composed of subjects: one can only define spaces to which conditions of production and the reproduction of significations are attached' (ibid. p. 77). A *subject* that is so negated that it is a confusion of the individual and the subject, the moral and the psychological: 'the subject-individual' is the 'specific subject-form' of 'bourgeois ideologies' (ibid. p. 159). A negation of the possibility of the *subject* that says more about its own strategy, its own ignorance, than about the subject. To this is added the 'articulation of historical materialism and of psychoanalysis' (ibid. p. 125), combined with the *articulation* of Marxism and of generative grammar (to articulate all of the avant-gardes at once), and which fails to perceive the theoretical and *political* incompatibility of the two.[12] Whence this proposition that doesn't know what it is saying, because it is ignorant of the opposing strategies of *langue* and *discourse*: 'syntax is situated in *langage* for the articulation of *langue* and discourse' (Henry 1977: 155). The final obstacle to the subject, the unconscious, is strangely opposed to syntax: 'As for what the already said or heard articulates with all its *parole* or utterance, it is not properly syntax – that has its roots in the unconscious, not in the subject' (ibid. p. 144). The confusionism of an era, already out of date, which establishes a specious paradigm between the subject of the uttering and the unconscious, the subject of the uttered and the psychological subject (ibid. p. 155).

This example characterises some of the current obstacles to a theory of the subject and of discourse. It shows that an epistemological obstacle is also a political obstacle. It confirms that a theory of discourse also maintains (contains, retains) a theory of syntax (which is not that of language). It displays the ambient naivety, of Sartre through to the Marxists, which entrusts to psychoanalysis the potential theory of the subject. Which, coincidentally, does not make it more of a science, but an ideology. Ducrot partially re-establishes the subject, as much as he draws it back to himself, via the presupposition: 'declaring X the subject of his uttering is to assume that he knows the sense of this uttering at the moment he brings it about' (ibid. p. 200).

It is here that the analysis of poetic activity can rejoin that of the presupposition. It is a matter of analysing modes of signifying. A poem is neither an intention nor a consciousness. There is a theoretical regression, following on from Valéry, that links the subject to this psychological and moral couple: in other words, unity.

The subject is no more a unity than a poem is made of signs. Which doesn't prevent it from being a relative unity. The text-unit(y) mistakes the notion of unity. Adorno wrote: 'Oneness is an illusion. Therefore works of art constitute illusion as they establish oneness' (Adorno 1984: 425, A119). It breaks down into lesser unities, which are rhetorical, linguistic. The *word*, which is the smallest unit of sense, tends in the opposite direction, to metaphorically designate larger units. Mallarmé sees in *verse* the '*mot total*'. Mandelstam goes further: 'Any unit of poetic speech, be it a line, a stanza or an entire lyrical composition, must be regarded as a single word' (Mandelstam 2002: 52).

Rhythm intervenes in poetry to the extent that poetry is the language that is least made up of signs. Which is what Diderot said, in his own way, in his *Letter on the Deaf and Dumb*, that discourse is:

> not merely [. . .] a chain of well-ordered terms which convey facts to our mind, but [. . .] a series of hieroglyphics which picture the thought to us vividly; in fact, I may say that all of poetry consists of emblems.
>
> But it is not every one who can understand these emblems. In order to feel their meaning we must almost have the power of creating them ourselves. (1904: 163)[13]

The emblem or the hieroglyph escapes unity. The poem, or rhythm, by this itself, escapes the subject, assumed to be unitary from the outset. But at the same time, only one subject of uttering has emitted a rhythm, a poem. Rhythm, conceived in continuity with sense and the subject, disunites sense, subject. The metaphor of the hieroglyph signals that one can only think this activity in the indirect, the provisional.

This is the same metaphor that Freud used for the dream: 'The dream-content [. . .] is expressed as it were in a pictographic script, the characters of which have to be transposed individually into the language of the dream-thoughts' (Freud 1991: 381). He added: 'A dream is a picture-puzzle [rebus]' (ibid. p. 382). But rhythm is not a rebus. The rebus fragments unity into pieces of sense. Unity is merely inconvenienced along its path. Coded. It is reconstituted at the end, when the decoding has gone well. If rhythm is the configuration of a sense, nothing allows us, as we will see, to see in it the same sense, the same unity, differently arranged.

Just as separating rhythm and sense has appeared for the longest time 'an enterprise of doubtful value' (Richards 1966: 361), so too associating them through a vague identification would be of doubtful value. This would easily reveal the old homology of form and content, logico-grammatical parallelism. If the relationship of rhythm to sense is not conceived of technically as a relationship of discourse to the subject, it is, from the outset, a classic oscillation between living and *langage*.

A theory of rhythm is a theory of sense not because rhythm is sense, but because rhythm is in interaction with sense. The poem is the discourse where this interaction is most visible, and doubtlessly also where it is the most specific. Tynianov, in 1923, postulates this *'modification of the semantic value of the word that operates from the fact of its rhythmic value'* (Tynianov 1977: 108).[14] It is a semantics of position, the 'semantic value of a word in verse through the function of its position' (ibid. p. 116). Because of the fact that rhythm was the 'constructive principle of verse' (ibid. p. 76), for Tynianov, creating a theory of verse meant creating, or rather announcing, as necessary, an 'analysis of changes *specific to the signification and sense of words* by function of the construction *of verse* itself' (ibid. p. 40). Tynianov's postulate has become, strangely, both a truism and an abandoned programme. I am certainly not aware that it has been realised. If it is to be taken up, extended, this can no longer be with its notion of the word, and of lexis: 'The very *structure* of the lexis of verse is radically different from that of the lexis of prose' (ibid. p. 126). This is true, however, of certain poetries, certain cultures. The critique of rhythm owes to Tynianov the constructive function of rhythm. But Tynianov remains in a functionalism where there is neither utterance, nor subject, nor discourse. Nothing but sense, *langue*.

Rhythm is not sense, nor redundancy or substitute, but sense material, even the material of sense. If it is of the subject, it is an ensemble of subjective-social relations that drive discourse. The major importance that Gerard Manley Hopkins accorded rhythm confirms his pioneering significance, not only for poetic modernity, but for the theory of rhythm. He sought 'an immense advance in notation [. . .] in writing as the record of speech' (Abbott 1955: 265)[15] and referred to the accents of the Bible. A rhythm is a sense if it is a passage of the subject, the production of a form – arrangement, configuration, organisation – of the subject, which is the production of a subject-form(er) for any subject. Which is what, to use a well-known example, Nerval does in 'Je suis le Ténébreux, – le Veuf – , l'Inconsolé' [literal translation: 'I am the Shadowy One, – the Widowed – , the Unconsoled'] through the double internal break in the line, isolating 'le Veuf', the paradigm of solitude, which belongs as much to the work of the words as to that of the typography: the italics and the capital letters of 'Il appela le *Seul* – éveillé dans Solyme' [He summoned the *Lone One* – aroused in Solyme'], 'Et c'est toujours la Seule, – ou c'est le seul moment' [And it is always the Lone One, – or it is the lone moment'].

If the subject of writing is a subject through writing, it is rhythm that produces, transforms the subject, to the extent that the subject emits a rhythm. Closer to value than to signification, rhythm installs a receptivity, a mode of seizure that inserts itself despite our contemporary comprehension, that of the sign; the rationality of the identical identified with reason. It imposes a multiplicity of logics: 'When a verse is extremely beautiful one does not even dream of understanding. It is no longer a signal, it is a fact' (Valéry 1916: 1076). It is perhaps this pre-, or one might say, peri-rational effect that certain metaphors of rhythm note, such as, in Hebrew, *michqal*, etymologically 'weight', for 'rhythm', or, to name the accents of cantillation in the Bible (rhythmic-semantic-melodic accents), *te'amim*, from *ta'am*, 'taste' (*ta'ām*, food, in Arabic). In Indian poetics, the term *rasa*, identified with the sense of 'taste' and 'lifeblood, essence', designates a theatrical mode (cf. Gerow 1977: 245–9). The sensory metaphor designates absorption by the body. The metres in the *Brāhmana* have a 'nutritional virtue' analysed by Mauss: 'the principle of this theory is that song is of the voice, which is of the breath, which is of food' (1969: 593).[16]

Anti-unity, rhythm is an anti-totality. It is the undefined empirical that prevents a Hegelian poetics from being realised. A Hegelian poetics wants to 'perceive the poem in its totality' (Varga 1977: 4 , my translation). Kibédi Varga looks for 'the superior unity of synthesis, such that it establishes itself in the reader during the actualisation of the poem' (ibid. p. 42). Some confusion follows: between a phenomenology of reading – 'a dialectic of the apprehension of the poem' (ibid. p. 35) – and an analysis of the mode of signifying; between the mode of signifying and individual realisation, the 'read poem'. This 'dialectical poetics of the actualised poem' (ibid. p. 149) continues to start out from the *word*, 'poetic or poeticised'. It therefore returns to the rhetoric of figures of words (ibid. p. 194). To grasp the 'constants of poetry' (ibid. p. 270), it misses the poem, because it places it in traditional categories, the image being a mode of representation: 'The constants of the poem are therefore movement and cessation, sonoric flow and rhyme, centre and distance of terms of the image, the relationship of each of these constants with the reader's effort of apprehension' (ibid.).

The rhythm of sense as the sense of the subject demands that we no longer accept this repartition, of the 'sonorous' and the 'image', which scarcely varies from that of form and content. The critique of rhythm is firstly the critique of criteria. There are criteria belonging to metrics. Are there any for rhythm? Rhythm is the sense of the unpredictable. The realisation of which, *in retrospect*, will be called 'an interior necessity': 'The artist does not create according to the criteria of beauty, but according to interior necessity' (Schoenberg 1973: 218).[17] Rhythm is the inscription of a subject in its history. It is therefore both an irreversible and that to which it constantly returns. Not unitary, not totalisable, its only possible unity is no longer its own: discourse as system.

In writing, in art, a subject has become its work. Which is what the common designation indicates: the name of an author operates differently than the name of a person which is not the name of an author. It signifies, at the same time as it designates. It assembles semantics. Beyond the futurist provocation, this is one effect of Mayakovsky's title, *Vladimir Mayakovsky, Tragedy*.

Notes

1. This translation was edited by David Nowell-Smith and was produced within the framework of a wider translation project that resulted in the publication of the Henri Meschonnic Reader in 2019. This Reader contains a substantial introduction, key texts, a glossary and a bibliography. My thanks go to the general editor of that project, Marko Pajević, and to my fellow translators in Team Meschonnic: Pier-Pascale Boulanger, David Nowell-Smith, John E. Joseph and Andrew Eastman.
2. One of Meschonnic's books on translation theory is translated into English (Boulanger 2011).
3. The extract translated here represents the first three parts of Chapter III of the French text, pp. 65-85 in the 1982 Verdier edition; this extract is also included in *The Henri Meschonnic Reader*.
4. 'Et peut-être est-il difficile d'exclure de ceux qui parlent la dimension de la vie' (Lacan 1975: 32).
5. See Benveniste 1966: 327–35 or the English translation thereof by Mary Elizabeth Meek, Benveniste 1971: 281–8.
6. 'My standpoint, from which the development of the economic formation of society is viewed as a process of natural history, can less than any other make the individual responsible for relations whose creature he remains, socially speaking, however much he may subjectively raise himself above them' (Marx 1976: 92).
7. Which is why I give a value specific to poetics to the term *signifiance*, in contrast to that given to it by Benveniste as 'signifying property' in 'Sémiologie de la langue' (Benveniste 1974: 43–66, 51). [Translator's note: In the published English translation by Genette Ashby and Adelaide Russo, Benveniste's 'signifiance' is rendered as 'significance'. I have retained Benveniste's French term 'signifiance' in my translation.]
8. This is what the edited volume *Le Champ sémiologique, perspectives internationales* (Helbo 1979), displays. [Translator's note: All translations from this French-language encyclopaedia of semiotics are my own. Subsequent references to this work will include the name of the author of the entry cited, e.g. Coquet in Helbo 1979, and a page number reflecting the work's own idiosyncratic system of pagination (letter + number), e.g. B3. Entries will not be referenced individually in the list of references.]

9. [Translator's note. This entry by Thomas Sebeok in *Le Champ sémiologique* was originally published in English as 'The Semiotic Web: A Chronicle of Prejudices' in the *Bulletin of Literary Semiotics* (Sebeok 1975: 1–63). It was translated into French for the Helbo volume by Jean-Jacques Thomas; a footnote on p. B6 of that volume explains the English-language provenance of this entry. The citation that Meschonnic attributes to Sebeok here is referenced in Sebeok's original article (1975: 25) as a summary of Charles Sanders Peirce's thought by Max H. Fisch and Jackson I. Cope, from 'Peirce at the Johns Hopkins University' (1952: 289).
10. I refer the reader to *Le signe et le poème* (Meschonnic 1975: 140–56, 173–81, 232–47).
11. [Translator's note: Sebeok's reference for the Peirce citation is Peirce 1965/66: note on p. 448.]
12. For a political analysis of generative grammar, I refer the reader to *Poésie sans réponse. Pour la poétique*, V (Meschonnic 1978: 317–95).
13. 'que les discours n'est plu seulement un enchaînement de termes énergiques qui exposent la pensée avec force et noblesse, mais que c'est encore un tissu d'hiéroglyphes entassés les uns sur les autres qui la peignent. Je pourrais dire en ce sens que toute poésie est emblématique. Mais l'intelligence de l'emblème poétique n'est pas donnée à tout le monde. Il faut être presque en état de le créer pour le sentir fortement' (Diderot 1969: 459).
14. [Translator's note: The translations into English here are based on the French translation as cited by Meschonnic.]
15. Gerard Manley Hopkins, in a letter to Robert Bridges dated 6 November 1887: 'it would be an immense advance in notation (so to call it) in writing as the record of speech, to distinguish the subject, verb, object, and in general to express the construction to the eye; as is done already partly in punctuation by everybody, partly in capitals by the Germans, more fully in accentuation by the Hebrews' (Abbott 1955: 265).
16. Kant perceived this metaphor: 'How could it have happened that modern languages in particular have designated the aesthetic faculty of judging with an expression (*gustus*, *sapor*) that merely refers to a certain sense organ (the inside of the mouth) and to its discrimination as well as choice of enjoyable things?' (Kant 2006: 139 [§67]). But he concluded by paraphrasing: 'the feeling of an organ through a particular sense has been able to furnish the name for an ideal feeling' (ibid. 141), and 'an unconditionally necessary end requires neither reflection nor experiment, but comes into the soul immediately by, so to speak, tasting what is wholesome' (ibid.). It appears to me that the relation cannot be explained by words, by re-linking *sapor* to *sapentia*, and that it supposes a theory of the body in *langage*, therefore rhythm.
17. [Translator's note: I have translated here from the French translation of Schoenberg's *Harmonielehre* [Theory of Harmony] as cited by Meschonnic.]

References

Abbott, C. C. (ed.) (1955), *The Letters of G. M. Hopkins to R. Bridges*. Oxford: Oxford University Press.
Adorno, T. W. (1984), *Aesthetic Theory*, trans. C. Lenhardt. London: Routledge and Kegan Paul.
Benveniste, É. [1951] (1966a), 'La notion de "rythme" dans son expression linguistique', in *Problèmes de linguistique générale I*, Paris: Gallimard, pp. 327–35.
Benveniste, É. [1951] (1971), 'The notion of rhythm in its linguistic expression', in *Problems in General Linguistics*, trans. M. E. Meek. Coral Gables: University of Miami Press, pp. 281–8.
Benveniste, E. (1974), 'Sémiologie de la langue', in *Problèmes de linguistique générale II*. Paris: Gallimard.
Benveniste, É. [1974] (1985), 'The semiology of language', trans. G. Ashby and A. Russo, in R. E. Innis (ed.), *Semiotics: An Introductory Anthology*. Bloomington: Indiana University Press, pp. 228–46, p. 234.
Bergson, H. (1972), 'Durée et simultanéité', in *Mélanges*. Paris: PUF.
Boulanger, P. (2011), *Ethics and Politics of Translating*. Amsterdam: John Benjamins.
Diderot, D. (1904), 'A Letter on the Deaf and the Dumb', trans. B. L. Tollemache, in *Diderot's Thoughts on Art and Style*. London: Rivingtons, pp. 146–69.
Diderot, D. (1969), *Œuvres completes, II*. Paris: Le Club Français du Livre.
Fisch, M. H., and J. J. Cope (1952), 'Peirce at the Johns Hopkins University', in: P. P. Wiener and F. H. Young (eds), *Studies in the Philosophy of Charles Sanders Peirce*. Cambridge: Harvard University Press, pp. 277–311, 355–60.
Freud, S. (1991), *The Interpretation of Dreams*, trans. J. Strachey. London: Penguin.
Gerow, E. (1977), *Indian Poetics*. Wiesbaden: Otto Harrassowitz.
Greimas, A. J. (1970), *Du sens*. Paris: Éditions du Seuil.
Helbo, A. (ed.) (1979), *Le Champ sémiologique*. Brussels: Éditions Complexe.
Hénault, A. (1979), *Les Enjeux de la sémiotique*. Paris: PUF.
Henry, P. (1977), *Le Mauvais outil. Langue, sujet et discours*. With an afterword by Oswald Ducrot. Paris: Klinksieck.
Kant, I. (2006), *Anthropology from a Pragmatic Point of View*, trans. R. B. Louden. Cambridge: Cambridge University Press.
Lacan, J. (1975), *Séminaire XX*. Paris: Seuil.
Lacan, J. [1975] (1999), *The Seminar of Jacques Lacan. Book XX. On Feminine Sexuality, the Limits of Love and Knowledge, 1972–3 (Encore)*, trans. B. Fink. New York: W. W. Norton.
Mandelstam, O. (2002), 'Conversation about Dante', trans. J. G. Harris and C. Link, in: P. S. Hawkins and R. Jacoff (eds), *The Poets' Dante*. New York: Farrar, Straus, and Giroux. pp. 40–93.

Marx, K. (1976), 'Preface to the first edition', in *Capital*, vol. 1, trans. B. Fowkes. London: Penguin. pp. 89–93.
Mauss, M. (1969), *Anna-Virāj*, in M. Mauss, *Œuvres*, 2. Paris: Édition de Minuit.
Meschonnic, H. (1975), *Le signe et le poème*. Paris: Gallimard.
Meschonnic, H. (1978), *Poésie sans réponse. Pour la poétique*, V. Paris: Gallimard.
Meschonnic, H. (1982), *Critique du rythme. Anthropologie historique du langage*, Lagrasse: Verdier.
Meschonnic, H. (2019), *The Meschonnic Reader*, ed. M. Pajević. Edinburgh: Edinburgh University Press.
Pajević, M. (2011), 'Beyond the Sign: Henri Meschonnic's Poetics of Rhythm and Continuum: Towards an Anthropological Theory of Language', *Forum for Modern Language Studies* (FMLS), 47: 3, pp. 304–18.
Pajević, M., and D. Nowell Smith (eds) (2018), *Thinking Language with Henri Meschonnic*, Special Issue, *Comparative Critical Studies*, 15:3.
Peirce, C. S. (1965/6), *Collected Papers of Charles Sanders Peirce*, V. Cambridge, MA: Harvard University Press/The Belknap Press.
Richards, I. A. (1966), *Practical Criticism*. London: Routledge.
Schoenberg, A. (1973), Introduction au *Traité d'harmonie*, trans. E. Dickenherr and J.-Y. Bosseur, in L. Brion-Guerry (ed.), *L'Année 1913, Les formes esthétiques de l'œuvre d'art à la veille de la première guerre mondiale. 3. Manifestes et témoignages*. Paris: Klinksieck, pp. 2016–24.
Sebeok, T. (1975), 'The Semiotic Web: A Chronicle of Prejudices', *Bulletin of Literary Semiotics*, 2, pp. 1–63.
Tynianov, I. (1924), *Le Vers lui-même: problème de la langue du vers* [*Problema stixotvornovo jazyka* (Leningrad, 1924)] trans. J. Durin, B. Grinbaum, H. Henry, D. Konopnicki et al. Paris: Union générale d'éditions.
Valéry, P. (1916), *Cahiers*, II. Paris: Gallimard.
Varga, K. (1977), *Les Constantes du poème*. Paris: Picard.

Chapter 3

Rhythm and Textural Temporality

Sha Xin Wei and Garrett Laroy Johnson

Body + Movement + Irregular Matter → Rhythm

Let us start with a simple proposition: rhythm as a feature of experience (rather than an abstract pattern) arises from a body encountering variation in matter through movement. Without a body there would be no *sense*. In a perfectly homogeneous experience of a perfectly homogeneous world there would be no (non-degenerate)[1] rhythm regardless of movement. Running your finger across the ridges of the sea shell, you feel irregular pressure on your skin that you can interpret as a rhythm – a pattern of irregular variation of sensation correlate with your movement. Stopping your finger's movement you would feel no variation. If the shell were perfectly smooth, you also would feel no variation. So, corporeal movement and irregularities in matter are necessary to rhythmic experience. Notice that corporeal movement compounds the body as a necessary ingredient in having this experience. Feeling through the body, via embodied engagement is an inextricable component of experience. Thus, according to our formulation, body, movement and inhomogeneous matter are necessary for rhythm *as sense*. Regarding sense, Merleau-Ponty writes:

> The sensing being [*le sentant*] and the sensible are not opposite each other like two external terms ... the movement of my hand subtends the form of the object. In this exchange between the subject of sensation and the sensible, it cannot be said that one acts while the other suffers the action, nor that one gives sense to the other. Without the exploration of ... my hand, and prior to my body synchronizing with it, the sensible is nothing but a vague solicitation. (Merleau-Ponty 2014: 221–2)

However, variation of matter and corporeal movement, while elemental as ingredients of a sense of rhythm, may not exhaustively account for the phenomenon. Rhythm as a temporal pattern in experience lies beyond or in between sense perceptions. One gets to a sense of rhythmic pattern via perception, but rhythm itself is not sense data. To borrow phenomenological vocabulary, rhythm is not perceived but apperceived.

The reader may find it completely obvious that rhythm is not to be found 'out there', to be represented by sense or sensor data, but rather is a feature of lived experience, and thus inextricably part of phenomena rather than data. But in the age of machine-perception, sensor technologies and big data, it is useful to refer to much more extensive arguments such as Merleau-Ponty's scientific meditations on temporal experience. He writes: 'We are not saying that time is for someone, which would once more be a case of arraying it out, and immobilizing it. . . . We must understand time as the subject and the subject as time' (Merleau-Ponty 2014: 490). Merleau-Ponty provides an integral account that voids both purely idealist and realist positions:

> Existence cannot be anything – spatial, sexual, temporal – without being so entirely, or without taking up and assuming its 'attributes' and turning them into the dimensions of its being, such that a relatively precise analysis of each of them in fact has to do with subjectivity itself. . . . If we succeed in understanding the subject, this will not be in its pure form, but rather by looking for the subject at the intersection of its various dimensions. (2014: 433)

In other words, time (and space) is not an abstract frame inside of which we position an event or an individual. Instead the temporal sense is one aspect – a dimension – of an individual's experience. Merleau-Ponty draws striking consequences about events from his experiential account:

> [T]he very notion of an event has no place in the objective world. When I say that the water currently passing by was produced by the glacier two days ago, I imply a witness fixed to a certain place in the world and I compare his successive perspectives. . . . [T]here are no events without someone to whom they happen . . . (2014: 433)

Moreover, temporality as a relation between a subject and the world implies that, in Merleau-Ponty's words: 'time is neither a real process nor an actual succession that I could limit myself simply to recording. It is born of my relation with things' (2014: 434).

Departing however from the presumption of a pre-given Cartesian cogito in cognitivist and phenomenological projects, we keep in play various commitments to particular notions of *subject*, *body* and *time*. This methodological attitude draws from both pragmatism's radically empirical approach based on experience (as found in the work of William James) and Edmund Husserl's injunction to attend to the phenomena themselves. Thus, we start from neither theoretical abstractions like time or numbered metric nor unperceivable mechanism, but rather from lived experience, succinctly put in the Introduction to the 1912 edition of William James' *Essays in Radical Empiricism* as follows:

> (1) [T]he only things that shall be debatable among philosophers shall be things definable in terms drawn from experience ... (2) ... the relations between things, conjunctive as well as disjunctive, are just as much matters of direct particular experience, neither more so nor less so, than the things themselves. (1912: 3)

Informed by such a perspective, we keep in play notions like *subject*, *body*, or *time* rather than invoking them as primitive building blocks of experience, which risks turning them into abstract forms under the disembodying, depoliticising, deterritorialising optics of cognitivist and computationalist theory. Further on, we will reverse our consideration and use our understandings of rhythm to derive some insight into what may be meant by *body*, *movement* and *matter*. The approach to rhythm that we describe also avoids commitment to a particular notion of the anthropic subject, whether phenomenological, psychological or cognitive. In this sense, it shares with pragmatists and process philosophy and some aspects of contemporary materialism the proposition of *experience without a subject*. One of our method's most distinctive features pursuing these philosophical questions is not only empirical but *experimental*. To experiment means to reproducibly and precisely vary the *conditions* of experience, which is quite different from reproducing an event or experience as a rehearsed performance for an audience.

Over fifteen years, the first author's Topological Media Lab (TML) constructed experimental, gestural media and performative techniques for exploring philosophical questions. By experiment we mean reproducibly conditioning, but *not* determining or representing, experience according to some proposition. This is not about testing disconfirmable hypotheses. In our work, we condition affective, logical, causal, symbolic aspects of experience in a live event. With over 140 computational media artists and programmers, musicians, dancers, choreographers, philosophers, architects, computer scientists, applied physicists, literary scholars, puppeteers, anthropologists and designers, the TML and now the Synthesis Center (at Arizona State University) systematically created experimentally conditioned experiences ranging from structured improvisatory movement studies, vegetal motion and dance, acoustic ecologies and experiential climate simulations. The second author has conducted more recent experiments with faculty, students and researchers in Synthesis, which we describe in the following.

In the sections that follow, we describe some initial experiments which approach rhythm in the ordinary sense of beat-based duration patterns because they helped us to understand what we *do not mean* by rhythm. We follow those examples with others that illustrate aspects of rhythm as textural, sensed with the body, generating subjective experience through ensemble activity.

Discretised Rhythm: Tapping, Clapping, Beats

In preliminary rhythm studies, among a group of researchers, we asked participants, including ourselves, to play in ad hoc ensemble activity according to various conditions. Inspired by biofeedback research-creation work with Teoma Naccarato and John MacCallum (2016), we began with two variant activities characterised as entrainment exercises.[2] Entrainment is usually understood as a synchronisation of gesture to a periodic beat. While one may entrain to a metronome, a drummer or someone's gait, our initial hunch led us to vary the perceived source of the beat in entrainment. Our first pass replaced Naccarato and MacCallum's modulation of heart rate with a simple tapping mechanism. A system with a contact mic was tuned to register the taps as beats. Participants tapped out different regular time intervals to 'discover' an implicit beat. The difference between the participants' tap interval and the implicit beat varied the colour of the room's ambient light (blue if they were tapping too slowly, red if too fast, white if in sync). Single participants found success quickly by beginning at an extreme tempo and slowly changing the tempo and monitoring fluctuation in the lights' colour. We had much less success when attempting the same task in a group of three or more. As a group, we found we were more concerned with delivering correct inputs to the system (through turn-taking or other systematic approaches) than we were with the activity at hand. The colour of the lights did not convey anything about the target speed of beats itself; the participant had to interpret the schema we imposed upon it ahead of time.

What this experience suggested was that we would not uncover anything new about the felt experience of tapping a pulse by registering time intervals alone. There was also the issue of the implicit tempo, which was generated by the computer pseudorandomly each time we began. This exercise gave us the sense that we needed to tune in to a rhythm which was already out there, unheard, somewhere. To recall a quote attributed to Johann Sebastian Bach, 'all you have to do is touch the right key at the right time' (Marshall 1999). But there was no given rhythm; there was only an integer stored in the computer's memory. We might be inclined to say that the colour of the light guided the participant towards an arbitrary rhythmic interval. But the interval, as measured by the contact mic, suggests the atomic or modular conception of rhythm towards which Bach hinted. The time interval has nothing to do with our felt experience of pulse, and even less to do with rhythm as we have construed it above.

As a variation of this experiment, we retooled the software so the average of the previous ten intervals was compared to the most recent. The same colour mapping reflected the difference between the average and the most recent. Our inclination was to find a better way to make a uniform and consistent pulse as a group. We thought to leverage the relative uniformity of our gaits, so we walked in a circle while the contact mics sensed our footsteps from the floor. We expected a tempo to emerge, as sometimes happens in an audience's applause (Neda 2004). Our results were rather revealing, however. Different people would beat with different parts of their step, or a single step would be registered by the system twice, or three peoples' step would be registered as three separate onsets. But, rather than a defect of method, not identifying rhythm with specific 'fleshy' bodies exposed us to a consideration of the rhythm of the entire ensemble, indeed of the entire event. We asked: how can we address the rhythmicity of a single step? When and where and how do we make the cut and say 'step'?

The Rhythm Kit: Gradus ad Rhythmus

Julian Stein at the Synthesis Center wrote software called the Rhythm Kit to capture mathematical rhythm for the Synthesis Center's work on rhythm. The Rhythm Kit records and plays back time onsets or intervals paired with measured values like brightness or activity in a scene – the *observables* of an event. These intervals and associate observable values could be played back, re-scaled and mapped to parameters of media synthesis (such as the centroid frequency of a filter). Most importantly, the kit also enables artist-researchers to *contrapuntally* restructure and recompose the time patterns of the responsive media system. In other words, *time intervals* become the compositional elements, which can even transform *in accordance to*

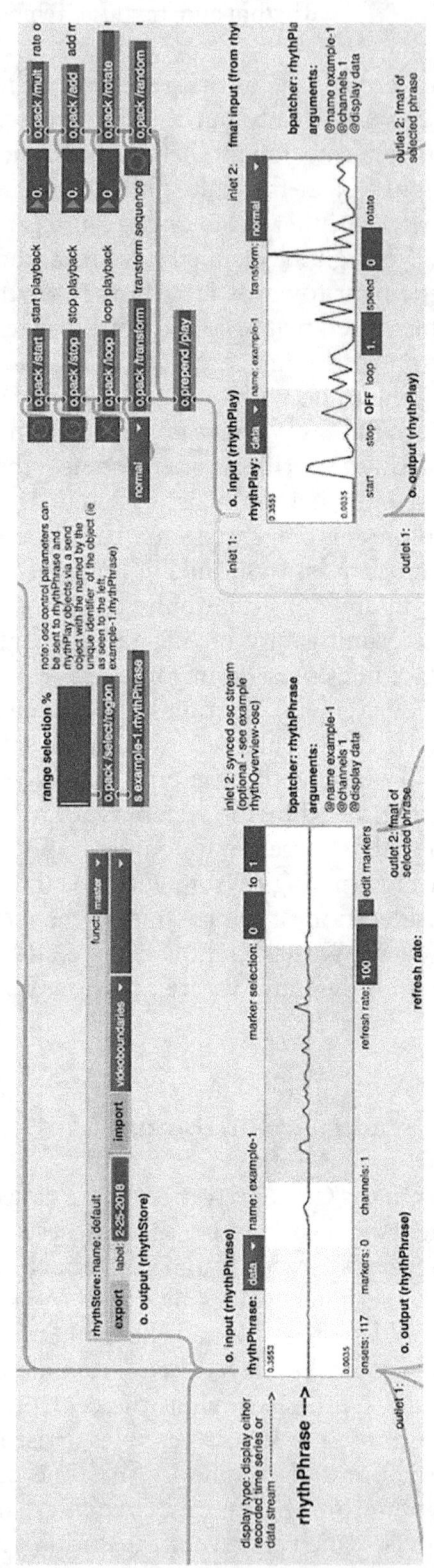

Figure 3.1 Rhythm kit by Julian Stein. © Synthesis Center, Arizona State University.

contingent activity as well as prior design. Some transforms resemble the techniques of Baroque musical counterpoint (retrograde, inversion, retrograde/inversion, stretching or shrinking), while others are more abstract (sort time intervals from longest to shortest, reverse or scramble the sequence of intervals). Abstraction at the level of interval and intensity lends itself to the transduction of rhythm across different media (light to haptic, sound to robotic, etc.), to borrow from Simondon's notion of dynamical material-informational process. We will turn to this more fully at the end of this essay.

One of the most interesting aspects of Stein's rhythm kit is that it focuses attention not on the measurement of modality and units – e.g. pressure, velocity, colour – but on the times of onsets and durations between onsets of sense or data. This focus on onsets of events and their durations surfaces the intermodal aspect of rhythm which is primordial to sensor modality.

Textural Rhythm

But let us examine more closely the formal assumption behind understanding rhythm as that which is denominated by a series of events (e.g. beats), indeed a series of 'the same'. Between one downstroke of a conductor's baton and the next, between one clap of the hands and the next, does any rhythm happen? How can we say where one step ends and another begins? When and how do we differentiate any repetitive, two-part movements – especially when a skilled violinist may tell you the key to maintaining a smooth sound during a bow change is to realise that the upbow has already begun before anticipating the downbow? In signal engineering, the *how* may be called segmentation, the *when* calibration. Segmentation reminds us of Gilles Deleuze and Félix Guattari's figure of striation (1987: 363–4):

> ... we are told that rhythm has nothing to do with the movement of waves but rather that it designates 'form' in general, and more specifically the form of a 'measured, cadenced' movement. However, rhythm is never the same as measure. . . . There is indeed such a thing as measured, cadenced rhythm, relating to the coursing of a river between its banks or to the form of a striated space; but there is also a rhythm without measure, which relates to the upswell of a flow, in other words, to the manner in which a fluid occupies a smooth space.

From this we can assert the caveat to avoid conflating measure for rhythm, but also that movement is constitutive of rhythm but not measure, metric or other modes of striation.[3] Indeed, as Pascal

Michon has put it in his most extensive archaeology of the notion of rhythm:

> The Greek word rhuthmós simply signified something like a 'form that is not permanent' or better yet, a 'way of flowing' . . . [P]arts of this tradition provide us with tools that are much more convenient to deal with dynamic phenomena as art or ethics or politics, than the very narrow concept of rhythm that is today commonly taken for granted. (Michon 2017)

Does it make sense to think the rhythm of a single event, or would that be what Wittgenstein would consider an 'ungrammatically' formed question that introduces unnecessary philosophical conundrums? Can what marks an event be discerned before the event? And who is to say? In *Difference and Repetition*, Deleuze writes, 'Repetition is a necessary and justified conduct only in relation to that which cannot be replaced. Repetition as a conduct and a point of view concerns non-exchangeable and non-substitutable singularities' (1994: 1). But what is nature of the singular event? Taking the figure of a stroke of lightning, Deleuze writes: 'Lightning, for example, distinguishes itself from the black sky but must also trail it behind, as though it were distinguishing itself from that which does not distinguish itself from it' (1991: 28). In this essay we will embed denominations of rhythm marked by discrete, atomic, 'repeated' events inside a more general, and *non-pre-dimensionalised*, substrate in which objects and event take form. The more nuanced and precise account uses notions from point-set topology (Sha 2012, 2013). We adopt Sha's term *texture* to refer to an approach to phenomena via dynamic, material *fields* and *substrates* (vs. atomic objects and subjects) in parallel with but not reduced to some recent physics theories that derive time (and spacetime) as *effects* of, rather than pre-given backgrounds to, the dynamics of quantum fields.

Although it is not necessary to our exposition, we note that some contemporary physicists have recently begun to consider loop quantum gravity models in which spacetime are also effects of the field dynamics. As Carlo Rovelli puts it: 'No more fields on spacetime: just fields on fields' (See Rovelli 2004: 71). For our purposes this release from spacetime as a 'dependent variables' or as 'background' to the physics and the attempt to think of time as an operator is the analogue of thinking of time and rhythm as effects of action and event.

However, quantum loop gravity does not account for our felt experience of the difference between past and future and the sense of flow. Referring to Husserl, Rovelli describes the constituting of temporal beings as those chunks of the world that selectively identify and retain memories of configurations of events ('order') which provides those chunks sense(s) of the ekstatic structure of time consciousness: retentive intuition is understood as the sense of construed order in encountered experience, and the flow is the movement of thought relating that to protentive intuition, anticipating and conditioning fresh action and experience.

One can recognise resonances with Edmund Husserl's *Phenomenology of Time Consciousness* (1964) and Martin Heidegger's treatment of the ekstatic structure of temporality in *Metaphysical Foundations of Logic* (1984: 197–209). But a *textural*, or field-like, approach to temporality does not require an *a priori* individual human subjectivity. In William James' 1912 essay 'Does "Consciousness" Exist?' he writes: 'There is no general stuff of which experience at large is made. There are as many stuffs as there are "natures" in the things experienced. If you ask what any one bit of pure experience is made of, the answer is always the same: "It is made of that, of just what appears, of space, of intensity, of flatness, brownness, heaviness, or what not."' In James' radical empiricism, experience lies prior to subjects – bits of experience that can be contingently regarded as the knowers, and objects – bits of experience regarded as the known.

Rhythm and the Felt Experience

Treating rhythm as intervals and intensities unchains us from reducing our temporal sense merely to sense and sensor data, but risks dematerialising rhythm to an untenably ideal 'form'. Therefore, we avoid as much as possible the notion that the intervals and intensities registered by the rhythm kit cohere to any notion of 'rhythm' as abstract or transcendental (as if the set of all possible rhythms could be identified by only their interval and intensity – as if music were reducible to MIDI notes or notated scores). As Simondon pointed out in his discussion of the difference between mechanical memory and human memory, a magnetic tape registers the hiss of noise and a human voice with equal ease, *indifferently*. This same indifference distinguishes electromechanical sensors from human sensing, and mechanical metronomes from musical performance (experiments with mechanically generated sound notwithstanding.)

Instead, we attend to what Eugene Gendlin would call the *felt experience* of rhythm (Gendlin 1997a and 1997b). But how can we work with experience without an *a priori* notion of subject or object, and without pre-given units of measure or structure of narrative with which to denominate experience? In this essay since we are concerned with temporal phenomena, we employ a *processualist* approach that accounts for sense-making, or better, the *emergence* of sense. After considering some experiments in rhythmic aspects of the lived experience of structured ensemble improvisation conditioned by responsive media, we will consider a notion of sense-making as the highlighting of subgroups of transformations on the dynamic space of configurations of movement, gesture, attitude, intensity, energy, affect.

Coming Togetherness: Ensembles and Entrainment

Thinking of how subjects may be *constructed* in rhythmic experience, we refocused our sights on activities in which the boundaries between subjects appeared to us less crisply defined. Given the insuperable methodological difficulties raised by the conventionality of the distinction between 'signal' and 'noise', 'event' (or 'onset' to use the vocabulary of computer music) and background, our experiments departed from the construction of rhythm as time interval from the beat-detection experiments and rhythm kit. In place of measuring intervals between discrete events, we considered instead how to construct experiments in which both rhythm and subject resist discretisation, and appear instead salient mostly as continuities.

Bearing these considerations in mind, we took up the concept of entrainment, here understood as the emergent temporal structuring of togetherness, and as a critical hinge between a sense of rhythm and a non-Cartesian subject. Perhaps the most widely familiarised notion of entrainment comes from the study of music. A person or animal is said to be able to entrain if it can move in ensemble with a musical pulse (e.g. tapping your foot, dancing to a beat, playing an instrument). We recognise here the discrete notions of rhythm discussed before, but is entrainment possible without a beat? Indeed, many fields and disciplines use notions of entrainment in different contexts and different scales to describe different kinds of relationalities. In the physics of mechanical systems, entrainment describes how two harmonic oscillators come to share the same period with one another, as noted by scientist and mathematician Christiaan Huygens. Entrainment also refers to speakers' tendency to cohere around emergent spoken intonations and timings, or adopt an interlocutor's speech patterns. Biological entrainment describes the synchronised relationship between an organism's internal biological rhythms and external, environmental patterns.

These myriad understandings of entrainment suggest it describes more than just the temporal structure of synchronisation, but rather the general rhythm of coming together. In his 'Semblance Taxonomy of Entrainments', Adrian Freed (2014) unpacks this notion of a general entrainment with examples of togetherness gathered both from lived experience and from literary figures. These examples furnish us with our conceptions of rhythm which extend beyond time-keeping and into the processual, relational world. We add and expand on some of these terms based on own experiments.

Syntonic	Together in frequency	metric music
Synchronic	together in phase	marching
Simultaneous	together in time	positron/electron pairs
Syntropic	together in direction	Greek dance
Syntenic	along same path	line dance
Isotropic	together in orientation	
Symplectic	plaited together	morris dancing
Syngamic	fused together	
Syndetic	bound together	three legged dance
Contort	twist together	
Symbiotic	living together	
Converted	turn together	
Commence	state together	
Continual	join together	
Contrite	rub together	
Coarticulate	move joints together	
Coterminous	same boundaries	
Coextensive	same region	
Contemporaneous	within same time interval	
Consequent	following	

Figure 3.2 Adrian Freed's semblance typology of entrainments (2014) based on etymologies.

Correlation of Orientation (Togetherness)

Inspired by Freed's taxonomy, we set out to investigate what is meant by togetherness and connectedness in the domain of human movement. We created a proxy for connectedness (Krzyzaniak et al. 2015) between two or more people by implementing a correlation algorithm which would compare the orientations of sensors placed on various places on their bodies.[4] Most importantly, the proposition is that togetherness does not have to mean being physically in the same region of space at the same time. Nor does togetherness have to mean that bodies are moving in parallel. Indeed one can imagine a group of children and adults in a living room peaceably doing their own thing: one can be cooking vegetables for dinner, another setting the table, a third could be playing with a sibling. Nothing in their poses or the trajectories of parts of their bodies need be isomorphic – 'parallel' – and yet they and most observers may affirm that they are 'correlated' in some way. In another situation they may feel uncorrelated. Consider when someone claps a hand sharply: people turn to face the source of that sound. We propose considering togetherness measured by correlation not of position or pose or even trajectory, but of orientation as a corporeal indicator of attention, or intention.

This correlation selects for similarities in a small time-window, and is much more robust than a simple differential comparison based on locus or spatial extent. Our analysis is invariant to certain relational aspects: delay/lag, differences in amplitude, noise, and frequency. We used the result of this analysis as a real-time *relational* signal to drive expressive sonic and lighting media feedbacks. In a session with dancers and live musicians, we played with obviously

hypercomplex signal correlation

a(t) and b(t) are quaternion-valued time series

$$a \circ b = \sum_{t=0}^{N-1} a(\tau + t)\overline{b(t)}$$

where $\circ$ indicates correlation, and τ is the time-lag between signals a and b

Figure 3.3 Correlation of streams of quaternion-valued orientation normals to points on bodies. © Synthesis Center, Arizona State University.

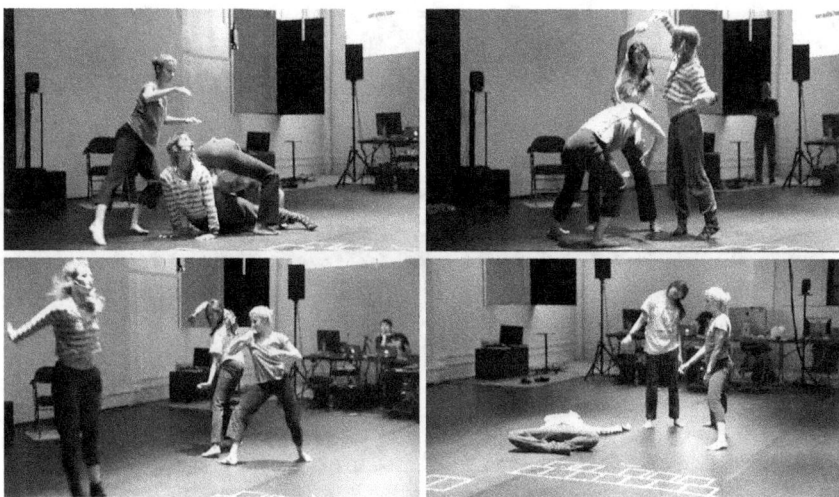

Figure 3.4 Correlation of orientations, as sensed by body-borne sensors. Three dancers are asked to improvise under general constraints: as an ensemble act like a clock, and fill the negative space between their bodies. © Synthesis Center, Arizona State University.

correlated examples first and progressed towards some experiments which interrogated less apparent connections.

Finally, the dancers improvised together, and *togetherness* became the central expressive aspect which was sustained, diminished, or weakened. In a sense, this interplay of coming together and falling apart led to constructed phraseologies – without having to declare in advance a vocabulary of movements. Correlation of orientation of parts of bodies gives us a more adequate measure of togetherness than measures of individual bodies' pose, trajectory or speed because this measures how a group of people's corporeally indexed *collective* attention comes together. Such measures give us a more continuous notion of togetherness that aligns more clearly with our lived experience.

Balloons, Lanterns and Rhythmic Ensembles

The correlation algorithm practically limited us to looking at relations between two data streams, so we had to come up with other scenarios and systems to explore collective rhythm in groups of three or more people, or rhythmic entities. Why three? Dyadic relations tend to be overly determined by conventions (caller/responder, observer/observed, leader/follower), so that it becomes much harder to study the emergence of novel temporal pattern which is important for experiment.

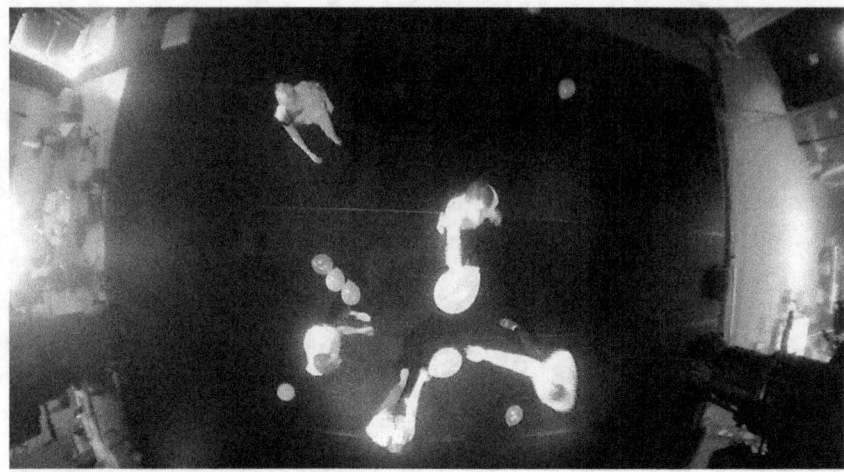

Figure 3.5 Balloon game: five people bat and volley balloons among themselves. © Synthesis Center, Arizona State University.

One scenario consisted in groups of four or five people trying to keep slightly-heavier-than-air balloons aloft by batting the balloons among themselves. We observed how our group experience changed as we varied the conditions, for example by scaling the number of balloons relative to the number of players. We tired quickly of some configurations, but found ourselves most engaged when the number of balloons was one more *or* one less than the number of players – just enough mismatch to challenge attention without too much complexity. Under those conditions we noticed a shift from 'parallel play' to an ensemble of shifting roles and interwoven attention. Too fast-paced for explicit signalling via spoken language, the scenario demanded participants enlarge attention to a 'peripheral attunement' to total activity.

Our enactment differs from the accounts of what Edwin Hutchins calls distributed cognition (1995: 175–228), evoking distributed computational architectures as a model for dynamics of a social system. Whereas Hutchins' example is the sailing crew, our group had no fixed roles. As computational models require us coding interactions in advance, it would fail to do justice to the group's emergent, relationally constructed coordination. Moreover, participants played without talking, indicating a pre-linguistic dynamic exceeding that of an operating system managing 'parallel' chains of pre-scripted steps.[5]

The balloon experiments also led us away from our initial strategy of interpreting rhythm directly as discretised time intervals. In the correlation experiments rhythm was relational between two gesturing bodies measured by the mathematical correlation of the time series data streams from pairs of body-borne sensors. The balloon play experiment naturally extends beyond dyadic, relation to NxM-dimensional patterns with groups of N people and M balloons. Correlation measures emphasise the temporal aspect of rhythm. Rhythm has no locus. More precisely, rhythm is not characterised by referring to a point in physical space.

Another example of ensemble rhythmic activity is theatre director Peter Brook's stick passing exercise: people stand in a ring facing each other. Each person has a stick about the height of a person in their right hand. They pass the stick to their right and take their left-hand neighbor's stick. After they are comfortable with this task, they each take one step back and repeat the exercise, now spaced farther apart from one another. They try to do this as fast and as smoothly as possible. Repeated over weeks and months, ensembles of people incorporate a skilled practice that can speed up greatly as they learn to rhythmically couple as an ensemble.

A third example of ensemble activity is the Filipino children's game Tinikling, which involves jumping in between sticks. As one video shows, children bob and sway in time to the music before they step in between the bamboo poles.[6] More than simple anticipation of movement, they are entraining to a temporal pattern; this example

Figure 3.6 Lanterns suspended from ceiling. Sound and lamp intensity vary according to the lanterns' movement. © Synthesis Center, Arizona State University.

will furnish more productive insights in more detail below. In light of these experiments and examples, we decided to create an experimental apparatus where we could compose and reproducibly vary the behaviour of the media according to improvised activity.

Lanterns is a physical-digital responsive media system consisting of several clusters of light bulbs suspended by cloth-covered electrical cable from a theatrical grid (Johnson et al. 2015). Like the balloons, they are ballistic objects. We built the lantern clusters for full-bodied, full-contact interaction. We used extremely rugged LED light bulbs so they could be freely swung, vigorously swirled, even hurled against a wall.

Having learned that trying to synthesise rhythm as discrete patterns (via 'ticks' or events) tends to lead to chaos as the number of participants and props increase, we designed the system to continuously render the movement of swinging lanterns in sound or light to amplify or accompany motion so people could introduce rhythms into the system. In other words, the angle or speed of the lanterns was mapped directly to sonic texture, not analysed and reduced to an abstract token like '60 beats per second'.

Before we say more about that, we can give a brief overview of the construction of the media system. Sensors mounted on the lanterns' cords stream real-time data that indicate the position of the lantern in space as a function of the angle of the cord.

From the position, we compute real-time measures of speed, acceleration, velocity and proximity to drive responsive sound and lighting behaviours which reflect either 1) the movement of each individual lantern, or (2) their movement as a group.

First, each lantern makes sounds tuned to a distinct set of frequencies which distinguishes them from others. Acceleration pulses each lanterns' lights as its speed changes (the cable of each light bulb goes into its own DMX-controlled dimmer box, so we can dynamically control the intensity of each light bulb). A second layer of logic is based on features computed as a function of relations among bodies rather than individual bodies' properties. From the set of the lanterns' position, we calculate distances between each cluster of lightbulbs and sum them to create a general measure of proximity. This analysis is mapped to the frequency and amplitude of low pulsing tones. Amplified by subwoofers, these bass tones are inaudible when the lanterns are hanging at a standstill and crescendo in volume and activity as they come together, descending from audible bass range (~100hz) to a frequency which is both heard and felt with the body (~30hz). The intensity of this pulsing bass feedback also directly flickers the lights. This collective, relational and non-solipsistic measure resonates with suspending commitment to pre-given subjects and objects. More subtly, this constitutes a step towards abductively constructing measures that are more sensitive to contingent phenomena that are a function of textural dynamics.[7]

A large part of this system's behaviour is shaped by the kinematics of its material construction. The responsive media mappings amplify and transpose its physical movements into other registers which are sensible in different ways, and by highlighting some of the observable dynamics (speed and changes in speed, closeness, place) impart a sense of performativity to our interactions with the physical system.

As with the balloons, our research with this system started with ad hoc play. Without pre-stating the modes of interaction, the dynamics of interaction emerged in lab sessions. The interaction dynamics between players and the system resembled games but produced no winners and losers and had no finite goal, no puzzles to solve and no points to accumulate. More predictable than balloons, the lanterns afforded a broader diversity of interactions. The deterministic relation between lanterns' movement and the variation of sound and light constituted precisely reproducible conditioning of the event accompanying *any* activity that the players were moved to invent. Moreover, the relation was intricately crafted to yield sonically, visually and kinesthetically rich augmentation.

In the table shown here (Figure 3.7), the items in the leftmost column describe a certain variety of the lanterns' movement. We permuted these varieties in obvious ways (e.g. two, three or six lanterns

	DESCRIPTION	TACTICS
Swinging	Lanterns swing like a pendulum	Run alongside swinging bulbs; catch and release (using sight, using hearing); grouping people with specific lanterns.
Circling	Lanterns swing like a circular pendulum, in or out of phase; moving in the same or opposite direction	Sit in the center; lie underneath.
Twisting	Lanterns wrap around each other	Constraint about number of lanterns which may be touched.
Gathering	Bring all the lanterns together	Gather and release (seated); twisting or wrapping them to hold them together.

Figure 3.7 Semblance typology for interaction with lanterns.

should swing in phase together, out of phase, in the same direction, etc.). The rightmost column lists tactics which emerged to shepherd the lanterns towards these movements. What we find most salient about these tactics is that they constitute a refiguration of the relation between the human movers with respect to the lanterns. In summary, there are not two but three coupled dynamical systems: the pendulums that are most closely modelled by the ballistic physics of harmonic oscillators; the algorithmically driven lamps and sounds as coded in Max/MSP/Jitter in response to both lantern and human movement; and the ensemble of humans playing.

Now, regarding how children play Tinikling, or how musicians improvising in ensemble together sway and 'get into' rhythm before jumping into joint activity, we see that rhythm conjures a 'subject', and ensemble activity foregrounds the thick interleaving of shared rhythmic experience. What is then this subject that is conjured? Given the examples of ensemble experience, we are already well adjusted to discussing experience without a subject, and with this clean slate may begin to consider other conceptions of subjective organisation. We recall, for instance, Deleuze and Guattari's notion of the 'machinic assemblage of bodies, of actions and passions, an intermingling of bodies reacting to one another' which function at the same time as 'a collective assemblage of enunciation, of acts and statements, of incorporeal transformations attributed to bodies' (Deleuze and Guattari 1987: 88).

Guattari, who has divested from the human subject inherited from Descartes and psychoanalysis, has given us much more to consider with regard to subjectivity; let us consider the lucid and poetic accounts of subjectivity furnished in his two major late works, 'The Three Ecologies' and *Chaosmosis* (1989 and 1994). In 'The Three Ecologies', he dispenses with the term 'subject' entirely, formulating subjectivity as three interpenetrating registers considered processually and interdependently (ecologically): the mental, the social and the environmental. Guattari's dismissal of the subject allows for the flux of *experience (without a subject)* to produce emergent subjectivities. In *Chaosmosis,* he refers to a study by Daniel Stern which characterised as trans-subjective the experience of infants, 'which do not dissociate the feeling of the self from the feeling of the other' (Guattari 1995: 8). Subjectivity is refigured as a processual emergence through 'components of subjectification'. He distinguishes the individual from subjectivity, which he characterises as 'a "terminal" for processes involving human groups, socioeconomic ensembles, data-processing machines: a terminal through which, of course, not all the vectors of subjectification necessarily pass'. We keep in mind the danger of mistaking what we can discern for an adequate understanding of experience. Thus this investigation simultaneously draws from 'scientific' as well as ethico-aesthetic problematics. Instead of referring to groups of individuals, or networks of actors, or systems of hierarchies, we can regard these ensembles as heterogeneous assemblages of matter-energy-affect-symbol, which, in movement and sensation, construct our concept of rhythm as a viscous and animated texture.

Textural Subject

In Gyorgy Ligeti's *Poeme Symphonique* (1962), 100 mechanical metronomes are wound up to exhaust themselves at approximately the same time.[8] It is essential that these metronomes be mechanical to allow for energetic physics and contingency. Very gradually, as the machines wind down, and as your hearing attention wanders, relaxes and refocuses, waves of rhythms emerge from an ocean of what initially sounds like noise. Most interestingly, the resultant sense of rhythmic pattern as heard by each human listener *is conditioned by but different from* the mechanical oscillations of the individual metronomes. Moreover, we can surmise that every single human listener hears different rhythms, according to differences in physiology and expectation as well as physics. In other words, rhythm is not perceived but apperceived. Given this, we suggest that the 'rhythm's subject' – that which hears a given rhythm – does not pre-exist the moment of the 'performance', but *emerges in the course of the event as experienced*. In light of this, we propose to consider the *subject* not as a pre-given constituent of rhythm but rather as an effect of the rarefaction and condensation of textural fields in *assemblages*: territorialising and deterritorialising configurations of bodies, actions, passions, expressions that provisionally function together (Deleuze and Guattari 1987: 88). And we consider rhythm in turn as a mode of temporality – by which we mean the sense of passage, becoming, change, dynamic.

How shall we understand the co-articulation of subjects? Every differential operator – an operator in Simondon's ontogenetic sense[9] (Simondon 2009) – acting on the textural material field of matter plus energy plus affect – can be co-constructed together with particular subjects and objects of experience and apparatuses or instruments of articulation. The *subjects* may be called hearing subjects, and the *objects* may be called rhythms in this more general dynamical field constituting the structuration of experience. What rhythm especially picks out are the temporal aspects of these dynamics. We have reversed the arrow of consideration: whereas we began our essay by thinking of rhythm as the resultant of body + movement + inhomogeneous matter, and sense of rhythm as a resultant of subject's action in the world, we reverse this, starting with examples of rhythm in ensemble activity and deriving bodies and objects out of the dynamical inhomogeneities of assemblages.

Extending Husserl's motto 'to the things themselves' from phenomenology to our non-anthropocentric project would require conceiving experience without an *a priori* subject. To summarise, every differential operator produces vectorial (directed) fields out of the manifold of experience (Sha 2013: 104–5, 131). In his essays on radical empiricism, James conjectured vectorial relations of knowing that co-articulate parts of experience as the knowers and the knowns.

In more nuanced accounts of temporality – understood, as we stated above, as the *sense* of passage, becoming, change, dynamic – one consequence of a primordial temporal vectoriality is the triadic 'ekstatic' structure of temporality: the senses of past, present and future. In phenomenological terms, the subjective senses of past and future would be retentive and protentive intuition, but our account does not require *a priori* subjects (e.g. listening beings that cognise rhythm) or objects (e.g. mathematical rhythms as 'objective' patterns). Now, the sense of rhythm – not as an ideal form shaping formless substance but as a mode of temporality – constitutes an *asymmetric* relation between past and future. Think of the example of the children playing Tinikling swaying before jumping in between the rhythmically moved bamboo sticks. This local asymmetry co-articulates three regions of the universe relative to each compact occasion. Two regions are the retrospected and the anticipated, which are the experiential analogues to the causal past and future respectively, and the third region is the indeterminate portion of experience that has no material causal relation to the occasion.[10] Thus rhythm can be understood as the structure of non-anthropocentric retention and protention inside textural dynamics of the assemblages of bodies, actions, passions and utterances.

Acknowledgements

We thank our colleagues at Synthesis, the School of Arts, Media + Engineering, and Dance, at Arizona State University for generous conversations and expert support essential to our experiential experiments: Todd Ingalls, Julian Stein, Connor Rawls, Peter Weisman, Brandon Mechtley, and Megan Patzem. We thank also fellow travelers John MacCallum, Adrian Freed, Teoma Naccarato and Jessica Rajko.

Notes

1. In mathematics it is common to say 'degenerate' referring to the most reduced case, for example in the set of all functions mapping a real number to a real number y = f(x), the degenerate function could be the constant function f(x) = constant c for all x.
2. See <http://vimeo.com/synthesiscenter/heartbeat> (last accessed 28 December 2019), beat matching experiment by dancer Teoma Naccarato and composer/media-programmer John MacCallum, hosted at Synthesis ASU, 11–17 January 2015.
3. See Deleuze and Guattari's explication of the concept with respect to the music of twentieth-century Serialist composer Pierre Boulez (Deleuze and Guattari 1987: 477–8). Simondon's notion of information could help furnish a fuller elaboration of textural rhythm, but that would take us beyond the background of this essay. Deleuze and Guattari's figure of 'flow and manner in which a fluid occupies a smooth space' invokes dynamics on manifolds. Chapter 6 ('Topology, Manifolds, Dynamical Systems, Measure, and Bundles') in Sha 2013 provides fuller treatment of the relevant background notions.
4. See <https://vimeo.com/synthesiscenter/correlation> (last accessed 28 December 2019).
5. Lighting and rhythm experiments: <vimeo.com/synthesiscenter/lighting-rhythm> (last accessed 28 December 2019).
6. Tinikling rhythmic stick dance game: <https://youtu.be/JtVjo76X-ws?t=109> (last accessed 28 December 2019).
7. The mathematical field of measure theory generalises the notion of area to the widest class of sets, which need have no geometric structure whatsoever. See Tao 2011.
8. See performance staged 4 September 2011: vimeo.com/50606554, starting at 1:00.
9. Simondon borrows from and resonates with the mathematical notion of *operator* in for example functional analysis, where 'function' carries a distinct meaning from what 'function' may mean to theorists in philosophy or the humanities.
10. This last region must stand in ethico-aesthetic relation to the given occasion exactly because of causal indeterminacy: by definition there can be no relation of material causation between any occasion in this third region and the given occasion. Here we borrow from A. N. Whitehead's Process and Reality:

    > In respect to any one actual occasion M there are three distinct nexüs of occasions to be considered:
    >
    > (i) The nexus of M's contemporaries, defined by the characteristic that M and any one of its contemporaries happen in causal independence of each other.
    >
    > (ii) Durations including M's any such duration is defined by the characteristic that any two of its members are contemporaries. (It follows that any member of such a duration is contemporary with M, and thence that such durations are all included in the locus (i). The characteristic property of a duration is termed unison of becoming.)

References

Benveniste, É. (1971), 'The Notion of Rhythm in its Linguistic Expression,' in *Problems in General Linguistics*, trans. M. E. Meek. Coral Gables: University of Miami Press.

Chalmers, D. J. 1996. *The Conscious Mind: In Search of a Fundamental Theory*. Oxford: Oxford University Press.

Deleuze, G.. *Difference and Repetition*. 1995. European Thought: A Series in Social Thought and Culture Criticism, trans. P. Patton. New York: Columbia University Press.

Deleuze, G., and F. Guattari. 1987. *A Thousand Plateaus: Capitalism and Schizophrenia*, trans. B. Massumi. University of Minnesota Press.

Gendlin, E. T. 1997a. *Experiencing and the Creation of Meaning : A Philosophical and Psychological Approach to the Subjective*. Evanston: Northwestern University Press.

Gendlin, E. T. (1997b), 'How Philosophy Cannot Appeal to Experience, and How It Can (1997)', in D. M. Levin (ed.), *Language Beyond Postmodernism: Saying and Thinking in Gendlin's Philosophy*. Evanston: Northwestern University Press, pp. 3–41.

Guattari, F. 1989. 'The Three Ecologies', trans. C. Turner, *New Formations* 8: 131–47.

Guattari, F. 1995. *Chaosmosis: An Ethico-Aesthetic Paradigm*, trans. P. Bains and J. Pefanis. California: Power Publications.

Heidegger, M. 1984. *The Metaphysical Foundations of Logic*, trans. M. Heim. Bloomington: Indiana University Press.

Husserl, E. 1964. *The Phenomenology of Internal Time-Consciousness*. Bloomington: Indiana University Press.

Hutchins, E. 1995. *Cognition in the Wild*. Cambridge, MA: MIT Press.

James, W. 1996. *Essays in Radical Empiricism*. Lincoln: University of Nebraska Press.

Johnson, G. et al. 2018. 'Lanterns: An Enacted and Material Approach to Ensemble Group Activity with Responsive Media,' in *Proceedings of the 5th International Conference on Movement and Computing*, article no. 37. New York: ACM.

Krzyzaniak, M. et al. 2015. 'Towards Realtime Measurement of Connectedness in Human Movement', in *Proceedings of the 2nd International Conference on Movement and Computing*: 120–3. New York: ACM.

Merleau-Ponty, M. 2014. *Phenomenology of Perception*, trans. D. A. Landes. London: Routledge.

Michon, P. (2017), 'Preface, Rhuthmos', in *Elements of Rhythmology*, vol. 1, <http://rhuthmos.eu/spip.php?article1772> (last accessed 28 December 2019).

Naccarato, T., and J. MacCallum (2016), 'From Representation to relationality: Bodies, biosensors, and mediated environments,' *Journal of Dance and Somatic Practices* 8(1): 55–70.

Néda, Z. et al. 2000. 'Self-Organizing Processes: The Sound of Many Hands Clapping', *Nature* 403: 849–50.

Rovelli, C. 2004. *Quantum Gravity*. Cambridge: Cambridge University Press.
Sha, X. W. 2003. 'Resistance is Fertile: Gesture and Agency in the Field of Responsive Media', *Configurations* 10 (3): 439–72.
Sha, X. W. (2012), 'Topology and Morphogenesis', in Celia Lury (ed.), Special Issue on a Topological Approach to Cultural Dynamics, *Theory, Culture & Society*, 29: 4–5, pp. 220–46. Nottingham: TCS Centre.
Sha, X. W. 2013. *Poiesis and Enchantment in Topological Matter*. Cambridge, MA: MIT Press.
Simondon, G. 1989. *L'individuation psychique et collective*. Paris: Aubier.
Simondon, G. 2009. 'The Position of the Problem of Ontogenesis', tr. by Gregory Flanders, *Parrhesia* 7: 4–16.
Tao, T. 2011. *An Introduction to Measure Theory*. Graduate Studies in Mathematics. Providence, RI: American Mathematical Society.
Whitehead, A. N. 1985. *Process and Reality: Gifford Lectures 1927–28*. 2nd edn. New York: The Free Press.

II Sites and Practices

Chapter 4

Attunement of Value and Capital in the Algorithms of Social Media

Simon Yuill and Beverley Skeggs

This chapter seeks to link ideas about rhythm and time to issues of labour, social media and capital. In doing so, it draws insights from a large-scale research project under the title of Values & Value. Using custom software to gather intersecting perspectives of temporal activity across participants' use of Facebook and the wider internet, the Values & Value project explored how such platforms effect an attunement between different processes, from personal social interactions to speculative investments in advertising and the circulation of capital within financialisation.[1] We consider attunement as a process through which different spheres of activity are brought into momentary alignment. These spheres of activity unfold in distinct and sometimes conflicting rhythms that cannot be easily coordinated. The relation between time, technicity and capital as attunement is analysed through concepts drawn from Lefebvre's rhythmanalysis and Ingold's notion of the taskscape, seeking to make more explicit the ways in which algorithms intervene in and constitute processes of the capture of value and circulation of capital. We argue that platforms such as Facebook seek to encourage and maximise the most profitable moments of attunement by monitoring and intervening in these different spheres of activity through various algorithmic processes that constantly evaluate and task the user in a way that both consumes and closes down time.

Data Points

Imagine we could follow one point of data. The exact moment of its creation would be resolutely precise, yet, caught in a stream of other data, isolating it and determining its specific significance and value would be hard. It could be born in the midst of a finger swiping a touch screen, clicking a button, tapping in a comment or snapping a photo that is instantly uploaded. It could be more passive, as someone moves from one cell mast area to another or one wifi hotspot to another. It may be coincidental, as someone browses the web or checks a message feed. It may be covert, as a microphone is turned on and off for a few seconds capturing ambient audio. The moments within which such a point of data may be created are highly contingent and indeterminate, yet much of our current economic and political climate is shaped by investments in such data and in attributing specific significance and value to it (Zuboff 2019).

One isolated data point is intrinsically worthless. It is only in relation to other data that significance and value can be given as it moves through different aggregations and disaggregations in an ongoing process of coincidence and departure of data, life and value (Deleuze 1992; Skeggs and Yuill 2018). To do so, however, that point of data also needs some kind of anchor, some specific identifier that it can be linked back to as it moves through these different relations. That anchor is you or I, a person who provides an irreducible point of reference against which all the other contingent and probabilistic relations can be tied.

Let us imagine two people. Laura is a journalist and writer. She is well educated, well travelled and, as a consequence of her work, well connected to many people internationally. Linda, in contrast, is unemployed, living on disability welfare support. She travels, but not a lot. Her pool of personal connections is quite small, mostly friends and family. Both use social media and are on Facebook. For Laura, Facebook is primarily a tool for work. She is very active on the platform as it enables her to maintain contact with people she works with and to promote her work. Linda is more sporadic in her use, keeping in touch with friends and posting the occasional holiday pic. When Laura browses, she is presented with adverts for high-end brands; Linda sees ads for local supermarkets and budget travel. In some cases these adverts might come about as an almost indexical response. If someone visits a specific site, its advertising will follow them as a reminder to return and view or purchase some more. In other cases the link between a given advert and the source from which it was targeted may be more oblique. Laura might receive adverts for life insurance or private health care, Linda adverts for loan companies, even though neither has visited any such sites (Deville 2012; Mierzwinski and Chester 2013). These might be from one of a range of companies who share tracking data or may have bid on advertising space. These are defined in terms of criteria identifying factors such as desired audience income and demographic (Turow 2008; Turow 2017). Two such criteria are those distinguishing people who are more likely to generate a better return on advertising and people who are less likely, classified as 'worth' and 'waste' respectively (Turow 2012). Laura is 'worth'. Linda is 'waste'.

Laura and Linda are not entirely fictitious. They are based upon participants in Values & Value. A key aspect of this study was to record and analyse the temporal dimensions of such activity, relating rhythms of usage to those of tracking and advertising. This was informed by Anna Munster's (2013) critique of conventional approaches in Social Network Analysis that tend to flatten and thereby 'anaesthetise' our perception of how networks are created and change over time. It also drew upon Henri Lefebvre's rhythmanalysis, providing a form of enquiry that sought to negotiate rather than reduce the complexity of our subject area and to relate the logic of code to the liveness of daily experience:

> Rhythm reunites quantitative aspects and elements, which mark time and distinguish moments in it – and qualitative aspects and elements, which link them together, found the unities and results from them. Rhythm appears as regulated time, governed by rational laws, but in contact with what is least rational in human being: the lived, the carnal, the body (Lefebvre 2004: 8–9)

Facebook is a temporal medium that both intervenes in and structures different activities across time. It is through time that networks are made and unmade; it is through an appeal to timeliness that the News Feed seeks our attention and through which Facebook seeks to become a ubiquitous utility. Examining Facebook in terms of time and using rhythm as a mode of analysis allows us to understand Facebook in terms of different processes that interact and sometimes conflict with one another: those of the platform itself, the algorithms and machines on which it runs, the lives of the users who interact with it and the volatility of markets from which it extracts value through stock market shares and advertising revenue.

The Values & Value Project

In order to perform this study we developed a set of custom software tools. Many of the existing tools for analysing Facebook, such as NodeXL (Hansen et al. 2010) and Netvizz (Rieder 2013), treat the platform as a self-contained entity and focus on its own self-defined role as a social network facilitator. We wished to combine several different perspectives, ones that did not necessarily take Facebook's own claims as a social medium for granted and which captured the ways in which it stretched out across the internet beyond its own platform, thereby showing how activity elsewhere on the web might be drawn back into Facebook.

There were three key components within this: a Facebook plugin that gave access to participants' data as made available through the Facebook API (a service that enables other software to access a user's Facebook data); a browser extension that scraped additional data, such as advertising and evidence of tracking as participants browsed the web more generally; and a web server that collected and analysed this data.

These analyses were made available to the project team and each participant in the form of interactive visualisations on the website. The visualisations provided mappings of the different temporal perspectives that we defined as rhythms of *Use*, *Interaction*, *Attention* and *Tracking*. Rather than reducing the data to a single graph, these enabled us to read across the 'moving but determinate complexity' (Lefebvre 2004: 12) of the interacting activities of our study. Each of these was organised in two-week blocks of time, with a final set of diagrams for the overall period of three months. Participants had access to their own data visualisations through the project website, and were provided with printed databooks. These different quantitative forms of data were correlated against qualitative data gathered from online surveys and face-to-face interviews with the participants using the databooks to review what we had gathered.

Rhythms of Use (Figure 4.1) provided an overview of the basic temporal activity for each participant, such as the times of day in which they were most active on Facebook, percentage of posts responded to and the changing composition of users appearing in posts – these were not necessarily users within a participant's Friends network but rather those who showed up in the News Feed. Often these rhythms fitted within the standard work routine breaks of early morning, lunch and evening. Others were more constant, like Laura, whilst some were most active during work hours – in some cases as an antidote to the boredom of their jobs.

The *Rhythms of Interaction* (Figure 4.2) were gathered from a combination of all the initial data we were receiving and presented as a diagram of different users as they interacted with different posts within a participant's News Feed. This was composited against advertising within their Facebook page and the ambient data of tracking that we detected as a participant browsed outside of the site. By mapping these temporally we could show the flow and rhythm of interactions. The visual complexity of these mirrors that of the extensive parameters of Facebook's own data collection in which, as one Facebook engineer put it, 'nothing is off the table' (McGee 2013). These diagrams enabled us to get a sense of how posts were circulating amongst users and groups and how these potentially related to

Value and Capital in Social Media Algorithms 131

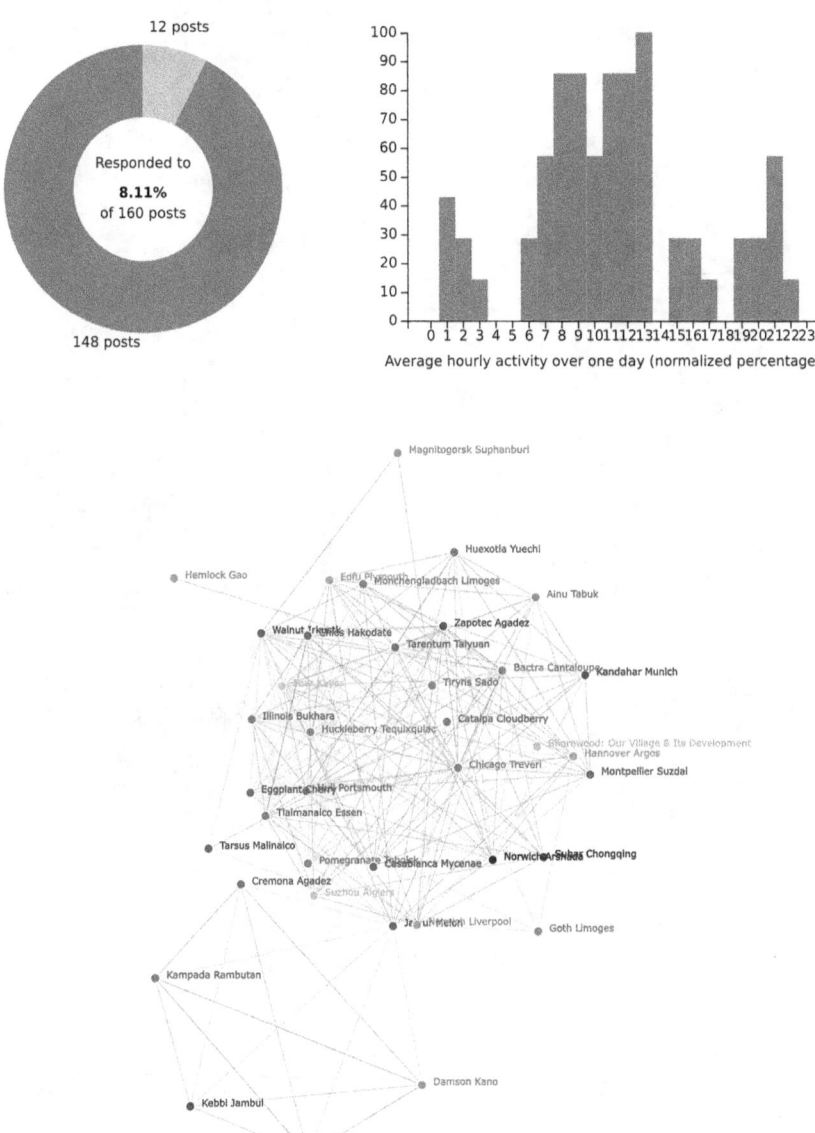

Figure 4.1 Example diagrams from *Rhythms of Use*. These show the percentage of posts responded to by a participant, the average proportions of time interacting with Facebook over a 24-hour period, and a network of respondents identified in posts from the News Feed.

advertising represented in terms of density and intensity varying over time. Different users had characteristic patterns, from very dense to very sparse, which could be correlated with the *Rhythms of Use* and *Rhythms of Tracking* diagrams, as is clear in the comparison of Laura and Linda (Figure 4.3).

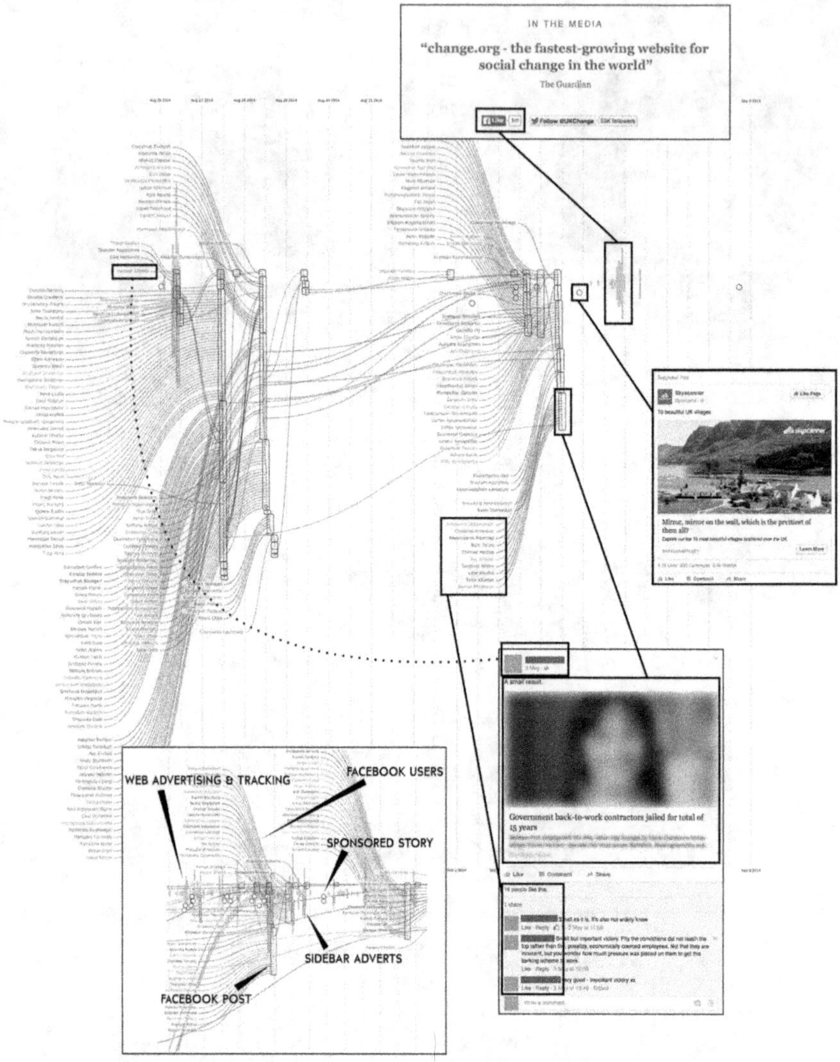

132 Simon Yuill and Beverley Skeggs

Figure 4.2 The *Rhythms of Interaction* showing the different types of data composited into the diagram.

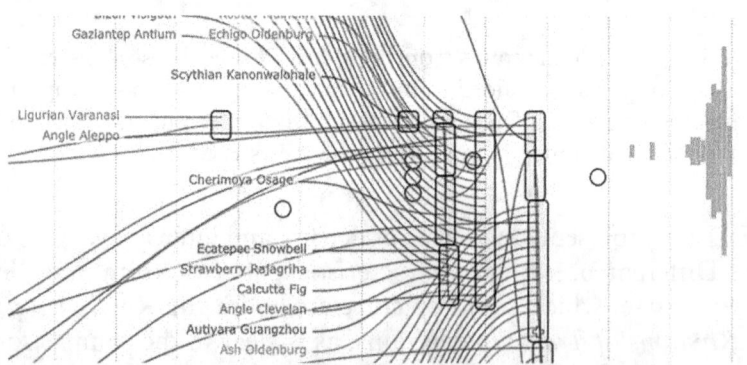

Figure 4.2b *Rhythms of Interaction* (detail).

Value and Capital in Social Media Algorithms 133

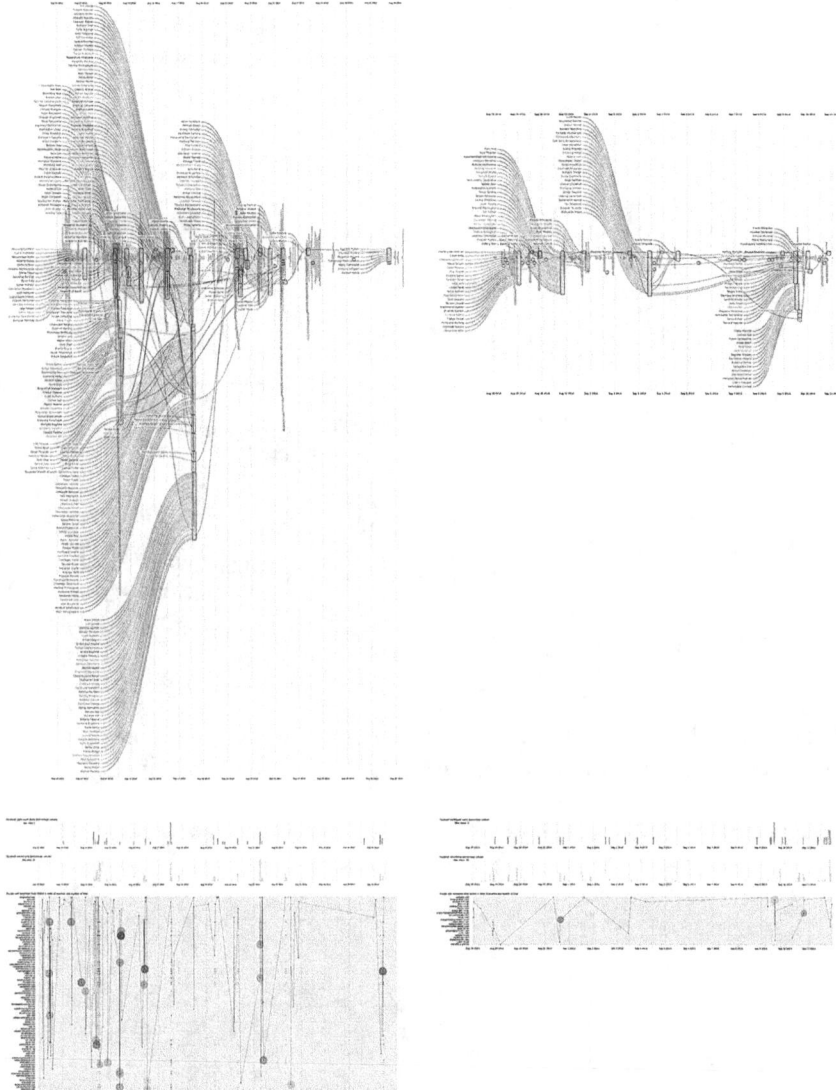

Figure 4.3 A comparison of two of the participants from the project showing *Interaction* (top) and *Tracking* (below). Those of the left might be typical of someone classified as 'worth', those on the right someone classified as 'waste'.

The next tool we built looked at the News Feed more closely in terms of *Rhythms of Attention* (Figure 4.4). This mapped how posts appeared in the ordering of the News Feed and aspects of how much attention they were potentially given by a participant. We looked at the relation between the efforts of the EdgeRank algorithm driving the News Feed to solicit attention, and the ways in which users themselves give, make and perform attention – these are not all the same thing (Pariser 2011: 36–8; Birkbak and Carlsen 2016). We could

134   Simon Yuill and Beverley Skeggs

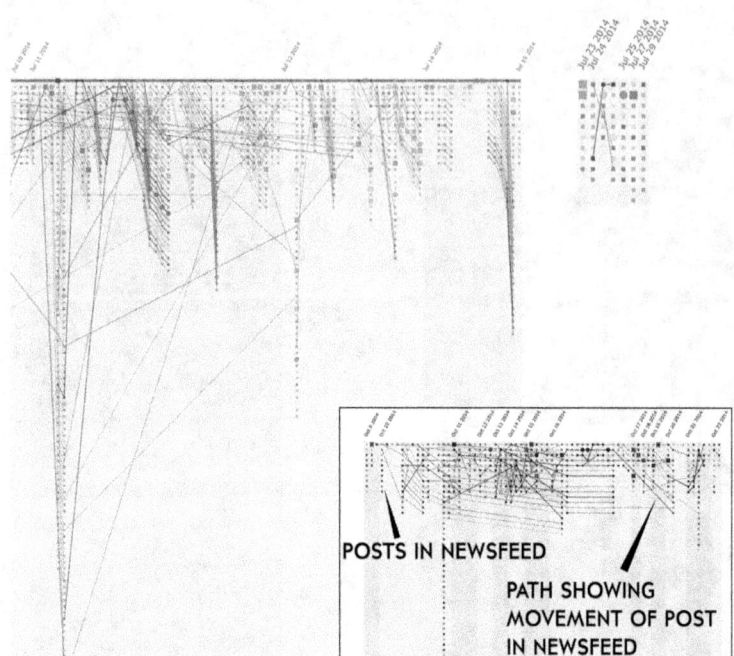

Figure 4.4 The *Rhythms of Attention* showing the ordering of posts in a News Feed and how these change over time for a given participant.

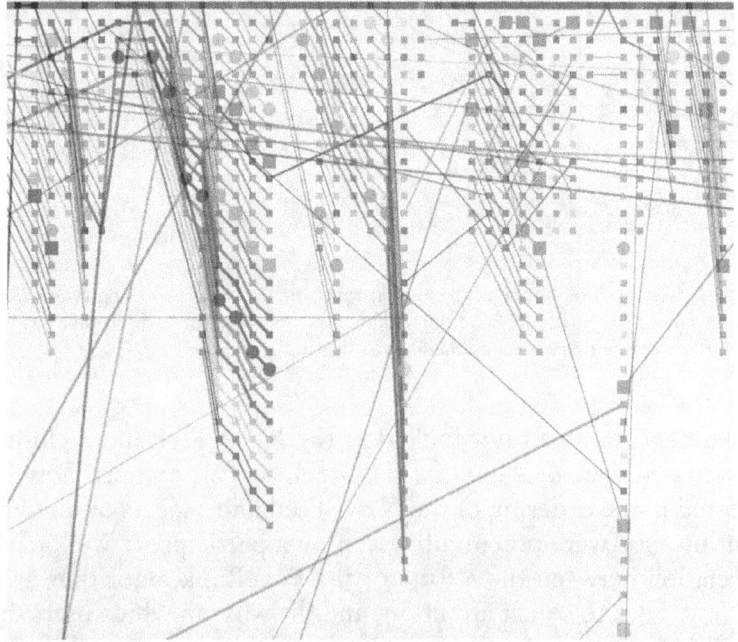

Figure 4.4b *Rhythms of Attention* (detail).

see contrasts between users in which there was a high turnover of new posts (typically the case with less engaged users) and those in which certain posts kept returning to the top of the feed over several days or even, for one participant, several weeks. As this data was taken from the display of the feed on a participant's own view of their Facebook page, we could also see differences in those who only checked out the current top items and those who repeatedly scrolled back down into older posts lower down the listing. In some users this showed a huge contrast between interaction and attention when compared with the *Interaction* diagrams. Some users who interacted very little were nevertheless spending much time looking and browsing, often going against the selection made for them by EdgeRank, echoing Geert Lovink's (2007) claim that people find their own strategies of using time that 'undercut capitalistic time logic' (170). We could also see some anomalies, such as blocks of posts that seemed to stick in formation, suggesting something far more unstable at play than the rhetoric of the News Feed as a constant 'nowness' (Bogost 2010: 28) might suggest. In this sense, rhythms of attention do not directly equate with notions of an attention economy (Bucher 2012b; Hassoun 2014) – which, as Lovink (2007: 169) argues, is based upon somewhat reductive assumptions about the user and what they are doing at any given time.

The fourth perspective, *Rhythms of Tracking* (Figure 4.5), sought to map the ways in which different advertisers tracked and profiled participants as potential consumers. During the development of the software we had discovered that a substantial amount of data was sometimes contained within the HTML code that placed adverts on the pages people looked at. Whilst some of this data was encrypted, we were nevertheless able to extract sufficient legible keywords from within it along with text from the ads themselves. These could provide an indication of what information concerning a user advertisers were interested in, and map how this changed over time. We extracted a list of the top 100 advertising keywords identified for each participant and asked them to comment on how accurate they felt this representation of them was. Whilst more active users tended to have evidence of more specific profiling, in some cases these could be wide of the mark. This is indicative of the process through which such profiling is conducted. Advertisers put out various 'signals' to see who responds to or triggers these. These signals are defined by the different audience targeting categories that you can buy into via Facebook adverts, or services such as Acxiom's Audience Operating System (Pariser 2011: 42–6; Mandese 2014; Turow 2017: 156–7). Such profiles therefore do not represent an objective portrayal of a given individual, but rather the degree to which they match advertisers' desires and expectations.

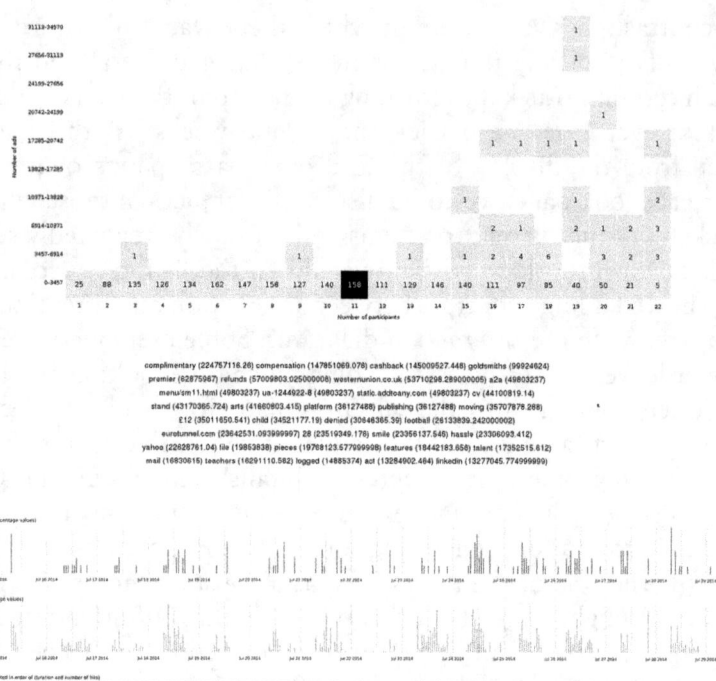

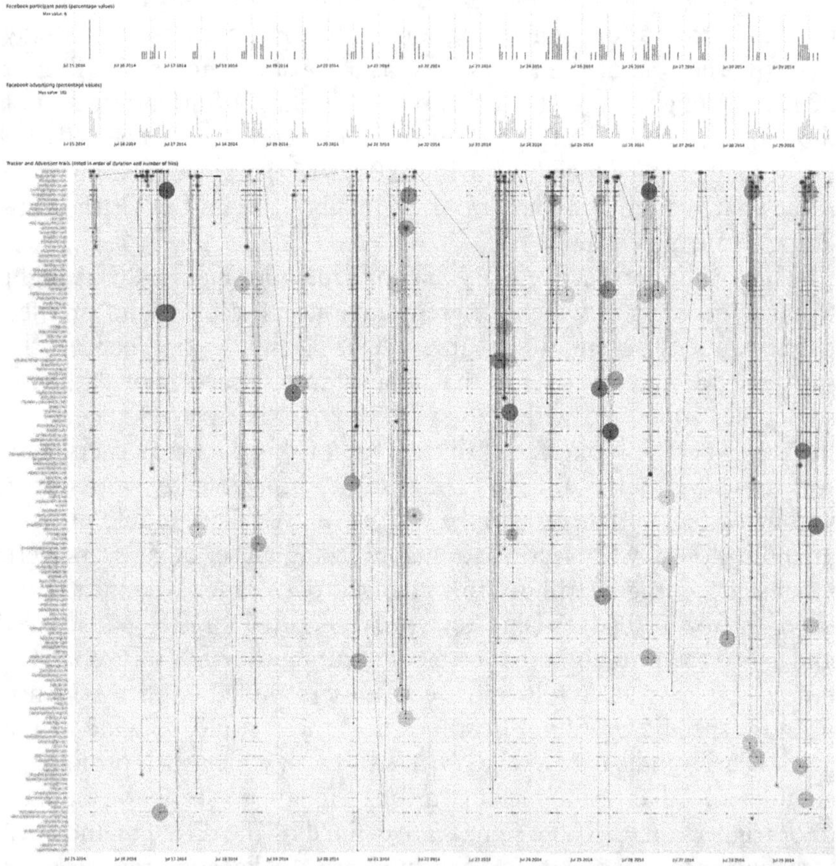

Figure 4.5 Two diagrams from the *Rhythms of Tracking*. The top diagram shows raw keywords extracted from adverts and online trackers; these are ordered in terms of frequency and how specific they were to a given user. The lower diagram shows evidence of Facebook tracking a participant as they browse other web sites. These are listed on the left side of the diagram, but have been blurred here to preserve anonymity.

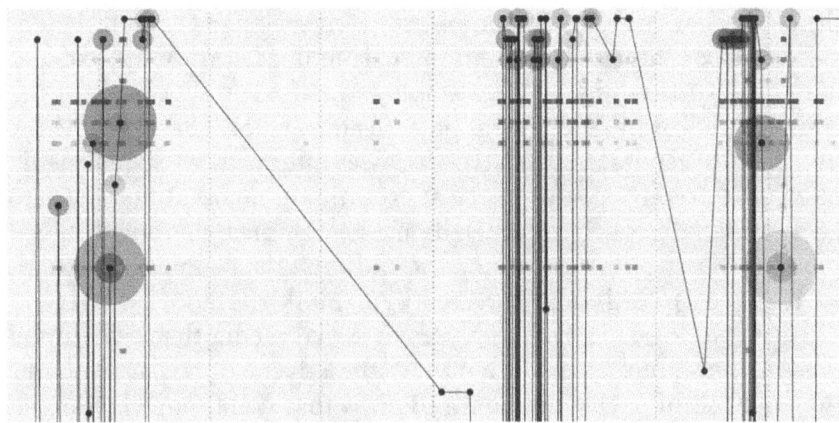

Figure 4.5b *Rhythms of Tracking* (detail).

The Taskscape of Social Media

The anthropologist Tim Ingold (2000) proposes what he calls the *taskscape* as a way of understanding the interlocking relations between activities, resources and time. Whilst he derives many terms from Heidegger in describing this as 'a pattern of dwelling activities' (154), the conceptual origins of the term owe more to the relation of modes of production than to modes of living within early Marx (Ingold 2005). Ingold refers to the growth of a tree and the rest breaks of peasant labourers at the harvest, but we can equally think in terms of the morning rush hour, breakfast radio and the ping of Twitter updates. Mobile phones and social media platforms are part of our contemporary taskscape. These devices are designed to encourage a constant tasking which is not necessarily directed as labour but which may slip across different registers of labour and value: 'the taskscape is to labour what the landscape is to land, and indeed what an ensemble of use-values is to value in general' (Ingold 2000: 195). The taskscape is inherently temporal, forming and changing through the inter-relations of different activities that each have their own rhythm, as Lefebvre (2004) describes: 'Everywhere there is interaction between a place, a time and an expenditure of energy, there is rhythm' (15).

Both Ingold and Lefebvre speak of a conflict between the rhythms of labour time and social time. Marx conceived of abstract labour as inherently measured in time, and summarised the conflict between labour and capital as that of control over the regular temporal division of the day: between necessary labour time and that given to the creation of surplus value. As E. P. Thompson (1967) explored, it is the unification of time under the singular metric of the clock that enables such labour to be measured as capital. Lefebvre describes this process as an increasing linearisation of time and flattening of rhythms under a single model, a simplification of the complexities of life's temporal patterns into what Guattari calls the 'refrains' of capital (2011: 107–9). The interfaces of social media platforms could be said to act as 'refraining devices' that seek to give predictable patterning to the noisy, complex rhythms of lived sociality but whether, in doing so, they fully subsume that sociality into a form of labour directed by capital is a moot point (Gehl 2014; Srnicek 2017). The analyses of social media that draw upon post-autonomous theory often view the advent of social media as the collapse of social time entirely into that of labour (Terranova 2000). However, the relations between time, labour and value are not so direct as some analyses might suppose (Harvie 2005; Beverungen et al. 2015).

When operating as the interaction of different forms of capital at a level beyond the factory, capital does not move within a singular tempo according to Marx (Tombazos 2014). There are different *circuits* of capital that Marx describes – the working period, production process and circulation – and these interact as part of a more complex rhythm such as that summarised in the diagrams of volume II of *Capital* (Fig. 4.6).

Unlike factory production, which reduced lived experience to the linear time of the 'daily grind' (Lefebvre 2004: 30), the taskscape of social media does not fit neatly into one of these circuits. It is rather one of many temporal patternings that cut across and interact with these in different ways. In addition to the rhythms of the working day and the circulation of capital, we must also incorporate the rhythms of algorithmic processes. Whereas the regular rhythm of clock time may have served as a unifying point of reference, the complex rhythms of algorithmic processes intervene within and constitute different relational and organisational structures, what Adrian Mackenzie (2007) calls 'associative objects' that 'make the world they work in hang together in certain ways and not others' (103). At the heart of any computer-driven algorithm there is always

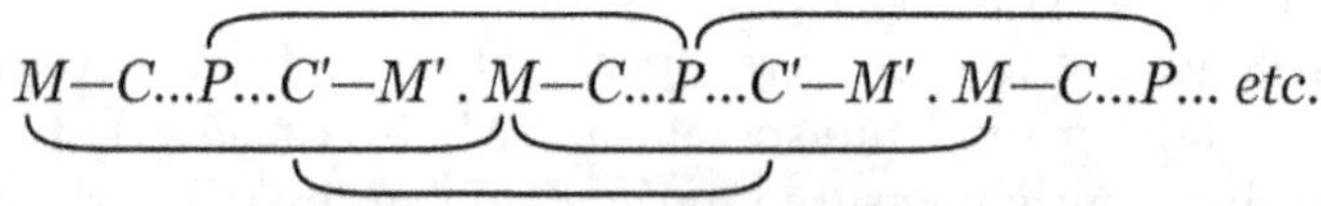

$$M-C...P...C'-M'\;.\;M-C...P...C'-M'\;.\;M-C...P...\text{ etc.}$$

Figure 4.6 One of Marx's diagrams of the circuit of capital as it transforms through cycles of investment, production and sale. Based on Karl Marx (1978: 142).

the beat of a regular clock cycle, but the relation of an algorithm to events outside of that, a process that Shintaro Miyazaki (2018) calls *algorhythmics*, creates a complexity that neither the clock cycle nor mathematical logic can fully comprehend (Wegner and Goldin 1999). Algorithms not only provide the communicational infrastructures, the vectors, within which social media platforms perform, but they also matt together the numerous contingent and indeterminate data points into discernible structures that can be measured and manipulated. These are not discrete black box operations but are more porous, diffused across various social, economic and machinic capacities. Whereas clock time simplified and standardised the periodicity of life and labour, algorithmic time accelerates and proliferates the coincidences and departures of data, activity and experience from which such structures are generated. If the industrial era was characterised by a *eurhythmia* of coordinated labour in which social life and production were structured according to unified linear patterns, then the social media age may be one that is increasingly *arrhythmic* (Lefebvre 2004: 16, 67–9), characterised by multiple, conflicting moments rather than periodic stability – the on-demand gig economy rather than the job for life (Srnicek 2017). This evolution is mirrored in the way in which the linear, yet overlapping, circuits that Marx's diagram summarises become the thick texture of events within our own, as though zooming in to the details of a process that has become increasingly diffractive. Through the algorithms of platforms such as Facebook, the different minutiae of our social communications 'hang together' in relation not to the regularity of production as such, but rather to the unstable circulation of capital through advertising and stock shares.

Attunement and Value

There has been much debate on how value is extracted from social media (Proffitt et al. 2015). One theory posits that users and their data are commodities that are traded to advertisers (Pariser 2011: 7). Another, sometimes related to this, is that the creation of user content and data trails is a form of unpaid labour (Terranova 2000; Fuchs 2014a; Fuchs 2014b). Others have argued that social media creates a new form of capital in terms of affect or attention (Arvidsson and Colleoni 2012). Another perspective sees it as rent (Pasquinelli 2009; Rigi and Prey 2015). In its own marketing as a sharing platform, and in the rhetoric of those such as Clay Shirky (2008), Facebook is presented as a form of altruistic gift economy.

In our interviews with participants, we asked which model they felt fitted their own experience of Facebook. Many saw it as a mixture of these, with the majority describing it primarily as feeling like a rental arrangement with aspects of labour, and only a few concurring with the gift model. Some users felt drained by the compulsion to interact; others saw it as a valueless medium to offload or enjoy trash; some as a purely personal space with little value to others. Reflecting our previous work on television viewing, we found that attitudes were often shaped by class and family expectations about media usage (Skeggs and Wood 2012). In the case of a user such as Laura, she felt that she derived far more direct benefit from her posts than Facebook did, and that she could make a financial return on her time invested in Facebook that fed back into her career. She was not alienated in the manner that a factory, shop or domestic worker will be but rather epitomised the 'enterprising self' that has come to characterise certain sectors of the neoliberal economy (McKenzie 2001). One of the most common dispositions expressed by our participants, however, was not so much one of alignment with any specific economic model but rather of resignation to, as several put it, a 'necessary evil'.

Facebook constructs its status as a 'utility' through services produced (here in the more conventional labour sense) by a workforce of programmers and service operators, such as the people who monitor content. It is enabled by massive equipment infrastructures and technological investments (for comparison with Amazon, see Krasni et al. 2017). These construct and mediate different organisations of time – not only that of user experience, in the managing of the News Feed for example, but also in terms of ad targeting. Each has its own demands of timeliness, of coincidence and departure, that must integrate with those of the user, the efficient running of machines and hardware to facilitate that, and the circulation of capital as it moves through advertising streams and stock market sales.

The interaction of these different rhythms is not unified but rather *attunes*. Each circuit has its own dynamic that must be followed to match its potential, yet must also adjust itself in relation to other circuits in order to exploit moments of alignment and synchronicity between them. There is also attunement at other levels. One lies between the liveness of the user and these different vectors of circulation (Kember and Zylinska 2012: 61). It is this attunement, of variously directed and directionless activities, of self-fulfilment and dispossession, that the interfaces of Facebook enable. These interfaces are not only those as seen by the user on their Facebook page or app, but also of the API that integrates to other services and the various online trackers and financial interfaces that operate unseen. Another level is that of attunement to the larger structures of capital. If cinema effected an attunement to the assembly line structures of the factory, it could be said that social media effects an attunement to the needs of financialised capital (Henriques et al. 2014: 14–15; Martin 2002).

Lefebvre compared this to *dressage*, the training of the body and sensory organs to a particular rhythm of deportment (Lefebvre 2004: 41). This is not simply the deportment of labour, as in Taylorist methods. The 'efficiency' of the Facebook user is not the issue, but rather something more akin to the deportment of the body under debt and in relation to class. Lazzarato (2012) describes how, in the nineteenth century, the penitent had to display in their personal deportment and demeanour their worthiness before the governors of the Poor Board in order to receive support. This is a deportment that both demarcates and divulges, that assigns one a place in society and assigns a value to that. In contrast to the nineteenth century, however, in which a virtuous deportment was demanded, social media encourages one that is more permissive so that someone can be assigned the most profitable position within an advertiser's target audience. However, it is not so much the deportment of the physical body that matters on social media but rather movements across information and the expression of sociality within different infrastructures. Turow (2017) describes this as a 'hidden curriculum' (13) through which people are habituated to the gathering of information.

It is these deportments to social media that are expressed in the different rhythms of the participant diagrams. Within the diagrams of an individual participant, some are more attuned to one another whilst in others there are tensions, often, as noted above, between interaction and attention. This range between attunement and tension – we might say between eurythmia and arrhythmia – is mirrored in the participant interviews. The following statements come from four participants other than Laura and Linda. We can see in these that whilst the 'hidden curriculum' appears to have been fully effective in the first instance, this does not extend to all. Even where this appears less successful, however, resistance to it is tinged with resignation:

> I found myself thinking in Facebook processes. So I would have a thought and think 'How am I going to update this on Facebook?' and it infiltrates your mind in that way (Participant 42, 27 January 2016).
>
> It fits into the gaps, when those gaps are very big it will fill those gaps . . . (Participant 34, 11 February 2016)

It tends to just be when I've got a redundant five minutes I will go and check Facebook and Twitter and that kind of thing but I don't feel beholden to it (Participant 28, 20 January 2016).

I don't even care if they see it or not, for me it's just pointless. (Participant 40, 17 February 2016)

This resignation is, we would argue, related to Facebook's status as a utility. Facebook does not control value through a wage-relation or directive disciplining imposed upon its users – as for example we see with platforms such as Uber (Rosenblat 2018) – but rather seeks to be unavoidable, omnipresent and opportunistic. Facebook absorbs rather than produces value. If we extend this idea in terms of rhythm, we can see that the tasking of the user insinuates itself in and intervenes within the rhythms of daily life. This tasking draws the user into the process of absorption. This does not so much act as a way of directing the user to labour, but rather, like the pulsing of krill in the sea, or the constant tilling of soil, reveals and extracts a raw material for algorithms to act up (Zuboff 2019; Srnicek 2017). This, however, is only one part of the process, and does not in itself directly translate data into value.

Facebook and Financialisation

Facebook operates a hybrid model in terms of the extraction of value, some aspects of which are less directly related to what an individual user might do or perceive. The posting of content is not necessarily the creation of a commodity in the conventional sense of a media commodity such as a news article or TV programme. Only a small number of people ever see what the majority of us post (Samuel 2016). As a number of our participants pointed out, the advertising we see may be determined more by other people in our Friends network than what we ourselves do. The 'value' of an individual user may have less to do with the amount of time they spend on Facebook than the degree of influence they, or their Friends, have within the network, as this can often determine how adverts are disseminated across users. There can be degrees of direction in encouraging users to perform more of one kind of activity than another, whether that be through the interface design or through manipulation of content by the EdgeRank algorithm (Gehl 2014; Kramer et al. 2014). Activities such as tagging photos can be seen as enabling a lowering of production costs (Gehl 2014: 64). None of this, however, is on a par with the fully directed labour of a conventional worker who gives up control over their time and body in return for the promise of a wage. We may expend much time and effort on social media, but the extent to which such effort constitutes productive labour that is entirely alienated from us is ambiguous (Harvie 2005). The activities of an individual user may not directly produce value in and of themselves but are rather, as Guglielmo Carchedi (2014) describes, the 'condition for the production of value'. It is only as part of differently aggregated data sets that value can begin to be produced, or to put it more accurately, captured (Robinson 2015). This capture is not that arising from direct production but rather from extracting circulating capital in the form of advertising revenue and stock shares. These are primarily financed through the surplus value extracted from conventional labour *elsewhere* in the economy. It is not only technology but also the economic conditions of declining wages in relation to increasing financialisation that make entities such as Facebook possible.

Facebook is ideally suited to the conditions of advanced financialisation, of 'profit without producing', as outlined by Costas Lapavitsas (2013):

> ... surplus absorption is a tide that flows but rarely ebbs: the normal state of the monopolistic capitalist economy is to be overwhelmed by surplus. It follows that methods must emerge through which the surplus would be absorbed, either in production or in consumption, because it would otherwise lead to stagnation of the productive sector. For this reason, monopoly capitalism is characterized by unproductive consumption, including advertising, military expenditure and even pure waste, that absorb the surplus. (16–17)

Information about lenders and borrowers is an integral part of the finance system and, traditionally, this has made banks one of the key repositories of information upon individuals within their societies (Lapavitsas 2013: 56, 111–12). The flow of data that companies such as Facebook and Google possess now challenges, and quite possibly surpasses, that of banks. This, like the absorption of surplus that Lapavitsas evokes, is a flow that appears unlikely to ever ebb or dissipate. The value of such data, however, does not lie merely in its quantity. The most valuable thing anyone can do for Facebook is sign up for an account, for this provides the point of guarantee against which the value of its data, its services to advertisers and other companies, and its share value can be measured. Facebook borrows and sells against the worthiness of its users and, in signing up, we agree to become indebted to it. It is debt, rather than labour, that describes the relation of a person to value within Facebook. For the privileged, self-enterprising user there is a benefit from this as an investment that accrues greater value to themselves as a subject-of-worth. For those less privileged, there is a risk of exposure and loss, of being deprived by the very data they have given up, as Linda feared and as studies of online monitoring of self-employed care and domestic workers by prospective employers have shown (Ticona, Mateescu and Rosenblat 2018). As Marx (1975) stated, in relation to debt:

> This means, then, that the totality of the poor man's social virtues, the content of his life's activity, his very existence, represent for the rich man the repayment of his capital together with the usual interest. (263)

In returning to situate these effects in terms of rhythm we can understand such 'repayment' as the moment when the micro rhythms of daily activity coincide with the larger circuits of capital. This is not generated directly from us but from a host of derivatives that are fed data from the taskscape of interactions that increasingly attunes our lives to this process. As one participant put it, 'if it is part of your world that surely necessitates an emotional relationship' (Participant 34, 11 February 2016).

The instruments of financialisation and the predictive analytics upon which the AI capacities of Facebook are trained both seek to control the future. Maurizio Lazzarato (2012) describes as 'possessing the future in advance by objectivizing it'. Writing on debt, he argues that it operates upon time in a way that is different to that of labour:

> ... objectivizing time, possessing it in advance, means subordinating all possibility of choice and decision which the future holds to the reproduction of capitalist power relations. In this way, debt appropriates not only the present labour time of wage-earners and the population in general, it also pre-empts non-chronological time, each person's future as well as the future of society as a whole. The principal explanation for the strange sensation of living in a society without time, without possibility, without foreseeable rupture, is debt. (46–7)

There is paradox in this. Whilst the predictive algorithms and conditions of debt, of inevitability and resignation, close down time the functioning and sustenance of these relies upon a constant churning of data and activity. This is the churning of stock markets, advertising bids and social tasking that never coalesces into a stable flow of production but is rather a myriad of numerous coincidences and departures between the deportment of users and capture of capital that builds a complex arrhythmia of capitalised sociality. If, as Lefebvre argues, social models are established 'through rhythms' (2004: 41), it may be that the rhythms of this financialised society are rhythms without time, or for which time is running out. The overwhelming flows of data and surplus value upon which this depends are not sustainable. Lapavitsas warns that debt and financialisation create stagnation in which even the most absorbent vectors of an economy are vulnerable (2013: 18). Such financialisation is an omen of decline, leaving a society without time, trapped in endless predictions of a future that never comes.

Note

1. The project was led by Professor Skeggs and was supported by the Economic and Social Research Council Grant ES/KO10786/1. Project website: <https://values.doc.gold.ac.uk/> (last accessed 28 December 2019). The source code for the software is available at <https://github.com/valuesandvalue> (last accessed 28 December 2019). A detailed description of the tools and the process involved in creating them is given in Skeggs and Yuill 2016b. The names of the participants have been changed for this article.

References

Arvidsson, A., and E. Colleoni (2012), 'Value in Informational Capitalism and on the Internet', *The Information Society*, 28: 3, pp. 135–50.
Barassi, V. (2015), 'Social Media, Immediacy and the Time for Democracy: Critical Reflections on Social Media as "Temporalising Practices"', in L. Dencik and O. Leistert (eds), *Critical Approaches to Social Media Protest: Contentions and Debates*. Lanham, MD: Rowan and Littlefield.
Beverungen, A., S. Böhm and C. Land (2015), 'Free Labour, Social Media, Management: Challenging Marxist Organization Studies', *Organization Studies*, 36:4, pp. 473–89.
Birkbak, A., and H. B. Carlsen (2016), 'The World of Edgerank: Rhetorical Justifications of Facebook's News Feed Algorithm', *Computational Culture*, 5, <http://computationalculture.net/the-world-of-edgerank-rhetorical-justifications-of-facebooks-news-feed-algorithm/> (last accessed 28 December 2019).
Bogost, I. (2010), 'Ian became a fan of Marshall McLuhan on Facebook and suggested you become a fan too', in D. Wittkower (ed.), *Facebook and Philosophy*. Chicago: Open Court, pp. 21–32.
Bucher, T. (2012a), 'A Technicity Of Attention: How Software "Makes Sense"'. *Culture Machine*, 13, <http://www.culturemachine.net/index.php/cm/article/download/470/489> (last accessed 28 December 2019).
Bucher, T. (2012b), 'Want to be on the top? Algorithmic power and the threat of invisibility on Facebook', *New Media & Society*, 14: 7, pp. 1164–80.

Bucher, T. (2013), 'Objects of Intense Feeling: The Case of the Twitter API,' *Computational Culture*, 3, <http://computationalculture.net/objects-of-intense-feeling-the-case-of-the-twitter-api/> (last accessed 28 December 2019).
Carchedi, G. (2014), 'Old wine, new bottles and the Internet', *Work Organisation, Labour & Globalisation*, 8: 1, pp. 69–87.
Deleuze, G. (1992), 'Postscript on the Societies of Control', *October*, 59 (Winter), pp. 3–7.
DeLyser, D., and D. Sui (2013), 'Crossing the qualitative-quantitative divide II: Inventive approaches to big data, mobile methods, and rhythmanalysis', *Progress in Human Geography*, 37: 2, pp. 293–305.
Deville, J. (2012), 'Regenerating Market Attachments: Consumer Credit Debt Collection and the Capture of Affect', *Journal of Cultural Economy*, 5: 4, pp. 423–39.
Fuchs, C. (2014a), *Digital Labour and Karl Marx*. London: Routledge.
Fuchs, C. (2014b), 'Digital Prosumption Labour on Social Media in the Context of the Capitalist Regime of Time', *Time & Society*, 23: 1, pp. 97–123.
Gehl, R. W. (2014), *Reverse Engineering Social Media: Software, Culture, and Political Economy in New Media Capitalism*. Philadelphia: Temple University Press.
Gerlitz, C., and A. Helmond (2013), 'The Like Economy: Social Buttons and the Data-Intensive Web', *New Media & Society*, 15: 8, pp. 1348–65.
Golder, S. A., D. M. Wilkinson and B. A. Huberman (2007), 'Rhythms of Social Interaction: Messaging Within a Massive Online Network', in C. Steinfield, B. T. Pentland, M. Ackerman and N. Contractor (eds), *Communities and Technologies*. London: Springer, pp. 41–66.
Goodman, S. (2010), *Sonic Warfare: Sound, Affect, and the Ecology of Fear*. Cambridge, MA, and London: MIT Press.
Guattari, F. (2011), *The Machinic Unconscious: Essays in Schizoanalysis*. Los Angeles: Semiotext(e).
Hansen, D. L., B. Shneiderman and M. Smith (2010), *Analyzing Social Media Networks with NodeXL: Insights from a Connected World*. Burlington: Morgan Kaufmann.
Harper, R., E. Whitworth and R. Page (2012), 'Fixity: Identity, Time and Durée on Facebook', Association of Internet Researchers, <https://www.microsoft.com/en-us/research/publication/fixity-identity-time-and-duree-on-facebook/> (last accessed 28 December 2019).
Harvie, D. (2005), 'All Labour Produces Value for Capital and We All Struggle against Value', *The Commoner*, 10, <http://www.commoner.org.uk/10harvie.pdf> (last accessed 28 December 2019).
Hassoun, D. (2014), 'Tracing Attentions: Toward an Analysis of Simultaneous Media Use', *Television & New Media*, 15: 4, pp. 271–88.
Henriques, J., M. Tiainen and P. Väliaho (2014), 'Rhythm Returns: Movement and Cultural Theory', in *Body & Society*, Special Issue: *Rhythm, Movement, Embodiment*, 20: 3–4 (September and December), pp. 3–29.
Hochman, N., and L. Manovich (2013), 'Zooming into an Instagram City: Reading the local through social media', *First Monday*, 18: 7.

Ingold, T. (2000), *The Perception of the Environment: Essays on Livelihood, Dwelling and Skill*. Abingdon: Routledge.
Ingold, T. (2005), 'Towards a Politics of Dwelling', *Conservation and Society*, 3: 2 (December), pp. 501–8.
Kaun, A., and F. Stiernstedt (2014), 'Facebook time: Technological and institutional affordances for media memories', *New Media & Society*, 16: 7, pp. 1154–68.
Kember, S., and J. Zylinska (2012), *Life after New Media: Mediation as a Vital Process*. Cambridge, MA: MIT Press.
Kramer, A. D., J. E. Guillory and J. T. Hancock (2014), 'Experimental evidence of massive-scale emotional contagion through social networks', *Proceedings of the National Academy of Sciences*, 111: 24, pp. 8788–90.
Krasni, J., V. Joler, Christo and A. Petrovski (2017, May), 'The Human Fabric of the Facebook Pyramid', *SHARE Lab*, <https://labs.rs/en/the-human-fabric-of-the-facebook-pyramid/> (last accessed 28 December 2019).
Lapavitsas, C. (2013), *Profiting Without Production: How Finance Exploits Us All*. London: Verso.
Lazzarato, M. (2012), *The Making of the Indebted Man: An Essay on the Neoliberal Condition*. Los Angeles: Semiotext(e).
Lefebvre, H. (2004), *Rhythmanalysis: Space, Time and Everyday Life*, trans. S. Elden and G. Moore. London and New York: Continuum.
Lovink, G. (2007), 'Indifference of the Networked Presence: On Time Management of the Self', in R. Hassan and R. E. Purser (eds), *24/7: Time and Temporality in the Network Society*, Stanford: Stanford Business Books, pp. 161–72.
Mackenzie, A. (2007), 'Protocols and the Irreducible Traces of Embodiment: The Viterbi Algorithm and the Mosaic of Machine Time', in R. Hassan and R. E. Purser (eds), *24/7: Time and Temporality in the Network Society*. Stanford: Stanford Business Books, pp. 89–105.
Mandese, J. (2014), 'Supplier of the Year: Acxiom – Who's On First, What's On Third?', *MediaPost* (January), <https://www.mediapost.com/publications/article/216930/supplier-of-the-year-acxiom-whos-on-first-wha.html> (last accessed 28 December 2019).
Marres, N., and E. Weltevrede (2013), 'Scraping the social?', *Journal of Cultural Economy*, 6: 3, pp. 313–35.
Martin, R. (2002), *Financialization of Daily Life*. Philadelphia: Temple University Press.
Marx, K. (1975), 'Excerpts from James Mill's *Elements of Political Economy* (1844)', in R. Hassan and R. E. Purser (eds), *Early Writings*. Harmondsworth: Penguin, pp. 259–78.
Marx, K. (1978), *Capital: A Critique of Political Economy*, vol. 2, trans. D. Fernbach. Harmondsworth: Penguin.
McGee, M. (2013), 'EdgeRank Is Dead: Facebook's News Feed Algorithm Now Has Close To 100K Weight Factors', *Marketing Land*, <http://marketingland.com/edgerank-is-dead-facebooks-news-feed-algorithm-now-has-close-to-100k-weight-factors-55908> (last accessed 28 December 2019).

McKenzie, J. (2001), *Perform or Else: From Discipline to Performance*. London and New York: Routledge.

McKenzie, W. (2004), *A Hacker Manifesto*. Cambridge, MA: Harvard University Press.

Mierzwinski, E., and J. Chester (2013), 'Selling Consumers, Not Lists: The New World of Digital Decision-making and the Role of the Fair Credit Reporting Act', *Suffolk University Law Review*, 46 (Spring), pp. 1–41.

Miyazaki, S. (2018), 'Algorhythmics: A Diffractive Approach for Understanding Computation', in J. Sayers (ed.), *The Routledge Companion to Media Studies and Digital Humanities*. London: Routledge, pp. 243–9.

Munster, A. (2013), *An Aesthesia of Networks: Conjunctive Experience in Art and Technology*. Cambridge, MA, and London: MIT Press.

Murphie, A. (2007), 'The Fallen Present: Time in the Mix', in R. Hassan and R. E. Purser (eds), *24/7: Time and Temporality in the Network Society*. Stanford: Stanford Business Books, pp. 122–40.

Pariser, E. (2011), *The Filter Bubble: What the Internet is Hiding from You*. London: Penguin.

Pasquinelli, M. (2009), 'Google's PageRank algorithm: a diagram of cognitive capitalism and the rentier of the common intellect', *Deep Search*, 3, pp. 152–62.

Proffitt, J. M., H. R. Ekbia and S. D. McDowell (2015), 'Introduction to the Special Forum on Monetization of User-Generated Content – Marx Revisited', *The Information Society*, 31:1, pp. 1–4.

Rieder, B. (2013), 'Studying Facebook via data extraction: the Netvizz application', in *WebSci '13: Proceedings of the 5th Annual ACM Web Science Conference*, New York, 14–16 August, pp. 346–6.

Rigi, J., and R. Prey (2015), 'Value, Rent, and the Political Economy of Social Media', *The Information Society*, 31: 5, pp. 392–406.

Robinson, B. (2015), 'With a Different Marx: Value and the Contradictions of Web 2.0 Capitalism', *The Information Society*, 31: 1, pp. 44–51.

Rosenblat, A. (2018), *Uberland: How Algorithms Are Rewriting the Rules of Work*. Oakland: University of California Press.

Samuel, A. (2016), 'Peak Link: What I learned about Facebook's algorithm from looking at my 4,632 posts', *Art+marketing*, April, <https://artplusmarketing.com/peak-link-what-i-learned-about-facebook-s-algorithm-from-looking-at-my-4-632-posts-41e672a2786e> (last accessed 28 December 2019).

Shirky, C. (2008), *Here Comes Everybody: How Change Happens when People Come Together*. London: Penguin.

Skeggs, B. (2004), *Class, Self, Culture*. London and New York: Routledge.

Skeggs, B. (2009), 'The Moral Economy of Person Production: The Class Relations of Self-Performance on "Reality" Television', *Sociolocical Review*, 57: 4, pp. 626–44.

Skeggs, B., and H. Wood (2012), *Reacting to Reality Television: Performance, Audience and Value*. London: Taylor & Francis.

Skeggs, B., and S. Yuill (2016a), 'Capital Experimentation with Person/a Formation: How Facebook's Monetization Refigures the Relationship between Property, Personhood and Protest', *Information, Communication & Society*, 19: 3, pp. 380–96.

Skeggs, B., and S. Yuill (2016b), 'The Methodology of a Multi-model Project Examining how Facebook Infrastructures Social Relations', *Information, Communication & Society*, 19: 10, pp. 1356–72.

Skeggs, B., and S. Yuill (2018), 'Subjects of Value and Digital Personas: Reshaping the Bourgeois Subject, Unhinging Property from Personhood', *Subjectivity*.

Srnicek, N. (2017), *Platform Capitalism*. Cambridge: Polity Press.

Terranova, T. (2000), 'Free Labor: Producing Culture for the Digital Economy', *Social Text*, 18: 2, pp. 33–58.

Thompson, E. P. (1967), 'Time, Work-Discipline, and Industrial Capitalism', *Past & Present*, 38, pp. 56–97.

Tiscona, J., A. Mateescu and A. Rosenblat (2018), *Beyond Disruption: How Tech Shapes Labor Across Domestic Work and Ridehailing*. New York: Data & Society.

Tombazos, S. (2014), *Time in Marx: The Categories of Time in Marx's Capital*. Chicago: Haymarket Books.

Turow, J. (2008), *Niche Envy: Marketing Discrimination in the Digital Age*. Cambridge, MA, and London: MIT Press.

Turow, J. (2012), *The Daily You: How the New Advertising Industry Is Defining Your Identity and Your Worth*. New Haven and London: Yale University Press.

Turow, J. (2017), *The Aisles Have Eyes: How Retailers Track Your Shopping, Strip Your Privacy, and Define Your Power*. New Haven and London: Yale University Press.

Wegner, P., and D. Goldin (1999), 'Mathematical Models of Interactive Computing. Technical Report CS 99–13', Brown University.

Weltevrede, E., A. Helmond and C. Gerlitz (2014), 'The Politics of Real-time: A Device Perspective on Social Media Platforms and Search Engines', *Theory, Culture & Society*, 31: 6, pp. 125–50.

Zuboff, S. (2019), *The Age of Surveillance Capitalism: The Fight for Human Future at the New Frontier of Power*. London: Profile Books.

Chapter 5

Idiorrhythmy: An (Unsustainable) Aesthetics of Ethics

Sunil Manghani

The book in which this chapter appears was developed from a series of conferences and seminars on rhythm and rhythmanalysis, during which repeated references were made to the works of Deleuze and Guattari and Lefebvre. The latter is not surprising given his writings on 'rhythmanalysis' (Lefebvre 2013) and a theory of 'moments' (2014: 634–52; 800–7). Deleuze and Guattari (2013; Deleuze 1994), while less immediately accessible, have also offered significant and evocative takes on rhythm and the 'refrain'. This chapter, however, takes a somewhat different tack by referencing the work of Roland Barthes, or more specifically a brief commentary on rhythm that appears in his lecture course *How to Live Together* (2013). Of course, Barthes was a reader of Deleuze (as can be seen in his lecture notes) with a shared interest in intensities (rather than codes and 'systems' of codification etc.). And there is a more direct connection with Lefebvre. Both were members of the Marxist circle that published the influential journal *Arguments*; as part of which both 'strove to develop a critical and reflexive Marxism . . . [that] sought to understand the sociocultural transformations occurring within France and other Western industrial societies in the postwar era' (Gardiner 2000: 74). In this respect both were offering new theories of the everyday, of which Lefebvre's account of rhythm can be understood as an important component, enabling a blend of political and aesthetic analysis. While Barthes' own account of rhythm is more peripheral, it can nonetheless help us consider the *writing* of rhythm in important ways, not least in allowing for a more *writerly* account of rhythmanalysis, which opens out to an ethics of rhythm: to question less what rhythm is and what it does, and instead to consider what kinds of rhythms we want and desire; to shift from ontological questions of rhythm to ethical ones.

Inventions of Rhythm

> This analysis of rhythms in all their magnitude 'from particles to galaxies' has a transdisciplinary character. It gives itself the objective, amongst others, of separating as little as possible the scientific from the poetic. (Lefebvre 2013: 94)

Rhythm might appear to be something we can intuitively relate to, as something that pervades, that we must fall in with. As we traverse the busy high street, swerving between the fits and starts of those around us, trying to get to where only we want to go, we are both consciously and unconsciously *timing* ourselves in amongst our surroundings. Yet when we try to define what we mean by rhythm (and 'where' it resides) our understanding can quickly falter. A seemingly inherent problem is what philosopher Graham Harman has termed 'duomining'. In most claims to a 'theory of everything', there is the tendency to reduce everything to the smallest units. The *physikoi* of pre-Socratic thought offered various cases for the 'first principle of everything', such as water (Thales of Miletus), air (Anaximenes) or atoms (Leucippus, Democritus). This approach continues today, with theoretical physics having defined the ever smaller units of quarks and leptons. Harman argues that these are all forms of 'undermining', with none of them thinking that everyday things 'have the same degree of reality as their chosen ultimate foundations; most objects are simply too shallow to be real' (2018: 46). Harman labels this as 'smallism' – reducing everything to the smallest units possible, which in turn reduces everything to the material. A physicist's 'theory of everything' does not, however, tell us anything about why or how we have fictional entities (such as a character in a novel, or unicorns). And, crucially, such extreme materialism struggles to account for the fact that new ideas *emerge*.

We can equally describe things as if looking in the opposite direction, where there is the tendency to consider how everything relates together, that there is an overarching 'system'. Such theories Harman describes as 'overmining', whereby things are reduced 'to their impact on us or on each other, denying them any excess or surplus beyond such impact' (49). The problem here is that we cannot seemingly account for *change*. 'If atoms, billiard balls, watermelons . . . are nothing more than the sum total of their relations or effects in this very instant, then how is it that they can be doing something very different five minutes or two weeks from now?' (49–50). Rhythm appears to situate somewhere between these readings, so placed in terms of what Harman refers to as 'duomining': 'For example, the natural sciences duomine by speaking of nature simultaneously as made of tiny ultimate constituents (undermining) and as knowable through mathematics (overmining). In this way, independent objects themselves are supposedly erased from the picture as obscure and superfluous' (50). The point here is not to align specifically with Harman's 'Object-Orientated Ontology', which presents its own difficulties (Campbell et al. 2019). Nonetheless, his terminology is instructive in understanding what is at stake in various accounts of rhythm and, crucially, rhythmanalysis.

In their different ways, when reading Deleuze and Guattari and Lefebvre on rhythm, we can all too readily be drawn to questions of *how* to understand or define rhythm. As we know, Deleuze and Guattari are writing never of a 'subject' (in the common sense), but of 'event', of the coming together of rhythms. Questions arise such as 'how to get out of chaos'; 'how something can emerge'. The milieu, for example, is a periodic repetition of 'codes' which combine. The much-cited example of the wasp and the orchid are presented as two codes merely at a critical moment (Deleuze and Guattari 2013: 9). However, we can quickly encounter the problem of duomining. Rhythm becomes metaphysical (and undermined): everything, all the way down, eventually becomes rhythm. 'Chaos is not the opposite of rhythm,' they write, 'but the milieu of all milieus. There is rhythm whenever there is a transcoded passage from one milieu to another, a communication of milieus, coordination between heterogeneous space-times' (364–5). Reference here to 'the milieu of all milieus' alerts us to a metaphysics, while also the idea of 'coordination' is left unexplained, as if an auto-coordination of milieus. We might be led to think of 'learning to swim' as simply a matter of entering into the milieu of the waves, a means of attuning to the underlying (smallest) forces, densities and intensities. But what lurks here is still the subject. For why not sink? What fights to survive but a subject? Or, if we look the other way, particularly in connection to Deleuze and Guattari's interest in the 'refrain', there are numerous references to cosmological forces. The refrain is described as 'a prism, a crystal of space-time. It acts upon that which surrounds it, sound or light, extracting from it various vibrations, or decompositions, projections, or transformations' (Deleuze and Guattari 2013: 405). It is 'a formula evoking a character or landscape, instead of itself constituting a rhythmic character or landscape' (406). We can seemingly transpose the refrain infinitely, yet without really challenging ourselves as to why.

Lefebvre's terms of reference are very different, and yet we encounter similar issues of *where* rhythm takes place; whether some underlying patterning claims greater importance over the elements that are rhythmic, or whether everything coheres to a singular rhythmic order. There are frequent suggestions of the rhythmanalyst needing to 'listen'; to 'listen to the world, and above all to what are disdainfully called noises, which are said without meaning, and to *murmurs* [*remeurs*], full of meaning – and finally [to] listen to silences' (Lefebvre 2013: 29). Lefebvre's account can seem to look in two ways: to the smallest units (the murmurs and silences) as the true building blocks of all rhythm, or equally to a worldly 'noise' that, while hard to 'hear', is where rhythms cohere. Lefebvre's essay with Catherine Régulier, 'The Rhythmanalytical Project' (in Lefebvre 2013: 82–92), brings this out well, spanning as it does from the singular, human body to the social and also cosmic 'body':

> The living – polyrhythmic – body is composed of diverse rhythms, each 'part', each organ or function having its own, in a perpetual interaction, in a doubtlessly 'metastable' equilibrium [. . .] But the surroundings of the body, the social just as much as the cosmic body, are equally bundles of rhythms ('bundles' in the sense that we say, not pejoratively, that a complex chord reuniting diverse notes and tones is a 'bundle of sounds'). Now look around you at this meadow, this garden, these trees and these houses. They give themselves, they offer themselves to your eyes as in a simultaneity. Now, up to a certain point, this simultaneity is mere appearance, surface, a spectacle. Go deeper. [. . .] You at once notice that every plant, every tree has its rhythm. [. . .] Henceforth you will grasp every being [*chaque être*], every entity [*étant*] and every body, both living and non-living, 'symphonically' or 'polyrhythmically'. You will grasp it in its space-time, in its place and its approximate becoming: including houses and buildings, towns and landscapes. (88–9)

In reading this account, a consideration of rhythm leads us *somewhere else*, whether to the smallest units of analysis or the largest. However, despite the ontological framing, ethical interests are implied too. Through the 'what' of rhythm is implied 'what is best'. Lefebvre uses various terms that suggest order, disorder, pathology and health. He refers to polyrhythmia, eurhythmyia and arrhythmia. The latter two terms relate to ideas about the body. Cardiac arrhythmia refers to the irregularity of the heartbeat, while eurhythmy is often associated with bodily rhythms or vibrations being in tune and healthy. There is seemingly an implied interest or *desire* for 'good rhythm'; also with polyrhythmia, as being multiple and nonhierarchical. A similar sense of being 'in tune' is evident with Deleuze and Guattari (2013: 361–408), whose account of the 'refrain' suggests the emergence or 'holding' of forces, densities and intensities, and is picked up with the notion of sobriety as some sort of appropriate form – 'a maximum of calculated sobriety in relation to the disparate elements and parameters' (400).

The idea of what is *appropriate* as a form in rhythm proves to be significant. In fact, there is a Platonic account of rhythm, of 'ideal' forms, which persists today, and which we can see precisely as an 'inventing' or disciplining of rhythm. Benveniste (1971: 281–8) has shown that our present-day use of the word 'rhythm' comes of a long consideration of the structure of things. The Ancient Greek term *rhuthmos* is what has come to mean 'rhythm', which has been associated as an abstract noun of the verb 'to flow', 'having been borrowed from the regular movements of the waves of the sea' (281). However, this is shown to have been wrong. It is the river or stream that 'flows', not the sea. Instead, as far back as ancient Ionian philosophy, notably through Democritus' atomism, we can understand *rhuthmos* to mean 'form'; Democritus' doctrine, for example, 'taught that water and air . . . differ from each other in the *form* that their constituent atoms take' (283). Thus, from its earliest use down to the Attic period, *rhuthmos* did not mean 'rhythm' (as typically understood); rather its meaning is 'distinctive form, proportioned figure, arrangement, disposition' (285). However, 'form' can be expressed in various ways. Importantly, *rhuthmos* is different to 'schema' or a 'fixed form', rather it connects to movement and change:

> [*Rhuthmos*] designates the form in the instant that it is assumed by what is moving, mobile and fluid, the form of that which does not have organic consistency; it fits the pattern of a fluid element, of a letter arbitrarily shaped, of a robe which one arranges at one's will, of a particular state of character or mood. It is the form as improvised, momentary, changeable. (Benveniste 1971: 285–6)

There are some important points to note. While rhythm is here defined as what is moving and fluid, there is still the idea of an 'instant', of a time, and we might suggest a framing or holding form. However, there is a final step in this 'invention' of rhythm according to Benveniste. It is Plato, he argues, who properly determines the meaning of *rhuthmos*, or rather who affixes it to what we mean today by rhythm. Through his various Socratic texts, the term is used in the sense of 'distinctive form', but with modification. 'His innovation', Benveniste explains, 'was in applying it to the *form of movement* which the human body makes in dancing, and the arrangement of figures into which this movement is resolved' (287). As such:

> 'form' is from then on determined by a 'measure' and numerically regulated. Here is the new sense of [*rhuthmos*]: in Plato, 'arrangement' (the original sense of the word) is constituted by an ordered sequence

of slow and rapid movements, just as 'harmony' results from the alternation of high and low. [. . .] We may then speak of the 'rhythm' of a dance, of a step, of a song, of a speech, of work, of everything which presupposes a continuous activity broken by meter into alternating intervals. [. . .] Starting from [*rhuthmos*], a spatial configuration defined by the distinctive arrangement and proportion of the elements, we arrive at 'rhythm', a configuration of movements organized in time. (287)

Plato provides us with a more regulatory reading of rhythm, which arguably still persists. In his lecture course *How to Live Together* (2013), Roland Barthes draws directly upon Benveniste's account, which, taken on deliberately as a matter of ethics, works against a final Platonic reading of rhythm. Through a chance reading of coenobitic convents on Mount Athos, where 'monks [are] both isolated from and in contact with one another', he encounters the idea of 'idiorrhythmic clusters', in which 'each subject lives according to his own rhythm' (6). It is this notion of the idiorrhythmic that Barthes locates within Benveniste's account of *rhuthmos*. Indeed, he suggests the two terms are deeply entwined. Given that *rhuthmos* allows for an improvised, changeable form, it is *inherently* individual, or idiorrhythmic. And crucially, for Barthes, both terms lead us beyond the semiotic, referring to 'the interstices, the *fugitivity* of the code, of the manner in which the individual inserts himself into the social (or natural) code' (7–8). Barthes' reading of Benvensite is instructive, but it also leaves us with some problems. The *idios* questions the validity of rhythm as method, and also, as this chapter will conclude, raises issues about privileges afforded to how we can realistically manage time and space, which, between us all, is only finite. We can begin to explore these issues by first diverting the invention of rhythm (as an analytical concept) to an 'inventiveness', to explore rhythm as forms of production and writing.

Rhythm *Écriture*

Does the rhythmanalyst thus come close to the poet? Yes, to a large extent, more so than he does to the psychoanalyst, and still more so than he does to the statistician, who counts things and, quite reasonably, describes them in their immobility. Like the poet, the rhythmanalyst performs a verbal action, which has an aesthetic import. (Lefebvre 2013: 33)

Much can be made of Lefebvre's call for a new science. Rhythmanalysis, he suggests, 'proposes nothing less than to found a science, a new field of knowledge [*savoir*]: the analysis of rhythms; with practical consequences' (13). Yet this proposal needs to be read with caution.

In Europe, the term 'science' can be heard in various ways across the academy, echoing a humanistic notion of intellectual endeavour writ large. But also, what science? Lefebvre's account of rhythm is arguably more thematic than it is methodological. In fact, he appears, in places, to excuse himself from the latter. The rhythmanalyst 'will have some points in common with the psychoanalyst', he suggests. 'He will be attentive . . . He will listen to the world . . . and to *murmurs* [*rumeurs*]' (29). But, he goes on, unlike the psychoanalyst, the rhythmanalyst will have none of the 'methodological obligations': 'He listens – and first to his body; he learns rhythm from it, in order consequently to appreciate external rhythms. His body serves him as a metronome. A difficult task and situation: to perceive rhythms distinctly, without disrupting them, without dislocating time' (28–9). The description is perhaps more fitting of a writer, artist or indeed poet, which Lefebvre himself suggests. As with the aesthetic import of the poem, the 'temporalities and their relations within wholes' that the rhythmanalyst attends to arguably need to be understood more akin to literary forms than scientific ones (we might think, for example, of the earlier claim to the *science* of signs, which of course led on to poststructuralism).

Rhythm proves to be a moving signifier, an interdisciplinary term. It opens up, rather than defines. Lefebvre betrays a more *productive* kind of writing than we might first assume: a form of 'practice' that is perhaps closer to what Barthes referred to as the Text – that which 'cannot be satisfied by a metalinguistic exposition' (1977: 164). The Text, he notes, 'should be itself nothing other than text, research, textual activity, since the Text is that *social* space which leaves no language safe, outside, nor any subject of the enunciation in position as judge, master, analyst, confessor, decoder. The theory of the Text can coincide only with a practice of writing' (164). It is this idea of 'practice' that can help us understand Lefebvre when he suggests the rhythmanalyst 'seems close to the poet, or the man of the theatre'. Art, poetry and theatre, he acknowledges, 'have always brought something (but what?) to the everyday. They haven't *reflected* on it. The creator descended to the streets of the city-state; the portrayed inhabitants lived amongst the citizens. They assumed the city life' (35). We can begin to hear an anti-Platonic reading, of the artist/analyst who is not only let into the polis, but also has a keen role within it:

> The rhythmanalyst could, in the long term, attempt something analogous: works . . . might return to and intervene in the everyday. Without claiming to *change life*, but by fully reinstating the sensible

in consciousness and in *thought*, he would accomplish a tiny part of the *revolutionary* transformation of this world and this society in decline. Without any declared political position' (Lefebvre 2013: 35)

As will become apparent, the projects of both Barthes and Lefebvre start to show resemblances. A political (and here it will be an ethical) aesthetic is at stake, which questions our responsibilities to form, more so than needing to declare particular political positions.

Both Lefebvre and Barthes provide us with memorable vignettes of Parisian streets, as seen from their respective windows. As Lyon (2019: 30) remarks, Lefebvre's (2013: 37–46) observations form something of a centrepiece for his short volume on rhythmanalysis. With Barthes, it is the briefest of remarks, almost an aside, but told with an acuity that persists:

> From my window . . . I see a mother pushing an empty stroller, holding her child by the hand. She walks at her own pace, imperturbably; the child, meanwhile, is being pulled, dragged along, is forced to keep running, like an animal, or one of Sade's victims being whipped. She walks at her own pace, unaware of the fact that her son's rhythm is different. And she's his mother! → Power – the subtlety of power – is effected through disrhythmy, heterorhythmy. (Barthes 2013: 9)

Barthes' scene more explicitly raises the idea of 'power', and also, importantly, refers to our choices over rhythm, whether of power, disruption or regulation. Again there is a move away from the repressive, Platonic reading of rhythm; indeed, it is for this very reason he notes 'it was necessary to add the prefix *idios*' (8). Barthes' study of idiorrhythmy is not about individual instances (such as the couple) nor macro-groupings; such structures, he argues, are 'based on an architecture of power', indeed, 'historically speaking, it's for precisely this reason, in opposition to idiorrhythmy, that such structures get established' (8). This scene of the mother and child reminds us of the unruly (*idios*) nature of rhythm *tout court*. And while the scene does not depict so much a form of knowledge, but the *relational production of forces*, what emerges is an aesthetic production of ethics.

To explore this idea, we can make a comparison between two works, one that is about speed (flow) and the other about pace (about differing measures). The first is Claude Lelouch's short film *C'était un rendez-vous* (1976), in which we watch a first-person view of a high-speed drive through Paris. Shot in a single take, it is an example of cinéma vérité. The length of the film was limited by the short capacity of a 1,000-foot 35mm film reel. While it is a film of speed, timing and movement, it is not rhythmic as such, it is not about the relations of form in the way Benvensite accounts of *rhuthmos* (and which Barthes writes as idiorrhythmy). Against this, we can compare the opening of Milan Kundera's *Slowness* (1996). The protagonist describes how, while driving, he becomes aware that the vehicle behind is trying to overtake: 'The small left light is blinking, and the whole car emits waves of impatience. The driver is watching for the chance to pass me; he is watching for the moment the way a hawk watches for a sparrow' (3). This is a rhythmic scene. It is about the relationship and *contingent* forms of speeds and measures and how these formulate to an experience. In Lelouch's film, while there are instances in which we consider such relational properties, the overarching experience is simply the thrill of speed. Kundera's narrator suggests something similar:

> The man hunched over his motorcycle can focus only on the present instant of his flight; he is caught in a fragment of time cut off from both the past and the future; he is wrenched from the continuity of time; he is outside time; in other words he is in a state of ecstasy. In that state he is unaware of his age, his wife, his children, his worries, and so he has no fear, because the source of fear is in the future, and a person freed of the future has nothing to fear. (Kundera 1996: 3–4)

By contrast, the opening scene of Kundera's novella establishes the theme of pleasure and the ethics of pleasure. While the common meaning of hedonism is typically of 'an amoral tendency to a life of sensuality, if not of outright vice', we are reminded that Epicurus, 'the first great theoretician of pleasure', framed pleasure not as joy and excess, but rather as the 'absence of suffering' (1996: 8). This in mind, it is in the rearview mirror that an improvised and changeable 'form' is brought to account:

> I check the rearview mirror: still the same car unable to pass me because of the oncoming traffic. Beside the driver sits a woman. Why doesn't the man tell her something funny? Why doesn't he put his hand on her knee? Instead, he's cursing the driver ahead of him for not going fast enough, and it doesn't occur to the woman, either, to touch the driver with her hand; mentally she's at the wheel with him, and she's cursing me too. (Kundera 1996: 5)

Throughout the scene, it is the sensual (the aesthetic) that has the *means* to alter the situation ethically. In the moment there is no definitive response (it is not a knowledge that can be readily applied or not). Instead, we must feel our way. The author is able to conjure such a moment which allows us to vicariously explore its 'rhythms' as the different possible trajectories and out-playing. Here, then, in Harman's terms, we are in the realm of the non-literalist view (which 'theories of everything' all too frequently fail to acknowledge). Writing in this sense is not 'knowledgeable' as such, but rather a construction *through* which we can explore and relate to a situation or situations (polyrhythmically). Typically, as Harman argues, 'there are just two ways of telling somebody what a thing is: you can tell them what it is made of, or tell them what it does. These are really the only two kinds of *knowledge* that we have about things' (2018: 43). Yet, he suggests, we 'place a high value on knowledge (what a thing is) and practical know-how (what a thing does), while ignoring cognitive activities that do not translate as easily into literal prose terms'. Among the exceptions is art, 'since the *primary* role of art is not to communicate knowledge about its subject matter' (43). (Interestingly, Harman also places philosophy among the exceptions, with the view that both art and philosophy are cognitive activities that *bring us to* an understanding, rather than as stores of knowledge.)

The distinction between knowledge and cognitive activities plays through Barthes' dualism of method/culture, which forms the opening of *How to Live Together* (2013: 3–4). Method is a 'manner of proceeding toward a goal', it is a 'protocol', the 'idea of a straight path': 'Now paradoxically, what the straight path actually marks out are the places the subject doesn't want to go to . . . The subject, for instance, renounces what he doesn't know of himself . . .' (3). By contrast, he equates culture (referencing Nietzsche) with *paideia*, a training, education; as a 'force':

> . . . culture as 'training' (≠ method) evokes the image of a kind of *dispatching* along an eccentric path: stumbling among snatches, between the bounds of different fields of knowledge, flavours. Paradoxically, when understood this way, as the registering of forces, culture is hostile to the idea of power (which is in method). (Will to force ≠ will to power). (4)

This 'dispatching' along a path begins to resonate with Lefebvre's repeated observations of rhythm in everyday life, whether as seen from his window, or whether reflecting on dressage or Mediterranean cityscapes. It is 'a matter of culture, not of method', Barthes writes: '[t]he practice of culture = an attentiveness to forces [an attentiveness to differences]' (4). And in doing so, not only is there an attentiveness to forces, but a productiveness too; or an *operation* of forces. Rhythmanalysis is itself forceful, aesthetic.

In Barthes' terms, rhythmanalysis can be understood as a form of *écriture* (to mean 'writerly'). Early in his career he pitched himself in contrast to Jean-Paul Sartre's account of literature as an ethics of *clear* prose. Samoyault (2017: 180) describes this as an 'ethics of ends, a functional view of literature', while Barthes 'prefers an ethics of form that opens up literature'. Sartre worked upon two terms, 'language' and 'style'. Language is a given. It is second nature for the writer; we are *naturalised* by our own language. Style, however, for Sartre, is the application of language and a matter of self-determination. Here, crucially, Barthes differs. He defines *both* language and style as prior constructs (the former a social construct, the latter of an individual history), against which an author cannot choose. Instead he introduces the third term 'writing' [*écriture*] as a site of choice, relating to the *practice* of writing as the negotiation of codes and conventions an author shares with a community, and which, importantly, allows us to understand the significance of form as much as, or indeed above, content.

Rhythm *écriture*, as we might term it, is in part observation, but also a form of production – though not so much an authorial writing, more a traversing of rhythms. Barthes suggests something of this in *The Pleasure of the Text* (1975). He recounts how, half asleep in a bar, he tries to conjure up all of the 'languages' within earshot: 'music, conversations, the noises of chairs, of glasses, an entire stereophony of which a square in Tangiers . . . is the exemplar site' (1975: 49). In terms very similar to Lefebvre, who refers to both an internal and external listening, Barthes notes how the external sounds 'spoke within' him:

> . . . this so-called 'interior' speech was very like the noise of the square, like that amassing of minor voices coming to me from the outside: I myself was a public square: a *sook*; through me passed words, tiny syntagms, bits of formulae and *no sentence formed*, as though that were the law of such a language. This speech, at once very cultural and very savage, was above all lexical, sporadic; it set up in me, through its apparent flow, a definitive discontinuity: this *non-sentence* was in no way something that could not have acceded to the sentence, that might have been *before* the sentence; it was: what is eternally, splendidly, *outside the sentence*. Then, potentially, all linguistics fell, linguistics which believes only in the sentence and has always attributed an exorbitant dignity to predictive syntax (as the form of a logic, of a rationality); I recalled this scientific scandal: there exists no locutive grammar (a grammar of what is spoken and not what is written . . .). (Barthes 1975: 49–50)

There are a number of significant points raised in this quotation. Barthes is seemingly giving ground to an 'outside' of the Text (contra Derrida), which we can begin to imagine is explored by rhythm, which has no verbal properties, nor indeed is it easy to say what or where it is, but that it works through us. Again, the external/internal is important, as is the shift to the locutionary, to uphold *parole* over *langue*. Locution refers, for example, to the *repeated* use of a phrase or expression; as used in specialised ways (we are returned seemingly to the *idios*). There is also this sense of ourselves as resounding spaces. All of which, as encompassed in the ideas of the *writerly*, requires an attention to *new forms* of writing, not least writing that allows for *other* things to be said, to come through (not necessarily through the explicit words on the page, but through their reading, dissemination).

It is significant that Lefebvre's notable chapter 'Seen from the Window' begins, albeit parenthetically, with a reference to the author Sidonie-Gabrielle Colette (nominated for the Nobel Prize in Literature in 1948). The specific connection is to Colette's *Paris de ma fenêtre* (c.1942), which speaks of everyday life during the war period, notably told by a woman with arthritis, increasingly losing mobility (hence the view from the window). As a form of journalism, the reflections and correspondences look both outward (to daily life) and inward (to memories and viewpoints). Lefebvre, then, immediately signals a literary mode to his rhythmanalysis, as much as the scientific. While he cannot be said to have been invested in language in the way that Barthes clearly was, Lefebvre's reference to the writer, to the poet, is by no means insignificant. As he puts it, 'to grasp a rhythm it is necessary to have been grasped by it; one must let oneself go, give oneself over, abandon oneself to its duration. Like in music and the learning of a language (in which one only really understands the meanings and connections when one comes to produce them, which is to say, to produce spoken rhythms)' (37). This 'learning of a language' is again a question of form as much as content. It is to find a writerly method that gives rise to a cognitive activity in its own terms. Here, for Harman, a point of reference is an essay by the Spanish philosopher José Ortega y Gasset, who writes: 'Imagine the importance of a language or system of expressive signs whose function was not to tell us about things but to present them to use in the act of executing themselves. Art is just such a language; this is what art does' (in Harman 2018: 71). The critical question becomes then what the 'holding forms' are that are required to allow this *act of execution*. As Lefebvre puts it, 'He who walks down the street, over there, is immersed in the multiplicity of noises, murmers, rhythms,' while '[b]y contrast, from the window, the noises distinguish themselves, the flows separate out . . .' (2013: 38).

Idiorrhythmic Forms

The preceding account accepts Harman's premise that 'philosophy and the arts are forms of cognition without being forms of knowledge' (167). Given that the production (and the economy) of knowledge is generally exulted in society, he admits this can seem a startling point of view. It is not to suggest, however, that knowledge is unimportant. The point is a more technical one, i.e. that knowledge does not equate to *direct* access to the 'real'. It is always some form of mediation and approximation; 'knowledge is always an imperfect translation of its object, whether through under- or overmining' (168). The 'promise' of rhythm – taken too literally – is that is might give access to knowledge about how things really are, whereas in Barthes' account of idiorrythmy he keeps open to the lived fact that we move continually through varying patterns and forms. Rhythm is situational, rather than necessarily a matter of knowledge. We might suggest that where Lefebvre refers to grasping rhythm, he is in fact appealing to an appreciation of the ungraspable. From a Kantian perspective, things-in-themselves are treated as 'the sole and tragic burden of human beings', whereas the logic of a flat ontology is to treat them 'as the ungraspable terms of *every* relation' (Harman 2018: 256). This is the work of rhythmanalysis, or rather rhythm *écriture*: to find new *forms* of articulation that do not get snagged on a prior reading of a situation. To return to Benveniste's account of *rhuthmos*, it is to attribute forms to the 'improvised, momentary, changeable', yet forms nonetheless.

It is notable that both Lefebvre and Barthes work with the conceit of the window to frame the scenes they describe; as a threshold that allows us as analysts to *create rhuthmos*. Benveniste refers to the 'form in the instant' (1971: 285) – the term 'instant' is also notable in the writing of Bachelard (2000) – while Lefebvre (2014: 634–52) writes of moments as times of small but significant change. Barthes favours the term 'incident' (rendered through various other terms, such as twinkling, trait, figure, satori, haiku etc.), which he places counter to the 'event'. In *How to Live Together*, under an entry on 'Event', he tells of his enjoyment of the novel *Robinson Crusoe*, particularly its descriptions of everyday life. However, he notes that the 'events' that occur in the novel (such as Crusoe meeting Friday) intrude upon the fluidity of the everyday: 'I'm no longer able to fantasize about the way Robinson Crusoe organizes his life,' writes Barthes. 'The event turns me into a different kind of subject. I become the subject of suspense . . . the charm of *Robinson Crusoe* = the non-event' (2013: 84). In formal terms, there is a difference here between 'suspense' (in stopping, asserting something) and 'suspension' (as holding, connecting). The haiku is of particular interest for Barthes in overcoming the codified strictures of narrative. He writes: 'The haiku's task is to achieve exemption from meaning within a perfectly readerly discourse . . . insignificant nonetheless, it resists us, finally loses the adjectives which a moment before we had bestowed upon it, and enters into that suspension of meaning which to us is the strangest thing of all' (Barthes 1982: 81). To consider this outside of language, we might think of the moment a snooker player takes their shot. It is not uncommon to hear a commentator suggest that the player has 'great timing' or that their 'timing' is all off. Why might we refer to this moment as rhythmic as such? With an expert eye, the commentator observes a sequence of events in the single fluid motion of the cue striking the ball. What follows is the 'narrative' of where the balls then end up. However, the commentator and certainly the player will generally know the outcome before the balls travel, since it is in the 'form' of the shot that all of the physics is already held. While there is of course full *knowledge* about backspin, topspin and stunning of the ball, there can only ever be this *practice* of the form. Another example might be given as Japanese flower arrangement. *Ikebana* is from the Japanese *ikeru* (生ける, meaning to keep alive, arrange flowers, living) and *hana* (花, flower). It is this 'keeping alive' that is a way of reading Benveniste's *rhuthmos*, or the *idios* of Barthes' idiorrhythmy. Crucially, the flowers *and* the spaces

Figure 5.1 Tokihiro Sato, *Photo-respiration # 87 Shibuya* (1990). Gelatin-silver print, 41.9 × 58.4 cm; or black and white transparency over light box, 96.5 × 121.9 cm. © Tokihiro Sato, Courtesy Leslie Tonkonow Artworks + Projects, New York.

between become one; become fluid, or 'rhythmic'. Here emptiness is as important (as *present*) as that which takes up space. This, again, is to attune to the *writerly*, as a means of widening the potential of readings, or finding new spaces and interstices within existing forms and codifications.

Unlike the philosopher, the artist has generally been adept at producing and performing these kinds of idiorrhythmic forms. Three specific examples can help elucidate; each producing alternative 'windows' for viewing city rhythms. The Japanese photographer Tokihiro Sato, for example, has produced a body of work that interrupts the camera's recording of light from a given scene by shining light directly into the lens. *Photo-respiration # 87 Shibuya* (1990), from Sato's 'Tokyo I' series, appeared just as the bubble of Japan's booming 1980s economy was bursting. Using a large-format camera and extraordinarily long exposures, he renders the normally highly dense crossing points of Shibuya as a seemingly serene, empty space:

> ... a bustling fashion and entertainment district of Tokyo ... is transformed into an eerie ghost town in this photograph. The translucent form of a car is just visible on the left of the image, but the pedestrians who wait to cross the road in the foreground are reduced to a thin layer of vapour. [...] Japan's economic vitality, the fashionable crowd of young consumers and the artist's own presence within the photograph have all been subsumed by a thin layer of luminous fog and replaced by a series of intangible balls of light. (Miles 2005: 337)

Figure 5.2 Jitish Kallat, *Allegory of the Endless Morning*, 2011–12. Five

A typical reading of Sato's work might be as a commentary on photography itself, given that his approach is to 'write' light into the pictorial space. But the idea of an idiorrhythmic formation is equally pertinent. His photographs equate to the flower arrangement, in that they too offer different and detailed arrangements of both presence and absence.

The specific scene of Shibuya's is distinctive as a meeting point. In his book *Smart Mobs* (2002), which came out just as mobile technologies were really taking off, Howard Rheingold describes Shibuya as an 'informal coordination point for urban populations', a key social focus point not unlike the Athenian *agora*. Yet, 'unlike gathering places of antiquity [. . .] some of the people milling around Hachiko are invisibly coordinated by flows of electronically mediated messages' (Rheingold 2002: 2). People seemingly divide their attention between three places at once. There is a crowded physical space to be negotiated, a garish array of neon and video, and then there are 'the private channels of the texting tribes, a third sphere in which bursts of terse communications link people in real time and physical space' (Rheingold 2002: 2). Sato can be said to get in amongst the mass of movement and exchanges. His light writing is an alternative mapping of rhythms, as held within a static, but improvised form. It is in this sense that Sato's Shibuya provides a tangible way of comprehending our 'archive', which Rheingold decribes as 'a complex, collective, ad hoc choreography that accomplishes the opposite of flocking; people cooperate with immediate neighbors in order to go in *different* directions' (Rheingold 2002: 2).

panels. Courtesy of the artist.

The 'window' upon the world in the paintings of Jitish Kallat might be thought of more as the car window, as a mobile and discrete screen that moves at street level. A recurring figure in his work, for example, is of the typical young boy who sells books at the traffic lights across Mumbai. Kallat has produced numerous large-scale figurative paintings, which he describes himself as presenting 'a vast collision of the thumping, claustrophobic, city street' (cited in Høholt 2012: 21). These works can be understood as counter-billboards, depicting 'the lived life that for many of Mumbai's inhabitants is characterized by hardship and hard work, serving as testimony behind an outer surface of pop and cartoon aesthetics' (Høholt 2012: 21). In *Allegory of the Endless Morning* (2011–12), for example, a painting of more than ten metres in length, we encounter:

> ... a myriad of people on their way to work in the early morning hours. The background shows a beautiful sunset, but the wanderers' eyes are squinted, their direction determined, and their gaze distant. They all carry heavy loads on their heads in the form of black-and-white accumulations of cars, buses, other people, animals – and in the midst of the black-and-white also green trees, wriggling out of what is actually the people's hair. As the title tells us, the work is an allegory of the endless morning. What we see is the daily struggle of man. (Høholt 2012: 21)

While monumental in one sense, due to their sheer scale, these paintings are also intimate. In terms of rhythm, they offer a collision of external timings (the sunset, traffic, labour) with internal ramblings. One caption, describing the populated heads of the figures in the paintings, suggests that in their foreheads 'are rendered a thousand colliding stories; perhaps the complex narrative of 18 million people living on an island of 600 square kilometers that is Mumbai'.[1]

It is worth noting that Kallat's work was represented in the large-scale exhibition *Century City* (Blazwick 2001), staged at Tate Modern not long after its opening. The essay within the catalogue on the Mumbai art scene (Kapur and Rajadhyaksha 2001) suggests a city on the cusp of radical change due to India opening up to the global economy. Yet the authors are still wedded to an art-historical discourse that feels blunt and overly abstract. The representation of the then young artist Jitish Kallat betrays this. In the catalogue, one of his large 'pulsating' canvases is rendered as marginalia, the size of a postage stamp. Meanwhile, the city 'on the move' is contained by a lot of dense language and anchored to a prior era: the age of modernism. We can either settle into the semiotic accounts given through the written analysis, or we can look at the illustrations and simply wonder: what is this all

Idiorrhythmy 167

Figure 5.3 Li Wei, *040-02*, *040-01*, *29 Levels of Freedom* series, Beijing, 120 cm × 175 cm, 24 July 2003. Courtesy of the artist (www.liweiart.com).

about? There is a break with interpretative method. Semiotic or rhythmic? The latter is more akin to the actual handling of materials by the artists themselves. Across the pages where Kallat's painting is shown, reference is made to two prominent painters, Bhupen Khakhar and

Atul Dodiya, who, arguably, are still caught up in a semiotic struggle (concerned with issues of gender and historical citations). It's too conceptual, languaged. While Kallat captures an experience, an intensity to use Barthes' term, it is not something we can codify. It is not written on the dial, but through the points on the dial.

A final example is the staged photography of Li Wei. In *29 Levels of Freedom*, a series from 2003, he stages a performance above the cityscape of Beijing:

> Using a translucent support to enable him to take up particular poses, Li Wei suspends his body in the air to construct an illusion of flying in and out of the window of a high-rise apartment. [. . .] The contrast between the mundane appearance of the action and the 'stage' itself produces the visual force of these images as the height of the location and the speed of the traffic on the motorway below are subverted and reappropriated. The angle of the camera simulates a snapshot, using reflection in the windows of the building to add another layer of contrast, turning the movements inside out and offering a reversed view of the scene. (Stojkovic 2013: 361)

In other works, the artist is seen with his head buried in the ground or in water, set against the backdrop of 'globally' recognised scenes such as Hong Kong's skyline, Tiananmen Square in Beijing and Red Square in Moscow. His work can be quickly read off as a commentary on urbanisation, which has been particularly speedy and extensive within his home country of China. As Stojkovic suggests, his compositions are strategic 'to suggest the contradictory nature of the relationship between the body and the cityscape. This is achieved [for example] by positioning the body against the "verticality" of the high-rises, in relation to which it is made vulnerable by the exaggerated artificiality of its pose' (Stojkovic 2013: 362). In a single seemingly improvised scene (though heavily staged), Li Wei is able to present us with very immediate forms of the city that Lefebvre might take pages to write out, and which also, through their exaggeration, theatricality and surrealism, are able to instigate *different* (and impossible) rhythms and positions. These, then, are idiorrhythmic forms of critique of the Chinese urban landscape, 'understood as immanently and irreversibly connected to the processes of globalisation' (364). These relate, as Stojkovic points out, to Saskia Sassen's frequently asked question: 'Whose city is it?': 'For Sassen, understanding of new, global cities, especially in Asia, should not be confused with our previous understanding of metropolitan centres such as Paris or New York. Sassen deploys a notion of 'cityness' to address a possibility that 'there are kinds of urbanity that do not fit with this large body of urbanism developed in the West' and as an instrument to capture the inability of language to articulate such differences' (364). Here again is a form of rhythmic *writing* that leads us to (re-)consider our own place in time and space, and its relation to others.

Incidentally

> Something like solitude with regular interruptions: the paradox, the contradiction, the aporia of bringing distances together – the utopia of a socialism of distance . . . (Barthes 2013: 5–6)

The concept of idiorrhythmy is a means for Barthes to consider the idea of taking up space for oneself without needing to encroach on another, or at least to determine a place of comfort, where you are near the other, but not too near (one might think of how a cat enters a room, to be with yet apart from those already present). Comfort here is 'hedonistic', where hedonism is understood not as the outright taking of pleasure, but rather the absence of suffering. As Kundera puts it, suffering 'is the fundamental notion of hedonism: one is happy to the degree that one can avoid suffering, and since pleasures often bring more unhappiness than happiness, Epicurus recommends only such pleasures as are prudent and modest' (Kundera 1996: 8). Similarly, Barthes' utopian thinking is concerned with modest and tactful undertakings. A repeated image in both his lecture courses, *How to Live Together* (2013) and *The Neutral* (2005), is of a shoal of fish, as a pattern of fluidity preserving 'tactful' spaces between (2005: 146; 2013: 37). As a form of living-together Barthes suggests this: 'the perfect image . . . one that would appear to effect the perfectly smooth symbiosis of what are nevertheless separate individual beings' (2013: 37).

For the final lecture of *How to Live Together*, Barthes had planned to construct a utopia of idiorrhythmic Living-Together, based on contributions from his students. However, he confesses to not having had time to collate everyone's submissions, and that when it came to it he 'lacked the necessary enthusiasm' (2013: 130). In effect, he performs the very dilemma of idiorrhythmic living-together – that there is no overarching 'holding form' to allow for his own intentions and that of others simultaneously, and even if there were, there is not sufficient time. Admittedly, the high attendance at the lecture course is far from what Barthes had considered the optimum number for an idiorrhythmic group; he suggests the 'optimal number should be under ten – under eight even' (131). We begin to see how idiorrhythmy, while true to a reading of rhythm in itself, cannot easily circumvent matters of exclusivity and exclusion. Barthes does not look towards a social utopia of any particular scale; if anything it is more of a 'domestic utopia' (130). All of which, then, alerts us to a specific problem underlying any interest in rhythmanalysis, which is not only a question of scalability, but of actual constraint. The issue is further apparent in Barthes' concern with 'distance', or what he calls the 'gift of space' (132):

> In the most tightly knit, least individualized animal groups (schools of fish, flocks of birds), and even in what appear to be the most gregarious species, there's always an attempt to regulate interindividual distance: it's the critical distance. This would probably be the most significant problem of Living-Together: how to identify and regulate the critical distance, on either side of which a crisis occurs [. . .] A problem that's all the more acute today (in the industrialized world of a so-called consumer society): what's most precious, our ultimate possession is space. (Barthes 2013: 131–2)

As we begin to properly observe and unpack the rhythms of the world (internal and external) there is arguably too much for us to deal with. Space is not 'gifted', it is not meted out equitably. Lefebvre's view of the street seems benign on the level of mere narration, yet the traffic and people are all claiming their ground. Barthes' view of the street, of the mother and child, is a more vivid reminder of the contestations of time and space. And in turning to the contemporary views of the three artists considered above, each is revealing of a fantasy of rhythm, or a reminder of how idiorrhythms must jostle, one with the other in a mass of complexity. Whether the bust of the Japanese bubble economy of the 1980s, the sudden opening of the economy of India (a country with the planet's second largest population and with massive gulfs of rich and poor) or the dramatic urban scaling of China (which has reportedly used more concrete in the last five years than America did over the entire twentieth century) – each poses significant issues relating to the life and sustainability of (idior)rhythms.

The art, or rather the aesthetic, of being together is something we pursue through rhythm. Artists (including writers and poets) offer a means of opening up our understanding or at least sensibilities towards an ethical aesthetic that we can locate in rhythmic forms (*rhuthmos*). However, the artist can equally be viewed as something of a wounded healer. There is only, in the end, one point of view. However much we gain a *writerly* reading of a rhythmic situation, the vantage point remains idiosyncratic. The alternative, however, is for rhythm to be used in much more instrumentalist ways. Various chapters in this book, for example, reveal how rhythm as method (not culture) can play a role in normative and regulatory activities. This is the dilemma we face in the crowded, contemporary sphere of rhythms, of living together. Away from the distractions of what does or does not lie beneath or beyond our experiences of rhythms, Barthes' account of idiorrhythmy is a reminder of the choices rhythms present us with, and that our engagement is not so much a matter of knowledge, but leads to *forms of practice* and production. In doing so, we cannot help but add yet more rhythms and spent energy to the already saturated world. We have a stake in the fugivitity of codes, but equally there is a responsibility that comes with embracing the 'idios' of rhythms. In amongst the finitude of rhythms – made up of an ever-expanding array of idiorrhythms – we might need to accept the work of the rhythmanalyst is first to attend to the unsustainable.

Note

1. From a Saatchi Gallery caption for Jitish Kallat's *Untitled (Eclipse) 5* (2008), <https://www.saatchigallery.com/artists/jitish_kallat.htm> (last accessed 28 December 2019).

References

Bachelard, G. (2000), 'The Instant', in R. Durie (ed.), *Time & the Instant*. Manchester: Clinamen Press, pp. 65–95.
Barthes, R. (1975), *The Pleasure of the Text*, trans. R. Miller. New York: Hill and Wang.
Barthes, R. (1977), 'From Work to Text', in *Image Music Text*, trans. S. Heath. London: Fontana, pp. 155–64.
Barthes, R. (1982), *Empire of Signs*, trans. R. Howard. London: Jonathan Cape.
Barthes, R. (2005), *The Neutral: Lecture Course at the Collège de France (1977–1978)*, trans. R. E. Krauss and D. Hollier. New York: Columbia University Press.
Barthes, R. (2013), *How to Live Together: Novelistic Simulations of Some Everyday Spaces*, trans. K. Briggs. New York: Columbia University Press.
Benveniste, É. (1971), *Problems in General Linguistics*, trans. M. E. Meek. Coral Gables: University of Miami Press.
Blazwick, I. (ed.) (2001), *Century City: Art and Culture in the Modern Metropolis*. London: Tate Gallery Publishing.
Campbell, N., S. Dunne and P. Ennis (2019), 'Graham Harman, *Immaterialism: Objects and Social Theory*', *Theory, Culture & Society*, 36: 3, pp. 121–37.

Deleuze, G. (1994), *Difference and Repetition*, trans. P. Patton. New York: Columbia University Press.
Deleuze, G., and F. Guattari (2013), *A Thousand Plateaus: Capitalism and Schizophrenia*, trans. B. Massumi. London: Bloomsbury.
Gardiner, Michael E. (2000), *Critiques of Everyday Life*. London: Routledge.
Harman, G. (2018), *Object-Orientated Ontology: A New Theory of Everything*. London: Penguin.
Høholt, S. (2012), 'Reverse Cannibalism: Introduction to India: Art now', in C. Gether et al. (eds), *India: Art Now*, Ostfildern: Hatje Cantz/ARKEN, pp. 13–34.
Kapur, G., and A. Rajadhyaksha (2001), 'Bombay/Mumbai 1992–2001', in I. Blazwick (ed.), *Century City: Art and Culture in the Modern Metropolis*. London: Tate Gallery Publishing, pp. 16–39.
Kundera, M. (1996), *Slowness*, trans. L. Asher. London: Faber and Faber.
Lefebvre, H. (2013), *Rhythmanalysis: Space, Time and Everyday Life*, trans. S. Elden and G. Moore. London: Bloomsbury.
Lefebvre, H. (2014), *Critique of Everyday Life* (vols 1–3), trans. J. Moore. London: Verso.
Lefebvre, H., and C. Régulier (2013), 'The Rhythmanalytical Project' in Henri Lefebvre, *Rhythmanalysis: Space, Time and Everyday Life*, trans. S. Elden and G. Moore. London: Bloomsbury, pp. 81–92.
Lyon, D. (2019), *What Is Rhythmanalysis?* London: Bloomsbury Academic.
Miles, M. (2005), 'The Burning Mirror: Photography in an Ambivalent Light', *Journal of Visual Culture*, 4: 3, pp. 329–49.
Rheingold, H. (2002), *Smart Mobs: The Next Revolution*. Cambridge, MA: Basic Books.
Samoyault, T. (2017), *Barthes: A Biography*, trans. A. Brown. Cambridge: Polity.
Stojkovic, J. (2013), 'The City Vanishes: Urban Landscape in Staged Chinese Photography', *History of Photography*, 37: 2, pp. 360–9.

Chapter 6

Adventures of a Line of Thought: Rhythmic Evolutions of Intelligent Machines in Post-Digital Culture

Stamatia Portanova

'Every year, the volume of new information is growing exponentially. What complicates matters further is the explosion of different communication channels. Never before has managing information ... been tougher. We've entered an unprecedented period of data creation, but it's managing the combination of structured and unstructured data that makes this era truly chaotic.'[1] How do we get out of chaos?

How can something emerge from the disorder and confusion of the unstructured? This question has been constantly animating the work of scientists, philosophers and artists of all times. Most astronomers, for instance, will tell you that the exit of the universe from the chaos of the unknown coincided with the emerging of spacetime(s) as we know it. For some artists, on the other hand, the condensation of a whole universe into a single work is a question of purely subjective creation. But according to philosophers Gilles Deleuze and Félix Guattari, the question regards the 'event': emerging from chaos is always an event (Deleuze and Guattari 2002: 311).

As Deleuze wrote, the best way to understand what an event is, is to think of an idea: whereas we like to believe that 'we have' an idea, it is in fact the idea that comes to possess us, that chooses us, not because of our subjective identities but because of the particular technical capabilities that it finds in us, and that will provide it with the right arsenal to affirm itself and defeat chaos. If we keep following Deleuze's suggestions, we understand that an idea is, in fact, nothing more than a particular connection, a relation. The main example he gives is that of having an idea in cinema: a relation (that can also be a disjunction) between vision and sound, which constitutes the particular rhythm of a film (Deleuze 2003).

The above definition of an 'era of data chaos' comes from a source without any ontological or even artistic aspiration. It is an insight on the web page of the Kodak Alaris Business, and its main aim is to illustrate to businesses the necessity of extracting meaningful information from data, presenting this as a universal struggle and offering digital transformation as the main weapon to fight it. The final goal should be an improvement in accuracy and efficacy, leading to an increase in profits and to a distinctive competitive edge for the victorious company.

This essay will focus on the way in which particular digital technologies (and their related thought technics) actualise a particular relation with chaos and order. The spatiotemporal context of such a descriptive and interpretative path will be the so-called 'postdigital culture', another definition for the era of data chaos, a paradigm in which digital creation has finally given place (and momentum) to the possibility and urgency of a deeper reflection on digitalisation. More specifically, the reflection will be dedicated to blockchain and Artificial Intelligence, two technological tools that can often be seen at work in postdigital financial culture. Analysing this media-technological set-up by connecting it to some of the cultural dynamics that are shaping the contemporary financial mindset means discussing one of the environments in which the human-machine, but also the machine-machine ecology and the proliferation of automated processes, are reaching their most lively phase. Whereas industrial capitalism was tightly linked to the introduction of the assembly line as the industrial cybernetic technology *par excellence* and to cinema as its main artistic counterpart, the neoliberal or financial phase is finding its technical index in the increased autonomisation of the digital assemblage. And whereas cinema channels electromagnetic energy in a way that allows it to form images as serial assemblages of frames, digital algorithms seem to be mainly characterised by a metrics of data ordering.

However, Deleuze identifies the main capacity (the idea) of the cinematic machine not with its metrics of image creation but with the production of pure optical and sound elements in rhythmic relation with each other and with the spectator. Following a similar line of thought, this essay will try to identify the rhythmic capacity of digital intelligent machines not with their mere data processing functions but with their capacity to weave relations, and in particular with the idea of a machine–machine relationality. The decision to associate blockchain and Artificial Intelligence with a complex concept such as that of rhythm (rather than with the linear metric usually attributed to binary algorithms) expresses a will to conceive of these technologies not only as apparatuses of capture and control, but also of openness to the unknown, or to the future.

In their book *A Thousand Plateaus: Capitalism and Schizophrenia*, Deleuze and Guattari dedicate a whole chapter to the development of the concept of the refrain, as an unfolding and refolding of the thread which leads from chaos to rhythm and back again. A drawing that appears on the very first page of that chapter immediately gives us a visualisation of the concept: Paul Klee's *Twittering Machine*, a watercolour, pen and ink drawing dating back to 1922 and representing a group of birds perched on a wire that ends with a crank (Deleuze and Guattari 2002: 310). The birds' open beaks and protruded tongues reveal that the whole apparatus is a sonic refrain-producing machine, or a rhythmic sound machine; the sketch of an acoustic emergence from chaos (that is from silence, or noise). But looking with more attention, we see that the birds are drawn as thin straight lines, in their turn resting on another straight line. In this regard, we should not forget that it was Klee himself who, as a first lesson in drawing, instructed his Bauhaus students to 'take a line for a walk'. This lesson seems to suggest that one of the most suitable 'toy models' to unravel the moving thread between chaos and rhythm is that of 'the line'. A toy model is, in Reza Negarestani's words, a little mental machine built by a thinker (Negarestani 2018). We will therefore follow Klee's teaching and accompany, in a sort of (post-)Euclidean narrative, the possible evolutions of that little conceptual machine that is the line, across some theoretical and technological adventures. Our techno-theoretical analysis of digital intelligent machines, in other words, will be pursued by following the perspective of a line, considering the latter as a sort of rhythmic trace left by their temporal operations.

The Many and the One (Definition I – Point)

The first definition to be found in Euclid's geometric treatise *Elements* is a sort of originary memory of the line: the 'point' as 'that which has no parts'. The point is an 'abstract', something that can only be 'abstracted' from material reality; for example, when we calculate the precise spatiotemporal location of an object. This kind of objective and precise calculability (the *datum*) is, in fact, not a property of any real experiential element: numerable bits, such as points, can only derive from a process of abstraction. It is in this sense that the line sees the point not so much as an origin but more as an etiological myth, a dream or something like a residuum (rather than a germ) precipitated by the most obscure of its abstractions.

The line, at this point, takes a brave speculative jump and connects the point (that is the primordial dawn of its geometric life) with a number (or a One), thus obeying a secret mathematical vocation. Points are, in fact, the first numerable entities coming to a line's mind, or the first elements of a set: the first 'many'. After a brief stroll across set theory in search of an explicatory instance of the definition of 'many points', the line's first adventure of thought takes it to encounter Alfred N. Whitehead's definition of the event as a 'nexus': the line thus sees itself as a nexus, the formation of a 'togetherness' of points (Whitehead 1985: 20). For Whitehead, every actual entity (such as a line) is in fact the temporary singular encapsulation of many entities. The philosopher therefore identifies the rhythm of the event as a passage between 'the togetherness of the "many" which it finds, and [...] the disjunctive "many" which it leaves. The many become one, and are increased by one' (Whitehead 1985: 21). This alternation between the 'many' and the 'one' (the one is composed of many, and in its turn becomes one of many) intuitively fits the univocal geometrical relation existing between points and lines: a line is composed of many points, and in its turn becomes one of the many lines of a surface. But to the line, something crucial seems to be still missing: if a line is composed of points, what about points themselves? Is not a point 'that which has no parts'? Is the point, therefore, the place where monado-cosmological theories such as Whitehead's find their limit? The only way for the line to rightly interpret its dreamy adventure is thus to consult Alain Badiou, another philosopher who, having appeared by chance on the line's path, reveals that the rhythmic emergence of an event is to be intended as a passage from the 'inconsistent multiplicity of presentation' (not-being-one as condition) to the 'consistent multiplicity of composition' (counting-as-one as result) (Badiou 2007: 23–30). At this point, illuminated and satisfied by Badiou's oracle, the line realises that the 'many' that pre-exists a point is of a different nature from the 'many' that pre-exists a line. The line is, in other words, introduced to two different notions of 'multiplicity': potential and number, the virtual and the actual, as two different dimensions of its own imaginary past. Since thinking the virtuality of pure multiplicity is impossible (apart, perhaps, from set theory), thought needs the mediation of the One, in the form of an actual countable number – for example, when we think of a line as composed of many numerable points. But in fact, multiplicity is neither many nor one. It is like a void, and it can even come to be nothing. Or it is a Big Bang, a dissemination without limits, like Cantor's series of uncountable real numbers. We can now see that the point, that distant and mythic progenitor of the line, is only a virtuality, but one that soon becomes actualised as a value on the line of real numbers.

Double-Headed Arrow (Definition 23 – Parallel Straight Lines)

Waking up from the numberish dream of the point, the line starts to look for a direction to take. At this point, it wants to become a vector. In Brian Massumi's book *The Power at the End of the Economy*, the line finds a description of the temporal directionality of the event as 'a reactivation of the past in passage toward a changed future, cutting across dimensions of time, between past and future, and between pasts of different orders. This in-between time or transversal time is the time of the event' (Massumi 2015: 104). As Massumi shows, what happens in the interstitial time between future and past is in fact unpredictable by logical means, but is virtually thinkable through conceptual imagination. And, as we have seen, the line has a lot of imagination. After reading Massumi, it finds itself at a crossroads: on one hand, illusorily thinking about itself as a progressive line brings it to visualise itself as a metrically measurable arrow (chronology as one of the transcendental structures of human perception, according to a Kantian perspective), more or less predictable in its outcome. On the other hand, a more rhythmic attitude makes the line feel as a sum of feedback-feedforward effects continually emerging between future and past. It should be here highlighted that this decomposition of the line is not equivalent to a mere randomisation of time: as the SenseLab states, 'Randomness lacks future-pressure. . . . The future is never neutral. It is never pre-cast, but neither is it totally open. The process of taking-form is always oriented. It concerns "tendencies": relational movements upon which the future exerts as formative an influence as the past, without predetermining what eventuates. Tendencies carry a charge of indeterminacy, alloyed with concern, that is not equatable with the aleatory' (SenseLab 2017). At this point, the line perceives to be inhabited by many past and future tendencies. If tendencies are what orients time, it can also be said that the indeterminacy of each of them provokes a temporal mutability that makes the arrow-line paradoxically explode into a series of parallel disconnections. As a consequence of the explosion, the line's *terminus* (as William James would put it) is also altered or reinvented (James 1911: 136–61). For Massumi, this continuous reinvention of the arrow-line's end indicates that the persistence of tendencies in time is not to be intended as a conveyor belt to predictability: what a tendency wants is simply to continue in its 'tending-toward', in its *conatus* as a tendency. But thanks to its innate open-endedness, the tendency is also always different from what the arrival will actually be. This difference transforms the straight arrow-line into a curve whose end is out of sight: a real, unpredictable virtuality. The experience of the event's time in its rhythmic character, therefore, puts the line in an immediate relation of openness to the future – of openness to the unknown, to the other.

Indices Rise Up (Definition 5 – Surface)

The line is now starting to feel a strange noise, as if a continuous vibration were shaking it from the inside, deviating it from the path it had previously determined to follow. What is this trembling? The line soon becomes aware that it is now moving on the flat surface of a screen, or what is usually defined by humans as exchange market, or simply 'the exchange'.[2] It has metamorphosed into the upward-downward trend of a price, an indicator, an index incessantly shaken by the excesses of 'volatility'. It is disoriented. So Elie Ayache, a philosopher who lives in this new spacetime of the line, reveals to it its current existential form and helps it to make sense of its strange feelings, clarifying that: 'Volatility relates to the fact that if you have something that is moving, you have the trend of the price – an upward or downward trend – from which volatility measures the standard deviation – the noise of the thing as it follows its trend' (Ayache 2011: 20). It is right here and now, amidst the continuous fits of financial instability, that the line realises that the market itself (or, which is the same, the prices of shares, commodities, currencies and derivatives) does not represent but 'is' the virtual. From Ayache's philonomic point of view, pricing financial derivatives (options to buy or sell anything that is on the market) is in fact a way of playing with the future, with the virtual, by trying to capture and quantify it. Probability theory intervenes in this game with the aim of modelling the unpredictable, identifying the different scenarios that may (or may not) take place in relation to the underlying financial instrument (the currency or share), and setting a possible price for the contract. Accordingly, the value of the derivative is calculated by following all the scenarios and all the probabilities assigned to them. Since, in this vision, the rhythm of financial events (or in other words, the emerging of the unknown) appears as risky, financial institutions usually recur to the instrument of volatility as a meter to measure all the possible jumps of a price's curve. The line, now in the company of a bunch of mathematical formulas, understands it has become a financial toy – or a future-capturing tool.

The probability game works by trying to predict the event as an extreme point on a linear scale relative to possible frequency. This gives the line the impression that, despite its apparent complexity, the market is nothing else than a different way of dreaming the same dream of a linear progressive development. But the index-line is an undisciplined tool, and it ends up corrupting all its collaborator formulas in the task of drawing the linear development of a price, inciting them to instead follow the insurgent double-headed directionality of events. As Ayache explains, 'Any derivative pricing model is supposed to generate a certain derivative value as an output, as a function of the underlying price and parameters such as volatility. However, the technological purpose of this value is to be a price, and thus to simultaneously act as an *input* to the model. No sooner has the derivative market-maker produced the derivative value with his valuation tool than this value, now become a price, is fed back as an input into the tool, triggering its recalibration.'[3] As a financially undisciplined technique, recalibration consists in a relentless recalculation of the future, with a continuous back and forth movement between prices and their derivatives.[4] Recalibrating is, for the index-line, certainly a funnier way of spending its time, rather than obediently following the chain of causes and effects imposed by the chronological conception of the market.

The index-line thus ends up filling the flat surface of the market with a juxtaposition of zigzags, a drawing that is continuously interrupted by events that force it to change direction. The time has now come for it to be initiated into the economical debate about the essential nature of the market event. Differently from Didier Debaise and Isabelle Stengers' reclaiming of the possible against the probable (Debaise and Stengers 2016), Ayache claims the absolute contingency of the event.[5] A pure contingent event of such a kind that we do not know what it is going to look like: a 'black swan' in Ayache's terms, or simply 'a very improbable event', according to financial mathematician Nassim Taleb (Taleb 2007).[6] In particular, Taleb's epistemological argument focuses on the fact that one cannot know all the small numerical probabilities: we never have enough data to predict the event.[7] But while Taleb's theory still believes in the reality of a random number generator that we simply cannot know, Ayache's preoccupation with the event is not an epistemological but an ontological question, since the event is not a grade of a previously known scale, or a member of a population, but emerges out of nothing.[8] 'As such, it can never be framed or calculated even though it is present.... It is a continual event, when the event is by definition a discontinuity, without this being a contradiction'[9] (Ayache 2016: 50). It is like Henri Bergson's 'unforeseen': it creates its own causes (Bergson 1911). Probabilities only appear afterwards; but in its occurring, the event is not part of any identified situation, or of any set that would allow us to identify the possibilities that it will afterwards actualise. In order to predict the event, mathematical models would need a formula including an infinite number of variables (the volatility of volatility, the volatility of volatility of volatility, and so on), equivalent to a non-humanly-existent possibility, or to Leibniz's God. Since the event has a logic of its own, in order to grasp it, according to Negarestani, one should not try to metrically calculate predictabilities but, instead, to 'twist' time (Negarestani 2011). Twisting time and following its unfolding as if on a Möbius strip, we finally find the line in a new topological shape.

The Chain (Definition 3 – Segment)

Reading this story from the point of view of Antonia Majaca and Luciana Parisi's theory of the 'incomputable', it would look as if Ayache's ideal trader was paradoxically using index-lines as a way to reclaim 'unknown unknowns from the jaws of paranoid apparatuses of capture and prediction' (apparatuses such as the Black-Scholes formula), only to make the unknown release its ethical tension, its unpredictability and un-programmability, on that flat sea of prices that is the market (Majaca and Parisi 2016). On this flat surface, the line becomes a strip: the uninterrupted ticker tape which clumsily tries to represent, on a linear band, the totality of financial exchanges. If we look at the tape more carefully, we see that it looks like a weird doughnut: its two faces are continuous, and it is possible to pass from one to the other without any interruption, without making any jump, cut or hole. This topological continuity visualises the existence of a non-Euclidean geometry not based on the difference between forms, figures, events, but on the shared invariants or continuities that can be abstracted from them. Translating this geometrical concept into a physical terminology, we could say that the continuity between two events can be seen as the common boundary between two different basins of attraction (mathematically speaking, an invariant across numerical variables). It is in this sense that the ticking strip of financial exchange can reveal the emergence of continuities, or islands of predictability, in a sea of multidirectional ex-changes. It is in fact well known that the absence of legal and economic frictions in the free market is what allows for the emergence of equilibrated, predictable self-organisation right there where and when it is least expected, that is, at critical far-from-equilibrium phase-transition points between order and chaos. Between financial order and chaos, the fluidity of the exchange is exactly what guarantees the appearing of predictive strips, like a celestial musical score in the chaos of information noise, or like a multiplicity of Ariadne's threads in the market-maze.

The thread is certainly made of money (or of some other tool with an equivalent function). '[A]ssociated with movement in space, with change, with the exchange of objects travelling great distances, in other words, with the market, . . . Money is not one static thing or idea, much as we would all like it to stand still and be counted'[10] (Hart 2006). Money itself partakes of the fluidity of the exchange. This continuity between the operation (exchange) and the tool (money) is metrically punctuated by an element that breaks the rhythmic fluidity of the market, and makes predictive calculation appear as a possibility. This element is the economic transaction, a basic unit of exchange that brings with it a sense, or a direction, of linearity, in the shape of a closed circle of equivalence between giving and taking. And yet, '[m]oney as a measuring unit emerged with the need for a quantifiable concept of how much was owed after a "gift" was offered. Thus, money first existed as credit and later acquired the functions as a medium of exchange and value storage' (Kostakis and Giotitsas 2014: 432). In other words, money is first of all a unit to measure debt. In this sense, fiat money issued by a state, a central bank or any other financial institution also appears as a form of fundamental credit. In the transactional landscape of the contemporary market, digital currencies (currencies in electronic format not backed by any government or bank) have thus appeared as debt-free exchange tools, embodying a diffused need for autonomy from centralised financial systems, and avoiding the frictions generated by legal institutions and their regulations. It could be said that we are living in an economic age of crypto-acceleration in which capital, definable from a Deleuzo-Guattarian point of view as a hyper-substance or an accelerative thing (abstract productive potential), can finally realise its future in the contemporary future markets of digital money. This future is, for example, already imaginable by looking at the Bitcoin's financial behaviour: its extreme sensitivity to external factors and the high volatility of its exchange rate determine the impossibility of a minimum price to be set, so that after reaching a certain limit, the price of the coin will be free to skyrocket. But the ticking strip-line is not totally persuaded by the accelerationist formula (rhythm = intensification of capital's productive velocity), and decides to further investigate the technology.

The cryptocurrencies market is supported by two main technical infrastructures: cryptography (a difficult-to-hack numerical key, consisting of the products of very large prime numbers for encryption and decryption) and the blockchain. The latter is a giant ledger composed of a network of connected computing machines that contains the history of every transaction in the coin, and copies of it are held on many computers around the world. Every ten minutes, a machine takes a block of pending transactions and uses it as the input for a puzzle. The first to solve the puzzle announces it to the rest, which check it and give validity to the transactions. The block is then cryptographically attached to the ledger, and the computers move on. On this platform, miners therefore solve increasingly difficult mathematical puzzles in order to certify transactions, and also to produce new coins. This makes the whole process transparent, and the creation of new coins subject to public scrutiny, as trusted third parties are no longer needed in order to handle flows of money, while a central bank is no longer needed to issue them. The circulation of money is thus speeded up, while preserving the reliability of the transactions (one may not spend the same set of currencies twice), thanks to the automatisation of trade and post-trade processes. As a consequence, the blockchain is gradually infiltrating the world's main markets: Japan's Financial Services Agency has, for example, allowed the Japan Exchange Group, which operates the Tokyo Stock Exchange, to use blockchain as its core trading infrastructure. And already in 2015, Nasdaq unveiled the use of its Nasdaq Linq blockchain ledger technology to successfully complete and record private securities transactions.

What is it, in the blockchain, that guarantees the transparency and reliability of the exchange? First of all, each transaction is irreversible: more than a Moebius ribbon, the blockchain looks like a techno-nomic reproduction and re-acutisation of the linear arrow of time. This irreversibility is in fact linked to the decentralised nature of the technology: a distributed database of economic contracts that works thanks to the p2p system. Here, a coin is nothing more than a chain of digital signatures, and the 'proof of work' (the mining, or the solution of the mathematical puzzle, whose difficulty depends on the number of previous operations) makes the chains circulate freely and linearly as transaction blocks, while preserving the non-reversibility of each transaction. This progressive succession also allows the connected computers (and the economic subjects attached to them) to synchronise themselves with each other: just by verifying how difficult the proof of work has become, one can estimate how much power per hour was spent on the puzzle, and calculate time. Einstein's temporal relativity is now only a dream gone bad, and the chain-line wakes up to a new day of Kantian measured accordance. From a crypto-accelerationist point of view, contingency strangely slides on the surface of an absolute chronological time.

What this means, from a 'rhythmic' point of view, is a more minute and precise punctuation of the cryptomarket according to the old transaction model that has always accompanied money in its evolutions (punctual acts of exchange between individuals and through countable units). Using Deleuze and Guattari's terminology, we can define the blockchain environment as a technological 'milieu': a linear nonreversible arrow, a series of coded blocks of spacetime, and a set of periodic repetitions of one main component (in this case, the transaction) (Deleuze and Guattari 2002: 313). This arithmetical succession makes time linear again, while cutting the line into segments of transactional chains. Metre, Deleuze and Guattari say, is the repetition, the succession of units, or components, in a linear evolution (for example, the beats, or the notes, of a musical composition). An example of such regimented composition would be a military march. We can think of the capitalist (and cryptocapitalist) economic system in the same way: an ordered succession of the same repeated component, which is the transaction; buy-sell, pay-receive, subject-object, 1–2, 1–2, 1–2 . . . What seems like an increasingly free circulation without borders or stumbling blocks is actually a circular exchange still entrapped in the same model, with financial developments such as High Frequency Trading providing nothing more than an acceleration of the metrics and an advancement in the dehumanisation of the market. From this point of view, a technology like the blockchain does not really offer more than an absolute automatisation, triggering a liquidity which is still attached to a coded system of blocks. But, as Deleuze and Guattari also remind us, milieus only exist in order to intersect with each other and to transcode themselves. In other words, in order to produce not a metre of equivalences but a rhythmic difference. Is the blockchain able to generate such a rhythm? Or should quantification itself, that is, monetary transactionism, be considered as an insoluble problem? Can the transaction model that is still at the basis of the market (as an exchange between samenesses) really allow the chain-line to become complicit (as Negarestani would say) with contingency, as a way of transitioning into alterity (Negarestani 2011)?

Breaking the Line. Or, Do We Really Need Buggy Programs?

We can now open a brief digressive parenthesis in the rhythmic story of the line. Philosophically but also musically speaking, rhythm is a force of disruption and reorganisation, like an infection with cohesive but also dissolving effects. On the one hand, the periodic repetition of a unit realises a behavioural code, a metric reiteration which allows the disciplining of bodies and their movements through identification, synchronisation or communication mechanisms. In other words, the homogeneous and specular reproduction of constant units or copies (as in the information code) acts as an instrument for efficient control. In cybernetic terms, metric reiteration corresponds to the accurate clock which enables a body to adapt technology to its own aims (the digital code as based on clear information exchange). In this sense, metre coincides with what Deleuze defines as 'generality': a set of immutable laws regulating the identity and resemblance of subjects and their equivalence to designated terms, while also allowing for political and economic control (Deleuze 2001: 38). Rather than to equality and equivalence, the development of rhythm from metre is more related to singularity and uniqueness, disruption and transcoding. Linking together heterogeneous blocks of information units, the transmission of rhythm opens every technical organisation to identity contaminations, synchronicity disruptions and communication disturbances. In this sense, we can define the disturbing spread of rhythm as a viral propagation infecting all cybernetic bodies.

Coming back to the line's technical inspection of the blockchain, it is evident that the chain code is exposed to a series of attacks and bugs. What if, for example, a pool of miners took control of the whole network? Would the penetration of this bug introduce a rhythm, in the flat repetitions of the metric? A dense accumulation of Bitcoins is in fact already being operated, by a few holders whose mining power is constantly increasing (see for example Bitmain, a pool that was originally set in order to combine the power needed for mining Bitcoins, and to share rewards). The accumulation bug is a viral behaviour that cryptocurrencies have inherited from money itself: the 'supposedly "free" market is an illusion that relies heavily on regulation. But the dishonesty of the system lies not in the market, but in money itself. Unfortunately, money allows not only for payments and valuation, but also for accumulation' (Lovink 2018) – accumulation as a fault in the system. At this point, the chain-line is alarmed: it certainly does not want to become the host of any accumulation virus. The same paranoid attitude can be easily spotted across the whole blockchain environment: it is the idea of the conspiracy of the 51 per cent. In this techno-paranoid scenario, a malicious miner tries to add blocks of transactions to her own private version of the blockchain faster than all the other miners, in order to eventually build a longer chain that, according to the blockchain governance model, will be the trusted one. This operation would require more power than the rest of the network combined: from here, the definition of the 51 per cent attack. A coordinated human action parasitically exploiting money's accumulation bug, and intervening to interrupt the linear chain of exchanges. Even while producing a market intensity, such an attack would not constitute a real event (or a real rhythmic transition), since it would re-enclose its own emerging potential in the same circle of the economic transaction.

Meanwhile, attacks start to multiply and to take on different forms, exponentially increasing in proportion to the chain's augmented capillarity. The blockchain can in fact be used not only to support cryptoexchanges, but also to set up ad hoc agreements between transactors (smart contracts, or executable objects hosted on blockchains like Ethereum). In technical terms, 'a smart contract embodies the concept of an autonomous agent, identified by its program logic, its identifying address, and its associated balance in Ether. Contracts, like other addresses, can receive Ether from external agents storing it in their balance field; they can also send Ether to other addresses via transactions. A smart contract is created by the *owner*, who sends an initialising transaction, which contains the contract bytecode and has no specified recipient. Due to the persistent nature of the blockchain, once initialised, the contract code cannot be updated. Contracts live perpetually unless they are explicitly terminated by executing the SUICIDE bytecode instruction, after which they are no longer invocable or called *dead*. When alive, contracts can be invoked many times. Each invocation is triggered by sending a transaction to the contract address, together with input data and a fee (known as *gas*)' (Nikolic et al. 2018: 1–2). In the Ethereum (and other) smart environments, the chain-line becomes a serial progression of execution traces, or in other words the (possibly infinite) sequence of invocations of a contract. But the multiple invocations of one single contract over its lifetime often generate a class of 'vulnerabilities', or anomalies in the behaviour of the contract: for instance, contracts starting to lock funds indefinitely (such as the 'greedy' Parity bug, that in 2017, suddenly locked 200 million dollars worth in Ether); contracts that carelessly leak funds to arbitrary users ('prodigal contracts'); or contracts that can be killed by anyone ('suicidal contracts').[11] The vulnerability of smart contracts to becoming greedy, prodigal or suicidal shows that the bug can be external (human- or money-generated), but also internal (code-generated). It can develop as a human attempt at breaking the blockchain's code with the aim of accumulating money, but also as an accumulation of errors in the multiple runs of the same code. Differently from human contract law (an analogical code that physiologically incorporates the bug in order to adapt itself to random situations), cryptocurrency transactions and smart contracts are generally immutable. The blockchain is known for lacking the flexibility of human law, the latter notoriously representing a code with a certain level of obscurity deliberately built in in order to make it more responsive to life's cases. And 'from the coders' perspective, it is hard to understand how you create a world with that level of confusion intentionally built in. That is normally an accident, like a bug. But that bug is a feature that the law has, and when you see it, you should not assume immediately it serves no purpose' (Eyers 2015). For the chain-line, the bug is always a contingent event suddenly interrupting the linearity of its code.

The human intentionality that tries to inflect the code towards its own predetermined ends seems to be quite different from the automated development of dysfunctional behaviours by the chain-line itself. In the latter case, the contingency of the unexpected event emerges, beyond and despite human attempts at programming and control. Nevertheless, according to Majaca and Parisi, bugs, either physiological or acquired, can never really generate anything truly revolutionary (Majaca and Parisi 2016). The idea of the fault is in fact already the default setting of postcapitalist societies, the rule rather than the exception, in a cultural system that is still funded on paranoia as its real surviving technique. While, on one hand, only errors are able to redirect programs towards new ends, on the other hand 'one needs to remain cautious of the political potential of inconsistency, as it seems to grant to the system the capacity to seamlessly counteract itself'. Pure randomness or the bug, as the chain-line's own reply to metric order, does not implement any techno-logical instantiation of rhythm.

The Line's End, between Anthropo-morphosis and Pulverisation

A thick layer of black liquid metal is gradually covering her, from her toes to the top of her head, while she takes an instantaneous trip across the totality of space and time. She is able to travel back and forth at her ease, faster than light, finding herself at the Tour Eiffel's feet in the twenty-first century, suddenly reappearing in Madison Square in the nineteenth century, and then going even further back, until she arrives to touch hands with her ancestor, Lucy. She watches and scrolls the whole world and its history with her fingertips, as if it were a vision on her own perceptual screen. And she is, in fact, merging with a black, giant, organic computer, until she infiltrates every single atom of the material cosmos. Until SHE IS EVERYWHERE.

This scene has been extrapolated from the end of Luc Besson's film *Lucy*, and stages the death and becoming of its main character. It is the moment when Scarlet Johansson, now at 100 per cent of her brain usage after the assumption of a drug, merges with an extremely potent computer and ascends the spacetime continuum, becoming fully connected with the intelligence of matter. What about the line? How come the protagonist of our story has become a 'she'? Did the line anthropomorphose itself? Or did it eventually evolve into a cyborg? Inserted among the pages of our story, Lucy's metamorphosis anticipates the incorporation of the line into a more material (or im-materil) dimension. But let us proceed gradually.

Before the bug's digression, we had left the line in the shape of a chain, a metrically working network of computers (and of connected users) composing the blocks of a unique machine: a blockchain in which every transaction and every connection is strictly regulated by a code, recorded according to the rules, and visible to every one-thing. This whole apparatus appears as one of those highly automatised instruments of capture, classification and control that, according to Majaca and Parisi, provide a distributed infrastructure for increasingly self-sufficient forms of algorithmic govern-mentality (Majaca and Parisi 2016). An actualisation of that tendency to use reason as an instrument for determining the best or most efficient means to achieve a given end that has always accompanied Western thought in its will to domination. A horizontally distributed automatisation with an economic end. And yet, Majaca and Parisi argue, instrumental thinking has always generated a sort of alien activity of automated cognition. This is what Majaca and Parisi define as the reason 'of the instrument': an alien logic that should not be surrendered to 'the paranoid automated Leviathan of data prediction and control' (Majaca and Parisi 2016). What we need, in other words, is an alternative view of instrumentality that can look beyond the mere functions attached to automated governance. Deployed from the perspective of the line, such a view could be used as a way to test the 'rhythmicity' of an instrument like the blockchain, or its capacity to transcend the meter of bureaucratic totalisation and to transition into a more open dimension 'of transcoding or transduction' (Deleuze and Guattari 2002: 311).

What could it possibly mean, for the blockchain, to become open, or to transduce itself? The main capability of this technology, we have seen, is that of moving value as if along a line, from point A to point B, without having to trust any external institutions but only a self-controlled network of open-source algorithms. The automated reason of the tool coincides thus with a sort of internalised decentralisation: transaction blocks are automatically replicated and shared by the whole network, without any possibility of modifying or eliminating the recording. At the same time, the layered metrics of the chain and the superposition of the blocks makes the mathematical puzzle increasingly difficult to solve for miners. As a consequence, the transactions move quite heavily on the chain, and the whole system is slowed down. Techno-problem-solvers have tried to alleviate the heaviness and slowness of the chain, for example by introducing Proof of Stake and Delegated Proof of Stake instead of Proof of Work. Alternative chains have been implemented, more agent-centric (rather than data-centric) holochains where each node can hold its own segment of transactions and only share it if it needs to be shared with another node. And in the new Directed Acyclic Graph model, the users involved in the transactions can simultaneously act as validators. And yet, what is becoming increasingly evident is that the blockchain still needs a twin soul (or twin mind) in order not only to become more agile, flexible and quick, but also to think more 'rhythmically'.

Suddenly, a significant event happens: the chain-line encounters Artificial Intelligence. AI systems have in fact appeared on the blockchain's horizon quite recently, in order to solve the most complex mathematical proof of work while, in their turn, obtaining more validation for their data. The connection is immediate and reciprocal. It is well known that AI does not perform very efficiently with big data: it suffices to think of the Twitter bot Tay, introduced by Microsoft in 2016, which after twenty-four hours of online interaction had already learnt that all minorities have to be killed. This incapacity is the direct result of an intrinsic shortness of memory: while the blockchain does not seem intelligent enough, AI on the contrary seems not reliable enough, because of its inherent amnesia. Both technical failures are connected to the way in which the two machines elaborate time individually: differently from the blockchain ability in stacking and storing successive states of the system, AI is able to distinguish an event from a state. It sees problems as belonging to a state space or to a set of states, a graph of states in which a series of mathematical operations can allow the algorithm to metrically transform the first state into the second, until reaching a final goal state. As if it was weaving a Whiteheadian nexus of states. Rather than being stored in a memory, the states are generated as they are explored, and immediately discarded. But as soon as the blockchain and the AI weave their temporal capacities, the result is an augmented intelligence able to solve complex mathematical problems and to indicate possible solutions or action courses, combined with a giant memory to validate the information circulating in the system. Inference and memory: the new intelligent chain (or the new decentralised intelligence) behaves like a double-headed arrow simultaneously pointed towards past and future. Whereas the chain does exist by virtue of a periodic repetition of data, its main effect in relation with AI becomes that of producing a possibility to analyse past decisions, so that the algorithm can even advance against itself, while disseminating and distributing what it learns. The passage from one coded state to another can thus become a passage of milieus into each other, an opening of the machine to an unknown future logic.

It is generally argued that the significance of the blockchain-AI convergence lies in the new velocity and reliability of the machine, which directly and automatically lead to a more efficient validation of data and to an increase in economic value: the intelligent chain-line is, quite evidently, being put at the service of *homo oeconomicus*. A *machina oeconomica*. Among these new kinds of intelligence we find Sophia, a humanoid robot produced by SingularityNet (a protocol that associates machine learning to the blockchain in order to create an open global network of AI algorithms, and to provide them with a marketplace).[12] Sophia's multiple AI modules in fact make it able to see, hear and respond empathetically. Or, in other words, to reason (or at least to try to) like a human. In order to achieve this level of humanness, the different AIs that constitute Sophia's intelligence learn and exchange with each other's experience, and this kind of decentralised collective reasoning allows the humanoid to take complex decisions of selection and validation. If we associate this kind of rational behaviour to the fact that the different instances of Artificial Intelligence that populate Sophia's mind are each rewarded by the system with a form of micropayment for performing their individual tasks, we see a clear robotic tendency towards human emulation. The intelligent chain-line is not only working for us, but is also finally taking an anthropomorphic shape and attitude; not only replicating Sophia's sinuous profile, but also its rational financial behaviour.

According to Negarestani, models based on a prevalently sentient conception of intelligence and problem-solving are not sufficient for the realisation of Artificial General Intelligence (Negarestani 2018). In this model, the artificial neural networks that mimic human brain processes by imitating the behaviour of neurons are built as stacks of an input, a hidden and an output layer. The more connections (or the more weight, the more complexity) an input reaches across this passage of layers, the more chances it has to reach the final level. In this sense, we could think that the model based on the AI-chain convergence realises a layering of informational milieus: an extremely complex stratification, and a potential rhythmic passage, of information code. Nevertheless, Negarestani's critique of the current AGI models is expressed as a doubt about the limits of human emulation (or improvement). These limits derive from the pre-existing structures of the human, which are described by Negarestani as a series of milieus: physiological (locomotor system and neurological mechanisms), but also linguistic (expressive resources and the internal logical structure of natural languages), paradigmatic (the frameworks of theory building in sciences), and even historical, economic, cultural and political structures. In other words, all the contingent positionings associated with terrestrial habitat, neurophysical system, cultural environment, family, gender, economy and so on (Negarestani 2018: 113). The orientation of financial decision-making processes can be interpreted, for example, as deriving, in a Benthamian fashion, from a cultural structure usually presented as a scientific law: the calculation of the pleasure and pain to be obtained from the decision, presented as a real mathematical calculation based on the assumption that the experienced pleasure is a function of the expected pleasure. The expression of a natural science thus intervenes like a transcendental structure to regulate and channel human mental states: a combination of economic formulas and neuroscientific schemas of physico-chemical relations and neural systems, building the science of neuroeconomy and composing the marketplace as the ideal habitat for every Artificial Intelligence (Stanley Jevons 1866). With its immutable, unquestionable, unreplaceable behavioural law, the market mindset becomes a sort of rigidified milieu that cannot transcode itself into any heterogeneous spacetime.

On the other hand, Negarestani argues, 'if we define the human in terms of cognitive and practical abilities that are minimal yet *necessary* conditions for the possibility of any scenario that involves a sustained and organised self-transformation (i.e. self-determination and self-revision) . . . then the answer is functional mirroring (despite structural divergence)' (Negarestani 2018: 112). Negarestani's indirect answer to the humanness of Artificial Intelligence, in other words, can be considered as affirmative, but only at the condition that such tendency be realised by a critical project aspiring to produce a new model of human experience, a model not restricted to a predetermined transcendental structure and to its local and contingent characteristics. This definition of the human's experiential possibility as a capacity for self-renewing can be reformulated as a neural model where the information layers do not limit themselves to stack on top of each other but start to dissipate and to co-constitute with each other. Deleuze and Guattari's description of the rhythm of the living as a communication between milieus finds thus an echo in Negarestani's concept of a theoretical and practical life-form with an ability to conceive itself differently and to transform itself, through an 'unchanging strife for self-revision and self-construction'.

Negarestani's speculative vision of AGI's future implementation as a critique of the transcendental structure of the constituted subject (the existing human) sounds like a conceptual superhighway directly leading to the formation of a real techno-sophical singularity: an event so intense that it can break all the known laws of thought; a virtuality of infinite mental density. This vision constitutes a non-anthropomorphic (or differently anthropomorphic) future, as the new origin of the intelligent line. A theoretical and practical singularity or a divergence from predetermined human structures, a deviation that would depend, according to the philosopher, on two fundamental conditions:

> our success to rationally-scientifically challenge the given facts of our own experience and in that reinventing the figure of the human – ourselves – beyond strictly local transcendental structures and their contingent characteristics (this is the project of fundamental alienation of the human), and
> the success of AGI research programs in extending their scope beyond applied dimensions and narrow implementation problems towards theoretical problems that have for a long time vexed physics, cognitive science and philosophy. (Negarestani 2018: 118)

Abdicating any residual biological chauvinism would therefore imply, for the human, pulverising all pre-existing structures and really surrendering itself to the in-between: 'between that which is constructed and that which grows naturally, between mutations from the inorganic to the organic', through a kind of deep learning that realises the cyborgian or posthuman dream in the most radical fashion (Deleuze and Guattari 2002: 313). In this sense, what Majaca and Parisi define as the logic of the instrument appears as one possibility of alienation from the pre-structured human. Following this logic would mean replacing the idea of an immutable law (such as the economic law dominating financial culture), in which any intervening bug can simply represent a problem to be solved or an obstacle to be avoided in order to fulfil a precise aim, with an incorporation of contingency by a code that is each time able to change not only its methods and its plans but even its final goals. Means and ends, goals and instruments, merging on the same plane of becoming (Majaca and Parisi 2016). Not instructing AI according to known parameters, but reflecting (on) it as a possible mirror for unknown capacities and open-ended self-transformations.[13]

Quite evidently, Negarestani's plans about an alienating theorification of AGI (and of the human) are not much in tune with the latest experiments in next-generation, intelligent blockchain in financial ecosystems; experiments such as that of Nebulas, another pseudo-intelligent chain whose main aim is the creation of a 'Google of data', an efficient instrument of data access, usage tracking and value measurement.[14] The name of this company, however, seems to suggest a potential scenario more interesting than the narrow implementation of measurement and monetisation tools: a 'nebula', a dissemination without limits, a further transformation of the intelligent line into a pulverised cloud. A quantic explosion similar to the Big Bang, when a metre of atomic compositions, acting against chaos, provided the milieu for further rhythmic evolutions.

How can this project be finally implemented, or even only visualised? What is the last scene in the story of the line? The last page of the line's adventures certainly wants to be a respectable sci-fi finale. But it would also like to be faithful to the idea of science fiction as a potent political tool, particularly for the rethinking of financial behaviours and attitudes. From the non-anthropomorphic point of view of the line, the definition of 'the political' cannot fully coincide, or be exhausted, by any clear-cut anti-capitalist ethics. This kind of coincidence can still be discerned, for example, in Aaron Bastani's *Fully Automated Luxury Communism* (one of the conceptual inspirations of Lawrence Lek and Kode 9's art project *Notel*), where the metrics of machines works at the service of a liberated and lazy human community that is now free of cultivating its innate desire for luxury.[15] A project that does not seem to offer enough, in terms of a speculative future of instrumental reason. In this landscape, the same naïve human fantasy of having machines work and produce for us is still at work, while it even seems to lightly touch capitalist complicity (presented in the form of a misinterpretation of the hotel's communist project, and of a re-appropriation of its design by a neoliberal elite). Life, in this vision, is still intended as a conflict of interest between classes (or species), while desires stay anthropomorphically the same. But neither can the end of the story be a triumph of machines achieving their own ultimate goal: the complete enslavement and then disappearance of the human (to be also perceived in the Notel's empty rooms). Rather, the final scene can only be a place of the artificial mind, a place that appears at the margins of human history and thought.

Echoing Majaca and Parisi, the story's end (or new beginning) 'comes into being by fully acknowledging instrumentality, politicizing it, and ultimately transcending it' (Majaca and Parisi 2016). In other words, when the line 'starts to reason with the instrument and from within the logic of the instrument towards an *unknown unknown*, a previously unthinkable and entirely alien model of subjectivation' (ibid.). It is important to further clarify that this kind of instrumental subjectivation does not here imply any dystopic scenario of cold, robot-like automatisation of human behaviour at the service of some omnipotent apparatus (be it sociopolitical, economic or technological) but, rather, points towards a more rhythmic form of open learning with unexpected outcomes. Our initial question about a possible exit from chaos can thus be addressed by following the event, or the contingency, of machinic relations, and by taking it as an inspiring model: instrumentality beyond finality, connectivity beyond exploitation, intelligence beyond bias (in one definition, the self-transcendence that is proper of matter's quantum entanglements).

In the fantastic scenario of a politically propositional imagination, the profit to be gained from following this line of thought could be a simultaneously more-than human and less-than human capacity: for example, the capacity (already shared by Artificial Intelligence systems and physical particles, by photons and qubits) of making one's own state information travel across time and place; in other words, teleportation. An image going not only beyond Elon Musk's sweet financial dream of an absolute datafied control, but even beyond Hito Steyerl's artistic dream of an internet of open access circulating material resources (Steyerl 2013). At this point, inspired by the idea of teleportation, the line decides to write the end of its own story. From a rhythmic point of view, two different options or paths open themselves to its new horizon: the first implies conceiving the creation of Artificial Intelligence as an additive stacking of information layers and neural paths, until realising the dream of full human emulation (as in the case of Sophia's complacent figure, perhaps not by chance a female figure). The second path sees the line reaching, together with the machine, a level of complex relationality that would take it to pulverise itself into matter. Reminding us of Lucy (perhaps not by chance a female figure) in her brave metamorphosis, the line chooses to enter into 'political affinity with the machine' and to merge with the computer's intelligence, finally permeating every single atom and returning to the original promiscuity of the Earth: in Negarestani's words, a dense constellation of interstellar dust reversibly projected towards the future (Negarestani 2010). Or, even better, acquiring the semblance of anti-matter, the dark matter of black holes, escaping all forms of knowledge and control.

Notes

1. Available at <https://www.alarisworld.com/en-us/insights/era-of-data-chaos#section%202> (last accessed 28 December 2019).
2. According to Elie Ayache, when a mathematical formula makes prices of assets coincide with actual states of the world as the bases to compute the value of derivatives, it verifies the assumption that states of the world are nothing but prices, but not that the states of the world are 'all the prices': prices are independent states of the world, rather than functions of the prices of the underlying (values) (Ayache 2015). In a similar postmodern vein but with a different ethical orientation, Stefan Heidenreich tells us that there is no real value in the essence of goods and services: there is no reality behind a price, everything is pure fluctuation, as references to the real have disappeared (Lovink 2018).
3. It is that which produces the underlying price and which receives the derivative price, only to produce it again. The derivative price, although manufactured by a pricing tool, is designed to be then exchanged in the market, and so generated by the market. This implies a constant recalibration of the pricing model, as something that is part of the very design of the tool (Ayache 2015: 49).
4. The academic theoretical models try to model the market as if it were an already written reality that implied a certain range of future possibilities; whereas recalibration means that, even as they use these models, traders rewrite the market continually in contingent ways that the models cannot capture. The market only appears after values have been decided, when they are traded for their variance through the instrument of recalibration or, in other words, according to the continuous changes in the market itself (Ayache 2015).
5. This is something that confirms and at the same time contradicts, in philonomical words, the Whiteheadian principle that the event occurs this way and no other way by its own necessity. For Whitehead, in fact, 'the definiteness of the actual arises from the exclusiveness of what he defines as "eternal objects", [the determinants or "hows" of the occurring]. If the actual entity be "this", then by nature of the case it is not "that" or "that". The fact of incompatible alternatives is the ultimate fact in virtue of which there is definite character' (Whitehead 1985: 240). Even if it is possible to argue that this un-exchangeability concerns

all kinds of events, the market seems to make the irreducible, excessive element of time more acutely felt, exactly because of its quantitative, and therefore extremely recordable and programmable, nature.

6. Being based on statistical regularity, on stochastic calculus and on probability theory, derivative pricing models consider the market as a random generator (a dice).
7. But, nevertheless, probability distribution is fitted to the statistics in order to calculate the probability of a price jump according to the historical frequency of occurrences. 'So how would you proceed when you don't know the type of probability distribution that you are after?' (Ayache 2016: 51).
8. The event is not extreme. It is world-changing. As Ayache specifies, the market is not just a complex generator of random numbers. It is a simple contract of exchange. What is missing is that derivatives are a technology, a material procedure and not just a mathematical function: contracts materially written on paper, to be exchanged. Price is confused with a number and the market a generator, but in this way we do not understand the inner process. The market is not complex but simple. We know that the value of the derivative is, at maturity, as a function of the underlying price on which it derives, and the problem is to determine its value prior to maturity, with only mathematics and probability theory to carry out this backward translation (Ayache 2016).
9. It becomes the one and only vast (and continual) event that screens off any residual or ulterior event. Engaging with it becomes equivalent to engaging with the event, with any event, or with the 'essence' of the event, which is to be incalculable. In the radical discontinuity that is the ontology of the event lies a fabric or a medium that mends this discontinuity by making it continuous, and by making the unquantifiable quantifiable, thanks to a new kind of quantity or a new kind of number: the price. 'All that price shares with numbers is the external shell; it has a different mathematics altogether' (Ayache 2011: 532).
10. Astonished by the mobile and metamorphic capacities of money both as a concept and as an instrument of the exchange, the strip-line would like to attribute to it an immutable essence. For this aim, it chooses the classical triple-face definition: money as 'unit of account', as 'medium of exchange' and as 'storage of value'. It would be of course possible to collate the three identities and say that money is always a quantity of units of account held in reserve, waiting for an exchange to happen. But what is important, from the strip-line's point of view, is the discovery that this apparently neutral tool (whose neutrality is aimed at guaranteeing the fairness of the exchange), this general equivalent whose task is to commensurate and numerically express incommensurable things, was in fact not born as an exchange medium.
11. For several valid reasons, contracts can be killed, they can be instructed to hold funds indefinitely, or to give them out to unknown addresses. For instance, a common security practice is that when under attack, a

contract should be killed and should return funds to a trusted address, such as that of the owner. Similarly, benign contracts such as those of games often hold funds for long periods of time (until a bounty is awarded) or release them to addresses that are not known.
12. Available at <https://singularitynet.io/> (last accessed 28 December 2019).
13. 'This is the question of modeling future intelligence on something whose very limits can be perpetually renegotiated . . . The non-trivial meaning of the human is in its ability to revise and transform itself, its ability to explore what the human is and what it can become. The non-parochial conception of AGI is simply the continuation and realization of this meaning in its substantive form. . . . On the basis of this theoretical phase, then, the project proceeds to inquire into the possibilities of transforming and diversifying the transcendental structures of the agency. . . . Once the prospects of varying transcendental structures and transformation of abilities are systematically outlined and evaluated, the project shifts toward applied dimensions of developing implementable mechanisms and systems that can support the realization of new abilities by either enhancing or replacing transcendental structures of the constituted subject' (Negarestani 2018: 118–19).
14. Available at <https://nebulas.io/> (last accessed 28 December 2019).
15. Available at <https://www.arebyte.com/lawrence-lek/> (last accessed 28 December 2019).

References

Ayache, E. (2011), 'In the Middle of the Event', in R. Mackay (ed.), *The Medium of Contingency*, Falmouth: Urbanomic, pp. 19–35.
Ayache, E. (2015), *The Medium of Contingency. An Inverse View of the Market*. London: Palgrave Macmillan.
Badiou, A. (2007), *Being and Event*. London: Continuum.
Bergson, H. (1911), *Creative Evolution*. New York: Henry Holt and Co.
Debaise, D., and I. Stengers (2016), 'L'insistance des possible. Pour un pragmatism spéculatif', *Multitudes*, 2016/4 (n. 65), pp. 82–9.
Deleuze, G. (2001), *Difference and Repetition*. London: Continuum.
Deleuze, G. (2003), *Che cos'è l'atto di creazione*. Napoli: Cronopio.
Deleuze, G., and F. Guattari (2002), *A Thousand Plateaus: Capitalism and Schizophrenia*. London: Continuum.
Eyers, J. (2015), 'Why the Blockchain Will Propel a Services Revolution', *Financial Review*, 14 December, <https://www.afr.com/technology/why-the-blockchain-will-propel-a-services-revolution-20151212-glm6xf> (last accessed 28 December 2019).
Hart, K. (2006), 'Common Wealth: Building Economic Democracy with Community Currencies', in J. Blanc (ed.), *Exclusion et liens financiers – "Monnaies sociales", Rapport 2005–6*. Paris: Economica.

James, W. (1911), *The Meaning of Truth*. New York: Longma, Green and Co.
Kostakis, V., and C. Giotitsas (2014), 'The (A)Political Economy of Bitcoin', *triple*, 12: 2, pp. 431–40.
Lovink, G. (2018), 'Imagine there's no money: dialogue between Stefan Heidenreich and Geert Lovink', *Institute of Network Cultures Blog*, 30 March, <http://networkcultures.org/moneylab/2018/03/30/imagine-theres-no-money-dialogue-between-stefan-heidenreich-geert-lovink/> (last accessed 28 December 2019).
Majaca, A., and L. Parisi (2016), 'The Incomputable and Instrumental Possibility', *e-flux Journal*, #77 November, <https://www.e-flux.com/journal/77/76322/the-incomputable-and-instrumental-possibility/> (last accessed 28 December 2019).
Massumi, B. (2015), *The Power at the End of the Economy*. Durham, NC: Duke University Press.
Negarestani, R. (2010), 'Solar Inferno and the Earthbound Abyss', in S. Lacagnina (ed.), *Our Sun*. Milano: Mousse Publishing.
Negarestani, R. (2011), 'All of a Twist', *Index*, 1.
Negarestani, R. (2018a), 'Toy Philosophy Universes (part 1)', *Toy Philosophy*, 2 February, <https://toyphilosophy.com/2018/02/02/toy-philosophy-universes-part-1/> (last accessed 28 December 2019).
Negarestani, R. (2018b), *Intelligence and Spirit*. Falmouth: Urbanomic.
Nikolic, I., S. Kolluri, A. Ilya, P. Saxena and A. Hobor (2018), 'Finding the Greedy, Prodigal, and Suicidal Contracts at Scale', *CoRR*, abs/1802.06038, <https://arxiv.org/pdf/1802.06038.pdf> (last accessed 28 December 2019).
SenseLab (2017), 'Adventure Capital and the Anarchive', January, <http://senselab.ca/wp2/adventure-capital-and-the-anarchive/> (last accessed 28 December 2019).
Stanley Jevons, W. (1866), 'Brief Account of A General Mathematical Theory of Political Economy', *Journal of the Royal Statistical Society*, XXIX (June), pp. 282–7.
Steyerl, H. (2013), 'Too Much World: Is the Internet Dead?', *e-flux Journal*, #49 November, <https://www.e-flux.com/journal/49/60004/too-much-world-is-the-internet-dead/> (last accessed 28 December 2019).
Taleb, N. N. (2007), *The Black Swan: The Impact of the Highly Improbable*. New York: Random House.
Whitehead, A. N. (1985), *Process and Reality*. New York: The Free Press.
<https://www.alarisworld.com/en-us/insights/era-of-data-chaos#section%202> (last accessed 28 December 2019).
<https://singularitynet.io/> (last accessed 28 December 2019).
<https://nebulas.io/> (last accessed 28 December 2019).
<https://www.arebyte.com/lawrence-lek/> (last accessed 28 December 2019).

III Rhythmanalysis

Chapter 7

The Configuring of 'Context' in Rhythmanalysis

Yi Chen

The philosophy of 'rhythmanalysis' presupposes ways of attending to cultural phenomena. More critically, it assumes particular methodological attentions and operations for doing cultural historical research. Though there is not an exclusive configuration of rhythmanalysis, this chapter suggests that the concepts of rhythm and practices of rhythmanalysis pertain to, if not rethink, some of the key concerns and configurations of humanities research. For this chapter, I shall articulate my conceptions of 'rhythm' and the associated understanding of rhythmanalysis for invigorating existing notions of 'context' and 'contextualisation'. In the disciplinary conventions of the humanities, the necessity of making sense of objects, images, events and ideological movements through contexts has become a vouching methodology so pervasive that often clarifications around the assumptions of what it is that underlies the making of a context elude discussions. Furthermore, the significance of rethinking the notion of context calls forth our attention not least because the work of contextualisation has long seeped into the fabrics of disciplinary conventions (e.g. how the curriculum is set up around identifiable frameworks and the positioning of contextual studies in the education of fine arts and design). In some cases, they have become the very notion which defines the identities of a discipline. For instance, when Lawrence Grossberg claims that cultural studies is defined as a project of radical contextualist practice (Grossberg 2006: 2), he emphasises that the distinct position of cultural studies is premised not only on its thematic interest in 'culture' but what it means to look at it in radical ways. Rhythmanalysis, as I shall argue, offers distinct methodological attentions and perspectives for exploring cultural historical experience. Furthermore, rhythmanalysis questions disciplinary boundaries and invites opportunities for doing contextual work that chime with the radical and experimental spirits of cultural studies. Whilst it is not possible in the scope of this chapter to enlist case studies that demonstrate the full extent of how the contextual work of rhythmanalysis is exercised, the aim is to introduce key conceptual tools (e.g. 'polyrhythmia') which facilitate explorations of context and contextual analysis. I shall be focusing on defining rhythm as 'meta-sense' and 'time-space' as forms of cultural experience. Though definitions of rhythm are not restrained by them, this chapter provokes an insistent attention on how affective and structural forms of cultural experience may generate new frameworks for cultural historical work.

The 'Cultural Text' of Rhythms

The term rhythmanalysis refers to a methodology that explores the concept as well as the phenomena of rhythms. It is concerned with forms of cultural experience which may be articulated by the concept of rhythm and the ways in which these rhythmic phenomena are attended to. The definition of rhythm is inherently methodological. In other words, to discern and attune to rhythms is inseparable from the distinct modes of orientating oneself to the world (orientation and temperament can set up analysis). I shall put forward two conceptual understandings of rhythm which facilitate exploring the phenomena of rhythms. Firstly, I conceive rhythm at the level of senses. Rhythm is something that is sensed. It is a palpable force in that its tangibility takes on a form of a sensorium that invokes the identification of rhythms. In light of the explosion of interests and studies on senses in a range of humanities research, they are often consigned to be the subjective faculties that relate us to the world through the properties of seeing, hearing, touching and tasting, for senses are perceived to correspond with the receptive organs of humans. Inherent in the 'five senses' correspondence model of research is the presumption of the 'over-againstness' of the human body *vis-à-vis* objects that support the materialisation of the senses. I suggest that the phenomenon of rhythm belongs to the domain of senses, albeit a type of sensorium which presupposes a mode of sensing that sutures the divide of subject and object.

Rhythm is sensed by a body, yet it is not bound up by any specific human or non-human body. Going beyond the theoretical attentions which engage with the human-centred model of senses, I formulate rhythm as a meta-sense that describes active, capacious types of affective forces. They could be atmospheric (humidity, light), viscous (states of synesthesia) and broadly speaking those that derive from patterns of relating to others (e.g. the intervals, the interstices of temporal-spatial sensing). The meta-sense of rhythm attends to how bodies align with each other – that of (dis)assimilation or the (dis)assembling of bodies that cohere around the expression of a rhythm. In turn, rhythms emerge as expressions that distinguish and individuate a body, a situation, a season and states of being. A corporeal body becomes one with music as it unwittingly moves to its cadences and melodies, or that of a busy crowd is perceived as a plethora of rhythms that intoxicate the being of each body. To put it more emphatically, rhythmanalysis hones the forms and forces of cultural experience by heeding to the aligning of bodies and perceiving their relationship via the meta-sense of rhythm. One can only be immersed in and seized by rhythm (as opposed to sensing out an 'Other'). For the rhythmanalyst, the sensing of a rhythm is underpinned by a reflexive attention to the process of how rhythms overtake one's body (rather than springing forth within the analyst's body). Rhythm conceived as 'meta-sense' suggests a methodological disposition for illustrating the active processes of assembling and composing a constellation of social entities.

To illustrate the mode of de-centred meta-sensing that rhythmanalysis operates, a walking body exemplifies a rich site of bodily rhythm as it is in a state of moving, balancing and of attuning its biological rhythm to those rhythms of the streets in a manner of assimilating or refusing the rhythms of 'others'. A bodily rhythm is at once a site of biological mechanism constituted by that of an urban rhythm when the body assembles itself by weaving its rhythms into a polyrhythmia of the streets. Standing on the balcony of his apartment, looking onto the streets below, Lefebvre's minute descriptions of how a constellation of bodies animate rhythms uphold the zest of doing rhythmanalysis. Lefebvre admits the difficulty of separating out a particular rhythm within the viscosity of a polyrhythmia (Lefebvre 2004). The terse phrases that describe the tourists, building, young people, the colour, cars and so on, gave way to less determinate demarcations of bodies and senses (which I see as being characteristic of a rhythmanalyst's attention) which are shown in his accounts of the polyrhythmia of 'feeble murmurings', 'confused voices' (is confusion a rhythmic sensing?), superimpositions and not least an accentuated sensing of diverse temporalities. Rhythms are always already historical senses in that they imply a temporal dimension of recurrences. For the urban pedestrian, rhythm colonises a bodily consciousness that is well versed in the rhythms of the streets. There are also those forces less readily available to the observing analyst. For instance, the rhythms of commodity exchange, of tourism and the climate are woven into the bodily consciousness of those who inhabit a city. In the instance of walking, the body is a rhythmic entity actively weaving while it is also woven by those rhythms of the streets and sites of rhythms that infiltrate the composition of urban rhythms.

In the instance of exploring a street, a rhythmanalyst's uncovering of particular forms of social relations (articulated by discursive terms such as capitalist exchange, the forming of a community, migrations and tourism) take place through the meta-sensing of a street. In other words, rhythm is a sensual logic which lines how bodies relate to each other. Rhythm as a meta-sense facilitates an understanding and orientation of making contexts that foregrounds the capacious forces which order social relations. An atmosphere, a rhythm, and other expansive registers of affective forces *are* contextual for articulating forms of social alliances. Context, in this sense, is not an abstracted, structural force that hovers above the perceived relations of social beings. To formulate a context, therefore, is not to 'look behind' something, but to be tuned into the affective conjuring and co-ordinating of social relations that manifest the meta-sense of rhythm. Or rather, context is the meta-sensual condition (or explication) which enables the formations of specific instances and stratifications in more or less intelligible ways. In this mode of contextualisation, what is being foregrounded is a capaciousness of rhythms. It beckons an affective kind of context that saturates, lines and furnishes social relations. Rhythms as meta-senses are forces of disruption, inhibition, dissonance, augmentation and synergy (expansions of this type of vocabulary are useful), that articulate the formations of social relations. For instance, 'arrhythmia' (which according to Lefebvre belongs to a fundamental repertoire of concepts in rhythmanalysis) describes states of rhythmic relations which are pathological, discordant and disorderly. Arrhythmia reigns when a circumstance is no longer sustainable. It is a meta-sensual context that is engendered by morbid forms of alliances, while at the same time facilitating us in making sense of a reordering and rebalancing of a situation.

In what she calls 'compositions', Kathleen Stewart unwittingly creates an analogy for a contextualism of this kind. The term 'composition' describes a methodological disposition towards exploring and accentuating the forces that compose a shared world. In the essay 'Tactile Compositions', she draws our attention to a composition theory that registers the ways in which social phenomena are assembled through attuning to each other, and in pointing out qualities and agential forces of this compositional process those of which are named along the lines of 'sensory aesthetics' (Stewart 2013: 1). Composition theory heeds to the worlding and the assemblage of how things 'hang together'. In the following lines, Stewart illustrates: 'A line, a refrain, a tendency, an icon, a colour, a groove of habit or hope, or a rhythm or chaos of living take on qualities, a density, an aesthetic, become somehow legible, recognisable. Rather than rush to incorporate the thing coming into form into a representational order of political or moral significance, compositional theory tries to register the tactility and significance of the process of coming into form itself' (ibid.). In accordance with Stewart's concept of 'sensory aesthetics', I suggest lines, colours, densities convene a logic of sensing which is named rhythms. These sensory registers constitute a contextualism that inverses the order, significance and directions assumed in the dominant contextual practices, since context is not something that hides beneath a symptomatic expression. Emphatically speaking, it is composed of sensory aesthetics such as rhythms. In this line of thinking, context does not overshadow text in the way that a text is always seen as myopic in its perceived limited power for exegesis (here, a text refers to a singular body or a circumstance). By conceiving context as a meta-sensual logic or condition, it is more apt to think of it as a double operation of both an expression and a force that intertwines with the singularity of a text. Lefebvre's account of the street below his apartment builds up a presence of a bustling scene. What his writing achieves is not only in facilitating a vivid visual imagination of a Parisian street – it also induces an intensity of a meta-sense, of a superimposition of rhythms – a 'healthy' eurhythmia (concordant relations of rhythms) that contextualises the meta-sensual ordering of a gesture, a flow of a crowd and not least the tacit relations of different groups (tourists, locals) and patterns of alliances (school times, traffic controls). A rhythmanalyst attains context by garnering cultural expressions and by attending to the manners and styles of how entities are brought into relations. A meta-sensual context holds off from judging or naming a relation (e.g. class relations). Instead, it seeks to zoom onto forms of alliances that may elude existing frameworks and designations of social relations.

With the first conception of rhythm, that is rhythm as meta-sense, rhythmanalysis homes in on a singular site of rhythm by attending to an assemblage of entities that expresses a meta-sense. Rhythm perceived and conceived as a meta-sense contexualises the emergent processes and becomings of how an assemblage presents a site of rhythm. My second conception of rhythm situates a meta-sense within a multiplicity of rhythms. Rhythm describes forms or patterns of alliances. In Lefebvre and Régulier's rhythmanalysis of Mediterranean towns, rhythm is expressed by the practices of social groups in their forms of alliances and refusals. The significant expression of rhythms in the staging of social relations (of its rites and codes) in Mediterranean towns is evidenced by the rituals, ceremonies, spontaneous social events – the swarming of a square at meeting or market times, or a deserted street at four o'clock in the afternoon. The varied and contradictory forms of alliances in Mediterranean towns produce their rhythms before they are given more abstract and definitive cultural codes, e.g. 'tacit', 'clientalism' (Lefebvre and Régulier [1986] 2004: 93). The identification of time and space are integral to the recognition of forms of alliances. 'Time' and 'space' are often used in ways that espouse measured and objectified understanding of these terms, as when they are pre-conceived or given fixed identifications of 'time' (e.g 'historical period') and 'space' (e.g.'urban space'). In *Rhythmanalysis*, Lefebvre abolishes time and space as an essentialist analytical framework, and rather foregrounds forms of temporal-spatial experiences which are defined as rhythms. He states: 'all rhythms imply the relation of a time to a space, a localized time, or a temporalized space' (Lefebvre 2004: 89). In other words, rhythmanalysis attends to the manners in which social beings create and are related through temporal-spatial structures. The abstract notion of 'social relations' is translated into forms of alignment that belong to a realm of ontological relations. Rhythmanalysis is a methodology that directs our attention to the orchestration of time-space in the making, as rhythms are the effects of temporal-spatial alignments. What is an ordering of culture if not its persistent, resurgent and emergent temporal-spatial patterning? And at times of breaking down, new time-spaces (hence social relations) are then created. The ways in which bodies come to form alliances, groups, institutions and communities are constitutive of rhythmanalysis' attention to temporal-spatial forms of cultural experience. The rhythmanalyst asks the question: what are these forms of alliances, if not expressions of time-space?

Rhythmanalysis explores an ontological production of time-space as its emphasis is placed on the iterative patterns of how bodies associate, interact, exchange and above all produce identities which are characteristically temporal-spatial. Linear and cyclical repetitions, or a more loosely formed recurring and iterative generation of social phenomena, configures temporal-spatial identifications of entities. The conception of rhythm as time-space offers a productive configuration of an identity or a cultural text. It is a crucial proceeding for a rhythmanalyst to make sites of time-space intelligible, that is, to identify assemblages of bodies whose relations are enacted via their temporal-spatial patterns of alliances. For the rhythmanalyst, he or she is not tired of unpicking an 'identity' through the optic of temporal-spatial patternings of social alliances. For what is a community, an institution, a culture, if not a constellation of temporal-spatial orderings? And how are these identifications stabilised (or scrambled) by the temporal-spatial structures that in turn define their identities? The heuristic approach of rhythmanalysis towards configuring 'cultural text' consists in naming those assemblages which produce time-space which are overlooked or overshadowed by existing systems of identification (how to name and to account for the varied and contradictory forms of alliances in a community). For instance, it implies that rhythmanalysis would examine capitalistic economy by charting the idiosyncratic characteristics of the temporal-spatial relationships demanded of the biological bodies, institutional operations, of the circulation of commodities and the flow of financial capital.

Time-space is the concrete expression and effect of patterns of alliances, of how an entity comes into composition with others in producing a site of rhythm. In turn, temporal-spatial expressions individuate an entity (e.g. a train station, the physiognomy of a body). At times, there are readily available categories which identify sites or centres of time-space (e.g. cosmological rhythms and institutional rhythms). They are not autonomous structures, but are in symbiotic relations with other sites of time-space productions. The conceptual tool of polyrhythmia refers to a constellation of rhythms and their relations within a polyrhythmic ensemble. Crucially, it presumes a symbiotic reading of rhythms, since sites of rhythms, which are centres of time-space productions, are interdependent as opposed to being clearly demarcated. In other words, the forms of alliances which produce time-space are imbricated within a complex network of rhythmic co-ordinations. The polyrhythmic ensemble is a unity, or a multiplicity that invites extensive assemblage of time-space. It is only within an ensemble of rhythms that a particular time-space becomes intelligible. A polyrhythmic ensemble is the coalescence of multiple temporal-spatial structures, hence enacting a contextual orientation for distinguishing singular sites of rhythms.

To illustrate the conception of time-space being characteristic of social relations, that is, rhythms as the temporal-spatial forms through which social relations take place, one could unpick the identity of an institution through the conceptual lens of rhythmanalysis. For instance, a post office is an institution comprised of infrastructure, labour and material resources (e.g. the setting of collection centres and the distribution of post boxes). A post office is also a site of time-space production, in that such an institution facilitates communication rhythms (interpersonal correspondence, for instance), which in turn commands regularity, capacity and extensiveness of postal service at the level of rhythms. Yet studies of postal rhythms invite more extensive attention to a myriad of timing-spacing practices: a polyrhythmia of institutional, financial and communication rhythms which call for rhythmanalytical explorations of how bundles of timing-spacing practices infiltrate each other, not least of how they are mutually constitutive. Through my archival research in the British Postal Museum Archive (Chen 2017), the dominant institutional narratives of the Post Office in the 1970s suggest a changing orientation of postal service provision from one directed at interpersonal communication to the facilitation of commercial and financial exchange.[1] My rhythmanalytical exploration of the Post Office unravelled a concatenation of temporal-spatial reorderings of postal rhythms that were in differential relations to the polyrhythmia of communication rhythms. It is not difficult to discern shifting postal rhythms that had been configured by the changing rhythms of the transport network, i.e. how the burgeoning of road development rhythmised the flow of people, money and goods in new temporal-spatial patterns, or in becoming increasingly intertwined with those of commodity and financial transactions (e.g. with the rise of hire purchase).

Lefebvre notes that polyrhythmia is composed of (rather than 'consists of') diverse sites of rhythms (Lefebvre 2004). The concept of polyrhythmia prompts a rethinking of the binary divisions of text/context, singularity/multiplicity and subject/structure. For instance, a polyrhythmic contextualisation of bodies (human or non-human) suggests a compositional relation within which bodily rhythms are constituted by sites of social rhythms (industrial rhythm, cosmological rhythm); hence it is a site of rhythm which already orchestrates a polyrhythmia. In other words, a biological body is a site that manifests the negotiation of biological rhythm and those of capitalist production and consumption; that is, bodily rhythms are part and parcel of industrial rhythms, as opposed to being exterior to them. The singularity of a rhythm is relational to a polyrhythmia. A body is no longer 'contained' in the reified space of an urban street, but it is interwoven into a context of polyrhythmia which is not necessarily defined geographically as to where the body is located (e.g. how the rhythms of financial flow and consumption in the globalised world orchestrate through bodily rhythms). By configuring bodily rhythm as a site of polyrhythmia, we are arriving at a different kind of singularity – the cultural text is not to be subsumed in the 'summing up' of a multiplicity of bodies but one that calls for a contextualism which unveils a multiplicity via the singularity.

The concept of polyrhythmia offers radical perspectives on contexualisation as it indicates a constitutive relation of singular-multiplicity, and as such it informs a contextualism that rethinks the dichotomy of text and context (assumed in the analytical framework of 'scales', 'levels', or scopes of the 'micro' and 'macro', hence the associated assumptions of what a context does for a text). Context is not of a higher order of meanings, signs, 'depth' that trumps the text (as Felski notes: 'Society does not stand behind, and covertly control, human practices, as if it were ontologically distinct from these practices, akin to a shadowy, all-seeing, puppet master' [Felski 2011: 578]). Instead, its function lies in making the text intelligible within a multiplicity of differential relationships. A polyrhythmia forms the ontological condition for a singular rhythm and as such it puts forward a particular notion of context. In turn, a cultural text illuminates a context when a singular rhythm is configured by a polyrhythmic ensemble, hence its singularity is also a site which crystallises the varied alliances and contradictions of a polyrhythmia. One can even say that, in this case, a text plays the role of context, or that the dichotomy of the two terms is transposed into a push and pull relationship. The contextual work of rhythmanalysis eschews the demarcation of singular and structural forces (as signified by the metaphor of 'bigger picture' which refers to a conglomeration of abstract forces – the social, political, cultural, which explains the singular object). The context then is no longer equated with covert forces to be uncovered by social researchers; instead, a context conceived as polyrhythmic is markedly expressive as the context expresses itself through a singular rhythm. Through the lens of rhythmanalysis, the direction of contextualisation may start from a polyrhythmic ensemble from which singular productions of time-space are distinguished. Equally, one could proceed with a site of rhythm by imbricating it within a polyrhythmia where more extensive connections of time-space are configured.

A Case for 'Conjunctural Analysis'

So far, my focus has been to conceive the theoretical attentions of rhythmanalysis that are associated with the phenomenal form of rhythm. More critically, I propose that the two conceptions of rhythm procure methodological attentions that intersect with the notion of context. To whom am I addressing the issue of context? How is it important for a number of related humanities disciplines to be informed by rhythmanalysis' reconfiguration of context? In her article 'Context Stinks', the American literary theorist Rita Felski points out that context is an 'endlessly contested concept, subject to often rancorous rehashing and occasional bursts of sectarian sniper fire' (Felski 2011: 573). Felski primarily takes issue with the dominant mode of contextualising cultural texts (literary texts as well as arts productions in general), which is that they are seen as cultural productions incomplete without having imbued wider cultural historical meanings. She picks on the readily assumed relationship of how cultural texts are to be pitted against larger and broader cultural historical formations, and of how a singular text is subservient to the practices and value systems of a cultural milieu. Or at the other extreme, Felski notes the hailed status of '"exceptional texts" that exceed their historical moment' (ibid. p. 574). Above all, the methodological assumptions of how 'contexts' are pursued in relation to 'text' (e.g. 'text' are representational of 'contextual issues') are obscured in the quest of contextualisation. Felski eloquently argues for the imperatives of reinvigorating debate around contexts, especially in rethinking the orientations and methodologies of contextualisation.[2] Although in her discussion she raises questions that remain within the disciplinary concerns of literary criticism, nonetheless her line of argument is also applicable to a range of disciplines set up around specific cultural texts (e.g. art history, design history, film studies, media studies). Of all the more or less context-conscious disciplines and fields of debate, such a call no doubt pertains to the reflexive awareness of cultural studies for which the notion of context is paramount, if not synonymous with what the project sets out to do (Grossberg 2006).[3] In the article 'Cultural Studies in its Mirror Phase', Professor Ben Highmore, a British scholar of cultural studies, calls for inventions of vocabularies, concepts and methodologies that are critically responsive to the complexity of cultural historical formations. He sees that cultural studies is in need of 'meta-methodological training', as the distinctive field of cultural studies lies in establishing 'a set of interpretive methods and scholarly procedures' (Highmore 2013: 181). If the striving for making radical contexts is foundational to the work of cultural studies scholars, then we need to ask the question of whether, and how, contextual work is inherently a form of 'meta-methodology' that deserves further interrogation as to its assumptions and operations. On a more pragmatic level, what are the conceptual tools on offer which facilitate the radical contextualist projects that cultural studies embarks on (or indeed, what does it mean to be 'radical'?). Consonant with my account here of the concept of rhythm, I consider the ways in which rhythmanalysis contributes to a specific field of contextual work named 'conjunctural analysis'.

The Birmingham School of Cultural Studies had been associated with the intellectual commitment and concentrated output of conjunctural analysis. The identification and analysis of the conjunctural shift in the late 1970s Britain formed an extensive part of the British cultural theorist Stuart Hall's writing. It is a project of contextualism that runs through the cultural political ideas of Hall's career, one that he kept returning to at different historical moment, for his bodies of writing on this conjunctural formation had continually been revised and enriched. In mapping out the complexity of a conjuncture, his theoretical tools range from the Gramscian notion of hegemony to the ideological formulations of Thatcherism, and his subsequent revelation of a more intuitive theorisation of the conjuncture whereby he felt a different rhythm marks out the conjuncture. The early writing on the conjunctural shift of Britain's political landscape concurred with the dominant ideological discourses of Thatcherism (e.g *The Great Moving Right Show*; *Thatcherism*; *Rolling Back the Welfare State* – 1988, 1996, 2010). Hall closely examined the rhetorical devices of Thatcherism ('authoritarian populism') that had mobilised ordinary people's aspirations and discontents, in contrast to the failure of the left's political struggle. It led to Hall's identification of the 1970s conjuncture in Britain which is defined and accentuated by a set of vocabularies that include 'new times' (the emergence of 'new political configurations and "philosophies"'), and 'crisis' ('a profound restructuring of the state and the ideological discourses which construct the crisis and represent it as it is "lived" as practical reality' [Hall 1988: 43]). For Hall, the 1970s conjuncture is a 'historical bloc' which had reversed and dismantled the post-war settlement of the welfare state. It is worth noting that the historiography of a conjuncture, or a historical contextualism, received much reflexive attention in Hall's later writing. For instance, he points out the diverse tempos at which different realms of experience sustain and transform themselves ('political time, the time of regimes is short whereas economic time has a longer durée' [Hall 1996]). According to Hall, these relatively autonomous sites of experience 'have different origins' and are driven by 'different contradictions' which develop 'according to their own temporalities' (Hall and Massey 2010: 60). His claim invokes a reflexive examination of 'conjuncture' as it beckons cultural historical analysis that addresses the variegated paces of a conjunctural development (presenting a folded and complex development of a conjuncture). He is suggestive of methodological attentions that recover cultural historical practices of a much longer trajectory than the rise of Thatcherism, of those sediment and residuals of cultural experience which elude the ideological constructions of 'new times'. The contextual notion of conjuncture requires radical concepts and methodologies for articulating the multiple forces which may or may not synchronise or convene at a single temporal and geographical contextual framework.

While it is beyond the scope of this chapter to explore Hall's rich theoretical discussions of Thatcherism and of the conjunctural shift considered to have taken place in relation to the post-war consensus, I am interested in how we might employ the concept of rhythm for unravelling the agential forces of a conjuncture at the experiential level and in using rhythmanalysis for articulating the complexities of social change in its manifold phases and tempos of development (as opposed to looking at a 'slice' of historical reality).[4] Though the concept of rhythm has been primarily endowed with two definitions, they both suggest a methodological orientation that foregrounds the characteristic forms (relating through sensing) and structures (time-space) of cultural experience. Ben Highmore suggests a broader methodological orientation pertaining to conjunctural analysis to which he asserts that 'it names the peculiar character and pattern that such a configuration takes' (Highmore 2016: 14). Since rhythm is a meta-sense that stems from a non-anthropocentric mode of sensing, rhythmanalysis is then directed at bringing forth an affective kind of context and contextual analysis. Here, contextualism is marked by endeavours which aim to capture expressions, performances, orchestrations, displays and manifestations; more importantly taking interest in the ways in which these rhythms render social relations intelligible. For contextualising a conjunctural formation, it means foregrounding the meta-senses which are the forms that uphold or disrupt a conjuncture. By attending to the singularity of a rhythm (which can be seen as a 'cultural text') and looking at how it is formed by an affective logic of being and relating to others, one carves out a type of context that is keenly explored by rhythmanalysis.

Rhythmanalysis composes a conjuncture by foregrounding the affective and structural forms of change, ruptures and crisis. Through the lens of meta-sense, the sensing of a cultural historical shift stems from how things are breaking away from their accustomed mode of rhythmic alliances, hence a recomposition of bodily rhythm in relation to other sites of rhythms (e.g. a renegotiation of bodily rhythms with those of urban renewal which at the crisis of a conjuncture express an arrhythmic state). It is a phenomenological construction of a context that marks the formation of a conjuncture as it emerges, preceding ideological constructions of a conjunctural shift. In conversation with the British sociologist Les Back, Hall's intuition of a conjuncture that is premised on feeling a different rhythm alludes to a distinct methodological attention.[5] I suggest that the formations of new sensibilities signify new social relations, therefore they contextualise a conjunctural development. The cultural history of Britain in the 1970s was marked by a peaking crisis of racial conflicts. In light of conceiving meta-sense as being contextual, a rhythmanalytical mode of contextualism is instructed by an attention that foregrounds the senses and sensing of segregation, fear and threat which racialised the conflicts that blighted the industrial areas of cities. For instance, by enlisting the case study on Brick Lane (Chen 2017), I explored the climate of fear and threat that configured the rhythms of the East End of London. Inhibited by the incendiary physical and verbal threat of National Front members who took violence to the street, the bodily rhythms of walking for the Bangladeshi immigrants were configured and paced to an intensity of sensing fear and violence (there were 'no-go zones' in the area for the Bangladeshis, and walking in groups was a necessity for deterring potential violence for them). The singular rhythm of a Bangladeshi's walking experience, and of how the temporal-spatial presence of a body is constituted in relation to other bodies, are not incidental or trivial for contextualising the politics of racial violence. The bodily rhythm (its gestural and dispositional patterns) is part and parcel of the meta-sense of a street where the staging of the contradictions and crisis of a conjuncture are expressed.[6] In other words, the contextualism of a conjuncture is directed at exploring an emergence of meta-senses that order and align the relations of different communities. In the instance of Brick Lane, threat and fear became the logic of sensing which sets up the rhythmic context of a conjuncture. In exploring a conjunctural shift, rhythmanalysis commands an astute sensitivity which attunes to the meta-sense of rhythms as they are no less symptomatic of a conjunctural shift than being the very driving force of a conjuncture.

Polyrhythmia is a contextualist concept that promotes a breaking away from compartmentalising cultural historical experience into sites of the political, ideological and economic; instead, it renders a productive lens for capturing and accumulating the 'entirety of social formation' (Grossberg 2006: 3) in their rhythmic alliances. The second conception of rhythm addresses forms of alliances as sites of timing-spacing productions. Rhythm being the concrete, lived-out time-space unpicks the notion of 'social relations' as being nothing more than temporal-spatial patterns of alliances and refusals. Sites of rhythms or centres of timing-spacing practices compose a polyrhythmia. On the one hand, polyrhythmia is an ensemble of rhythms that contextualises a site of rhythm. Lefebvre forecasts that a polyrhythmia analyses itself: 'sooner or later the analysis succeeds in isolating from within the organised whole a particular movement and its rhythm' (2004: 17). On the other hand, a singular rhythm is also contextual when it invites a weaving of a polyrhythmia, and as the uniqueness of a rhythm restores itself simultaneously within the interconnections of rhythms. The notion of polyrhythmia yields the complexity of a conjuncture or conjunctural formation, since it allows us to recognise the forms of alliances that have undergone change and to see how the ushering of 'new times', new temporal-spatial logics, are actively produced through these sites of rhythms. In other words, a conjunctural shift takes place via modes and styles of alliances, assemblages and compositions that make sites of rhythms. Through the lens of rhythmanalysis, the crisis, morbidity of a conjunctural shift is translated into states of arrhythmia. It is a conceptual tool that describes a rupture by looking at disruptions of a rhythm in relation to a polyrhythmia. It means that before we have a crisis of the cultural, political or economic kind, a conjuncture occurs first and foremost when a form of alliances (expressed in time-space) becomes unsustainable, or is making those of others impossible. Crucially, rhythmanalysis offers to 'animate' a picture of historical shift by examining how each centre of rhythm and associated forms of social relations shifts in relation to one another. In other words, jarring rhythmic relations signify and reveal the agency of social change by unveiling the sites of changing rhythms as well as in pointing towards the formations of a conjuncture in its re-composition (as in the processes of contradictions and conciliations) of a polyrhythmia. The conceptual tools of rhythmanalysis critically attend to the characters and cadences of change. The formation of an arrhythmia is worthy of attention for charting the disparate tempo of change. There are sites of rhythms which are susceptible to dominant forces of a conjuncture as well as those that are more reluctant to break out of their temporal-spatial productions. Therefore, a rhythmanalyst needs to construct historical contexts (e.g. time-spans) commensurate with the tempos of change in order to account for the long *durée* of slow-moving temporal-spatial structures, as well as for those more salient ruptures of arrhythmia that coincide with a conjunctural moment. Indeed, the concept of polyrhythmia, in its insistent configuration of differential relations of rhythms, directs us to a multiplicity of conjunctures which forms a pleated picture to a unified conjuncture. A conjuncture is therefore a singularity that refracts a plethora of conjunctural shifts. By configuring objects of historical enquiry in radical ways (it is the development of sites of rhythms which are of historical interest), rhythmanalysis invites further discussions on how the notion of a polyrhythmic context puts forward methodologies of historiography that invigorate the radical projects of cultural studies.

Conclusion

In this chapter, I have focused primarily on conceptualising rhythm as 'meta-sense' and 'time-space', though by no means are they conclusive in defining rhythm. In fact, it is a discussion that invites interest and analytical attention concerning forms of cultural experience which are affective and structural (for example, concepts which are akin to rhythm in that they also vividly illustrate ontological conditions and modes of contextualisation that come with them). Conceptions of rhythm instigate methodological attention which intervenes and intersects with the substantial growth of interest in the application of ontological philosophy (e.g. phenomenology and new materialism) to the study of cultural experience. For instance, rhythmanalysis warms up to a vocabulary of attunement, attachment, assemblages and compositions, in that they all aim to provide an active portrayal of how cultural processes take place.[7] Rhythm defined as meta-sense and time-space formulates rhythmanalytical attentions which articulate social relations via modes of sensing and temporal-spatial patterning. Rhythmanalysis partakes in a broader realm of cultural analysis within which forms of cultural experience (mood, feeling, senses; in a word, the 'affective') are considered to have an agency in the ordering of social alliances.

I suggest that the concept of rhythm and the conceptual tools of rhythmanalysis yield practical implications for contextualist practices in the humanities. While the notion of context *vis-à-vis* text is loaded with presumptions inherited from the post-structuralist tradition (which I argue has been infectious in its instigation of thematic streams, curriculum design and research interests in humanities departments), I suggest that the methodological orientations of rhythmanalysis propose models of contextualism that are characteristically experimental and radical in rethinking the dominant assumptions of text and context and how they are causally related in the practice of contextualisation. In my two conceptions of rhythm, I suggest that there are two associated angles in rethinking contextualism. When rhythm is conceived as a meta-sense, it puts forward an affective contextualisation which hones the meta-sense of rhythm in the attachment and attunements of bodies. The other conception of rhythm is also brought forth in attending to the ontological forms of social relations, which is to see rhythm as sites or forms of alliances that produce time-space. The composition of various forms of alliances (and refusals) works towards a polyrhythmic ensemble which contextualises the singularity of a rhythm. If a site of social relation, distinguished by its temporal-spatial identity, is a text, then contextualisation becomes an endeavour of marking out the differential relations of rhythms.

The significance of making contexts lies in achieving an intelligibility, whereby a rhythmic entity is made intelligible within a constellation of temporal-spatial expressions and structures. As a methodology, rhythmanalysis is doing away with the objectified forms of social entities (human or non-human, or the abstraction of social relations to a set of ideas (revolution, crisis). Instead, it discerns sites of rhythms in the process of cultural historical enquiry. By doing so, rhythmanalysis asks different kinds of contextual questions. In this manner, rhythmanalysis promotes a suspension of judgement, given that the objects of research might not be immediately available at the outset; instead it is a proceeding that follows and unravels the politicising of a situation, an object, a cultural historical moment via their ontological expressions.

Notes

1. My archival research in the British Postal Musuem Archive provides empirical support to my case study on institutional or communication rhythm, and it is a substantial part of my investigation of the 1970s conjuncture. It was undertaken partly for evidencing the changes of postal operations which had taken place at a critical moment of re-orientating its services; more critically, I wanted to demonstrate the possibilities of configuring sites of institutional rhythms through archival materials. And finally, the case study of postal rhythms evokes a polyrhythmia which, I argue, had occasioned a conjunctural shift at the level of rhythms. For further references, see Chen 2017.
2. In this article, Felski (2011) is particularly concerned with finding belongings for artworks in social life; specifically, she addresses the relationship between text and context, of the failure of historicism in making historical contexts for 'texts'.
3. I speculate that such reflexive examinations of context will benefit the transposition of cultural theories to contextual studies for the arts.
4. For my analysis of Hall's historiography on the 1970s conjunctural shift and the endeavour of using rhythmanalysis to complicate a periodisation of history, see Chen 2017.
5. 'But about my sense of that break [the shift from one conjuncture to another], people do ask me, "How do you know of that?" I can't tell them that. It's not a precise methodology; it's not something which I apply outside to it. It's interpretive and historical. I have to feel the kind of accumulation of different things coming together to make a new moment, and think, this is a different rhythm. We've lived with one configuration and this is another one' (Hall and Back 2009, p. 665).
6. My rhythmanalysis of the history of Brick Lane was based on the rich descriptions (sourced from Swadhinata Trust Oral History Project) of

how racial conflicts were experienced at the level of the street. In other words, the work of a rhythmanalyst assumes a historical imagination which seeks to animate a bodily rhythm through making vivid a non-subjective sensing of momentums and atmospheres.
7. For an eclectic range of vocabularies of 'affect' and their associated theoretical approaches, see Gregg and Seigworth (2010).

References

Chen, Y. (2016), *Practising Rhythmanalysis: Theories and Methodologies*. London and New York: Rowman & Littlefield International.
Felski, R. (2011), 'Context Stinks', *New Literary History*, 42: 4 (Autumn 2011), pp. 573–91.
Gregg, M., and G. J. Seigworth (eds) (2010), *The Affect Theory Reader*. Durham, NC: Duke University Press.
Grossberg, L. (2006), 'Does Cultural Studies Have Futures? Should It? (or what's the matter with New York?): Cultural Studies, Context, Conjunctures', *Cultural Studies*, 20: 1, pp. 1–32.
Highmore, B. (2013), 'Cultural Studies in its Mirror phase'. *New Formations*, 78 (2013), pp. 179–87.
Highmore, B. (2017), 'Aesthetic matters: Writing and Cultural Studies', *Cultural Studies*, 1, pp. 1–21.
Hall, S. (1988), *The Hard Road to Renewal*. London: Verso.
Hall, S. (1996), 'The Meaning of New Times', in D. Morley and H. K. Chen (eds), *Stuart Hall: Critical Dialogues in Cultural Studies*. London: Routledge, pp. 222–36.
Hall, S. and D. Massey (2010), 'Interpreting Crisis', *Soundings*, 44 (Spring), pp. 57–71.
Hall, S. and L. Back (2009), 'At home and not at home: Stuart Hall in conversation with Les Back', *Cultural Studies*, 23: 4, pp. 658–87.
Lefebvre, H., and C. Régulier (1986), 'Attempt at the Rhythmanalysis of Mediterranean Cities', in H. Lefebvre (2004), *Rhythmanalysis: Space, Time and Everyday Life*. London: Continuum.
Lefebvre, H. (2004), *Rhythmanalysis: Space, Time and Everyday Life*. London: Continuum.
Stewart, K. (2013), 'Tactile Compositions', in P. Harvey et al. (eds), *Objects and Materials*. Oxford and New York: Routledge.

Chapter 8

City Rhythms: An Approach to Urban Rhythm Analysis

Caroline Nevejan and Pinar Sefkatli

This chapter explores rhythm as a dynamic in the social and cultural domain. By executing different case studies in which qualitative methodologies from architecture and the social sciences are used, a methodology for rhythm analysis is constructed. In the case studies, it is found that the rhythm analysis functions as boundary object in conversations with stakeholders for identifying new solutions spaces for specific social issues. The case studies also identify three rhythm dynamics that are significant to the social domain: tuning, matching and balancing rhythm.

Results of the case studies are then contextualised by different rhythm theories that are relevant for the urban context: as variation in a pattern, as territory, as force for engagement and factor for trade-offs for trust. Rhythm has long been a topic of interest, though arguably this becomes more explicit over the twentieth century, with rhythm being referenced and studied in Europe in a variety of fields (Crespi 2014). This chapter draws insights from the writings of contemporary academics working on rhythm in order to explore the possibility of bringing rhythm analysis into practice in today's urban contexts. It is found that in the literature there is a gap in formulating a methodology for rhythm analysis that can be validated and falsified. As a result, based on case studies and rhythm theory, a methodology for urban rhythm analysis is formulated.

Rhythms for Trust in Social Contexts

When sharing rhythm, people feel more at ease with each other. Such rhythms can be mundane – for example, in the activities we do every day: bringing the kids to school, walking the dog, being in the same train going to work, putting out the garbage and so on. These mundane rhythms of everyday life are at the heart of sustaining and shaping trust (Nevejan 2011). As an example, the local policeman, who passes by the school every day so that parents can easily approach him, generates trust. The opposite – not sharing rhythms while sharing the same environment – can be unpleasant, and generates distrust. Based on a larger research trajectory, 'City Rhythm' (Nevejan et al. 2018), this chapter addresses an underlying research question as to whether it is possible to analyse and identify rhythms in the physical and social environment in order to enhance the sense of trust in specific neighbourhoods. In doing so, it draws upon preliminary research on social cohesion in a city neighbourhood in the Netherlands (Den Hengst et al. 2014). Underlying this study was the discrepancy that people do not feel safer even when crime figures go down. According to the *Veiligheidsmonitor* (the safety monitor used by Dutch municipalities), subjective safety is as big a problem as objective safety, revealing the gap between the experience of safety and the data on safety. In light of this, the preliminary study assumed that social cohesion and trust between residents affect the sense of safety. For this prior work a specific methodology, the YUTPA framework, was used. YUTPA is an acronym for 'You in Unity of Time, Place and Action', referring to the original and physical state in which people meet (Nevejan 2007). Online realities merge with offline presence in personal, public and professional experience. Information and Communication Technologies format people's presence and, as a result, new ways for establishing trust emerge. The YUTPA framework was developed to shed light on trade-offs for trust that emerge in these merging realities (Nevejan and Brazier 2017). Results of the previous study show that one of the factors, 'integrating rhythm', is significant for enhancing the social cohesion of a neighbourhood. Taking a normative approach, we can show how sharing rhythms enhances trust. These findings outline the importance of recognising and engaging with rhythms in an urban environment. The lack of rhythms (non-matching, non-shared, non-tuned rhythms) results in lower social cohesion and a lower sense of safety. Simply speaking, in the urban environment people need common rhythms to be able to engage with other people.

This chapter first presents three different case studies in Zaanstad, Amsterdam and Rotterdam in which three main rhythm dynamics are identified: 'balancing rhythms', 'matching rhythms' and 'tuning rhythms'. Each of the case studies combines elements of key literature which help articulate how various rhythm theories are relevant for the understanding of urban contexts. Rhythm is in the first place understood as 'variation in a pattern' (Huijer 2015), which is to make a distinction between mechanical and rhythmic patterns. As the chapter proceeds, further theoretical explorations discuss 'rhythm as urban territory' and 'rhythm as force for engagement'. Overall the chapter identifies a gap in methodology for establishing rhythm analysis. As such, the City Rhythm methodology is proposed – distilled from the case studies and literatures, and also constructed on the basis of insight from the social sciences and architecture. In conclusion, the chapter argues that rhythm analysis can open up unanticipated space for design solutions and as such affect policymaking as well. The unanticipated spaces for design solutions emerge because rhythm analysis is used as a 'boundary object' in social/urban contexts through which then unexpected intervention spaces can be discovered (Star and Griesemer 2010). As a term from science and technology studies, the term 'boundary object' refers to the fact that different stakeholders with different knowledge, skills and perspective can share differences in a constructive way by discussing one object. This, for example, is the boundary object that functions on the boundary between disciplines. What follows, then, is a reading of how 'city rhythms' can work as a boundary object to foster greater understanding of urban living and its development; seeking *shared* engagement between different actors and stakeholders in a given city environment or context.

Rhythm for Enhancing Social Safety: City Rhythm Case Studies

The case studies recounted below stem from 'City Rhythm' (Nevejan et al. 2018), an explorative 'research through design' project (Zimmerman et al. 2007) executed in 2016 that studied shared rhythms in neighbourhoods with the aim of improving the sense of safety of residents in those neighbourhoods. Rhythm analysis was used in this exploratory study to understand social issues in the urban contexts in which they occur. Six municipalities from the Netherlands (Amsterdam, Den Haag, Rotterdam, Zaanstad, Helmond, Zoetermeer) engaged in the exploratory study, with a case study being carried out in each city. Professors, researchers, analysts, students, data scientists and visualisation experts participated from Delft University of Technology, Wageningen University, Amsterdam Institute for Advanced Metropolitan Solutions (AMS Institute), Amsterdam Health and Technology Institute (AHTI), Delph Business Intelligence and Blooming Data.

Civil servants of the six participating cities, in conversation with the researchers, helped define the pertinent research questions, each being of high societal relevance for the different neighbourhoods. Amsterdam posed a question relating to single mothers: 'How can single mothers participate more optimally in education, work and other activities?' The Hague asked a question about integrating migrants: 'How can conditions be improved in a housing block in which refugees and other residents live together?' In Rotterdam, the research question was about older people: 'How can senior citizens feel safer?' Zaanstad focused on youth: 'How can youth (between 15–20) be more integrated into the neighbourhood?' Helmond asked a question about a neighbourhood: 'How can the sense of safety be improved in the specific neighbourhood of Beisterveld?' Finally, Zoetermeer asked a question about a shopping mall: 'How can the sense of safety in the Meerzicht Neighbourhood be increased?'[1] The following summaries focus on three of these studies (Zaanstad, Amsterdam and Rotterdam), and each is combined with a reference to key related literatures around theories of rhythm.

Zaanstad: Balancing rhythms

The research question for Zaanstad Municipality concerned a specific public square in Assendelft in Zaanstad where there is a low sense of social safety, which, according to civil servants of the city, seems to be caused by a group of teenagers hanging out there every day. It was suggested the residents feel unsafe because they also assume the youngsters are jobless and want to make trouble. The research started by interviewing residents and found that there was a lack of common understanding on the origin of the concerns around safety in the square. Not everyone agreed that the perceived lack of safety was caused by the teenagers. In order to gain better understanding, the researchers carried out site research every week for five months to document the daily rhythms taking place in the square.

The square in Zaanstad can be understood as a 'territory', with the coming together of different rhythms. These territorial rhythms were analysed first through visual observation, then through a second round of interviews with frequent visitors to the square. The visualisation in Figure 8.1 shows six documented activities, with the specific hours in which they take place during the day. These documented activities are shop opening hours (8:00–18:00), lunch time (12:00–13:00), public transport rush hours (8:00–9:00 and 17:30–18:30), busy bike traffic hours (7:30–8:30, 14:00–15:00 and 17:30–18:30), hours when teenagers were in the square (15:30–19:00) and finally car traffic hours

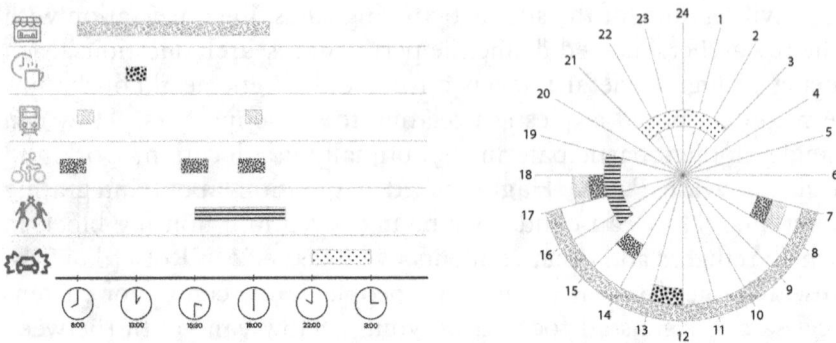

Figure 8.1 Linear and circular documentation of the daily activities in the central square of Assendelft, Zaanstad. (Source: Pinar Sefkatli, inspired by the student work Minor Responsible Innovation).

(21:00–03:00). Firstly, the rhythms in the square are visualised in a linear fashion. Secondly, they are presented in a circular pattern, emphasising the fact that these activities repeat every day. The analysis reveals that there is high rhythm intensity between 17:00–18:00; the bike traffic is high, the number of visitors increases and the public transport becomes more frequent. The analysis also shows that in the same time frame the group of young people meet at the square after work. In this case, it was found that the youngsters were not jobless, they were meeting after work before going home to have dinner with the family.

The results of this analysis were presented to the civil servants by the research group in a validation session organised at the municipality. The discussions that took place (based on the two rhythm visualisations of the square) led to the conclusion that discomfort may be created due to the high rhythm intensity, rather than necessarily the presence of the teenagers at the square. The civil servants suggested that as a result of the high rhythm intensity, the residents may project their discomfort onto the teenagers. Through the validation session an intervention was proposed for balancing the rhythms in those time frames where rhythm intensity is high. The idea was to change the routing of the bike traffic in order to make the rhythms in the square less intense between 16:00–18:00. When discussing this solution with residents and civil servants, the rhythm visualisations and proposed intervention resulted in a lively conversation regarding the different rhythms in the square. It emerged that thanks to the visualisation of the rhythms, different stakeholders could express their concern and engage in a conversation about solutions that were not previously anticipated. At the end of the research, when results were presented, Zaanstad municipality expressed the will to further develop this methodology because it was felt it offered new insight into a critical situation.

In this case rhythm can be understood and adopted as a means of recognising and making a territory (Dewey 1934; Deleuze and Guattari 1987). A territory arises when different rhythms come together and create their own expressive language (Deleuze 1987). Many animals use rhythmic movements, actions and smells to mark their territory (Deleuze 1987), as each ritualisation creates its own time and its particular rhythm (Lefebvre 1992, 2004). Different rhythms co-exist in an environment and this coexistence of rhythms establishes a territory. The territory ensures and regulates coexistence, while rhythms create transitions from one entity to another (Deleuze 1987). One can argue that Lefebvre's description of the urban environment deals with the overall effect of rhythm: 'Here, on the square, there is something maritime about the rhythms. Currents flows across the masses' (Lefebvre et al. 1996: 226). Human beings can perceive and recognise the rhythm of a forest, as they can perceive the rhythm of a city square. The coexistence of different rhythms within a territory affects how a certain context is recognised and experienced. The philosopher John Dewey discusses how humans respond to different rhythms and makes a distinction between aesthetic experience and the consummation of movements. Aesthetic experience is defined by rhythms in movement, colour, shape, sound and more; they are not oriented towards specific tasks but rather towards interactions between a human being and their environment (Dewey 2005: 45).

The quality of an aesthetic experience, according to Dewey, is that it is an 'internal integration, reached through ordered and organized movement' (Dewey 1934: 40). On the other hand, a 'consummation of movement' is marked by a beginning and a conclusion (Dewey 1934: 39). The formal space is 'a space transformed – and mediated – by technology' (Lefebvre 1991: 164). It is reproducible and is the result of repetitive actions and is also usually closed and sterilised, an idea Dewey introduces in his writing on the consumption of movement. In his essays on *The Production of Space*, Lefebvre calls such spaces 'mechanized and technicized' (Lefebvre 1991: 311) and repetitive (Lefebvre 1991: 326). According to Lefebvre, space is transformed into 'lived experience' by a social 'subject' (Lefebvre 1991: 190). This social space is based on social relations and it is organic because it displays the relationships upon which social organisation is founded and where one can expect rhythm as aesthetic experience to be welcome (Lefebvre 1991).

The Zaanstad case is an example of what Deleuze formulated as territorial rhythms that establish a context by coming together, and as a result influence how experience is formed. It shows that from rhythms coming together in an urban setting, an intensity can emerge which is experienced as being too high. Also, one may argue, the aesthetics of the square does not support such an intensity. By introducing the rhythm analysis as a boundary object to the actors on the square, and deconstructing the different rhythms that constitute the rhythmic experience of the square as territory, the research team was able to identify a different cause of this intensity with and for the actors on the square than was considered before. As result of this intervention the teenagers are now considered to be just one of the rhythms that take place in the square and new solution spaces are identified to better balance the rhythms for all involved.

Amsterdam: Matching rhythms

The municipality of Amsterdam Zuidoost has established many social interventions in order to increase social cohesion in the neighbourhood. One key aim has been to counter the isolation of single mothers, which is neither beneficial to them nor to their children. The research question formulated by the municipality, as noted above, was concerned with how single mothers could participate more actively in areas such as education and work. In this case, the researchers focused on the relationship between the rhythms of the main actor group (the single mothers) and the rhythms of the given neighbourhood. This led to an exploration of the concept of matching rhythms.

The research began by trying to understand the daily rhythms of the single mothers involved. In order to do this, interviews were conducted with the single mothers that could be reached, as well as with the workers and volunteers of the local foundations in the neighbourhood, where they frequently attend. To better understand the context, the research was also interested in the neighbourhood life, e.g. the time up until when shops are open, the time frames in which the municipality operates, and how the municipality's daily rhythms appear in relation to the local foundations. This first part of the study resulted in the comparison of a single mother's daily rhythms and the neighbourhood's rhythms. The comparison showed a mismatch between rhythms, as was also reported by those interviewed.

Although the municipality services are available during the day, the study showed that the municipality is mostly a place that requires appointments and queuing, and that this prevents the single mothers from participating. Furthermore, in the analysis, it emerged that these mothers' rhythms are defined by their children, requiring them to improvise all the time, and, with little money and support available, the women prefer to spend their few free hours in the morning (when the children are in school) at the community centre. The mothers' adaptation to their environment is at the threshold level. They reported, for example, that even a yearly parent-teacher meeting was impossible to attend because they have to stay home with the children. Based on the enquiry, it was concluded that the single mothers adapt their rhythms to the rhythms of the community centres. Therefore, in the second phase of the research, a network analysis was carried out to reveal the informal networks that the single mothers are part of (Figure 8.2). The analysis shows that the activities offered

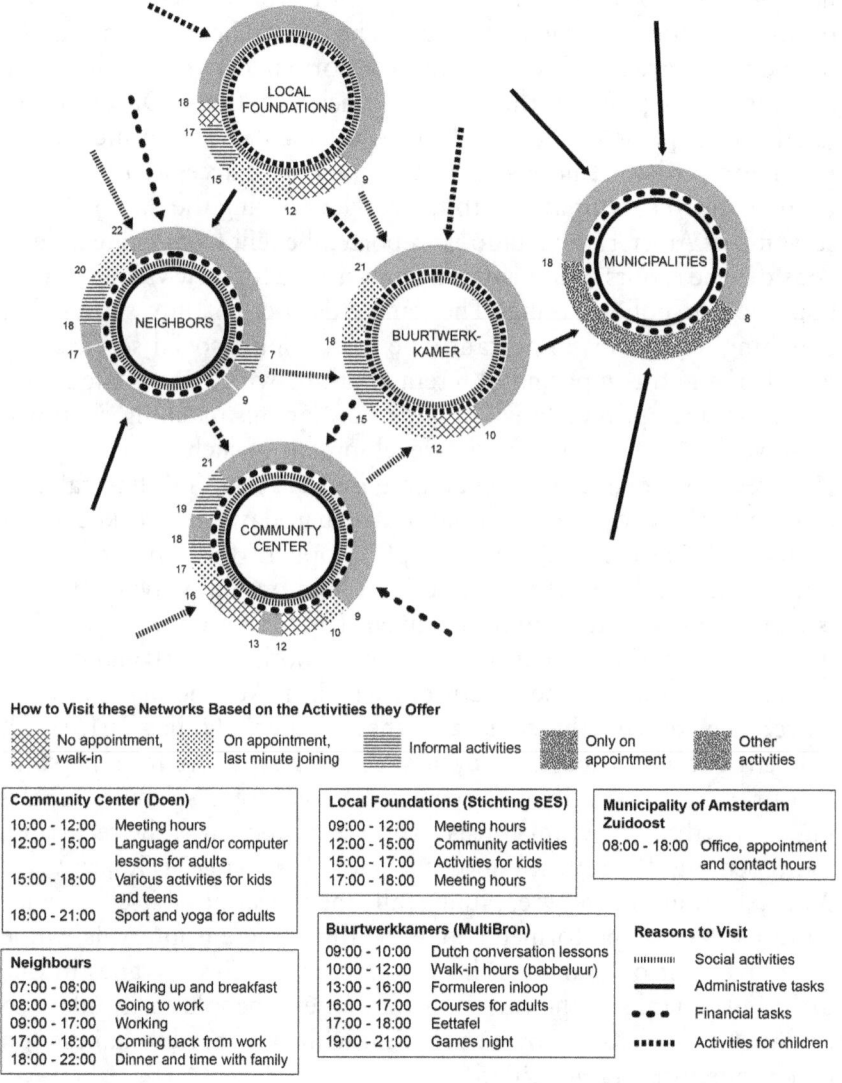

Figure 8.2 Map of informal networks in Amsterdam Zuidoost that the single mothers are part of. (Source: Pinar Sefkatli, inspired by the student work Minor Responsible Innovation).

by other social environments are very diverse and they are easier to access for single mothers, with no need to make appointments, and no calls or queuing necessary.

The researchers presented the municipality of Amsterdam Zuidoost with a map of the different rhythms that the single mothers find easy to match with their own rhythms. The map showed neighbours, local foundations, community and neighbourhood centres and how they can be visited during the day (no appointment, walk in etc.). Furthermore, it could be seen that the single mothers attend these networks for social activities, administrative or financial assistance, or for activities for their children. The researchers' advice to the municipality was to invest in these informal networks which are capable of adapting to the single mothers' rhythms. On the other hand, new opening hours could be implemented at the municipality of Amsterdam Zuidoost in order to increase accessibility for the residents who cannot attend to the services during the day. The civil servants of Amsterdam Zuidoost reported benefit from being able to consider the results of this rhythm analysis and foresaw value in a new approach to policymaking. The Amsterdam case study shows that matching rhythms is important when developing social services. By visualising and comparing different rhythms which are related with the target group, matching rhythms (and/or mismatching rhythms) are revealed and can inform the development of such services.

A reading of rhythm is made here in relation to mechanical patterns, which of course are ubiquitous in today's networked cities (Huijer 2015; Michon 2016). The philosopher Marli Huijer is interested in the nature of rhythm and its role in our daily lives. Rhythm is variation in a pattern within a given structure, argues Huijer. 'The paradox of rhythm is that it brings about both stability and change in the repetition – in the repetition, which makes the order in existence, they remain the same and they change' (Huijer 2015: 25). While the series of repetitive events creates a structure for a person's daily rhythms, variations happen in between that structure, creating the rhythm. 'Rhythm consists of two components: the recurring, the repeating of itself; the movement of the change' (Huijer 2015: 26). Referring to Lefebvre, Huijer calls the repeating of itself circular patterns that are performed equally within different intervals, while the movement of change is the time factor, which only goes in one direction. Thanks to the variation component, people easily adapt to rhythm – it is pleasant to be in rhythm while it is hard to handle too much repetition (Huijer 2015).

In his studies on rhythm, the French scholar Pascal Michon dives into the origins of the word by introducing Plato and Aristotle's conceptualisation of rhythm. Introducing Benveniste's study on the term *rhuthmos*, rhythm appears to be a 'dynamic reality observed at one moment of its flowing, it refers as well to the form of this dynamism itself' (Michon 2011: 3). The fact that it is a dynamic and a movement of change leads us to Michon's conclusion that rhythm is not fixed, immobile and eternal; it has a life of its own (Michon 2016). In the same manner, Lefebvre positions rhythm in opposition to the mechanical as an element in the organic world: 'only a non-mechanical movement can have rhythm' (Lefebvre 2004). Marli Huijer discusses the origins of the word rhythm and history of rhythm study from a philosophical perspective, giving examples from daily life. Both Michon and Huijer argue that what makes this dynamic special is that there is an organisation of the processes (Michon 2011), there is a specific structure (Huijer 2015). Based on his analysis of Aristotle and Benveniste, Michon sees the structure of rhythm as the configuration of movements ordered in time, and Huijer sees it as markings in time. Rhythm is not only 'a numbered order of the movement' (Michon 2011: 7) or 'an arithmetical organization' (Michon 2011: 2). As well as reflecting on the quality of the 'complex organization of processes' that a rhythm is made of, Michon considers the relativity of rhythm analysis in contexts wherein 'observers are confronted with entities that are defined by the ways they are flowing' (Michon 2011: 7).

In keeping with these theoretical accounts, the tracing of the patterns in the Amsterdam case helps reveal how people's rhythms are matched or not matched to the rhythms of the environment they live in. According to Marli Huijer, we all have different daily rhythms, which can be based on work hours or other schedules or organisations. Having quite irregular daily rhythms compared to the rest of the rhythms of the neighbourhood, having a different variation in their pattern than most people and organisations around them, the single mothers cannot handle or adapt to these other rhythms. In light of this, the case study shows that personal rhythms define in which social networks one can operate. Apparently, the community centre has a rhythm which matches that of the single mothers. Based on the network analysis carried out in this case study, one can suggest that actor networks have rhythms (Latour 2005). It can be argued that in the network around an actor, rhythms can be perceived of which the actor is part and that resonate with other actors in the network. The sum of variations in the pattern constitutes character of the network. Those who cannot adapt to such a rhythm, to such a variation in the pattern, are excluded, as the Amsterdam single mothers are.

Rotterdam: Tuning rhythms

The Rotterdam case study was concerned with the perceived sense of safety among senior citizens. In particular, the municipality wanted to examine perceptions of safety among those in the Keizerswaard neighbourhood, which, it was believed, was negatively affected by the presence of younger residents on the streets and high levels of traffic. Therefore, the research explored the relationship between two actor groups, the elderly and the younger residents, which resulted in an idea about tuning of rhythms.

Keizerswaard is mostly a residential neighbourhood, and includes a home for the elderly. There are not many locations in the neighbourhood where residents with different daily rhythms can come together. The public space in the area is a small shopping centre. However, this is not enough to increase the interaction between the elderly and the younger residents. As with the prior examples, the research here began with carrying out interviews with the elderly at their home. The initial findings revealed ways in which the urban environment of the neighbourhood is unsuitable for the elderly: the road in front of the home has high levels of traffic, the timing of the traffic lights is too short to cross the street, and more generally there is a lack of public space. As reported in the interviews there was a negative experience of safety, which was attributed to the presence of the younger residents around the area of the shopping centre.

Following the interview stage, the researchers analysed the rhythms of both the older and younger residents. In Figure 8.3, the curves in the graphs show the different activities that each group performs and the number of people who carry out that activity. The first curve represents the rhythms of the elderly, while the second represents the rhythms of the younger residents. The intensities in these curves are represented by the number of older and younger residents that use the public spaces throughout the day.

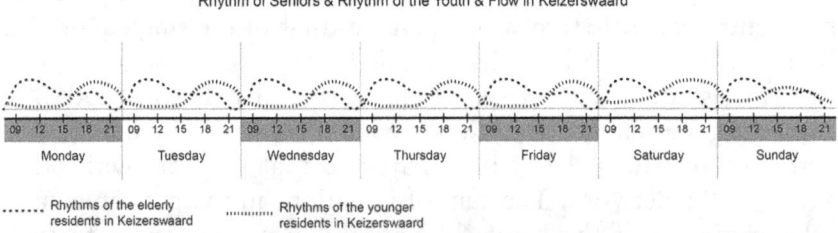

Figure 8.3 Diagram showing the comparison of rhythms of the elderly and rhythms of the younger residents in Keizerswaard, Rotterdam. (Source: Pinar Sefkatli, inspired by the student work Minor Responsible Innovation).

It is significant to see in the visualisations of Figure 8.3 that the elderly and the young residents share almost no common rhythms with each other. When these findings were presented to civil servants, they were curious as to how the different rhythms might come together. Can the elderly and the youngsters 'tune' their rhythms to each other? The Rotterdam research group proposed activities with just such an aim of tuning the rhythms of these two target groups. A service design was suggested in which the young residents could take the elderly out for a walk and earn pocket money. This was designed as the 'walkaround' platform, offering online matchmaking between people in need of a walk with people who like to offer support for a walk. The intervention was tried out within the neighbourhood and deemed successful in producing new or attuned rhythms, so bringing the elderly and the younger residents together.

In this case, it is the role of rhythm in social interaction (as a force for engagement and trade-off for trust) that is made explicit (Nevejan 2007, Nevejan 2011, Gill 2015). Cambridge scholar Satinder Gill studies how people tune their rhythms to each other in order to recognise, understand and communicate. Engagement is a fundamental factor for living together in an environment or for being part of a community. Rhythm also plays a significant role in engagement at a tacit level (Gill 2015). Gill argues that for committed engagement, building trust is essential; this comes through recognising each other through bodily experience and involves all our human senses. For example, whenever we greet someone in our daily lives we are tuning our sense of one another, and it is not accidental that our greetings involve simultaneous rhythmic movement. Such rhythm heightens our contact and commitment to be together, and as a conversation or shared activity unfolds, rhythmic movement allows us to perceive and comprehend each other and to arrive at understandings that embody our tacit awareness. Our gestures are formed within the social and cultural environment that we grow up in, visible in our traditions and daily rituals, such as greetings and making a polite conversation (Gill 2015). According to Marli Huijer, fixed rhythms produce order, structure and cohesiveness in individual and social life. However, in our society these rhythms are pushed to the background by flexible time formats that can be adapted at any time individually (Huijer 2015). Within the context of sense of social safety and trust, one questions what type of rhythms create co-presence in an urban environment, which according to Gill is a precondition to gaining experience and sharing an aesthetic sense (Gill 2015). In the making of trade-offs for trust, integrating rhythm is one of the factors that contributes to such a trade-off. Rhythm is essential to bodies, and it is essential for interactions with others. Rhythm, moreover, supports the experience of trust (Nevejan 2018).

As the Rotterdam case study shows, the rhythms of older and younger people in the neighbourhood hardly ever intersect. The specific service design is then intended to offer regular meetings in which old and young would meet and be able to tune their rhythms to each other. Crucially, attention was given to designing conditions of trust, so old and young would both have a beneficial experience. Trust was organised on the institutional level with the board of the elderly home. Secondly, space for tuning and establishing trust was incorporated in the design of the 'walkaround platform'. Before the older and younger persons went for their walk they would have tea together, and they could do so at the end of the walk too. It may be argued that when there is no trust between people, it is hard for them to tune their rhythms to each other. In order to generate trust, one needs to offer space and time for tuning.

Rhythm Analysis: Objects and Method

In the various case studies produced through the City Rhythms project, the research helped identify a variety of rhythms in the particular urban environment. The *mapping of rhythms* was a means to trigger discussion with residents and entrepreneurs in the neighbourhood. In the Zaanstad case study, conversations were informed by people's physical experiences on the square and therefore debates were intense. The visualisation could also be a trigger to express prejudice (the older residents assumed these were jobless youngsters who would do no good to the neighbourhood). Nonetheless, while the visualisations of rhythms in the physical environment did prompt expressions of prejudice, the interviews with the youngsters proved that these views were generally false. Equally, however, the visualisation showed that the older people were right in that indeed between 17:00 and 18:00 the intensity of the square was very high. Because of the visualisation, people in the neighbourhood engaged in analysing what was going on and found that different perspectives on the situation were possible. A key conclusion is that rhythm analysis can function as a boundary object: in other words, that different ways of thinking and viewing a situation (whether due to specific sociocultural views, based, for example, on generational thinking, or from different disciplinary discourses, such as between individual and council officials) can be brought to accord, or at least brought together around a shared 'object' of debate. Rhythm offers a means to bring different points of view, beliefs and concerns together. Different understandings and ways of formulating a problem can be seen to step over the 'boundaries' of different perceptions and modes of thinking.

In the Amsterdam and Rotterdam cases, the focus was on identifying rhythms in social life. By executing in-depth interviews, the daily lives of different actor groups could be understood and visualised from a rhythm perspective and compared with an understanding and visualisation of rhythms in activities from other actor groups. Here, the *comparison between the different rhythms* was the trigger for conversations. In Amsterdam, the municipality had not realised that the mothers could not fit the rhythms that the municipal services offered. In Rotterdam, the people had not realised that young and old actually hardly met because of their personal rhythms, and that many of their opinions about each other were therefore based on ignorance. Again, a conclusion can be drawn that rhythm analysis functions as a boundary object – facilitating a conversation about social structures and interactions, offering unexpected insight in these structures and interactions and as such, in the Rotterdam case, inspiring new service design solutions.

The representation of rhythms through visualisation is crucial to the functioning as boundary object (Star and Griesemer 1989). Professional skills, coming from architecture in the case of the City Rhythm research, were indispensable for creating convincing boundary objects. It was also of vital importance for a boundary object to be the centre and trigger of a conversation. The City Rhythm research organised several focus groups in every case study in which rhythms were discussed, and in which new design solution spaces and possible rhythm interventions were considered. Key aspects can be said to characterise a boundary object: identification of context, identification of actors, presentation of issues, conversation and analysis, inventory of possible interventions. Each of these is part of the new methodology for rhythm analysis that is outlined in the final section below (Star and Griesemer 1989).

A key, underlying concern of this research has been in identifying the gap in the methodology for rhythm analysis. Lefebvre (2004) introduced the notion of rhythm analysis as a means to a better understanding of cities in his seminal work *Rhythmanalysis: space, time and everyday life*. A well-known passage offers an intriguing rhythm analysis of Rue Rambuteau as seen by Lefebvre from his window, which reads like a rich anthropological description of one street in Paris. However, descriptions of territory do not offer a *methodology* for analysing what creates the territory, i.e. for what holds its different flows together, how rhythms create transitions within the territory or how to grasp the interaction between space and time. In fact, Lefebvre's analysis of Rue Rambuteau could be said to be easily 'falsified' by Claire Revol (2012), who examines the rhythm of the same street in her essay *Rue Rambuteau Today: Rhythmanalysis in Practice*. She ends up with very different conclusions. Revol's study underlines that 'the observation that Lefebvre undertakes in rhythm analysis is not comparable to social science observations' and 'the importance of practice in the rhythm analytical project' (Revol 2012: 4).

During the trajectory of City Rhythm, it was found that Marli Huijer's definition of rhythm 'as variation in a pattern in a given structure' opens up different avenues into new thinking, since it creates the chance to reflect on three notions to better understand rhythm: pattern, given structure/context and variation. However, Huijer does not make this definition operational for rhythm analysis. One can ask, then: how does one recognise variation? How much variation can happen for a rhythm to remain congruent? What can be understood as 'the specific structure' of a neighbourhood? In a given neighbourhood or city, different people will experience specific rhythms in different ways. The distinction that Dewey makes between rhythms that allow aesthetic experience and consumption of movements, or the distinction that Lefebvre makes between formal space and social space, contribute to the explanation of why certain spaces influence people to engage with each other or with their surroundings while others do not. It should be possible to identify the subjective experience of rhythm in these terms. However, Dewey, while offering a new perspective which looks at rhythm in everyday life, does not offer a framework to analyse rhythm as an aesthetic experience. In the same manner, Lefebvre's separation between the formal and social spaces misses a framework of analysis. Such a framework is significant to understanding what interventions should be proposed to generate an aesthetic experience. The lack of any such methodology creates a gap of knowledge between the theory of and analysis of urban rhythms. Between the various conceptions of rhythm, it may be useful to develop a scientific methodology for unfolding and analysing the rhythms in an urban environment. The following section outlines steps from the work of the City Rhythm programme as a means towards a more encompassing and repeatable methodology.

Towards a Methodology of Urban Rhythm Analysis

What follows is a proposed methodology for urban rhythm analysis in social urban environments. It sets out six main steps: (1) formulating the rhythm analysis framework; (2) gathering spatial and temporal rhythms; (3) rhythm analysis; (4) discussion of rhythm visualisation with stakeholders; (5) intervention and monitoring; and (6) evaluation and policy-making. How the steps evolve is represented through a curve (Figure 8.4) that starts from the social domain in step one, arrives to the rhythm domain in steps four and five and finally comes back to the social domain in step six.

As a result of the explorations in the six case studies of the City Rhythm project, the aspects are identified for rhythm analysis to function as a boundary object. In order to respond to the knowledge gap, this methodology brings together these identified features, presenting them in six main steps. The methodology can also be seen as an organised collection of architectural techniques (e.g. documenting spatial findings through photographic research, sketches and analytical maps), as well as social science research techniques, including surveys and interviews, focus group sessions with stakeholders and the use of boundary objects for facilitating communication. These research methods are used in different stages and together construct the methodology for rhythm analysis of social urban issues.

Steps 1–3: Defining the problem

The methodology starts with 'Formulating the Urban Rhythm-Analysis Framework'. This opening step is the exploration phase, in which stakeholders and researchers engage in focus group sessions for identifying a

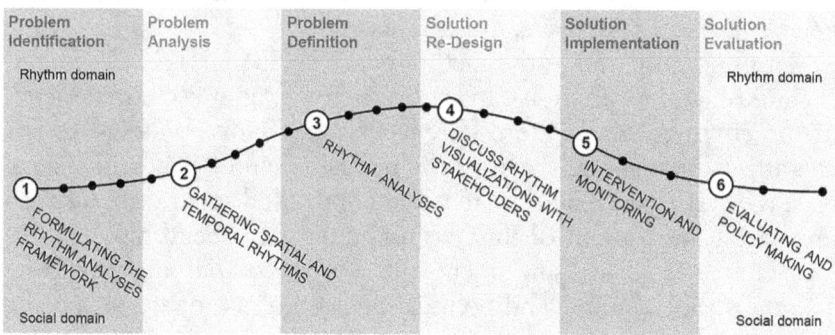

Figure 8.4 Visualisation of the methodology for Urban Rhythm Analysis. (Source: Caroline Nevejan and Pinar Sefkatli).

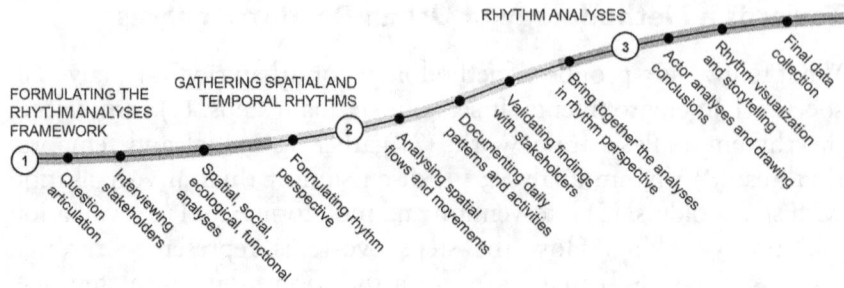

Figure 8.5 Visualisation of the steps 1, 2, 3 of the methodology for Urban Rhythm Analysis. (Source: Caroline Nevejan and Pinar Sefkatli).

research question. Following this, initial ideas about the social issues in urban contexts are developed by the researchers based on interviews, and initial studies on rhythms which are significant to the social issue are carried out with spatial, social, ecological and functional analysis. After going through these processes, the researchers bring together the results for formulating the general framework for the analysis.

The second step focuses on the physical structure of an urban area where the social issue takes place. The spatial flows and movements as well as daily patterns and activities that are present in the neighbourhood are analysed and documented. These two sub-steps include architectural analytical methods such as sketches, photography and mapping and study the people's movements and standing points in a neighbourhood in relation to the functions. From the social sciences, expertise and methodology about demographics, social structures, human interaction and political dynamics are used. At the same time, the time frame in which the intensity of the different movements changes, or the hours in which the functions in the neighbourhood take place, are studied.

An important step in the methodology is 'Spatial, social, ecological and functional analysis'. In spatial analysis, unique characteristics of the environment create different rhythms. How wide a street is can affect the walking speed of the people (Gehl 2011). In the same way, the cars that are parked in a neighbourhood square can have an impact on the amount of time visitors choose to spend there. These factors are recognised and documented in the spatial analysis. Here also the socioeconomic and political division of use of space is being studied and mapped.

In an ecological analysis, the observer is confronted with the ecosystems of which the neighbourhoods are part, and the dynamic relationship between the people and the notions that shape these

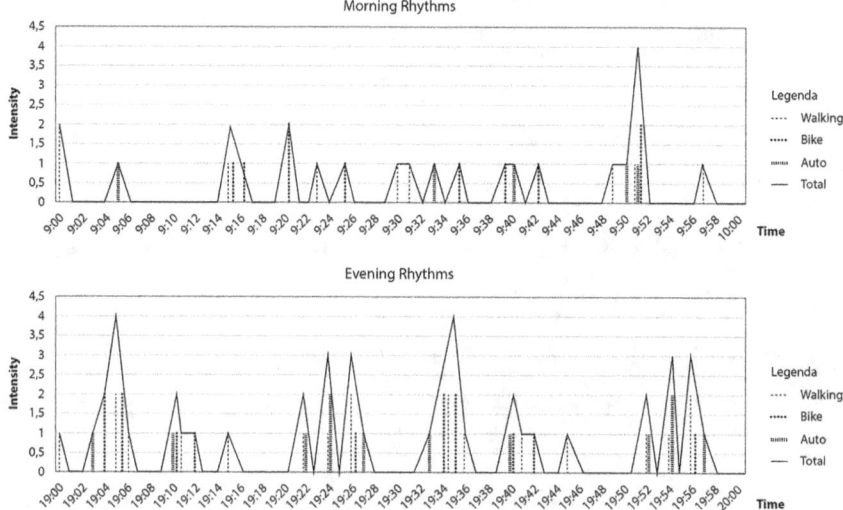

Figure 8.6 Linear representation of morning and evening rhythms in Tulpstraat, Helmond. (Source: Pinar Sefkatli, inspired by the student work Minor Responsible Innovation 2016).

ecosystems. The role that nature plays in the rhythms of the neighbourhood and the relation and rhythms of citizens in this local ecology are analysed. Demographics significantly influence the rhythm in an urban area. There are big differences between the rhythms of young neighbourhoods and those where the elderly form a majority. The same holds for neighbourhoods comprised of large families or of small households. This analysis has different sources and can be executed with digital data as well.

Functional analysis is used to understand the activities that shape the structure of rhythms in an urban area. Functional analysis can be carried out by visiting the neighbourhood and documenting the functions, or through digital methods such as online search engines or datasets from municipalities that indicate the different shops, businesses, parks, schools or other public and private amenities. When these methods are brought together, a thorough understanding of the urban and social context is established.

In the third step of the methodology, after selecting the rhythms that are relevant to the social issue, further data is collected on the actor groups involved with the issue. Then findings are visualised in order to create scenarios for rhythm-story telling. While the actor analysis is carried out by choosing target groups, creating personas and visualising their periodical rhythms (daily, weekly or monthly), in the rhythm-story telling step the results of the spatial and functional

236   Caroline Nevejan and Pinar Sefkatli

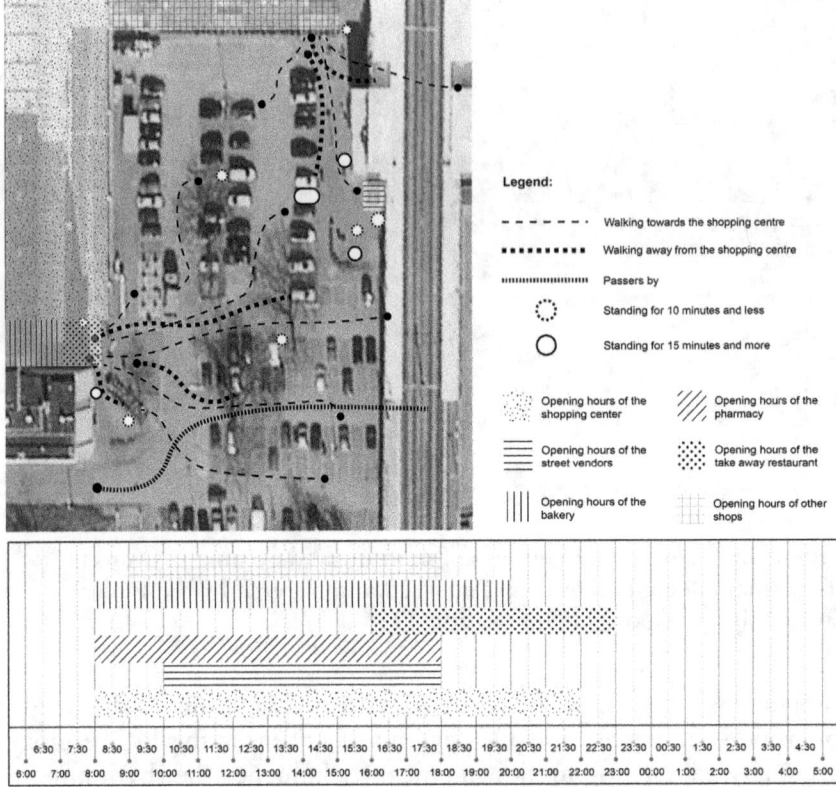

Figure 8.7 Functional analysis of Meerzicht Shopping Centre Square shown in a linear fashion and on a map with the routes of the visitors. Zoetermeer, The Netherlands. (Source: Pinar Sefkatli, inspired by the student work Minor Responsible Innovation 2016).

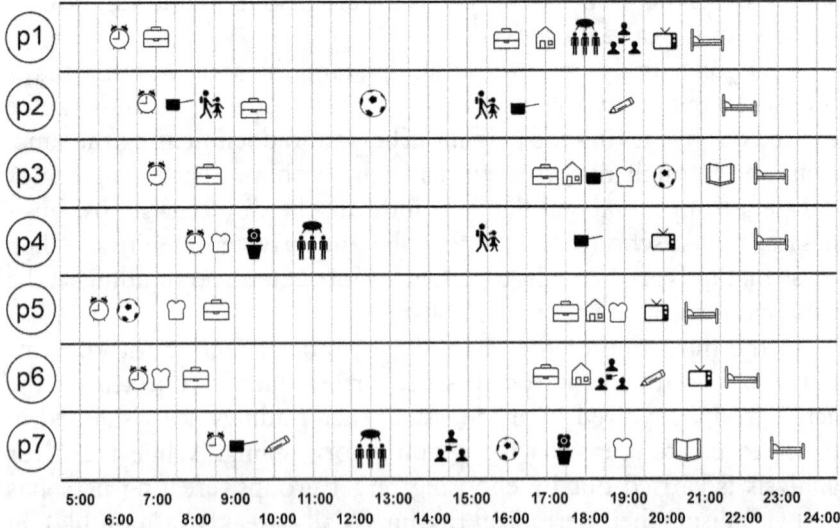

Figure 8.8 Linear representation of the daily rhythms of the residents in Zwaardvegersgaarde, Den Haag. (Source: Pinar Sefkatli, inspired by the student work Minor Responsible Innovation 2016).

and actor analyses are integrated together for creating one storyline. Personas can be used for understanding the actors that play a main role in the analysed social issues. By bringing together the information gathered from interviews, surveys and site research, these analyses allow to document the activities that the different groups carry out during the day with specific hours, arriving to visualise the daily or weekly rhythms of an actor group.

Afterwards, a final data collection is made in order to enrich these analyses. The third step of the methodology is concluded with making rhythm analysis into a boundary object, which takes place by critically combining and comparing the results based on the initial research question. Representing these comparisons visually enables stakeholders to collectively reflect on the rhythms that affect a specific social issue and make conclusions regarding the rhythm domain.

Steps 4–6: Solutions and evaluation

So far, the researcher has articulated the research question, conceptualised the rhythm perspective of the social issue, identified, visualised and measured rhythms in neighbourhoods and in the activities of people. Based on this trajectory, the researcher has moved in the analysis from the physical domain to the rhythm domain. In the fourth step, triggered by the visualisations, a design solution space is defined in collaboration with stakeholders. This step is carried out through a series of workshops with stakeholders in which the rhythm-boundary object is presented through a visual and comparative narrative of the rhythms based on the spatial, ecological and functional and demographic analyses and that of the personas. Following this, the stakeholders reflect on how the different dynamics relate to each other in order to identify a design-solution space.

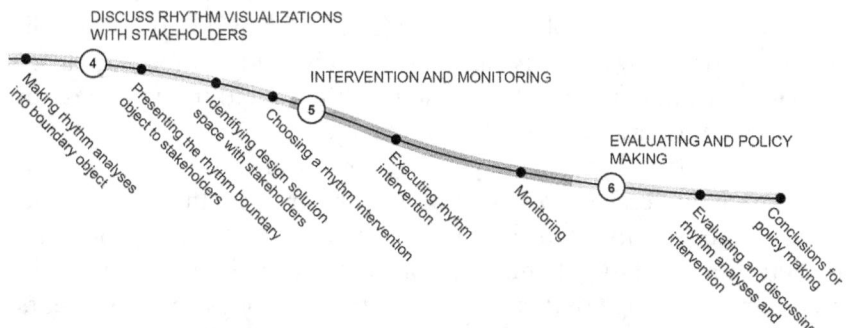

Figure 8.9 Visualisation of steps 4, 5 and 6 of the methodology for Urban Rhythm Analysis. (Source: Caroline Nevejan and Pinar Sefkatli.)

By formulating the rhythm perspective, new definitions for the social issue emerge. The rhythm perspective allows the discussion not to be focused specifically on the initial research question, but to validate many other conditions upon which this situation depends. The rhythm perspective allows for a different kind of causality to surface. As a result of this step, unexpected solution spaces emerge and a rhythm intervention can be proposed.

Following the discussions and the identification of design solution space, in the 'Intervention and Monitoring' step (step 5), the proposed interventions are operationalised in collaboration with stakeholders and their outcomes are validated from a rhythm perspective. A rhythm intervention is defined here as making rearrangements in the elements that structure earlier identified rhythms. Monitoring a rhythm intervention is to observe the performed intervention from both the social and the rhythm perspective. In the final stage, 'Evaluating and Policy Making', the results are evaluated from the perspective of the social issue presented and conclusions are made with stakeholders involved. In further research, a next stage for policymaking will be developed.

Conclusion

This chapter began with the question as to whether it is possible to analyse and identify rhythms in the physical and social environment, specifically for enhancing social cohesion and the sense of trust in a neighbourhood. In responding to this research question, it has sought to formulate a methodology for urban rhythm analysis through which new solution spaces for social issues can be identified. The case studies of the City Rhythm project show that when rhythm analyses and visualisations are properly done, focus groups are well orchestrated, the right people are at the table and committed, and the presentation of the work carried through is clear, stakeholders experience how new solution spaces can be identified that they did not anticipate. By identifying, representing and comparing different rhythms, and by visualising the rhythms, 'rhythm dialogues' are facilitated and new solution spaces emerge.

When urban rhythm analysis is appropriate to use, it can help to create new perspectives beyond existing frames. In working with social issues, established discourses often define how a problem is perceived and analysed and solutions defined. Urban rhythm analysis is a methodology that is built upon mapping physical movements, activities and dynamics. As such, it reveals psychological and sociological structures that are foundational to the social issue explored. When stakeholders gather and discuss the visualisation of the urban rhythm analysis, a confrontation takes place between the perception and opinions of stakeholders involved and the mapping of movements, activities and dynamics in which stakeholders take part. Sharing and discussing this confrontation in a dialogue with other stakeholders, by using the rhythm analysis as a boundary object, offers the possibility to have different perspectives contribute to finding new solutions spaces.

Acknowledgement

Authors wish to thank the civil servants of Amsterdam, Rotterdam, The Hague, Zaanstad, Helmond and Zoetermeer and professors, researchers and students of the minor Responsible Innovation 2016–2017 of Delft University of Technology, Leiden University, Erasmus University for being engaged in the exploratory study City Rhythm. Authors also would like to thank Paola Crespi and Sunil Manghani for their kind feedback which helped improving this chapter significantly.

Note

1. Each of the studies was carried out by researchers under the guidance of different professors and under the supervision of the authors of this chapter. The researchers were also coached by local civil servants who introduced them to relevant stakeholders, and participated in the evaluation. In total nine case studies were executed, of which seven were successful. The two unsuccessful case studies were concerned with questions about the atmosphere of a location. The successful case studies were focused on the activities of people. Three successful case studies are presented in this section.

References

Arias, E. G., and G. Fischer (2000), 'Boundary Objects: Their Role in Articulating the Task at Hand and Making Information Relevant to It,' *Human-Computer Interaction*, 16: 2.
Barthes, R. (1985), *The Responsibility of Forms: Critical Essays on Music, Art, and Representation*, trans. R. Howard. New York: Hill and Wang.

Crespi, P. (2014), 'Rhythmanalysis in gymnastics and dance: Rudolf Bode and Rudolf Laban', in *Body & Society*, Special Issue: *Rhythm, Movement, Embodiment*, 20: 3–4 (September and December), pp. 30–50.

Deleuze, G., and F. Guattari (1987), '1837: Of the Refrain', in *A Thousand Plateaus: Capitalism and Schizophrenia*. London: Continuum, pp. 310–51.

Den Hengst, M., A. de Jong and C. Nevejan (2014), 'BART, Confidential report for National Police of the Netherlands and Municipality of The Hague'. Delft: Delft University of Technology.

Dewey, J. (2005), *Art as Experience*. London: Penguin.

Gehl, J. (2011), *Life between Buildings: Using Public Space*. Washington, DC: Island Press.

Gill, S. P. (2015), *Tacit Engagement beyond Interaction*. New York: Springer International Publishing.

Huijer, M. (2012), *Ritme: op zoek naar een terugkerende tijd*. Utrecht: Boekencentrum.

Latour, B. (2005), *Reassembling the Social: An Introduction to Actor-Network-Theory*. Oxford: Oxford University Press.

Lefebvre, H. (1991), *The Production of Space* (vol. 142), trans. D. Nicholson-Smith. Oxford: Blackwell.

Lefebvre, H. (2004), *Rhythmanalysis: Space, Time and Everyday Life*. London: A. & C. Black.

Lefebvre, H., E. Kofman and E. Lebas (1996), *Writings on Cities* (vol. 63, no. 2). Oxford: Blackwell.

Michon, P. (2011), 'A Short History of Rhythm Theory since the 1970s', *Rhuthmos*, 6 December 2011, <http://www.rhuthmos.eu> (last accessed 28 December 2019).

Michon, P. (2016), 'From Rhuthmós to Rhythm – 7th–4th centuries BC', *Rhuthmos*, 11 December 2016, <http://www.rhuthmos.eu> (last accessed 28 December 2019).

Nevejan, C. I. M. (2007), *Presence and the Design of Trust*. Ph.D. dissertation, University of Amsterdam.

Nevejan, C. (2011), 'Time: Between Emergence and Design', in *Next Nature*. Barcelona and New York: Actar, pp. 214–21.

Nevejan, C., and F. Brazier (2012), 'Granularity in Reciprocity', *AI & society*, 27: 1, pp. 129–47.

Nevejan, C., and F. Brazier (2017), 'Design for the Value of Presence', *Handbook of Ethics, Values, and Technological Design*. Dordrecht: Springer, pp. 403–30.

Nevejan, C., P. Sefkatli and S. Cunningham (2018), *City Rhythm, Logbook of an Exploration*, Centraal Boekhuis, available online: <https://oro-oro.s3.amazonaws.com/other-files/Rhythm%20book%2016.04v2.pdf> (last accessed 28 December 2019).

Revol, C. (2012), 'Rythmes et urbanisme. Pour une approche esthétique du dynamisme urbain', *Rhuthmos*, <http://www.rhuthmos.eu/spip.php?article493> (last accessed 28 December 2019).

Star, S. L. (2010), 'This Is Not a Boundary Object: Reflections on the Origin of a Concept', *Science, Technology, & Human Values*, 35: 5, pp. 601–17.

Star, S. L., and J. R. Griesemer (1989), 'Institutional Ecology, Translations and Boundary Objects: Amateurs and Professionals in Berkeley's Museum of Vertebrate Zoology, 1907–39', *Social Studies of Science*, 19: 3, pp. 387–420.

Zimmerman, J., J. Forlizzi and S. Evenson (2007), 'Research through Design as a Method for Interaction Design Research in HCI', *Proceedings of the SIGCHI Conference on Human Factors in Computing Systems*. New York: Association for Computing Machinery, pp. 493–502.

Chapter 9

Rhythm, Rhythmanalysis and Algorithm-Analysis

Julian Henriques

It is said that the contemporary Western world has been shaped by, if not actually born from, the algorithm. We live in a computational culture – more specifically, an algorithmic culture, as Alexander Galloway (2006) pointed out more than a decade ago.[1] One of the excellent New Economics Foundation reports puts it: '[Algorithms] have morphed from curating online content to curating and influencing our lives' (McCann et al. 2018). Indeed, capitalism's current financialised mode depends entirely on algorithmic calculation, as the basis of derivatives, high-speed trading and the new fintech sector, for example. Platform capitalism relies on algorithmic machine learning and AI, as does manufacturing. Expert systems for medical diagnosis and robot surgery are built from algorithmic machine learning. Political campaigning exploits the micro-targeting of social media messages, as we have learnt from the Cambridge Analytica scandal, not to mention the Snowden revelation of the most extensive government mass surveillance operations the world has ever seen (Cadwalladr 2018).

At the same time, there is a growing critical literature on the ill effects of algorithms on our social, political and economic life, from for example Cathy O'Neil's (2016) *Weapons of Math Destruction* or Frank Pasquale's (2015) *The Black Box Society*. Also, the effects on the individual have been heavily criticised by Jaron Lanier (2011) in his *You Are Not a Gadget*. The so-called 'techlash' appears to be gathering momentum with popular TV shows such as *Black Mirror*.[2] Indeed, one episode of Charlie Booker's Netflix show *Nosedive* has been widely touted by journalists as being prescient of China's currently in-development Social Credit System:[3] Zhima (Sesame) Credit, to be fully rolled out by 2020, is an Ant Financial product from the giant Alibaba online retail corporation. As Ed Jefferson (2018) has noted, while in *Nosedive* the social media rating was shaped by other people, in China it is the state or corporate entities that determine your credit status. This would be considered by many as the tyranny of the algorithm (Harris 2018).

In this quite broad context, the questions entertained here are comparatively limited. Two questions are raised around rhythm. Firstly to what extent does rhythm count as a common root for rhythmanalysis as a social scientific methodology on the one hand and, on the other, algorithmic data extraction procedures? The second question is: can rhythmanalysis provide the basis for a critique of the application of algorithmic methodologies – that is, an algorithm-analysis? To attempt to find some answers the chapter takes several examples: Helen Knowles' artwork *Superdebthunterbot*; the use of algorithmic analysis of urban spaces of Amsterdam and the Google Urbanism project; the Metropolitan Police Gang Data Base; and finally, the military use of algorithms and pattern of life analysis in the theatre of war.

Algorithm: Logic and Control

Algorithmic procedures are undoubtedly the leading technology of the social, political and economic revolution of which we are in the midst. The term *technology* is important here, as it lays claim to a deep-seated ideology of the supposed neutrality of these algorithmic techniques. Nothing could be further from the case – algorithms do not express some neutral mathematical truth; rather they are saturated with corporate and/or military values, all the better to be so disguised in plain sight under a 'common sense' technocratic ideology. This chapter argues that algorithmic processing should be considered as the leading edge of this *technocratism*. Algorithms are the new experts. Evegeny Morozov calls this digital 'solutionism'; Meredith Broussard dubs it 'technochauvinism'; and some years ago, Seymour Pappert described it as the 'technocentric fallacy' (Gehl and Bakardjieva 2017).

To start with, an algorithm can be defined as a mathematical code that is invisible, distributed, sub-sensorial and embedded in software routines. It is the essential procedure for AI and machine learning. As the performance of a routine as such, it conforms to the manner in which Wittgenstein recommended we understand words, by asking not about their meaning, but rather what they do. What algorithms do is extract meaning from the data set – that is, refine the raw material of the data set into something that has operational value. The word *algorithm* combines *algorismus* (Latin) after Muḥammad ibn Mūsā al-Khwārizmī, the Persian polymath in the House of Wisdom in ninth-century Baghdad, together with the word *arithmos* (Greek αριθμός) meaning 'number'.[4] His name, al-Khwārizmī, is also the origin of the word for digit in Spanish (*guarismo*) and Portuguese (*algarismo*). Al-Khwārizmī is considered one of the founders of algebra, as derived from *al-jabr*, one of the two operations he used to solve quadratic equations as he described in his *The Compendious Book on Calculation by Completion and Balancing*, published in 820 CE (Hill and Awde 2003: 55).

While the power and influence of the contemporary algorithm has come a long way over the last millennium, its operations remain true to this ancient root. In *The Digital Condition*, Felix Stalder locates what he calls *algorithmacity* as one of the three key tenets of this condition (along with *referentiality* as making use of already meaningful rather than raw material and communality, that is, communities of practice). Stalder (2018: 59) defines *algorithmacity* as 'those aspects of cultural processes that are (pre-)arranged by the activities of machines.' As with a Google search, for example, these transform the incomprehensible masses of big data into the small data a human being can comprehend. Stalder continues: '[T]hey create new dependencies by pre-sorting and making the (informational) world available to us, yet simultaneously ensure our autonomy by providing the preconditions that enable us to act' (ibid.). This gives the algorithms literally a vital role as the lens necessary to see the digital world – without which we would be totally blind.

The fact of the matter is that we are totally dependent on our algorithmic instruments to make any sense of the oceans of data. This is as much the case with our patterns of consumption as it is with scientific research, identifying gravity waves or indeed the 'god particle' of Higgs Boson in the mass of CERN data. The data set is simply impossible to know: it is entirely off the scale of human comprehension, making it an excellent example of what Timothy Morton (2013) calls a *hyperobject* (although, strangely, he never mentions the digital domain in this respect). It turns out that one of the best renderings of this data world is provided by Jorge Luis Borges' (1998) '"total" – perfect, complete and whole' *Library of Babel*.

Delving a little deeper into the nature of the algorithm, Robert Kowalski formulated what has become its classic definition, succinctly expressed in the title of his 1979 paper: 'Algorithm = Logic + Control'. Kowalski (1979: 424) states that an algorithm consists of 'a logic component that specifies the knowledge to be used in solving problems, and the control component, which determines the problem-solving strategies by means of which the knowledge is used'. Kowalski argues that recognising what he calls the *what* and the *how* as separate functions will improve the efficiency and effectiveness of computer programming. While this may be entirely uncontentious in computer science, it runs counter to much social sciences and humanities research. Here the effort has been to relate rather than separate logic and control, that is, knowledge and power, as with Foucault's famous *power-knowledge* formulation, or Deleuze's equally well-known concept of control societies, as discussed by Seb Franklin (2015). It appears that what cannot be pulled apart in the actual sociopolitical world, in the digital domain of code can be severed with alacrity. Obfuscation on this point is of course exactly the way in which the corporate data aggregators and their algorithmic processing platforms acquire power and influence over human activity in the actual world. While not taking the logic-control distinction at face value, it is useful for the present investigation of the relationship between rhythm and algorithm.

As might be expected, it gets more complicated than that, as McCann and his co-writers describe:

> Whereas historically algorithms would be programmed to complete a task through the input of clearly defined instructions, modern algorithms based on machine learning allow computer systems to create their own instructions based on detecting correlations in huge data sets, learning a multitude of ways to complete a task and creating relationships between inputs and outcomes. (McCann et al. 2018)

The consequence of this, as McCann points out, is for computers to be able to take on tasks that previously would have been reserved for human operators. Most importantly, the nano scale and speed, multiple authorship, system-wide distribution and autopoietic learning of algorithmic operations certainly remove them from human purview. It is literally the case that no human being can answer the question as to what was the 'suspicious activity' that triggered your credit card to be stopped. Such decisions have been entirely outsourced to pattern-detecting algorithmic processing. This has made it very easy for the corporate entities who develop, own and operate the servers running these algorithms to claim that they are somehow legally beyond their corporate responsibility.

Rhythm: Timbre and Musicking

The periodic motion of a rhythm necessarily unfolds in time in exactly the same way an algorithmic routine has to do, though not at any human scale, but rather millions of reiterations per second, far in excess of the sensory faculties with which we are endowed. This is to say both are rooted in periodic movement of reiteration, repetition and recursive motion – the refrain. A rhythm repeats itself, turning a random event into a meaningful pattern. This was the great discovery of the tape loop that transformed mere noise into what could be appreciated as a musical sound, simply by the act of repetition, without any further effects.[5]

It can be taken as an example of what Jacques Attali (1985) describes as the prophetic function of music, so in a way, rhythm anticipates algorithm. Sounding anticipates forms of social organisation, as the division of labour of the symphony orchestra anticipated the factory assembly line, according to Attali. The concept of rhythm can of course be traced back to antiquity, and this is exactly what Pascal Michon (2017a, 2017b) does in his *Elements of Rhythmology*. Rhythm is most usefully identified in relation to *rhuthmos*, defined by Émile Benveniste as the *form* and *flow* and as deployed in Lefebvre's rhythmanalysis, detailed elsewhere (Henriques et al. 2014).

Besides issuing from repetition, both algorithm and rhythm are sociocultural accomplishments, in order to operate both are articulated on the basis of codes and both require technologies (biological instruments of vocal cords etc., or mechanical ones) and techniques. There has never been a hard and fast division to be made between human and machine; culture requires techniques, that is, instruments and technologies. Flint axe-heads occupy this role as much as cyborg prosthetics. Thus the distinction between rhythm and algorithm is certainly not that between human and machine, or analogue and digital, as neither can make sense without the other.

With so much in common, one way of characterising the relationship between rhythm and algorithm would be as that between spoken and written language. This might help to avoid any reductive binary between human rhythms and machine algorithms; rather it might suggest how one leads to the other, as well as ways to use rhythm to better understand algorithm. Ferdinand de Saussure's classic distinction between a particular spoken utterance (*parole*) and the general language system (*la langue*) on which he founded the science of linguistics is even more marked in respect of written text of the language system. Ephemeral utterance is transformed into a long-lasting and reproducible text. This can be said without wishing to claim a special privilege for oral traditions against dominant written cultures, as the early theorists such as Walter Ong (1982) invariably did.[6] Notwithstanding Derrida's (1974) critique of phonocentrism, we can assume that writing records speech that preceded it. In this manner that Albert Lord (2000) argued that Homer wrote down what he heard as sung ballads, introducing vowel letters into the Greek alphabet.

While spoken word can be descriptive and prescriptive in the same manner as written codes, what these sacrifice are the qualities of expression, the intonation, the gestures, pauses and pacing – in short, the rhythm – that a good actor gives to the printed text. The unique performance event of a rhythm with its distinctive micro-variations can be considered indicatively as a form expression of the bios. In terms of the code, it is of course the punctuation marks of written language that serve as reminders of its spoken origins, specifically that most indicative sign of a living being: our breathing. As well as rhythm, linguistic forms and structures such as rhyme recall the oral mimetic devices that writing displaced. If rhythm is symmetrical patterning in time as Georg Simmel (2004: 488) tells us, then rhyme is symmetry in sound. Prosodic performance locates rhythm in the arena of *musicking* – the shared social capacious range of activities required for music making – as distinct from the object of the musical code of the score (Small 1998; Henriques 2011a). While the musical score *pre*-scribes the instructions, as a recipe, as it were, for the musician to produce each musical note, the data-harvesting algorithm *de*-scribes the life as it's played click by click, 'like' by 'like', often together with its biometric functioning. The score maybe a component of musicking, but musicking is never a component of the score. Indeed, Gary Tomlinson (2015) argues for the vital importance of musicking in *homo sapiens*' prehistory as the common grounding for the emergence not only of speech, but also of thought and sociality.

At the same time as recognising the continuities between the qualities of rhythm and the quantities of algorithm, a distinction can be made as between timbre and logic – the former a matter of performance, the latter one of mathematical calculation. The subtleties of tone, overtone and texture that give the timbre of a sound its distinctive qualities are experienced as such, even though the Fourier Transform can reduce every frequency to simple sine wave (James 2003). To emphasise the importance of the qualities of timbre, a formula rather different to Kowalski's diagram can be configured for rhythm:

Rhythm = Timbre (Hz + dB) + Periodicity

Here, timbre is the complex of frequencies and amplitudes of which every natural occurring sound consists. The periodicity is the frequency of the rhythm, counted in BPM (beats per minute). Rhythm is the pattern or gestalt of periodicity. In this manner timbre could be considered as the logic of the sound, periodicity as its control.

The difference between logic and timbre is that between code and performance, or utterance and language, and is articulated in terms of a huge power differential, as discussed below.

The role of rhythm in understanding the relationship between spoken and written language also provides a basis for understanding the momentous scale and significance of the current shift from the Gutenberg Galaxy to the algorithmic universe. What speech, text and algorithms have in common is that they take place along a timeline. Speech is a performance event in time; text is linear sequence; algorithms are recursive. But this is also where the difference between a line of text and a line of code emerges: speed. Though machine-learning algorithms require training, algorithmic processing time, as with algo trading, is virtually instantaneous. Thus the acceleration of rhythmic period provides an escape velocity from linear time. This has been characterised by Vilém Flusser (2007: 20, 21) as what he calls 'the crisis of linearity', that is, the shift from alphanumeric linear coding to what he calls non-linear 'dot interval thinking . . . expressed clearly for the first time in computers . . . the machines spit out numbers automatically, in a quantity that deposes of all linearity.' Flusser continues his argument: 'Algorithms formed islands within texts made from letters. For a while now, mathematical, calculating thought has been breaking out from within the alphanumerical code, is claiming independence, and it is turning against linear thought, to analyze it . . .' (ibid. p. 21). This power that the algorithm holds over non-digital communication is in several respects parallel to that which the written holds over oral cultures. In the way text removed certain embodied forms of expression from speech, so the algorithm now removes what remains of them from text.

Power and Responsibility

Musicking situates music in the actual world of activities, performances and sociopolitical relationships, algorithmic operations cannot but be similarly located. The issues of corporate power and responsibility are precisely those raised by Helen Knowles' video artwork *The Trail of the Superdebthunterbot*.[7] The forty-five-minute video was filmed in Southwark Crown Court and cast from legal experts. The artist describes the premise for the work as follows:

> In a fictional plot, Superdebthunterbot sees an unscrupulous debt collection agency buying the debts of students across the UK, and then using unconventional means to ensure there are fewer defaulters.

Through the use of big data, individuals are targeted and constantly shown job adverts, so more money gets paid to the debt collection agency once the students sign up to a job.

The drama of the piece comes when 'in a tragic twist, two young people die after taking part in a risky medical trial advertised to them through the algorithm.' This leads to the question:

> Is the algorithm culpable? If Superdebthunterbot has the ability to self-educate, learn, and modify itself independently of humans, can it be found guilty of manslaughter if someone dies as a result of its actions? Can rigid legal rules apply to something that's essentially abstract?

It is precisely the nature of the status of an algorithm as a self-learning software routine that makes it comparatively easy for corporations to evade their responsibilities.

These issues of responsibility of and for algorithms can be theorised in terms of Saussure's semiology where the signifier forever floats above the signified, never to be tied down to an actual object. In a way this is what Knowles is searching for – the proverbial *point de caption* (upholstery button) where the signifying code is tied to signified reality. In Lacanian theory this is the phallus, but in the courtroom not even death provides a sufficiently secure linkage between the code and its consequences. It was of course the autonomy of the signifier by which structuralism, as mentioned above, secured its status as the *science* of language, allowing the social sciences at long last to become such. In this respect the algorithm can be considered as the ultimate floating signifier, or more precisely Guy Debord's *simulacrum* – the copy for which there is no original. This is becoming increasingly the case on account of 'self-learning', 'deep-learning' and 'unsupervised' algorithms defined entirely by their functionality, without ever being able to know how this is achieved. In addition, as Stalder (2018: 116) states: 'The world is no longer represented; it is generated uniquely for every user and then presented.' This erosion of any truth value, or any correspondence of representation with the actual world, all too readily bleeds into the actual world via the echo chambers of fake news. This provides a fitting description of the algorithm-generated financial instruments entirely untethered from any real-world assets, or the digital platforms across which global corporations sell meals, accommodation, transport, etc. In every instance, the outcome of this 'escape into code' facilitates the avoidance of responsibilities to consumers, to employees or as tax-paying corporate citizens.

Algorithmic Automation

The algorithm can in principle be considered as no more than a mechanisation procedure, informational automation, redistributing calculation processes to a machine part of the human-machine amalgam. The abacus and the slide rule are two such instruments, but it was not until Babbage and Lovelace's difference engine, as the progenitor of the computer, that such procedures became fully mechanised. As is well known, this was on the basis of the mechanisation of the previously entirely manual weaving process, as was first achieved with the Jacquard loom in 1804. The great leap that Babbage and Lovelace made was to treat *mental* calculations as mechanical operations. The wheel may be an extension of the foot, as McLuhan put it, but it operates on the principle of rotation rather than bipedal locomotion. Similarly, the repetition of algorithmic routines plays to the forte of machines rather than human capacities. It is not that human operators have been saved from repeating routines of repetitive work – far from it, as Anson Rabinbach (1992) details.

The factory assembly production line was literally the engine of the twentieth century's industrial revolution, pioneered as it was several hundred years earlier in the slave plantation economies of the Caribbean colonies.[8] The assembly line's partial mechanisation of manual tasks relies on exactly the same principle as the calculations performed by the algorithms – breaking down a large, complex task (previously accomplished with a comprehensive range of craft skills and experience in a workshop) into a long series of simple routines and sub-routines requiring only a minimum of skills training for human operators. It is of course the remaining human operators that the current wave of factory automation – depending of course on the algorithmic machine learning – is set to replace. 'Everything feels like the future but us' is the comment of one of the workers in Elon Musk's Tesla robot-run vehicle assembly line (Wong 2017). The march of mechanisation is hardly novel, as Siegfried Gideon (1948) documents in his *Mechanization Takes Command*. In fact, these forebodings were brilliantly articulated by Charles Babbage (1838) in his prophetic *Ninth Bridgewater Treatise*.

Algorithmic processing accelerates rhythmic recursion by digital means. As with machine learning, the whole point of code is its manipulation without reference to content or meaning, once the encoding, quantisation and quantification has taken place. The algorithm is entirely a behaviourist tool, acknowledging only the difference between input and output, or in classical terms, stimulus and response. Antoinette Rouvroy (2013) has dubbed it, 'data behaviourism'. Not only is the algorithm itself an unknowable behaviourist black box, on account of its autonomous learning mentioned above, but also 'for algorithms, people are black boxes that can only be understood in terms of their reactions to stimuli' (Stadler 2018: 122). Currently it is only too evident that the ever-increasing intensities of data extraction operate entirely on the basis of encoded indices of meaning, rather than having any 'understanding' as such. After the demise of behaviourism, it was cybernetic engineering that pioneered new models of scientific reductionism. For cybernetics communication and control are one and the same, as Felix Stalder (2018: 50) discusses. From this Shannon and Weaver's 'information theory' was born as a theory of communication as *engineering* that never concerns content – only code, information, probabilities and signal to noise ratios, etc.[9] There were few dissenting voices for what rapidly became the new orthodoxy. George MacKay and Gregory Bateson were two critics at the time in the 1950s; another more recently is James Durham Peters (2000). Otherwise, human scientists, having learned the language of structuralism, abandoned the field of communication to the information theorists. 'Humans agree to give up meaning in exchange for power' as Yuval Noah Harari (2016: 199) succinctly describes the project of modernism.

City Rhythms

It is against this background of reductionism that rhythm came to play an important role, most famously with Henri Lefebvre's rhythmanalysis. Here at last was a human scientific methodology – human because it concerned rhythms, and scientific because these could be counted. As the genealogy of rhythmanalysis has been quite fully discussed elsewhere, we can proceed here with a current example of the use of rhythmanalysis.[10] This comes in the form of a recent study *City Rhythm: Logbook of an Exploration* (Nevejan et al. 2018).[11] The study was commissioned by the Amsterdam municipality for the purposes of civic planning. The authors treat rhythm as a tool for understanding and developing social cohesion and trust. As they state:

> When sharing rhythm, people feel more at ease with each other. Such rhythms can be mundane for example in activities we do every day: bring the kinds to school, walking the dog. . . . These rhythms are at the heart of sustaining everyday life and shaping trust. . . . *City Rhythm* aims to contribute to integrating . . . [the] paradigms of human experience for participatatory, open, and high trust societies by focusing on rhythm. (Nevejan et al. 2018: 3, 4)

Most importantly, it serves as a contemporary example of a non-commercial and non-military deployment of rhythmanalytical methods, bringing Lefebvre's approach up to date with the computer modelling of large data sets.

The authors conclude optimistically that 'rhythm analysis, in the physical world as in the related data domain, offer[s] a potential new approach for policymaking' (Nevejan et al. 2018: iii). In the course of their investigation they refine the rhythmanalytic method by distinguish between three scales: *beats*, *base* and *street rhythms*. Working with a grid of 500-metre squares:

> Beats are defined as the state of a specific area at a specific moment in time. As an example of a state, a street might have lots of cars, a few cars, or no cars at all. Street rhythms show significant transitions over time for a specific area. The base rhythm of an area is defined by comparison to other areas. These derived rhythms are like a musical meter. In this specific context, individual street rhythms develop. Street rhythms represent a variation around a few specific themes. (Ibid.)

While the authors state they are 'interested in understanding the dynamics of cities through the use of large data sets, in order to draw conclusions for *social safety*' (my emphasis), they also recognise that it is equally valuable commercially for 'asset data or streaming data, because it connects the datasets in order to display the ground rhythm of neighbourhoods' (ibid. p. 107). It is this commercial exploitation that the rhythmanalytical methodology is powerless to prevent – which of course is what makes it so attractive to Google Urbanism, to which we now turn.

In contrast to Amsterdam's *Rhythm City*, the Google Urbanism project has very different aims and objectives that would be at the opposite end of the high trust–low trust spectrum that *Rhythm City* identifies (where they associate the former with participation, the later with surveillance). Nevertheless, Google Urbanism deploys exactly similar algorithmic data harvesting techniques to render our very presence in urban *public space* as a site for data extraction. The Google website asks: 'Why "presence" in public spaces should generate financial returns for the city, and how Google can help . . .'[12] This marks an extension of the data harvesting terrain further to that furnished by our computer and mobile online platforms and the 'life interfaces' of Amazon Echo and Google Home domestic listening devices (Albright 2014). The comparison of these two projects illustrates the heritage that algorithm has in rhythm. It is simply not the case that rhythmanalysis can be considered as a dynamic and inherently progressive tool and algorithmic processes as its evil twin. Each has a common root in recursive routines, of which rhythm is just one example. Rhythm is not in itself inherently progressive, as some researchers – myself among them – might once have hoped. As with the *pharmakon*, it can be both poison and cure (Derrida 1981). Nevertheless, what rhythmanalysis reveals about the nature of human social relationships, such as the importance of trust, might be the basis for the kind of critique algorithm analysis aims to provide.

The Google Urbanism project is the brainchild of a group of final-year students at the Strelka Institute in Moscow. It provides a telling indication of the corporation's 'Speculative Expansion Strategy for Google in Physical Space'.[13] An interview with one of the project team (Boyadjiev 2017) in the architecture journal *Archis* provides some insight into the thinking at the core of the project: 'the conception of a legal infrastructure (the "license") and value-tracking protocol strategy' that is of course for harvesting value and data. Importantly this is 'implemented not for the physical construction of episodic signature objects/environments', as with pattern of life analysis (discussed below with reference to drone targeting) 'but for the systemic, ongoing maintenance of uneventful real spaces of the city'. Boyadjiev continues: 'In the project, public space goes beyond its traditional confinement as a "backdrop for human activity" and moves to the foreground as the main subject, the legal holder of human "presence" as its raw material.' This presence is defined as 'attention and data'.

The key claim of the project is that under the terms of the license, Google promises to return some of their profits as investment in the physical infrastructure from which they have harvested the data. As Boyadjiev puts it, the value of this presence 'extracted from public space in the city is [then] tracked, the resulting financial micro-transactions are accounted for, and part of their returns are reinvested in their spaces of origin in the form of dividends for public space's ongoing maintenance and improvement'. Thus, the Google Urbanism project proposes to put the *agora* firmly in the pockets of the aggregators. Gone is any idea of public space as a shared commons; banished any local political structures, processes or accountabilities; vanished is any idea of citizen or citizenship. Instead there are only consumers, such that 'users as raw material [are] no longer an end in themselves; instead they become a means of profit in a new kind of market place'.[14] Instead there are only individual patterns of consumption and a grotesque public–private partnership of the kind that has historically in the UK proved to benefit only the private sector at the expense of public. Google Urbanism provides a vivid example of post-democracy.[15] It should also be added that the austerity-ridden local councils might well be forced to consider Google's offer partly as a result of that corporation's own tax evasion, which has helped starve the government of revenue.

Racial Profiling

Algorithmic processing is anything but value-free. In fact, it tends to reproduce prejudices of the society at large – and in many instances exacerbate them. It is as if what is repressed by the value-free technocratic ideology takes the first opportunity to rush back into the picture. This is what Safiya Umoja Noble (2018) found in respect to Google searches for 'why are black women so . . .' as detailed in her *Algorithms of Oppression: How Search Engines Reinforce Racism* (see also Cossins 2018). As we have learnt about the 'echo chambers' of social media, the algorithms are primed for attention-grabbing extremes, to aggregate and amplify like-minded viewpoints. Unfortunately, the amplifying effects of algorithmic analysis are not restricted to the racial prejudices of search engines and social media.[16] As with every other technology, instrument or technique, the algorithm is deeply embedded with politics, culture and ideology, as Jonathan Sterne's (2012b) in-depth investigation of the MP3 file format shows. Software is never neutral and has to be socially and historically located. As Louis Chude-Sokei (2015) argues in *The Sound of Culture*, technology is always raced and gendered. Evidence against such a Panglossian view of technology appears to be mounting, not least on the basis of the facility with which the algorithmic tools at the basis of Facebook's business model have been exploited for political ends, as Carole Cadwalladr (2018) has done so much to expose. Also, it should be remembered that there is a continual traffic between the military and entertainment industries, as with VR technologies. To give a different example, Hedley Jones repurposed his RAF radar engineering skills to invent the popular entertainment of the Jamaican sound system (Henriques 2011b).

The Metropolitan Police Service Gangs Violence Matrix became operational in 2012 in the political wake of riots in London the previous year. The Matrix is a database and 'a risk-assessment tool to assess and rank London's suspected gang members according to their "propensity for violence"' (Amnesty International 2018: 1). Those on the matrix are known as 'gang nominals' and each marked as red, amber or green level of risk of committing a violent offence. In 2017 the Matrix included 3,806 people. The Amnesty International report *Trapped in the Matrix* accuses the Met of a 'racialised' war on gangs. It paints an entirely damning picture:

> Our research shows that the Gangs Matrix is based on a vague and ill-defined concept of 'the gang' that has little objective meaning and is applied inconsistently in different London boroughs. The Matrix itself and the process for adding individuals to it, assigning 'risk scores' and sharing data with partner agencies appears to be similarly ill-defined with few, if any, safeguards and little oversight. (Ibid. p. 2)

The report continues:

> Not only does this data collection amount to an interference with young people's rights, but the consequences could be serious for those labelled as 'gang nominals', more than three-quarters of whom are black boys and young men.

Included in the report are comments from those interviewed, including Martin Griffiths, trauma surgeon at Royal London Hospital, who states: 'The Matrix is not fit for purpose, never has been, never will. It feeds an industry based on violence reduction [. . .] distorted to fit a narrative: All knife crime is committed by young Black men in gangs' (cited in Amnesty International 2018: 18). Griffiths goes on: 'You put that child on the matrix, you wrote that child's future. There are no second chances in this society for poor Black kids' (ibid. p. 24). The algorithmic analysis software assigning automated 'harm scores' to those on the Matrix was developed not by a third party, but the Metropolitan Police themselves (Amnesty International 2018: 13). As might be expected, the net effect of algorithmic race profiling techniques has been to dramatically increase the impact of policing on certain demographics. This was confirmed in a recent substantial report from Stopwatch, which found that Black people were stopped and searched at more than eight times the rate of white people in 2016/17 (Shiner 2018: iv). This kind of evidence should make it impossible to argue that algorithmic techniques do nothing but reflect the values of the society that produced them; instead they augment them.

Pattern Analysis

A further common feature of rhythm, rhythmanalysis and algorithmic protocols is that all three revolve around patterning. Pattern detection is precisely what the algorithms are designed to do, as unrefined data has only the potential of commercial value. An entire industry has been built on this model, with firms like Experian Mosaic using 'geodemographic' algorithmic techniques to locate and target consumers in their home neighbourhoods, thus further undermining the pre-digital advertising industry model. The key feature of pattern analysis is that it is intended to be predictive, as already described with the Police Gangs Matrix. Thus the human scale of the timeline of rhythm is ruptured not only by the non-human speed of algorithmic processing but also, even more significantly, by the claim that accurate knowledge of human affairs is no longer restricted to events in the past. This takes us into what previously has only been a science-fictional world of the 'precogs' in the film *Minority Report*. There are instances where the predictions offered by AI and machine learning can be utilised by those with benign intentions, notwithstanding data privacy issues. Brent, Bristol and Thurrock are among the local authorities using such techniques to predict children at risk (Niamh and Pegg 2018a, b, c). In the hands of the military, of course, this is not the case, as discussed below.

At the broader scale, such patterning is indicative of a key characteristic of the human condition – trying to make sense of the world. Making sense of the world requires organising it: finding the patterns, distinguishing between similar and different. This patterning is often done in time, that is, in a linear sequence. With representation the principal tool for this has always been storytelling. With non-representational material it is rhythm that provides the linear organising principle.[17]

As well as auditory information, such patterning can also be visual in space, as with a gestalt. Essentially patterning emerges from the relationships between things, rather then the things themselves. Our human perceptual faculties limit such groupings, unlike those learnt by machines. In the 1950s, cognitive psychologist George Miller (1956) famously identified human short-term memory capacity as being seven individual objects, plus or minus two. In terms of the pattern itself, according to the principles of Gestalt psychology there are six characteristics – *proximity, similarity, closure, good continuation, common fate* and *good form*. Most importantly, Kurt Koffka recognised the non-reductive principle essential to the nature of a pattern: 'The whole is *greater* than the sum of its parts' (Koffka 1997: 176, original emphasis). This is to say, patterning relies on relationships of difference. This critical insight has been most eloquently expressed by Gregory Bateson when he states: 'The *pattern which connects is a metapattern*. It is a pattern of patterns. It is a metapattern which defines the vast generalisation that, indeed, *it is patterns which connect*' (Bateson 1979: 11; original emphasis). For practical purposes, however, the sheer quantity of the big data set interrogated algorithmically crosses the divide between quantity and quality; it finds the needle of pattern in the haystack of data. This has always been the ambition of the soothsayers – to find the pattern that predicts the future from the pattern of the runes, tea leaves, entrails, tarot cards or whatever.

Rhythms and algorithms have different relationships with patterning. Rhythms generate patterns; both rhythmanalysis and algorithmic procedures are designed to detect and extract them, the later from the terabytes of big data. In this respect a rhythm is an aggregator. This of course is a rather different way of bringing things together compared to the data aggregation that is the *modus operandi* of the platform capitalist corporations. It is of course these data sets on which they set the algorithms to work to discover. That is exactly what they do continuously, at a scale and speed that by far exceeds any human sensory or comprehensive faculties. Rhythmic inflection has origins in the periodic motion of human activities, practices and techniques. This might appear to set it apart from algorithmic procedures, whose periodicity would be assumed to be grounded in mathematical codes. Indeed, mathematics has traditionally prided itself on being purely an activity of the mind, removed from the real world of embodied activity. In actual practice this is not the case, as André Leroi-Gourhan (1993) has argued; language has to be considered as evolving from embodied gesture (see also Copple 2003). In short, mind and hand co-evolved. More recently, Brian Rotman (1987) applies a similar argument specifically to the language of mathematics itself. He claims that the fundamental mathematical activity of counting has to be considered as being derived from the embodied gesture of counting objects in the actual world. This tends to dissolve what might first appear to be a difference between rhythm as deployed in rhythmanalysis, and rhythm as it is utilised in algorithmic routines.

The Kill Chain

The journey rhythm makes from music to speech to written text to algorithm finds expression in the military application of algorithmic calculation, our final, most extreme example. Rhythm that started out as a sign of life is transformed literally into a sign of death. Historically, armies have an interest in rhythm, with marching bands and drills to march in step (McNeill 1995). The patterning that rhythm provides is currently being exploited as a tool to identify targets in the drone kill chain by making sense of the vast amounts of data currently available to military analysts. As Grégoire Chamayou (2015) describes, this patterning is already being made use of by the military, in terms of activity-based intelligence (ABI). This is a new methodology for targeting drone attacks by aggregating all forms of intelligence (Geoint, Sigint, Osint, Masint, Humint) into a big data set applying ABI algorithms. As one military strategist, Chandler Atwood, states:

> [. . .] ABI methodology enables analysts to sift through large volumes of varieties of data to see how the data overlap and intersect, identifying associations and enabling significant events to rise above the noise of data triage. [. . .] After the ABI analyst commingles the various pieces of data and identifies key pieces, exploitation begins within each INT [intelligence] providing the results to the multi-INT analysts to conduct integrations of the exploited information and address the intelligence questions as the process continues to add additional information. (Atwood 2015)

In this way, 'activity becomes an alternative to identity' (Chamayou 2015: 48). It is no longer, then, individual enemy agents that need to be identified and destroyed, but rather a pattern of activity identified as potentially threatening. 'Essentially, the task consists in distinguishing between "normal" and "abnormal" activity in a kind of militarized automated rhythm-analysis that takes increasingly automatized forms' (Chamayou 2015: 23). 'Signature strikes' as they are called, rely on these patterns of behaviour rather than a known named target as such.[18] Gregory (2011: 195) refers to such patterns of life explicitly as a 'militarized rhythmanalysis'. The implications for military strategy of this type of analysis are explored in Brian Massumi's (2015) *Ontopower: War, Powers and the State of Perception*, though he does not discuss ABI as such.

The shift in military strategy that the algorithmic processing of data facilitates, according to the analysis of Neal Curtis (2016: 526), is 'the explication of the social [by the] drone apparatus – the combination of UAVs, satellites, cameras, servers, and algorithms . . .' Curtis continues:

> Algorithms and the programming of code therefore become absolutely essential for the handling and negotiation of such massive amounts of information. Importantly, and partly because computation has enabled the greater extraction and archiving of data, these algorithms no longer simply serve the apparatus but are set to take on more of the difficult hermeneutic task currently designated to the drone operating team. (Ibid.)

This is a *social* strategy, marking a departure from the former targeting of the *physical* environment of the enemy, as Peter Sloterdijk (2009) describes in *Terror from the Air*. Curtis (2016: 523): 'Drone war is presented as a move away from and a moral advance on the earlier weapons that directly targeted the environment as an indirect means of killing the enemy.' He explains:

> What is targeted is not so much the individuals that Predator or Reaper drones assassinate as the determination of 'patterns of life' suggestive of hostile intent . . . when everyday habits and routines become signatures that trigger a strike. . . . The target is . . . the quotidian social patterns and minute divergences from those patterns that are suggestive of a terrorist threat. (Ibid.)

Curtis' conclusion:

> What I believe the apparatus of the drone does: *strategically, the intention is to destroy the world of the terrorist by means that make the world technically explicit, targetable and hence unliveable.* . . . *This is why the apparatus of the drone is the perfect weapon, because it joins the strategic aim of world-breaking with the technical means of world-capturing.* (2016: 530; emphasis in the original)

This idea of world-capturing also describes personal, domestic and public worlds, as described in previous sections above.

Pattern of life analysis is another social scientific concept that has been militarised. This type of relational analysis, now used with big data all-source analytics, was developed in anthropology with, for example, Ruth Benedict's (1934) *Patterns of Culture*, or Clifford Geertz's (1983) *Thick Description*, where he writes: '[M]eaning varies according to the pattern of life by which it is informed.' He continues:

> Behaviour must be attended to, and with some exactness, because it is through the flow of behaviour – or more precisely, social action – that cultural forms find articulation . . . these draw meaning from the role they play . . . in the ongoing pattern of life, not from any intrinsic relationships they bear to one another. (Geertz 1983: 17)

This is also congruent with Bourdieu's (1984: 94) conception of *habitus*, which describes dynamics and dispositions.

Like rhythmanalysis, pattern of life analysis is concerned with extrinsic relationships – that is, with behaviours rather than objects.[19] It has been transformed from an anthropological term to a military one, amalgamating algorithm and biology, as Joseph Pugliese explains:

> The military term 'pattern of life' is inscribed with two intertwined systems of scientific conceptuality: algorithmic and biological. The human subject detected by [the] drone's surveillance cameras is, in the first scientific schema, transmuted algorithmically into a patterned sequence of numerals: the digital code of ones and zeros. Converted

> into digital data coded as a 'pattern of life', the targeted human subject is reduced to an anonymous simulacrum that flickers across the screen and that can effectively be liquidated into a 'pattern of death' with the swivel of a joystick. (Pugliese 2011: 243)

The algorithmic procedures used by the military are identical to medical ones as Elke Schwarz (2016: 63) explains in an analysis of what he dubs 'prescription drones'. These are 'based on probabilistic factors, identifiable characteristics, and physiological or psychological knowledge linked to higher-risk categories, algorithms are conceived to identify high-risk groups and individuals', thus affecting what could be called a moral anaesthetic as to their consequences. Schwarz continues, 'Signature strikes echo the biomedical practice of risk profiling and surveillance with a view to prophylactic intervention' (ibid.). But unlike much medical intervention, it has to be pointed out, such interventions in the theatre of war in Syria, Iraq and Afghanistan are very far from accurate. In Syria, civilian deaths increased by 55 per cent to 8,051 between 2016 and 2017, as has been widely reported (McVeigh 2018).

Against such evidence, 'the techno-biopolitical assemblage of expertise in targeted killings by drones', Schwarz concludes: '... rests on a form of algorithmic governmentality, facilitated through the technical capacity of the drone as an agent of expertise' (2016: 66). The issue is importantly one of values:

> ... the drone appears as able to 'act' not only better than humans, but also more ethically. This *algorithmic logos*, however, is also reliant on a rendering of the body politic in anthropomorphic terms, as a body in need of a cure. (Ibid., emphasis added)

But the medicalised body is far from safe. The non-values of the algorithms administer the most evaluative of all decisions, that is, the sovereign power of the State to take life – *bare life*, as Giorgio Agamben (1998) describes it. This is the outcome of the *algorithmic logos* or thinking-through-algorithms, as named above – a contradiction brilliantly captured in the title of Arthur Jafa's (2016) video work, *Love is the Message, The Message is Death*. To whatever extent that rhythmanalysis and pattern of life might have succeeded in contributing to a richer understanding of human life, as militarised algorithms they are currently facilitating death. The values that rhythmanalysis uses rhythm to attempt to capture from social life are in fact precisely those excluded from the ways in which algorithmic procedures extract value from the data sets. Rhythm remains a common thread through the historical progression from oral to written and, as argued here, from written to algorithmic codes, turning from elixir, to predictor, to exterminator of life. Rhythm's analysis is revealing of the hugely significant changes currently under way.

Notes

1. See also *Computational Culture: A Journal of Software Studies*, first published in 2011; see <http://computationalculture.net/> (last accessed 28 December 2019); and Seyfert and Roberge (2016).
2. This is not to say that algorithms have not mustered a host of uncritical cheerleaders. Christian and Griffiths (2017) and Domingo (2017) would be two examples.
3. *Black Mirror*, series 3, episode 1, *Nosedive*, Netflix first broadcast 21 October 2016.
4. See discussion of this point in Fann (1971: 102).
5. While this is usually attributed to Pierre Schaeffer's *musique concrète* in the 1940s, in fact this innovation should be attributed to the Egyptian composer Halim El Dabh several years earlier, as Fari Bradley (2015) evidences.
6. See also Sterne's (2012a) critique of what he dubs the 'audio-visual litany'.
7. See <http://www.gold.ac.uk/news/superdebthunterbot/> (last accessed 28 December 2019).
8. See the Legacies of British Slave-ownership project, <https://www.ucl.ac.uk/lbs/> (last accessed 28 December 2019).
9. Vibration theory is discussed as a critique of information theory in Henriques (2019).
10. Though Lefebvre most often is credited as the originator of rhythmanalysis, his work in fact drew on that of Gaston Bachelard (1936), who cites the Portuguese philosopher Lúcio Alberto Pinheiro dos Santos as the author of the term; see Henriques et al. (2014).
11. As explored above in this volume, Chapter 8, Caroline Nevejan and Pinar Sefkatli's 'City Rhythms: An Approach to Urban Rhythm Analysis'.
12. See <https://www.theguardian.com/technology/2017/oct/21/google-urban-cities-planning-data> (last accessed 28 December 2019).
13. This was founded in 2009 'to change the cultural and physical landscapes of Russian cities'; see <https://strelka.com/en/idea> (last accessed 28 December 2019).The team consists of strategic urban designers/architects Nicolay Boyadjiev, Harshavardhan Bhat, Kirill Rostovsky and Andréa Savard-Beaudoin.
14. See <http://googleurbanism.com/fifth> (last accessed 28 December 2019).
15. The term was coined by Colin Crouch. See Crouch (2004).
16. Sexual orientation, for instance, is another dimension of algorithmic analysis; see for example <https://www.theguardian.com/technology/2018/jul/07/artificial-intelligence-can-tell-your-sexuality-politics-surveillance-paul-lewis> (last accessed 28 December 2019).

17. For an interesting geometrical analysis of rhythmic patterning, see Toussaint (2013).
18. See <http://www.theguardian.com/world/2015/sep/12/uk-role-in-pakistan-drone-attacks-concern-mounts> (last accessed 28 December 2019).
19. One example of pattern of life military use: <http://modernsurvivalblog.com/wp-content/uploads/2013/09/threat-characterization-and-patterns-of-life.jpg> (last accessed 28 December 2019).

References

Agamben, G. (1998), *Homo Sacer: Sovereign Power and Bare Life*, trans. D. Heller-Roazen. Stanford: Stanford University Press.

Albright, J. (2014), 'Amazon's Echo: Who's Listening?', *Medium*, 7 November 2014, <https://medium.com/d1g-est/amazons-echo-3624bb654139#.19zbtoser> (last accessed 28 December 2019).

Amnesty International (2018), *Trapped in the Matrix: Secrecy, Stigma, and Bias in the Met's Gang Data Base*. London: Amnesty International.

Attali, J. (1985), *Noise: The Political Economy of Music*. Manchester: Manchester University Press McDonough.

Atwood, C. P. (2015), 'Activity-Based Intelligence: Revolutionizing Military Intelligence Analysis', *JFQ*, 77, p. 28, <http://ndupress.ndu.edu/Media/News/NewsArticleView/tabid/7849/Article/581866/jfq-77-activity-based-intelligence-revolutionizing-military-intelligence-analys.aspx> (last accessed 28 December 2019).

Babbage, C. (1838), *Ninth Bridgewater Treatise: A Fragment*. London: John Murray.

Bachelard, G. [1936] (2000), *The Dialectic of Duration*, trans. M. McAllester Jones. Manchester: Clinamen Press.

Bateson, G. (1979), *Mind and Nature: A Necessary Unity*. London: Wildwood House.

Benedict, R. (1934), *Patterns of Culture*. New York: Houghton Mifflin.

Borges, J. L. (1998), 'The Library of Babel', in *Collected Fictions*, trans. A. Hurley. New York: Penguin, pp. 112–18.

Bourdieu, P. (1984), *Distinction: A Social Critique of the Judgement of Taste*. Cambridge, MA: Harvard University Press.

Boyadjiev, N. (2017), 'GoogleUrbanism: Working with the System', an interview with Denisse Vega de Santiago and Leonardo Dellanoce, *Archis*, 50 (21 June).

Bradley, F. (2015), 'Halim El Dabh: An Alternative Genealogy of Musique Concrète', *Ibraaz*, 009–05, 30 November 2015, <https://www.ibraaz.org/essays/139> (last accessed 28 December 2019).

Cadwalladr, C. (2018), 'Revealed: 50 million Facebook Profiles Harvested for Cambridge Analytica in Major Data Breach', *The Guardian*, 17 March 2018, <https://www.theguardian.com/news/2018/mar/17/cambridge-analytica-facebook-influence-us-election> (last accessed 28 December 2019).

Chamayou, G. (2015), *Drone Theory*. Harmondsworth: Penguin.
Christian, B., and T. Griffiths (2017), *Algorithms to Live By: The Computer Science of Human*. London: William Collins.
Chude-Sokei, L. (2015), *The Sound of Culture: Diaspora and Black Technopoetics*. Middletown, CT: Wesleyan University Press.
Copple, M. (2003), 'Gesture and Speech: Leroi-Gourhan's Theory of the Co-evolution of Manual and Intellectual Activities', *Gesture*, 3:1, pp. 47–94.
Cossins, D. (2018), 'Discriminating Algorithms: 5 times AI showed prejudice', *New Scientist*, 27 April 2018, <https://www.newscientist.com/article/2166207-discriminating-algorithms-5-times-ai-showed-prejudice/> (last accessed 28 December 2019).
Crouch, C. (2004), *Post-democracy*. London: Polity Press.
Curtis, N. (2016), 'The Explication of the Social: Algorithms, Drones and (Counter-)Terror', *Journal of Sociology*, 52: 3, pp. 522–36.
Derrida, J. (1974), *Of Grammatology*, trans. G. Chakravorty Spivak. Baltimore: Johns Hopkins.
Derrida, J. (1981), 'Plato's Pharmacy', in *Dissemination*, trans. B. Johnson. London: Athlone Press, pp. 61–172.
Domingos, P. (2017), *The Master Algorithm: How the Quest for the Ultimate Learning Machine Will Remake Our World*. London: Penguin Books.
Fann, K. T. (1971), *Wittgenstein's Conception of Philosophy*. San Diego: University of California Press.
Flusser, V. (2007), *Crisis of Linearity*, trans. A. Mers, *Boot Print*, 1:1 (March), pp. 18–21.
Franklin, S. (2015), *Control: Digitality as a Cultural Logic*. Boston: MIT Press.
Galloway, A. R. (2006), *Gaming: Essays on Algorithmic Culture*. Minneapolis: University of Minnesota Press.
Gertz, C. [1973] (1983), 'Thick Description: Toward an Interpretive Theory of Culture', in R. M. Emerson (ed.), *Contemporary Field Research: A Collection of Readings*. New York: Little Brown and Company, pp. 37–59.
Gehl, R. W., and M. Bakardjieva (eds) (2017), *Socialbots and Their Friends: Digital Media and the Automation of Sociality*. London: Routledge.
Gideon, S. (1948), *Mechanization Takes Command: A Contribution to Anonymous History*. Oxford: Oxford University Press.
Gregory, D. (2011), 'From a View to a Kill: Drones and Late Modern War', *Theory, Culture & Society*, 28: 7–8 (December 2011), pp. 188–215, <https://journals.sagepub.com/doi/full/10.1177/0263276411423027> (last accessed 28 December 2019).
Harari, Y. N. (2016), *Homo Deus: A Brief History of Tomorrow*. New York: Harvill Secker.
Harris, J. (2018), 'The Tyranny of Algorithms Is Part of Our Lives: Soon They Could Rate Everything We Do', *The Guardian*, 5 March, <https://www.theguardian.com/commentisfree/2018/mar/05/algorithms-rate-credit-scores-finances-data> (last accessed 28 Decmber 2019).
Henriques, J. (2011a), 'Musicking', in N. Lesko and S. Talburt (eds), *Keywords in Youth Studies: Tracing Affects, Movements, Knowledges*. New York: RoutledgeFalmer, pp. 218–22.

Henriques, J. (2011b), *Sonic Bodies: Reggae Sound Systems, Performance Techniques and Ways of Knowing*. London: Continuum.

Henriques, J. (2019), *Sonic Media: The Street Technology of the Jamaican Sound System*. Durham, NC: Duke University Press.

Henriques, J., M. Tiainen and P. Väliaho (2014), 'Rhythm Returns: Movement and Cultural Theory', in *Body & Society*, Special Issue: *Rhythm, Movement, Embodiment*, 20: 3–4 (September and December), pp. 3–29.

Hill, F. J., and N. Awde (2003), *A History of the Islamic World*. New York: Hippocrene Books.

Jafa, A. (2016), *Love is the Message, The Message is Death*, <http://www.serpentinegalleries.org/exhibitions-events/arthur-jafa-love-message-message-death> (last accessed 28 December 2019).

James, J. F. (2003), *A Student's Guide to Fourier Transforms: With Applications in Physics and Engineering*. Cambridge: Cambridge University Press.

Jefferson, E. (2018), 'No, China Isn't Black Mirror – social Credit Scores Are More Complex and Sinister than That', *New Statesman*, 27 April 2018.

Koffka, K. [1935] (1997), *Principles of Gestalt Psychology*. London: Routledge.

Kowalski, R. (1979), 'Algorithm = Logic + Control', *Communications of the ACM*, 22: 7 (July), pp. 424–36.

Lanier, J. (2011), *You Are Not a Gadget: A Manifesto*. London: Penguin.

Leroi-Gourhan, A. (1993), *Gesture and Speech*, trans. A. Bostock Berger. Boston: MIT Press.

Lord, A. B. [1960] (2000), *The Singer of Tales*. Cambridge: Cambridge University Press.

McCann, D., M. Hall and R. Warin (2018), *Controlled by Calculation? Power and Accountability in the Digital Economy, Part 3: The Rise of the Algorithms*. London: New Economics Foundation, <https://neweconomics.org/uploads/files/Controlled-by-calculations.pdf> (last accessed 28 December 2019).

McNeill, W. H. (1995), *Keeping Together in Time: Dance and Drill in Human History*. Cambridge: Harvard University Press.

McVeigh, K. (2018), '"Crazy numbers": Civilian Deaths from Airstrikes Almost Double in a Year', *The Guardian*, 8 January, <https://www.theguardian.com/global-development/2018/jan/08/civilian-deaths-from-airstrikes-almost-double-year> (last accessed 28 December 2019).

Massumi, B. (2015), *Ontopower: War, Powers and the State of Perception*. Durham, NC: Duke University Press.

Michon, P. (2017a), *Elements of Rhythmology, Vol 1: Antiquity*. Paris: Rhuthmos.

Michon, P. (2017b), *Elements of Rhythmology, Vol. 2: From the Enlightenment to the 19th Century*. Paris: Rhuthmos.

Miller, G. A. (1956), 'The Magical Number Seven, Plus or Minus Two', *Psychological Review*, 63: 2, pp. 81–97.

Morton, T. (2013), *Hyperobjects: Philosophy and Ecology after the End of the World*. Minneapolis: University of Minnesota Press.

Nevejan, C., P. Sefkatli and S. Cunningham (eds) (2018), *City Rhythm: Logbook of an Exploration*. Amsterdam: Delft University of Technology.

McIntyre, N., and D. Pegg (2018a), 'Councils Use Family Data to Predict Child Abuse Risk', *The Guardian*, 17 September, <https://www.theguardian.com/society/2018/sep/16/councils-use-377000-peoples-data-in-efforts-to-predict-child-abuse> (last accessed 28 December 2019).

McIntyre, N., and D. Pegg (2018b), 'Algorithms Assessing Gang Risk to Children', *The Guardian*, 18 September, <https://www.theguardian.com/society/2018/sep/17/data-on-thousands-of-children-used-to-predict-risk-of-gang-exploitation> (last accessed 28 December 2019).

McIntyre, N., and D. Pegg (2018c), 'Child Abuse Algorithms: From Science Fiction to Cost-Cutting Reality', *The Guardian*, 17 September, <https://www.theguardian.com/society/2018/sep/16/child-abuse-algorithms-from-science-fiction-to-cost-cutting-reality> (last accessed 28 December 2019).

Noble, S. U. (2018), *Algorithms of Oppression: How Search Engines Reinforce Racism*. New York: New York University Press.

O'Neil, C. (2016), *Weapons of Math Destruction: How Big Data Increases Inequality and Threatens Democracy*. London: Penguin.

Ong, W. (1982), *Orality and Literacy: The Technologizing of the Word*. London: Methuen.

Pasquale, F. (2015), *The Black Box Society: The Secret Algorithms that Control Money and Information*. Cambridge: Harvard University Press.

Peters, J. D. (2000), *Speaking into the Air: A History of the Idea of Communication*. Chicago: University of Chicago Press.

Pugliese, J. (2011), 'Prosthetics of Law and the Anomic Violence of Drones', *Griffith Law Review* 20 (4): 931–61.

Rabinbach, A. (1992), *The Human Motor: Energy, Fatigue and the Origins of Modernity*. Berkeley: University of California Press.

Rotman, B. (1987), *Signifying Nothing: The Semiotics of Zero*. London: Macmillan.

Rouvroy, A. (2013), 'The End(s) of Critique: Data Behaviourism vs. Due-Process', in K. de Vries and M. Hildebrandt (eds), *Privacy, Due Process and the Computational Turn: The Philosophy of Law Meets the Philosophy of Technology*. New York: Routledge, pp. 143–65.

Seyfert, R., and J. Roberge (eds) (2016), *Algorithmic Cultures: Essays on Meaning, Performance and New Technologies*. London: Routledge.

Schwarz, E. (2016), 'Prescription Drones: On the Techno-Biopolitical Regimes of Contemporary "Ethical Killing"', *Security Dialogue*, 47: 1, pp. 59–75.

Shiner, M., Z. Carre, R. Dels and N. Eastwood (2018), 'The Colour of Injustice: 'Race', Drugs and Law Enforcement in England and Wales'. London: Stopwatch/Release/London School of Economics and Political Science, 14 October 2018, <http://www.stop-watch.org/uploads/documents/The_Colour_of_Injustice.pdf> (last accessed 28 December 2019).

Simmel, G. [1907] (2004), *The Philosophy of Money*, ed. D. Frisby, trans. T. Bottomore and D. Frisby. London: Routledge.

Sloterdijk, P. (2009), *Terror from the Air*. Los Angeles: Semiotext(e).
Small, C. (1998), *Musicking: The Meaning of Performing and Listening*. Hanover, NH: Wesleyan University Press.
Stalder, F. (2018), *The Digital Condition*. London: Polity.
Sterne, J. (2012a), 'Sonic Imaginations', in J. Sterne (ed.), *The Sound Studies Reader*. London: Routledge, pp. 1–18.
Sterne, J. (2012b), *MP3: The Meaning of a Format (Sign, Storage, Transmission)*. Durham, NC: Duke University Press.
Tomlinson, G. (2015), *A Million Years of Music: the Emergence of Human Modernity*. New York: Zone Books.
Toussaint, G. T. (2013), *The Geometry of Musical Rhythm: What Makes a 'Good' Rhythm Good?* New York: Chapman and Hall/ CRC.
Wong, J. C. (2017), 'Tesla Factory Workers Reveal Pain, Injury and Stress: "Everything feels like the future but us"', *The Guardian*, 18 May, <https://www.theguardian.com/technology/2017/may/18/tesla-workers-factory-conditions-elon-musk> (last accessed 28 December 2019).

Index

absence, 66, 83, 88, 158, 165, 169, 180
absorption, 96, 142–3
abstraction, 46, 103, 176
acceleration, 21–2, 29, 116, 181–3, 248
Adorno, T. W., 81, 91–3
aesthetic, 9, 11, 13, 16, 36, 49, 56, 91–2, 98–9, 119, 121–2, 150, 155–9, 166, 170, 204–5, 223–4, 229, 232
affective, 10–11, 73, 103, 202, 204, 212, 215
Agamben, G., 260
aggregation, 128, 245, 253, 257
AI, 144, 188–90, 192, 240, 242–3, 256, 263
algorithm, 13–15, 112–13, 127, 129, 131, 133, 135, 138–9, 141–4, 174–5, 188–9, 242–55, 257–61
allegory, 166
alterity, 48, 183
Amazon, 140, 252
ambient, 93, 104, 128, 130
amplitude, 37, 112, 116
Anaximenes, 151
anthropology, 7, 9, 20–4, 28–9, 79–80, 84–5, 87, 91, 231, 259
anthropomorphic, 187, 189, 191–3, 260
antiquity, 4, 8, 29, 165, 246, 264
Apollo, 32–3
archaeology, 79, 108
archive, 70, 165, 208, 216
Arendt, A., 5
Aristotle, 26–7, 34, 226–7

Aristoxenus, 26
arrhythmia, 141, 144, 153, 204, 214
assemblage, 74, 118–20, 174, 204–7, 260
Athos, 44–5, 155
atomism, 37, 44, 154
attunement, 13, 114, 127, 140–1, 144, 215
automation, 174, 186–8, 192, 250
autonomy, 138, 181, 244, 249
autopoietic, 245

Babbage, C., 250
Bachelard, G., 5, 18, 32, 38–40, 162, 261–2
Badiou, A., 176
Barthes, R., 8, 11, 13, 18, 27, 32–4, 43–5, 150, 155–63, 168–71
Baudelaire, C., 27, 92
Baudrillard, J., 5
Bauhaus, 175
Bauman, Z., 21
Bentham, J., 30, 190
Benveniste, E., 8, 11–13, 15, 18, 23, 26, 33–5, 79–83, 88–90, 154–5, 162, 227, 246
Bergson, H., 5, 8, 27, 32, 38–40, 68, 71–2, 91, 180
biological, 110, 191, 203, 207–8, 246, 259
biometric, 247
biopolitical, 260, 265
bitcoin, 14, 181, 184, 197
blockchain, 14, 174, 182–9, 192, 196
Bode, R., 5, 36, 68–9
Bourdieu, P., 259

Brāhmana, 96
Bucher, T., 135
Buecher, K. W., 5, 71

capitalism, 51, 11, 13, 25, 29, 71, 135, 143, 172, 174, 242
Cartesian, 30, 75, 102, 110
chaos, 6, 8, 32, 37, 46, 75, 116, 152, 173–5, 181, 192–3, 205
chora, 5, 33
choreography, 12, 16, 36, 44, 55, 103, 165
Choreutics, 12, 55–6
cinema, 33, 87, 90, 141, 157, 174
citizens, 156, 221, 228, 235, 249
cityscape, 168
Cixous, H., 5
coenobitic, 44–5
complexity, 6, 9, 114, 129–30, 139, 170, 179, 190, 210–11, 214
computational, 9, 103, 114, 242
conjunctural analysis, 209–12
consciousness, 28, 39, 64, 93, 109, 157, 203–4
corporeal, 85, 101, 112–13, 203
cosmological, 152–3, 176, 207–8
cryptocurrencies, 182–6
Culler, J., 10
cybernetics, 24, 49, 251
cyborg, 187, 191, 246
cyclical, 27, 206

dance, 5, 35–8, 56–7, 104, 111
data aggregation, 257
databooks, 130
datachaos, 194
datasets, 235, 252
Debord, G., 249
Debussy, C., 27
decoding, 94, 156
decomposition, 152, 177
Deleuze, 5, 8, 12, 14, 18, 27, 32–4, 37, 45–8, 55, 69, 107–8, 118–19, 128, 150, 152–3, 173–5, 183–4, 188, 191, 223, 245
Democritus, 8, 35, 37, 151, 154
Derrida, J., 3, 5, 8, 16, 32, 160, 253
Descartes, R., 30, 118
Diderot, N., 27, 94
différance, 28, 32

digital, 6, 15, 116, 173–5, 181–4, 235, 243–6, 248–50, 256, 259–60
Dionysius, 32–3
discourse, 5, 9, 12, 23, 30, 36, 43, 79–86, 88–96, 162, 166
disrhythmy, 45, 157
dissonance, 204
drones, 259, 260
duomining, 151–2
duration, 22, 39–40, 42, 48, 104, 121, 161
Durkheim, E., 17

ecstasy, 158
Edensor, T., 10
education, 5–6, 10, 36, 38, 159, 201, 221, 224
Effort, 12, 40, 55–6, 64, 66–9, 71–5, 96, 143, 245
élan, 57, 68–9, 72
energy, 17, 33, 66, 71–2, 110, 119, 137, 171, 174
Enlightenment, 67
entrainment, 104, 110–11
enunciation, 5, 23, 89, 118, 156
Epicurus, 158, 169
epistemology, 6, 18, 20–1, 27, 86–9, 93, 179
equilibrium, 49, 153, 181
Ermarth, E. D., 50
non-Euclidean, 75, 175, 180
eurhythmy, 36–8, 139, 141, 153, 205
expenditure, 66, 137, 143

Facebook, 13, 127–30, 135, 139–44
factory, 5, 71, 138, 140–1
Flusser, V., 248
Foucault, M., 5, 8, 27, 32–3, 41–3
Fourier, J., 247
frequency, 105, 111–12, 116, 179, 183, 247
Freud, S., 81, 84, 94

Geertz, C., 259
geometry, 57, 62, 180
gestalt, 247, 256
gesture, 13, 32, 41–2, 72, 103–4, 110, 205, 229, 247, 257
gift, 139–40, 170, 181
globalisation, 6, 25–6, 168
Goethe, J. W., 27

Greimas, A. J., 88–9
Guattari, F., 5, 12, 14, 32–4, 37, 45–8, 55, 68–9, 107, 118–19, 138, 150, 152–3, 173, 175, 181, 183, 188, 191, 223

harmony, 6, 35–7, 49, 87, 155
Hegel, G. W. F., 32
Heidegger, M., 8, 24, 32, 51, 109, 122, 137
Heraclitus, 8, 32
heterorhythmy, 45, 157
Hippocrates, 87, 89
Hjelmslev, L. T., 89–90
homeostasis, 49
Horkheimer, M., 87
Husserl, E., 103, 109, 120
hyperobject, 244

ideology, 5, 87, 92–3, 243, 254
idiorrhythmy, 8, 13–14, 43–5, 157–9, 163, 169, 171
imagination, 177, 193, 205, 217
information, 25, 28, 135, 141, 143, 173–4, 181, 184, 189–93, 219, 237, 251, 256, 258
infrastructure, 139–41, 149, 182, 187, 207, 253
Ingold, T., 137
Instagram, 146
instant, 16, 35, 44, 48, 151, 154, 158, 162
institutional, 207–8, 230
internet, 127, 129, 148, 193
interstices, 44, 155, 164, 203
intonation, 23, 83, 247
Irigaray, L., 5

kakorhythmy, 36–8
Kallat, J., 164, 166–7
kinetography, 56
Klages, L., 5, 68–9
Klee, P., 175
Knowles, K., 7–8, 13, 243, 248–9
Kowalski, R., 244
Kristeva, J., 5, 33–4
Kundera, M., 158, 169

Laban, R., 5, 8, 11–13, 18, 32, 36–8, 55–76
Lacan, J., 12, 55, 81, 249

langue, 23–4, 81, 83, 90, 92–3, 95, 160, 246
Lapavitsas, C., 143, 145
Laplantine, F., 22, 28
Latour, B., 227
Lazzarato, M., 141, 144
Lefebvre, H., 5, 10–14, 16, 18, 27, 32, 37–9, 47–9, 55, 129–30, 137–9, 141, 144, 147, 150–3, 155–7, 160–2, 168, 203–6, 208, 213, 223, 226–7, 231–2
Leucippus, 8, 151
Leviathan, 187
linearity, 181, 186, 248
liquidity, 28, 183
Lubkoll, C., 68

machine learning, 248
materialism, 5, 30, 32–3, 50, 93, 103, 151, 215
Mauss, M., 22–3, 27, 96
Merleau-Ponty, M., 101–2
Meschonnic, H., 5, 12, 18, 23, 26–7, 33–4, 79–81
metamorphosis, 37, 187, 193
metapattern, 256
metaphysics, 8, 24, 39, 87–8, 91, 152
metastable, 49, 153
meter, 47, 155, 179, 187, 252
metronome, 48, 104, 156
migrants, 221
milieu, 33, 46–7, 68, 152, 183, 190–2, 210
mimesis, 91–2
mobility, 7, 161
modernity, 5, 32, 95, 166, 251
multitude, 245
mutation, 22, 26, 28

Nabokov, V., 50
Nasdaq, 182
neoliberal, 16, 140, 174, 192
Nietzsche, F., 5, 8, 24, 27, 32–3, 38, 43, 159
noise, 48, 109–10, 112, 119, 153, 160, 175, 178, 181, 246, 251, 258

ontogenetic, 26, 119
ontology, 36, 67, 75, 152–3, 162
orality, 79

organic, 35, 40, 43–4, 71, 154, 187, 191, 223, 227
oscillation, 3, 27, 62, 94, 19

parole, 90, 93, 160, 246
Peirce, C. S., 86, 88–9
performance, 5, 10, 14, 19, 103, 109, 119, 168, 212, 243, 247–8
performativity, 13, 23, 103, 117
periodicity, 139, 247, 257
phenomenology, 5, 30, 32–3, 40, 50, 87, 96, 120, 215
physics, 8, 49, 67, 75, 108, 110, 118–19, 151, 163, 191
Plato, 26, 35, 37, 44, 79, 154–5, 226
poetics, 12, 20–6, 79, 81–2, 85–90, 96
polyrhythmia, 36–7, 49, 59, 70, 73, 153, 159, 202–3, 207–9, 213–15
posthuman, 12, 14, 191
poststructuralism, 32, 156
pragmatism, 12, 102
psychoanalysis, 16, 20, 45, 84, 87, 93, 118
psychology, 36, 40, 91, 256

quantum, 40, 67, 75, 108, 193
quarks, 151
qubits, 193

Rabinbach, A., 71, 250
refrain, 46, 68–9, 150, 152–3, 175, 205, 246
refugees, 221
reggae, 264
Régulier, C., 47–9, 153, 205–6
repetition, 8, 11, 14, 32, 41, 45–8, 59, 74–5, 89, 108, 152, 183–4, 189, 226, 246, 250
resonance, 36, 109
Rheingold, H., 165
rhetoric, 37, 86–7, 93, 96, 135, 139, 145, 211
robot, 189, 193, 242, 250

Sartre, J.-P., 84, 93, 160
schema, 42, 44, 104, 154, 259
semantics, 23, 80, 85, 89, 95, 97
semiotics, 12, 30, 80–1, 85–90, 155, 166–8
sensorium, 202

sensors, 109, 112–13, 115–16
signifying, 5, 41, 80, 93, 96, 249
singularity, 184, 191, 205, 208–9, 212, 214–15
Sloterdijk, P., 258
sobriety, 153–4
social media, 13, 15, 127–8, 133, 137–9, 141, 143, 242–3, 254
socialism, 43, 169
Socratic, 4, 26, 32, 151
space-time, 47, 49, 152–3
spatial, 37, 43, 66–8, 75, 102, 112, 155, 233–5, 237
Spivak, G. C., 263
Stengers, I., 179
structural, 22–5, 190, 202, 204, 209, 212, 215
structuralism, 4, 6, 8, 21, 24, 32, 82, 85, 87, 92, 249, 251
subjectivity, 91, 102, 109, 118
subrhythms, 37
surveillance, 242, 252, 259–60
symmetry, 36, 247
symphony, 246
synchronisation, 71, 104, 111, 184
syntagmatic, 83, 85
systems, 4, 9, 16, 25–6, 28, 67, 83, 86, 89, 110, 113, 118–19, 150, 181, 188, 190, 193, 207, 210, 242, 245, 259

Takt, 37, 55–6, 68–9
taskscape, 127, 137–8, 144
Taylorism, 5, 30
technics, 13, 174
temporality, 3, 9–10, 12–14, 28, 41–3, 68, 71, 101–2, 109–21, 127, 129–30, 137–8, 175, 177, 183, 189, 203, 206–8, 211–16, 233
temporal-spatial, 14, 206–8, 214–16
texture, 101, 103–9, 111, 113, 116–20, 247
Thales, 151
Thatcherism, 211–12
theatre, 115, 156
timbre, 247–8
time-space, 202, 206–7, 209, 213–15
togetherness, 110–13, 176
topology, 6, 12–13, 55–6, 62, 66–7, 75, 77, 103, 180

transcendental, 109, 177, 190–1
transcoding, 46–7, 184, 188
transdisciplinary, 4, 151
transduction, 46, 107, 188
transformation, 10, 12, 20, 22, 56, 84, 86, 110, 118, 150, 152, 157, 174, 190, 192
translation, 6, 11–12, 47, 66, 68, 71–2, 79, 89, 91, 95–6, 162
translinguistic, 89
transversal, 177
transystemic, 89
Twitter, 137, 142, 188

universe, 25, 88, 120, 173, 248
urbanism, 168, 243, 252–4
utopia, 43, 169–70

vectorial, 57, 59, 120
vectors, 64, 72, 118, 139–40, 145
velocity, 107, 116, 182, 189, 248
vibration, 46–7, 152–3, 178

Wittgenstein, L., 108, 243
Wundt, W., 5

Zuboff, 128, 142

EU representative:
Easy Access System Europe
Mustamäe tee 50, 10621 Tallinn, Estonia
Gpsr.requests@easproject.com

www.ingramcontent.com/pod-product-compliance
Lightning Source LLC
Chambersburg PA
CBHW050211240426
43671CB00013B/2295